UNBECOMING LANGUAGE

UNBECOMING LANGUAGE

Anti-Identitarian French Feminist Fictions

ANNABEL L. KIM

THE OHIO STATE UNIVERSITY PRESS
COLUMBUS

Copyright © 2018 by The Ohio State University.
All rights reserved.

Library of Congress Cataloging-in-Publication Data is available online at https://catalog.loc.gov.

Cover design by Angela Moody
Text design by Juliet Williams
Type set in Adobe Minion Pro

CONTENTS

Acknowledgments		vii
INTRODUCTION		1
CHAPTER 1	Sarraute's Indeterminacy: A Universe without Contours	36
CHAPTER 2	Inside Wittig's *Chantier*: To Build a Trojan Horse	79
CHAPTER 3	Garréta: No Subject Here	125
CHAPTER 4	Toward a Poetics of Unbecoming; or, Language Has a Body	165
CONCLUSION	Unbecoming Language	234
Bibliography		241
Index		251

ACKNOWLEDGMENTS

IT'S ONLY FITTING that in a book that tracks influences, I acknowledge my own.

At Williams, Brian Martin and Kashia Pieprzak opened up my horizon of possibility, making me want to become a professor of French (and a person) like them.

At Yale, Alice Kaplan taught me to think for myself, and her gift of and with language continues to inspire. Thank you, from one A. K. to another. Margaret Homans was an early believer in my work and her interest and engagement were invaluable. I'm grateful that Howard Bloch and Maurice Samuels have continued to support and encourage my work throughout the years. Agnès Bolton sustained me through more crises of faith than I can count. The anagram Ange(s) Bolton is a fitting one.

At Duke, the Contemporary Novel Group, the Triangle French History and Culture Seminar, Nancy Armstrong, Michèle Longino, Helen Solterer, and Kate Costello were thoughtful interlocutors indispensable to the crucial work of reframing the project and discovering what shape it was supposed to take. Anne Garréta pushed me to write freely without looking to her for approval or permission. Rey Chow's quick laughter and careful listening and reading modeled an intellectual engagement and generosity to which I aspire. Robyn Wiegman showed me how important the psychic dimension of writing is, and how much of it is craft and labor. Karen Bell and Tiwonda Johnson-Blount's warmth and kindness reminded me of the humanity that all this work is about and for. I'm grateful for the Provost's Postdoctoral Fellowship for my two formative years there.

Across the Atlantic, Suzette Robichon was a stalwart supporter who taught me much about French feminism, and Olivier Wagner guided me through Sarraute's papers at the BnF, helping me get a sense of the texture of the real lives that were hers and her interlocutors' and serving as an incisive reader and critic of her work.

I am thrilled to have landed in the Romance Languages and Literatures department at Harvard to finish this book. I thank Alice Jardine for helping me, at a crucial juncture, gain perspective on how to tell this story. Harvard French was so important in bringing French feminism to the United States and starting this conversation—I'm humbled by the opportunity to contribute.

I couldn't have done this without my editor, Kristen Elias Rowley, and her unflagging support in seeing this through from its earliest iteration to what it's now become. The comments of the Press's readers, anonymous and known, have improved the book immensely. Many thanks to Jennifer Willging for a generous and meticulous reading that attended to both content and form. I do not have sufficient words to thank Lynne Huffer for the labor and care with which she read the manuscript and pushed my thought to where it needed to go. If the final product reflects just half her brilliance, I will be satisfied.

No acknowledgments would be complete without my family, who've always believed in me, and my friends, especially fellow academics—Raisa Rexer, Julie Elsky, Kristin Okoli, Kevin Holden, Marika Knowles, Joy Kim, Taylor Moore, Durba Mitra—for their solidarity, and in Durba's case, for kicking my introduction into shape.

Finally, in all these places listed, and every page, Hannah Frydman was there. During this project of reimagining the world through literature, she's made this world we live in my (feminist) home, and this text we've lived in a true *chantier littéraire*.

Part of Chapter 3 was originally published as "The Riddle of Racial Difference in Anne Garréta's *Sphinx*." © 2018 Cornell University. This article first appeared in *Diacritics*, Volume 45, Issue 1, January 2017, pages 4–22.

Publication of this book was generously supported by subventions from Harvard's FAS Tenure-Track Publication Fund and the Romance Languages and Literatures Department's Potter Publication Fund.

INTRODUCTION

WHAT ABOUT THE WORLD needs to be undone? This book turns to the French writers Nathalie Sarraute, Monique Wittig, and Anne Garréta for answers. For Sarraute, it's the categorizing social forces that impose deadening contours onto our otherwise boundless subjectivities and flatten us into socially legible types and characters. For Wittig, it's the straight mind, that purportedly universal thought that animates the dominant social order and sorts humanity into the various identity categories that constitute the hierarchy that heteropatriarchy requires and is built on. For Garréta, the response could be articulated positively as a call to queer the world. For all three writers, though, their works problematize and resist difference, understood as the concept that makes categories possible. My concern here is with those categories that produce hierarchy and oppression (e.g., sex, race, class, sexual orientation, and nationality). Deployed as identity, difference has a stranglehold on the way we live. Its categories are the ones that govern how we navigate the world and know it or, at least, claim to know it. These categories are so natural to our thought and our processes of knowledge formation that they seem indispensable—givens. Sarraute, Wittig, and Garréta, however, write novels that refuse to accept these categories as givens and reject the idea that difference is a necessary condition for human existence. In their writing, difference does not work the way it normally works in the extratextual world that both writer and reader live in. *Unbecoming Language* tells the story of this literary fabrication of a way of being where difference is not necessary.

This book thus tells a political story—the story of literature's political potential, and of how the novel not only thinks, to use Nancy Armstrong's phrase,[1] but how it can act. This book is also a feminist story, as it takes as a starting point the premise that feminism is a theory and practice that aims for the end of identity-based oppression. In my view, feminism should be concerned not only with sex- or gender-based oppression but also with hierarchy, the conceptual foundation for such oppression, which is the same foundation for all other forms of oppression such as racism, classism, homophobia, etc. Feminism, then, as I use it, locates the origins of its political drive in a consciousness-awakening around gender-based oppression that radiates centrifugally to expose the way all systems of oppression are imbricated such that, to combat one, one must combat the others.[2]

This book can also be thought of as a supplement to accounts of French literature that treat Sarraute, Wittig, and Garréta, but not their interrelationship—the intergenerational chain of influence where Sarraute is a central influence on Wittig's writing, and Wittig is, in turn, a central influence on Garréta's writing. Treating Sarraute, Wittig, and Garréta together as a literary configuration loosens each writer's anchoring in the groups or collectivities with which she is associated (the New Novel for Sarraute; the radical lesbian feminist movement and the Mouvement de Libération des Femmes [Women's Liberation Movement], or MLF, for Wittig; and the Oulipo for Garréta), and articulates a strain of anti-difference feminist thought that has been largely forgotten in our (Anglo-American) histories of French feminism.

Anti-difference French feminism (i.e., feminism that rejects the idea of essential or constitutive sexual difference to argue that it is instead constructed) has largely been relegated to and compressed within the tumultuous decades of the MLF's action and organizing—the 1970s and 1980s. While histories and accounts of this strand of French feminist thought and action exist,[3] anti-difference French feminist thought hasn't been taken up by scholars and critics as the foundation for a feminist poetics and literary practice the way differentialist French feminist thought has. Where literature's intersection with feminism is concerned, the differentialist poetics of *écriture féminine*— the writing of feminine difference through a writing of the female body—as articulated and theorized by Hélène Cixous, has dominated and continues to

---

1. Armstrong, *How Novels Think*.
2. See hooks, *Feminist Theory*, which speaks powerfully to the need for feminism to contest more than sexism and misogyny.
3. See Duchen, *Feminism in France*; Picq, *Libération des femmes*; Collectif, "MLF."

dominate our sense of feminist literary possibility.[4] As a result, anti-difference thinkers such as Monique Wittig, Colette Guillaumin, and Christine Delphy have existed in the long shadows cast by their differentialist counterparts.[5]

This book thus also reframes not only literary histories but the history of French feminism and the adventure of its transatlantic life. When we think of French feminism, we most often think of differentialist feminism, which dominates Anglo-American accounts of French feminism. Accordingly, one of my hopes is that this book will make a persuasive case for the anti-difference poetics of Sarraute, Wittig, and Garréta (whose relationship to difference cannot be adequately represented by the prefix *anti*, a point I will return to later), and for the anti-difference feminist thought their writing enacts, so that we might have a different framework for perceiving French feminism. Differentialist and anti-difference French feminism are concomitant strands of thought that have both given rise to compelling and rich bodies of literature. The anti-difference stance that I take in this book is not meant to dismiss the theory and literature that have emerged out of a commitment to and engagement with difference—I recognize that Cixous, Irigaray, and Kristeva's work has invigorated feminist thought and writing. However, while there has been sustained scholarly and critical engagement with differentialist French feminism, anti-difference French feminism has been largely treated as a historical footnote—more materialist, less literary, and less theoretically complex than its headier differentialist counterparts. In *Unbecoming Language*, I call attention to a body of thought and literary production that has been overlooked but that constitutes an original feminist poetics, which, alongside and in contradistinction to the poetics of *écriture féminine*, suggests ways to refashion the world to make it more just.

---

4. For instance, Weil, "French Feminism's *Écriture Féminine*," gives a measured and thoughtful account of the relationship between French feminism and writing that acknowledges the plurality and heterogeneity of the modern French feminist movement and the artificiality of the Cixous-Irigaray-Kristeva grouping. Nonetheless, she binds Wittig with these other three writers and thinkers of difference and sees all four "creating the feminine in their own work [. . .] to provoke women to participate in reimagining their lives and their world" (169).

5. Cixous, Irigaray, and Kristeva's complex poststructuralist- and deconstructionist-inflected work has continued to engage scholars to the present day, a success that parallels the larger importation of such figures as Roland Barthes, Jacques Derrida, Gilles Deleuze, and Jacques Lacan into the American intellectual universe as exemplars of French Theory. For more on the creation of French Theory, see Lotringer and Cohen, *French Theory in America*; Poel, Bertho, and Hoenselaars, *Traveling Theory*; Cusset, *French Theory*.

There has recently been a renewal of interest in this anti-difference, materialist strand of French feminism, but those seeking to call attention to thinkers like Delphy and Wittig have reinforced and confirmed the narrative of their feminism as an overlooked one. See Disch, "Christine Delphy's Constructivist Materialism"; Hemmings, *Why Stories Matter*.

Readers will probably be familiar with at least one of the writers I examine: Sarraute is a canonical figure in twentieth-century French literature, somewhat akin to a French Virginia Woolf; Wittig enjoys a certain canonicity in her own right in feminist and lesbian circles; and Garréta, as a member of the highly publicized literary group Oulipo and a recipient of the Prix Médicis as well as a member of its jury, is a well-known and respected member of contemporary French literary circles.[6] But these writers are not known together. By being known together, each of their corpora takes on a new, collective dimension that speaks not only to their own work but to the greater question of what literature can do. My conviction, which I hope will be shared, is that the answer is a firm "a lot."

Through their experimentation with language, Sarraute, Wittig, and Garréta stage a different relationship with respect to language from what we find in conventional realist novels. These three writers demonstrate that literature can hollow out difference and rework our subjectivity. The reworking of subjectivity is not a given, however, and is only realized if we have a proper experience of literature. In an interview with *The Paris Review,* Garréta speaks to this need to experience literature:

> Nowadays, people don't read literature the way they should read it. They read it to find an example of something they have thought about earlier. Just an illustration, if you will. Very few people are willing to undergo the real experience of reading a book. It's also possibly because so many books are formulaic, so it's not an experience any longer.

When asked to articulate what she means by *experience,* Garréta responds by describing what reading the way we should accomplishes:

> Well, you embark on the thing and you don't necessarily know where you're going, and as you experience the book—or it can be a movie or a piece of art—it reorders the circulation of your affects, of your perceptions, in a way which is not always easy to figure out because it's, once again, very opaque. [. . .] But—something happens. It manipulates your desires, your perceptions, your affects in ways that aren't predictable.[7]

---

6. As the journalist Alain Salles put it, "Anne Garréta, like Pascal Quignard, is a well-known writer." Salles, "Grasset retrouve son rang." All translations in *Unbecoming Language,* unless otherwise noted, are my own.

7. Gerard, "States of Desire."

Sarraute, Wittig, and Garréta are able to effect this opaque reworking of our subjectivity, this "something," if and when we really read them. What reading them entails is an openness to being compelled, by their reworking of language and rejection of the formulaic, to rework our own relationships to language so that we might be able to experience ourselves as subjectivities without subjecthood. To be a subjectivity without subjecthood is to have a conscious experience of the world that is located specifically in our individual way of being in and perceiving the world—what we might call the self—without that experience and location then being immediately defined and delineated by subjecthood.

Subjecthood is the container in which we can be identified, interpellated, and taken up as a subject, be it the much maligned liberal subject who embodies an irresponsible and arrogant individualism, or the psychoanalytic subject divided by the unconscious, or the biopolitical subject ordered and disciplined by various apparatuses and networks of power. Subjectivity without subjecthood constitutes a radical reconfiguration of what it means for us, as human beings, to be in the world. It is neither the transcendence of being desubjectivated, of being outside oneself or no longer oneself (through self-shattering *jouissance* or otherwise),[8] nor is it the immanence of *assujettissement*, to use Foucault's term for subjectivation, in which individuals are produced as subjects through submission to power. Subjectivity without subjecthood is *itself*, without being mired in immanence, fixed or constrained by identity, pinned down by the various kinds of difference by which the social order would seek to immobilize it.

Literature, in the hands of Sarraute, Wittig, and Garréta, is an important corrective to what we increasingly do to language and what it does to us. Their formal experiments draw attention to the way language is always a fabrication and always in the process of fabricating. By drawing attention to the process by which they create fictional worlds, alternative textual realities, they open up a space where we might stop being passive consumers of a language that determines the shape of who we are and what sort of a life we lead—a space in which to encounter a language that reworks us. Literature, when it rejects the

---

8. This self-shattering *jouissance* is associated with queer theory's engagement with negativity and the anti-relational. See Bersani, "Is the Rectum a Grave?," which puts the language of self-shattering *jouissance* on the conceptual map; Edelman, *No Future*, which takes up the mantle of Bersanian anti-relationality to argue for a queer embrace of embodying the death drive; Puar, *Terrorist Assemblages*, which displaces self-shattering onto the figure of the suicide bomber. For an interesting take on desubjectivation that sees it as an ethical, and thus relational, site, see Lynne Huffer's engagement with Foucault in *Mad for Foucault* and *Are the Lips a Grave?* I take up the question of queer theory's sustained engagement and association with negativity and self-shattering or self-undoing later in the introduction.

tyranny of a self-identical, referential real and embraces the fictive, interrupts the flow of "reality" long enough for us to stop coinciding with the identities that have been assigned to us by forces beyond our control (i.e., disciplinary bodies such as the social order, the state, the community). It makes it possible for us to exist differently—freed, at least momentarily, from the determinism of difference. This subjectivity without subjecthood—where one is fully in oneself but free, fluid, unfixed, potential—is what I call *unbecoming*.

We are immediately *assujettis*, subjected from the moment we enter into life,[9] language, and consciousness—pushed toward a predetermined path of becoming who it is that we have been told we are (woman, man, straight, white, American, etc.). Consequently, this state of subjectivity without subjecthood will always succeed the becoming-identity we all undergo. It will always be a negative reaction to what we've become. Unbecoming is thus an act of erosion (eroding those categories we ostensibly correspond to and are contained by) and of excess (becoming more than our identitarian limits would have us be, spilling out past the contours that used to delimit us). Sarraute describes this state of subjectivity without subjecthood as follows: "On the inside, I feel myself to be everything and nobody. When, sitting here in this armchair, I speak to you, I don't know who's in front of you. Of course, one can say what the social person is, we can say what our social roles are . . . There, already, we're dealing with several persons, but I don't feel myself to be any of them. To whom are you speaking? I does not know [*je ne sait pas*]. [. . .] We are such an immensity, so many things happen in us that, seen from the inside, there is no identity."[10] Unbecoming is the process by which one attains this non-identitarian state of plurality and possibility, and it passes through an encounter or relationship with language, which is precisely what Sarraute, Wittig, and Garréta enact in their writing.

Beyond freedom from identitarian strictures, unbecoming provides a way out of the epistemological impasse in which we find ourselves today. In contemporary thought, one of the most significant developments in the last decade or so has been the new materialist turn—a return to the material, regularly invoked as the real, which entails moving past the linguistic turn that dominated the intellectual landscape of the late twentieth century with its attention to the discursive construction of reality and insistence on the instability and multiplicity of meaning.[11] In *Becoming Undone*, Elizabeth Grosz, a

---

9. See Stryker, "My Words to Victor Frankenstein," 249–50, for a discussion of birth pronouncements of gender such as "It's a girl."
10. Benmussa and Sarraute, *Entretiens avec Nathalie Sarraute*, back cover, 121.
11. Prominent new materialist thinkers include Jane Bennett, Bruno Latour, Mel Chen, and Elizabeth Grosz, who hail from different disciplinary backgrounds.

thinker of new materialism, argues for feminist theory to move beyond identity politics, the subject, and the epistemological, and "turn, or perhaps return to questions of the real—not empirical questions regarding states of affairs (for these remain epistemological), but questions of the nature and forces of the real, the nature and forces of the world, cosmological forces as well as historical ones. In short, it needs to welcome again what epistemologies have left out: the relentless force of the real, a new metaphysics."[12] Grosz's argument is based on an opposition between the epistemological and the metaphysical, the representational and the real, the conceptual and the material, where epistemology is always at odds with a direct experience of the real. I propose unbecoming as an abstention from having to choose between epistemology and ontology. Unbecoming, just as it reworks subjectivity, cutting subjecthood loose, also reworks epistemology.

Unbecoming subjectivity is experiential, open to and attentive to the material (in particular, the materiality of language, where this materiality is not simply material in its effects but in itself).[13] It is cognitive, but it is not knowing. Sarraute, Wittig, and Garréta use language to suspend the ways in which language consolidates and produces knowledge. Instead of language enabling the subject to know the world and thereby master self and world, language here erodes and exceeds the subject, transforming it into a consciousness that cannot use language to consolidate knowledge and the identities that are the objects of such knowledge. The only thing that unbecoming subjectivity can be is itself—not an identity, or a subject, but a consciousness that experiences itself as unbounded. It can only exist in its experience, and it is powerless to decant that experience into discrete epistemological units or bodies such as knowledge and truth. The subjectivity without subjecthood does not know anything—it experiences its own unknowingness and, in that experience, is freed from compulsory knowledge, compulsory identity, a compulsory way of being. Cognition without *connaissance*—that is the humble position of unbecoming subjectivity. It takes in experience and lets it go, at a point of equilibrium between materiality and knowledge, where neither the material nor the conceptual have taken up their positions of opposition and incompatibility. Unbecoming is thus a state of radical neutrality, neither purely epistemological nor purely ontological, but a state that, as it dissolves the boundaries of itself, refuses to be contained in either knowledge or the material. It is, to draw again on Sarraute's language, "this self-evident fact—or

---

12. Grosz, *Becoming Undone*, 85.
13. In Chapter 2, I discuss the materiality of language that emerges in Sarraute, Wittig, and Garréta's writing and its difference from the materiality theorized by new materialisms.

is it madness?—that each of us is an entire universe unto ourselves, that we feel infinite, without contours."[14]

So, who are Sarraute, Wittig, and Garréta, these writers of unbecoming? Their unbecoming poetics emerges through reading them together as forming a collective project of anti-identitarian writing, where each writer's individual corpus is shaped by her own approach to and conception of difference, which is informed by her particular historical moment. In the next section, I will situate and describe each writer in chronological order, so that the reader may familiarize herself with authors that she may not otherwise know and obtain a sense of the historical context of each writer's literary production. Afterward, the remainder of the introduction will be devoted to addressing methodological issues.

NATHALIE SARRAUTE (1900–99)

Nathalie Sarraute (born Nathalie Tcherniak), an author whose works have been translated into more than thirty languages and immortalized in Gallimard's prestigious Pléiade collection in 1996 while she was still alive, is one of the major French novelists of the twentieth century. She is considered a central figure of the *Nouveau Roman*, or New Novel, a group of experimental writers including Alain Robbe-Grillet, Claude Simon, and Michel Butor, who, in the 1950s and 1960s, became famous in some circles and notorious in others for pursuing literary innovation through the refusal of such conventions as well-developed characters or plot-driven linear narratives, which they associated with the traditional—and to them, outdated—Balzacian realist novel.

Born July 18, 1900 in Ivanovo, Russia, to a well-off, cultured, secular Jewish family, Sarraute first came to France in 1902 following her parents' divorce to live in Paris with her mother, Pauline Chatounowski, who wrote under the pen name N. Vikhrovski. She spent two months each year in either Russia or Switzerland with her father, Ilya Tcherniak, who was a chemist of such repute that the tsar issued him a special dispensation permitting him to live in Ivanovo even though he was Jewish. Sarraute, who was already being raised by her parents to be bilingual in French and Russian, spent the first part of her education in the French system, where she learned to read and write. Sarraute went back and forth between Russia and France until her father became the

---

14. Sarraute, Prière d'insérer to *"disent les imbéciles."*

primary custodial parent in 1909, at which point he'd already immigrated to Paris because of political persecution in Russia.

An excellent student, in 1920 Sarraute obtained her *licence* (the French equivalent of a BA) at the Sorbonne in English literature. Her studies also took her abroad: she started, but didn't finish, a BA in history at Oxford, and spent several months in Berlin studying sociology, history, and working on her German. Sarraute returned to Paris and went to law school, where she met her husband and lifelong reader, Raymond Sarraute, who would prove to be enormously influential in introducing her to his literary and artistic tastes. Sarraute practiced law until the German occupation of France in World War II made it impossible for Jews to do so. She left the bar but refused to wear the yellow star, going instead into hiding until the Allied Liberation of Paris, at which point she returned to Paris and, no longer a practicing lawyer, dedicated herself to writing, which would be her principal occupation for the rest of her life.

In 1932, Sarraute started to write what would, after years of working and reworking, end up being *Tropismes*. Her manuscript, completed in 1937, was rejected by numerous Parisian publishers before finally being accepted by Denoël in 1939, but would not be well-received until it was republished in 1957 by the Éditions de Minuit.[15] Her second work, the novel *Portrait d'un inconnu* [*Portrait of a Man Unknown*] (1948), hardly did better: despite a preface by Jean-Paul Sartre, national hero and intellectual, whom she'd met during the Occupation, the manuscript was rejected by Gallimard and published by Robert Marin, who bought back the novels at the cost of paper and freed Sarraute from her contract after the novel sold only 400 copies.

It took a long time for Sarraute to establish herself as a writer. It was only in the 1950s, when the New Novel movement was in the air and the subject of much press and media attention, that Sarraute began to enjoy more success, with Gallimard publishing two novels—*Martereau* (1953), *Le Planétarium* [*The Planetarium*] (1959)—and a collection of literary criticism, *L'Ère du soupçon* [*The Age of Suspicion*] (1956), which would come to stand alongside Alain Robbe-Grillet's *Pour un nouveau roman* [*For a New Novel*] (1963) as the two most important theoretical works on the New Novel. In refusing to create novels with traditional characters, plots, or narrative, the New Novelists refused identification with either the explicitly political and ideologically charged *littérature engagée* [committed literature] that Sartre had made influential in the postwar years, or the depoliticized, dilettantish right-wing literature of the Hussards. Their writing constituted a literary example of Théophile Gautier's

---

15. The lack of success of the Denoël edition may have had something to do with its unfortunate coinciding with the beginning of World War II, in addition to the difficult and experimental nature of her writing.

call for "art for art's sake," and this aestheticism put them at the modernist front of French literature.

With the advent of the New Novel, Sarraute was finally able to establish herself as a writer. After the publication of *Le Planétarium*, she was invited by universities all around the world to give talks about her work and contemporary literature (especially the New Novel). While much of Sarraute's success surely had to do with her association with the intensely mediatized New Novel, and no study of the New Novel omits her name, Sarraute always maintained a certain distance from the group, disidentifying with the label New Novelist. Her differences from the New Novel are manifold: Claude Ollier, Robert Pinget, Claude Simon, Samuel Beckett, Alain Robbe-Grillet, and Michel Butor were all writers with Minuit,[16] while she was a writer with Gallimard;[17] Sarraute was a generation removed from them, a good twenty years older; Sarraute insisted on an approach to writing that focused not on the objective, surface world, but on interiority and psychology, rejected by the other writers, especially Robbe-Grillet; and, most visibly, she was a woman, while they were all men.

Sarraute insists on her singularity even though (or perhaps because) critics and readers try to inscribe her in categories, tacking on to her such labels as Woman, Jew, New Novelist. It's easy to understand this tendency to identify her: these identities correspond to the realities of her lived life and make her more legible as an individual—she *was* a woman, Russian, Jewish, and closely associated with that group of writers that became known as the New Novel. As a portrait of her published in the popular press magazine *Télérama* attests, "Sometimes, when the sun set too early in winter, she would let herself be taken over by a deep melancholy that could stem from either *her Russian soul or her Jewish memory*."[18] This statement embodies precisely the categorizing, reductive powers of language to which Sarraute was always so sensitive throughout her entire writing career: it tries to identify and explain her by packaging her person into discrete categories—Russian, Jewish, etc. But Sarraute always rejected identity, insisting not on the differences between individuals but on how we are all the same, each of us as alike as two drops of

---

16. While Ollier and Butor also distanced themselves from Minuit and Jérôme Lindon's careful curation of his New Novelists, at the time of the iconic photo of those writers gathered in front of the Minuit offices, which came to be the face of the New Novel, both those writers were still with Minuit.

17. This difference in publishers is significant. Minuit, which began publishing Resistance materials during World War II, had a political identity grounded in resistance, subversion, and the contemporary. It was a young press compared to Gallimard, which was well-established—a bastion of prestige and guardian of literary tradition.

18. Gazier, "Nathalie Sarraute." My emphasis.

water.¹⁹ Sarraute thus refused to identify as a woman writer, a Russian writer, a Jewish writer, a New Novelist. For her, to write was to be no one. In no uncertain terms, she would reject the idea of writing as an expression of her individual identity, saying: "Who am I? What am I? Here are questions I've never asked myself while writing," and "When I write, I am neither man nor woman nor dog nor cat."²⁰

This is not to say that she was devoid of ego: her papers, available in the archives at the Bibliothèque nationale de France,²¹ show her to be someone of great precision who sought to be in control of her own life and image. And, though writing was never easy for her,²² Sarraute did not see herself as a minor writer. This desire for control can be seen in Sarraute's publication in 1997 of *Ouvrez*, her last published work, a year after Gallimard effectively had turned the page on her life and work by publishing her *Œuvres complètes* [*Complete Works*] as a Pléiade edition in 1996. For Sarraute, the idea of selfless writing meant that writing was an act and a space that did not consolidate or depend on a self endowed with identity—a self forged in and through difference. Instead, writing was where selves could disappear and subjectivities, unencumbered by identity, show themselves to be radically equal, without difference but not the same. While Sarraute's manuscripts will not be open to the public for several more decades, I would wager that whatever she was working on at the time of her death will prove to be yet another instance of our radical equality before and through language.

MONIQUE WITTIG (1935-2003)

Unlike Sarraute, whose life has been well documented and can be represented in a clear chronology,²³ there is little that's known publicly about Monique Wittig. There are no biographies, authorized or unauthorized (although Wittig's sister, Gille Wittig, self-published a short book consisting of text and photographs remembering their shared childhood).²⁴ Wittig's biography, then,

---

19. Finas, "Nathalie Sarraute," 4.
20. Sarraute, Prière d'insérer to *"disent les imbéciles"*; Rykiel, "Quand j'écris," 40.
21. Fonds Nathalie Sarraute, BnF Richelieu, Département des Manuscrits, NAF 28088.
22. Rambures, *Comment travaillent les écrivains*, 152–53; Leduc, *La Folie en tête*, 65.
23. The Pléiade edition of Sarraute's complete works includes a detailed chronology of her life compiled in consultation with the author herself. For more on Sarraute's life, see Bouchardeau, *Nathalie Sarraute*. Ann Jefferson, one of the editors of the Pléiade edition, is currently working on a biography of Sarraute.
24. Many thanks to Suzette Robichon for giving me a copy of this work, *Ma sœur sauvage* [*My Wild Sister*]. This work is doubly unauthorized insofar as it does not have an ISBN assigned to it and thus exists outside library catalogues and official records.

remains the property of those who actually knew and shared their lives with her. But we do know that Wittig was born in 1935 in Alsace, where she grew up in the rural town of Dannemarie. And we know that Wittig came to Paris to study at the Sorbonne in 1950.[25] Beyond that, little information has been made available. What we know of Wittig emerges, then, primarily out of her entry into public life through her writing, her feminism, and her life as an academic in the US.

Wittig, as is made clear in her posthumously published work, *Le Chantier littéraire* [*The Literary Worksite*] (2010), which is both an *ars poetica* and an homage to Sarraute, was deeply influenced by the New Novelists and their rejection of literary convention. Their experiments in form inspired her own, and her debut novel, *L'Opoponax* (1964), garnered critical acclaim, winning her the Prix Médicis and Sarraute's lifelong respect. When Wittig's literary creation collided with her feminist activism in the MLF, however, it resulted in what seemed to be a marked change in her literary course, which took on an overtly political lesbian bent with such novels as *Les Guérillères* [*The Guérillères*] (1969); *Le Corps lesbien* [*The Lesbian Body*] (1973); *Brouillon pour un dictionnaire des amantes* [*Lesbian Peoples: Material for a Dictionary*] (1976), co-authored by Sande Zeig; *Virgile, non* [*Across the Acheron*] (1985); the play *The Constant Journey* [*Le Voyage sans fin*] (1984), and a collection of short stories, *Paris-la-politique* (1999). What had been present as a thematic element in *L'Opoponax*—the protagonist is a little girl who comes to realize and own her love of another girl—became the driving force and logic of Wittig's subsequent works.

While Wittig is considered an important writer by academics and literary critics and her works enjoy cult status among a certain lesbian and/or feminist subset of readers (made possible by Wittig's works having been translated widely), she is probably best known for her feminism. Like many other members of the Mouvement de Liberátion des Femmes, Wittig had been involved in the revolutionary, Marxist student-worker uprisings of May '68, which nearly brought down De Gaulle's government. Revolted by the sexism of their male co-revolutionaries, who took for granted that women would serve them in a domestic and sexual capacity instead of being equal members in the movement, Wittig, along with other disenchanted women, initiated

---

25. These are the two lines of the biographical essay, authored by the Wittig scholar Diane Crowder, that deal with Wittig's early life that are published on the website maintained by the Monique Wittig Literary Estate (http://www.moniquewittig.com/bio/bio.html), as well as in a more recent biographical essay authored by Sandra Daroczi (https://modernlanguages.sas.ac.uk/research-centres/centre-study-contemporary-womens-writing/languages/french/monique-wittig). This is also the only biographical information one can find in encyclopedias.

what would become the MLF to fight for the liberation of the class of women.[26] In 1970, along with her sister, Gille Wittig, Margaret Stephenson (who would later change her name to Namascar Shaktini), and Marcia Rothenburg, Wittig co-authored and co-published "Combat pour la libération des femmes" [Combat for women's liberation] in the leftist newspaper *L'Idiot International*, which would act as a manifesto for the MLF. In addition, Wittig was one of the original ten to participate in the act of putting, on the tomb of the unknown soldier, a wreath dedicated to the one even more unknown than he—his wife—for which she and her fellow protestors were arrested. This act would be mediatized and then mythologized as inaugurating the MLF as a movement with real visibility.[27]

Wittig left France in 1976 with her partner, Sande Zeig, a dancer and choreographer, and taught in French departments at a number of American universities and colleges such as Vassar College and UC Berkeley before assuming a permanent position at the University of Arizona, where she would eventually also join their Women's Studies program. Wittig remained in Arizona until her death from a heart attack in 2003. Her trajectory as an academic overlaps considerably with her trajectory as a feminist, as many of the essays she published as part of *The Straight Mind* were first presented at academic conferences and published in academic journals. For instance, Wittig's oft-cited declaration that lesbians are not women was made during the 1978 meeting of the Modern Languages Association (MLA)[28] and the essay that communicated this idea in written form was first published in the academic journal *Feminist Issues*.[29] Because of Wittig's life in the academic sphere, she has been taken up and taught as a major theorist of materialist, anti-difference feminism, and is known primarily for *The Straight Mind* (1992), which was revisited and published in French translation as *La Pensée straight* in 2001. She has had a lasting impact on both feminist and queer studies for her unrelenting conviction that difference is a constructed, not natural, category, and that just as language created difference, it can undo it.[30] And, because of Wittig's insistence on the

---

26. See Picq, "MLF: 1970, Année Zéro."
27. The MLF was not a unitary group but rather a diverse coalition of smaller, constitutive groups that allied together and arrived at decisions through consensus. Wittig was herself involved with a number of different subgroups, such as *Les Gouines rouges* [*The Red Dykes*] and *Féministes révolutionnaires* [*Revolutionary Feminists*].
28. See Shaktini, *On Monique Wittig*, 197.
29. Wittig, "One Is Not Born a Woman."
30. Wittig has become a household name in feminist theory in large part because of Judith Butler's sustained engagement with her in *Gender Trouble*. Whether Butler should be judged a good reader of Wittig or not has been the subject of debate. Anne Garréta dismissed Butler's reading of Wittig as "la bouillie pour chat" (literally, "mush for cats," and figuratively, "rubbish"

specificity of a lesbian politics in the feminist struggle against patriarchy, she has been taken up by some as a queer or proto-queer figure.

In 2007, the journal *GLQ: A Journal of Lesbian and Gay Studies* published a special volume on Wittig entitled "Monique Wittig: At the Crossroads of Criticism," which brought together essays that had originally been presented at a conference at Harvard University held in Wittig's honor after her death.[31] These essays are both academic commentary and homage, an accounting for Wittig's work and a remembrance of her life. They operate as a collective testimony to the importance of her thought and presence. The essays display a remarkable diversity, ranging from the anecdotal and rigorously intimate to the more familiar rigor of academic analysis, from the attempt to channel Wittig's voice and style to an explicit affirmation of one's distance and distinction from her (with these seemingly contradictory impulses often cohabiting the same essay). The special issue gives some sense of the richness of Wittig's writing and thought, the influence and impact she's had. It shows what it can look like to remember Wittig as a feminist, theorist, politically engaged activist, writer, or lesbian; as having an unrelenting focus on recuperating subjectivity; as constituting a figure of queer possibility; as unassimilable to genealogies of queerness. While the special issue demonstrates just how portable Wittig is, and the many ways she can be taken up, we should remember that in her own eyes, as is made clear in her writing, both published and unpublished,[32] she was first and foremost a writer who wrote because of language, because of all the things language could make and unmake.

ANNE GARRÉTA (1962–)

Garréta's literary career began with a splash. *Sphinx,* published in 1986 when Garréta was a twenty-three-year-old *normalienne,* as female students of France's elite *écoles normales* are called,[33] received critical acclaim for the feat of erasing gender from a love story written in the highly gendered French language. Garréta was brought onto Bernard Pivot's popular literary television

---

or "baloney") in her keynote address on Wittig and Foucault for Sciences Po's 2013 Queer Week. For a written articulation of the disagreement, see Garréta, "Wittig, La Langue-Le-Politique," which charges Butler with misreading Wittig.

31. Epps and Katz, "Monique Wittig."

32. Wittig's letters to Sarraute, housed in the Sarraute archives at the BnF, attest to the importance of literature and writing to Wittig.

33. While the American and French education systems are very different, one could liken the *écoles normales* to the Ivy League, where membership in this elite sphere guarantees access to social, intellectual, and economic capital and resources not otherwise accessible.

program, *Apostrophes*, and hailed as a young writer to look out for.[34] Garréta went on to publish a philosophical pamphlet in the manner of eighteenth-century Enlightenment texts, entitled *Pour en finir avec le genre humain* [*To Do Away with Humankind*] (1987) before pursuing a PhD in seventeenth- and eighteenth-century French literature at New York University. Garréta has gone on to pursue a dual academic career in both France and the United States, teaching at the Université de Rennes II and Duke University.

After *Sphinx*, Garréta published two more novels, *Ciels liquides* [*Liquid Skies*] (1990) and *La Décomposition* [*Decomposition*] (1999), before she was inducted (or co-opted, to use their term) into the Oulipo, or Ouvroir de Littérature Potentielle [Workroom of Potential Literature],[35] a highly publicized and public literary group composed of writers and mathematicians who produce literary texts and seek to renew literary potential through adherence to certain constraints.[36] Since her entry into the Oulipo in 2000, her novel *Pas un jour* [*Not One Day*] (2001) won the Prix Médicis, and she has co-authored a novel, *Eros mélancolique* [*Melancholy Eros*] (2009), with the Oulipian poet Jacques Roubaud. Most recently, in 2017, she published a novel, *Dans l'béton* [*In Concrete*], a ludic and linguistically playful narrative of childhood.[37]

Garréta is a difficult writer to pin down. She exemplifies hybridity and a disregard for the consistency or coherence that we demand from or expect of identities. Like Sarraute, Garréta resists being defined by clear contours and corralled into neatly demarcated identities. She is feminist, but insists on her queerness.[38] She is French, but also lives and works in the United States and is equally at ease in French and English—less bilingual and bicultural than translingual and transcultural, operating through a constant movement between these two linguistic and cultural poles. She is Oulipian, but maintains an ironic stance on the way literary potential is attributed to individuals (such as the way a commitment to literary potential doesn't prevent a cult of personality from setting in). While trained as a scholar of seventeenth- and

---

34. Pivot, "Pendant la campagne électorale lisez des romans."
35. While *ouvroir* is often translated as *workshop*, I opt for the more literal *workroom*.
36. Some famous members of the Oulipo include Raymond Queneau, its co-founder, Georges Perec, and Italo Calvino. One particularly famous constraint is the lipogram, or omission of a letter, as illustrated by Perec in his novel *La Disparition*, which is written without the letter E.
37. The novel was published too recently for me to be able to include it in my discussion of Garréta's corpus, but it confirms the strong influence of Wittig, as there is an incredibly rich intertextual engagement with *L'Opoponax*. It also continues Garréta's work of suspending identity by maintaining, for a substantial portion of the text, the sort of non-disclosure of the narrator's gender we find in *Sphinx*.
38. Garréta, during a writing workshop held at the fourth annual Queer Week held at Sciences Po in March 2013, said, "I'm feminist, but not at the price of forgetting I'm queer."

eighteenth-century literature,[39] she also works with contemporary fiction and queer theory. Her literary and intellectual influences are eclectic, including Barthes, Proust, Rousseau, Rancière, Foucault, Sedgwick, and Wittig.

Where Garréta is consistent is in a commitment to indeterminacy, her investment in the freedom to move unhampered by categories. Garréta's combination of the contemporary—the queer, the postmodern—and of the early modern is logical insofar as both can be seen as coalescing around a rejection of division and the identification and definition (and the ensuing hierarchy) that follow,[40] and around a demand that everything be accessible, manipulable, in play. Garréta has described her affinity for early modern literature as follows:

> I like 17th- and 18th-century literature because the disciplinary division between literature and philosophy, between narrativity and ideas, hasn't yet happened. Because sticking literature inside the limits of a pure narrative plot is to sterilize it. Literature's great strength is precisely not having a territory. Not even a vague one. It's absolutely universal in the sense that it's the putting back into play of all the world's variety.[41]

Viewed in light of her investment in queer politics and her postmodern aesthetic sensibilities that have her combining the preciosity of early modern French with the language of video gaming,[42] Garréta might not seem to resemble Sarraute or Wittig, but she shares with them a sense of literature's possibilities. In this language of putting back into play all the diversity of the world—that is, experiencing the world in its differences without its being ordered by difference, given that hierarchy is inimical to play and the freedom of play—we can see a vision of literature as a space where the concept of territory no longer applies, where such boundaries and contours disappear.

Garréta, living in the twenty-first century, is wary of the language of universalism even as she evokes literature's universality.[43] Rather than get caught

---

39. Garréta, "Fins de romans, XVII(e)—XVIII(e) siècles."

40. Admittedly, the Enlightenment was actually a time of great division and taxonomical knowledge (see Foucault, *The Order of Things* and his discussion of the classical episteme), but Garréta's predilection for the early modern is grounded in the fact that it hasn't been taken over entirely by such categorization and still enjoys a certain intellectual or conceptual fluidity.

41. Garréta, interview with Frédéric Grolleau from September 1, 1999, reproduced at http://cosmogonie.free.fr/paru2.html.

42. This combination of disparate elements and citations of older forms embodies Fredric Jameson's conceptualization of postmodernism as characterized by pastiche. See Jameson, *Postmodernism*, 17.

43. Garréta, in conversation with me, has, half in jest, likened Wittig's attempts to appropriate the universal to trying to steal a motorless vehicle when it might be better to walk to one's

up in the question of whether to use the language of universality and universalism to describe the literary project of a writer who has a vexed relationship with these deeply French notions, I want to instead place Garréta, along with Sarraute and Wittig, under the sign of unbecoming, which describes the state of subjectivity without subjecthood enacted by these writers without tying it to an ism (like universalism), which denotes ideology. Unbecoming is a state, not an ideology. It is an experience, not a position—one that is open to any and all readers.

CONNECTIONS

The fact that all three writers pursue unbecoming writing is not a coincidence. A direct chain of influence connects Sarraute to Wittig to Garréta. Wittig knew and was inspired by Sarraute's work, and Garréta knows and is inspired by Wittig's, which means that the poetics of unbecoming can be seen as transmitted from one writer to the next, and not only transmitted, but transformed, according to each writer's own historical moment and situation.

The connection between Sarraute and Wittig is the clearest, as these two writers knew each other well. They enjoyed a long and close friendship, marked by mutual support and admiration, which lasted the decades between Wittig's meeting Sarraute through the publication of *L'Opoponax* and Sarraute's death in 1999. Wittig was one of Sarraute's most constant friends, and they spent each summer together at Sarraute's country house in Chérence.[44] Wittig's letters to Sarraute reveal a friendship that had its origins in passion, and her earliest letters include explicit declarations of love. What becomes evident, though, from reading Wittig's side of her correspondence with Sarraute, is that while that initial passion was romantic, it wasn't so much Sarraute as Sarraute who inspired it, but Sarraute as writer. Wittig fell in love with Sarraute not because of Sarraute's physical person, but because of Sarraute's language, because of the Sarraute Wittig found in Sarraute's books. Wittig's critical works are a testament to Sarraute's influence. Beyond *Le Chantier littéraire*, which is a sustained reflection on and engagement with Sarraute's writing, *The Straight Mind*, in addition to its well-known essays on feminist

---

destination instead. Garréta is deeply ambivalent about the question of the universal, however, and this remark is not a simple dismissal of Wittig's attempts at appropriating universality. As Garréta clarified at a later point, for her critique to stand, the term *universal* would need to be clarified conceptually, and Garréta's and Wittig's different *situations d'énonciation* [situations of enunciation—essentially, speaking positions] would need to be historicized.

44. For more on the camaraderie between Sarraute and Wittig, see the chapter on Sarraute in Hewitt, *Autobiographical Tightropes*.

theory, includes several essays devoted to Sarraute's writing. This juxtaposition speaks to how Wittig saw Sarraute's writing and language as playing a fundamental role in forming her own political and aesthetic project. While Wittig's initial encounter with Sarraute was one of love at first reading, her continued relationship with Sarraute and Sarraute's language resulted in an unwavering, sophisticated reflection on literature as a joining together of the political and the aesthetic, as seen throughout Wittig's œuvre.

While Garréta hasn't published book-length works consecrated to Wittig the way Wittig did for Sarraute, the impact Wittig has had on Garréta is undeniable. We can think of Wittig as a catalyst for Garréta's writing. Plenty of other literary figures inform Garréta's work, but it is to Wittig that Garréta confesses a debt. It's Wittig that Garréta cites as a condition of possibility for her debut novel, *Sphinx,* as I discuss in Chapter 3. Garréta's relationship to Wittig might not have had the intimate dimension that Sarraute and Wittig's had, but it is nonetheless also characterized by a fierce investment in Wittig not so much as a biographical character, but as a singular vision and experience of language.

Unbecoming Language consists of four chapters. The first three chapters examine each writer's use of language to unbecome, to combat a regime of seemingly compulsory difference. The fourth chapter examines all three writers' relationships to language to theorize a poetics of unbecoming—an original feminist poetics grounded in an experience of a language endowed with a body and agency. These chapters are anchored in my own close encounters with the novels I discuss, and thus remain largely within a world delineated by textual, rather than historical, boundaries. Nonetheless, the historical dimension is important, and in what follows, I attend to the way each writer's use and conception of language is itself historically conditioned. Language, at the moment of writing and at the moment of reading, can feel like a transcendent experience, where the text is the fruit of a now-ness of and with language, but it is in fact constantly both pulling and being pulled by the waves of history.

As Sarraute, Wittig, and Garréta belong to different generations, each of them originates from a different set of possibilities and constraints than is the case for the others. In considering how each of these writers lives and works under a particular set of historical conditions, I do not presume to account for the historical evolution of what it meant and means to be a woman, a subject which would require multiple volumes, nor, similarly, to provide a history of French literature in the twentieth century, which would also require a book unto itself. Rather, I want to consider, more modestly, some of the implications of what it means for Sarraute's, Wittig's, and Garréta's respective historicity to be filtered through the categories of writer and of woman concomitantly (which doesn't mean, however, considering their historical specificity through the filter of Woman Writer, an identification that misses the point of their unbecoming writing). The simple fact that each of them writes and lives in different moments means that their experience of both literature and difference is different for each.

Of the three, Wittig's historical specificity could be seen as the most obvious. Her writing career coincides with the political, revolutionary energy and the social turmoil of the MLF. It is evident that the sorts of feminist utopias of lesbian lovers and warriors that Wittig stages in works like *Les Guérillères, Le Corps lesbien*, and *Brouillon pour un dictionnaire des amantes* are related to her own active engagement within the MLF—to her experience in this coalition of women who created feminist spaces and identities for themselves in their struggle to create a world other than the one imposed on them by patriarchy. But these novels were not simply the imagining of other worlds: they were attempts at creating a history and a language for women who, up till that moment, did not have either. Wittig writes in *Les Guérillères* of the need to create such a history and language: "You say there are no words to describe this time, you say it does not exist. But remember. Make an effort to remember. Or, failing that, invent."[45] This imperative to create a history, to tap into a memory that one didn't even know one had, can be seen as part of the feminist zeitgeist of the 1970s and 1980s, which, in addition to political struggles in the streets and in consciousness-raising groups, permeated the academy on both sides of the Atlantic. We can see this in the beginnings of women's history as a discipline, as recounted in the pioneering work of feminist historians such as Michelle Perrot, Christiane Klapisch-Zuber, Joan Kelly, Nancy Cott, and Gerda Lerner, to name a few who, in the face of much resistance and scorn from the academy, gave a voice to women across the centuries whose lives had been relegated to silence.[46]

Wittig's later works such as *Virgile, non* and the short stories of *Paris-la-politique* mark a dramatic shift in tone from heady utopianism to bitterness. These works, which feature women incapable of acting in their self-interest or of striving toward emancipation, reflect Wittig's own experience of both physical and temporal distance from a feminist movement that ultimately failed to end patriarchy and was torn apart by internecine conflict, seen in the way a strong faction such as Antoinette Fouque's differentialist Psychanalyse

---

45. Wittig, *Les Guérillères*, 89.
46. Perrot, *Une histoire des femmes*; Klapisch-Zuber, *Culture et pouvoir des femmes*; Kelly, *Women, History & Theory*; Cott, *Root of Bitterness*; Lerner, *The Woman in American History*.

et Politique (Psychépo, or Psych et Po, for short) took over the movement and worked to legitimate and anchor the difference that was anathema to Wittig's politics.[47] And in a pre-MLF work like *L'Opoponax*, a bildungsroman where the protagonist's coming of age coincides with a becoming-lesbian, we can see the germ of the optimism Wittig and other lesbian feminists must have held in the years leading up to the MLF, of the energy without which such a movement and reclamation of marginal subjectivity would not have been possible. Wittig, whose life is marked by a deep political engagement, produced works that bear the mark of that exuberant moment in the 1970s when a whole new world—revolution—was just around the corner.

Wittig's writing, just as it bears the marks of its political moment, bears the marks of its literary one: her pursuit of formal innovation and rejection of novelistic conventions such as plot and character can be seen as the fruit of her exposure to the work of the New Novelists who had done away with them and demanded that writers write differently. The two strands of Wittig's feminism and her writing are tightly tied together. Without the New Novel's—and in particular, Sarraute's—influence, Wittig might have written novels that had traditional plots and featured heroic female protagonists, a simple and fantastic counterpoint to the classic realist novel, or heavy-handed novels in the vein of *littérature engagée*. And without the influence of the MLF, Wittig might have written formally innovative texts that continued in the "difficult," inaccessible vein of the New Novel by engaging in self-conscious reflection on *genre* as genre, but not as gender, producing works divorced from feminist political ends—art for art's sake. Wittig could have been cleaved into two: into Wittig the feminist activist and into Wittig the writer. Or she could have been simply one or the other. She was both, however, and this was made possible by the convergence in her life of both the New Novel's literary energy and the MLF's political energy.

Garréta's writing is more difficult to map onto the sorts of seismic political and literary movements that marked Wittig and made possible her becoming-Wittig, in large part because Garréta is a contemporary writer, still alive, still writing, and so her corpus (and hence, any evaluation of her work) is provisory. As Garréta explicitly articulated at a conference in France held in Wittig's

---

47. Under Fouque's leadership, Psychépo trademarked the name and logo of the MLF in 1979, ending what had been a diverse and pluralistic movement. Fouque took this legal action to take over the MLF and ostensibly save it from the parts of itself that identified as feminist, as she was vocally anti-feminist, seeing feminism as an attempt to destroy sexual difference (see Fouque, "Femmes en mouvements"). For feminist reactions to Fouque's actions, see Perrot, "MLF: 'Antoinette Fouque'"; Fourest, "Le Féminisme pour les nuls"; Collectif, "MLF." For a history and account of the MLF from Fouque's point of view, see Fouque and Mouvement de libération des femmes, *Génération MLF, 1968–2008*.

honor, whose proceedings were published under the title *Lire Monique Wittig Aujourd'hui*, she owes her entry into writing to Wittig:

> Monique Wittig is an extremely important writer for me. In a way, she made possible my first novel [. . .]. I thus have a debt, which isn't a debt, but that obligates me nonetheless—it isn't that I owe Monique Wittig something but that she opened up a possibility for me.[48]

But Garréta's voice is entirely her own, and her corpus, while it has a political spirit, is markedly different from Wittig's—Garréta is no Wittig Junior.

Garréta's writing, as we will see, is melancholic and dark—dystopian rather than utopian in its energies and tone. In addition, the strategy that Garréta employs for writing against difference and identity is not that of Wittig's lesbianization of her textual world in order to give lie to the false universalism of the white, straight male. Rather than attempt, as Wittig does, to reclaim the universal and recuperate the vilified, marginalized subjectivity of the lesbian,[49] rather than establish utopian spaces as a positive alternative to the damage difference and identity have done in creating structures of oppression in the world, Garréta instead occupies a negative position and destroys said world in her texts. She privileges destruction and desolation, as seen in *Sphinx, Ciels liquides, La Décomposition*, and even a seemingly autobiographical work like *Pas un jour*.

These departures from the Wittigian corpus might be attributed to Garréta's coming of age and into writing in the 1980s—after the fizzling out of the adventure of the MLF, whose aspirations were assimilated into the Socialist government of François Mitterand, a political mainstreaming that effectively domesticated feminism by taking it out of its revolutionary context—and to her taking up of gender and queer studies, distinctly American bodies of thought and work.[50] With both the movements of May '68 and the MLF hav-

---

48. Garréta, "Wittig, la langue-le-politique," 25. See Chapter 3 for a closer examination of Garréta's indebtedness to Wittig.

49. It's important to remember that for Wittig, the lesbian doesn't represent an identity per se. Instead, it's a refusal of sociality, of identity as a source of privilege and power. It's a fugitive subjectivity that's anarchic in its rejection of traditional power structures. As Wittig puts it, the point isn't to replace patriarchy with matriarchy, to simply invert who's in power and who's not, but to do away with hierarchy altogether. Wittig, *The Straight Mind*, 10. While one could argue that Wittig's stance of militant lesbianization doesn't in fact live up to Wittig's aspirations for it, it's important to recognize that the figure of the lesbian is conceptualized not as a stepping-stone to a different kind of hierarchy but as a means for its destruction.

50. Garréta's fluency in these fields is part of her formation as a hybrid individual. In particular, her taking up of gender and queer studies can be seen as an Americanization of her intellectual landscape, as these fields, though they are indebted to French poststructuralist

ing drawn to a close, and with familiar forms of power still in place, assuming a utopian vision must have seemed impossible or naïve. Garréta's writing thus imagines not the ebullient collectivities of Wittig's novels, but stages instead subjectivities that are marked by their alienation and isolation, a solitude that cannot be escaped, that prevails against any attempts to forge a durable relation. Garréta's melancholy could be seen as a mourning of the political possibility that used to be but is no longer.

Garréta's corpus, however, still speaks to a sense of political possibility for literature. This possibility is marked by queerness, understood in broad strokes as an anti-identitarian, anti-normative positionality. Emerging in the 1990s out of poststructuralist theory, queer—as taken up by queer theory—brought deconstruction to bear on sexuality in order to denaturalize it, and showed how heterosexuality is in no way natural, but the product of imposed and assimilated norms. This critique of normativity produced both a critique of compulsory heterosexuality but also of the categories of gay and lesbian identity that had become a rallying point for non-heterosexuals oppressed by a straight social order: *gay* and *lesbian* were also problematic in their mobilization, or rather, immobilization, around a homosexual norm and hetero/homo binary. Queer theory's denaturalizing critique and resistance soon expanded beyond sexuality to target all forms of normativity. Against compulsory identity, queer theory thus proposes fluidity, mobility, and the destabilization of categories.

In Garréta's work, the influence of queerness can be seen in her overturning of normativity (*La Décomposition* celebrates murder as a method to attain aesthetic perfection; *Ciels liquides* features an angelic character who might be considered queer par excellence as an immanently non-normative being existing outside the categories of gender as well as of the human), and in her embrace of a proliferation of meanings as a way of resisting the oppressive normativity of epistemological closure and certainty (e.g., *Sphinx*, a text that predates queer theory by some years, lends itself to a number of different possibilities—a love story between two men, two women, a man and a woman, or something else). But while Garréta's work can be considered queer, it goes further than queer, in my view. Queer theory is by and large content to operate through destabilization of normative identity categories and practices. I see Garréta's work as going beyond destabilization, as being animated by the ambition to destroy them altogether. The Wittigian nature of this ambition

---

theorists such as Foucault and Derrida, are considered by the French to be distinctly American products. For more on the vexed national character of these fields and the transatlantic exchange that produces them, see Berger, *Le Grand théâtre du genre*; Costello, "Inventing 'French Feminism,'" and, most recently, Perreau, *Queer Theory*.

calls for Garréta to be read with Wittig, and thus, with Sarraute, which is a reading that should not be subsumed solely under the aegis of queer. I will return to and develop this point more carefully in the last section of the introduction, where I will be able to paint a less reductive picture of the decidedly non-monolithic conceptual field of queer theory.

Finally, Sarraute's writing is even harder to map onto the sorts of seismic political and intellectual movements that mark Wittig and Garréta, partly because her writing remains so consistent in tone and intention even as the twentieth century, which served as the backdrop for the nearly seventy years of her writing career, was marked by constant social and political changes. To situate Sarraute historically in terms of what would have been the context for her entry into a writing against difference, it may be helpful to place her within what is called, reductively, first-wave feminism, in which case we can then situate Wittig and Garréta within second- and third-wave feminism, respectively.[51] First-wave feminism describes the feminist activism and theory from the mid-nineteenth century to the mid-twentieth century that was primarily concerned with obtaining suffrage. Behind the struggle for suffrage was the greater project of legal equality, which animated the liberal feminism that the first wave is identified with—a feminism concerned with access to equal opportunities and rights such as the right to vote, to hold property, to work freely, and to not be considered minors under the law, as stipulated by the Napoleonic Code. Sarraute, in interviews, has identified her feminism as being outside the literary realm: "I am politically engaged as a citizen, not as a writer."[52] For Sarraute, feminism was more about improving concrete conditions and obtaining equal rights than about concepts or theory. While Sarraute thus did not see her writing the way I do, as a concerted and coherent feminist project of writing against difference, there was no shortage of ways her life as a woman in the first half of the twentieth century posed constraints—constraints first-wave feminism was fighting to change. Of course, Wittig and Garréta also faced (or face, in Garréta's case) certain limitations as a result of being women (or rather, of being interpellated and identified as such by the state and social order), but they began writing and publishing when there was at least a semblance of equal status under the law.

---

51. The wave model of feminism has been rigorously critiqued on many fronts, and it certainly has the infelicitous consequence of overly distinguishing one moment in feminism from the others (e.g., there were first wave critiques of essentialism, and it isn't as if the third wave of feminism hasn't been concerned with questions of economic access and equity), but it still remains a useful model for thinking through feminism's progress and evolution throughout the twentieth century by accounting for what struggles came to dominate a given period.

52. Huppert, "Nathalie Sarraute," 14.

To understand how being a woman who wrote was necessarily different for Sarraute than it was for Wittig or Garréta, take the example of suffrage. Sarraute wrote and published *Tropismes* (1939) before French women received the right to vote in 1944.[53] To write and to publish necessarily means believing that one's voice deserves to be heard, and Sarraute was attempting to make her literary voice heard even though the French state made it clear that her voice as a citizen did not count. Sarraute's legal inferiority manifested itself in other ways as well. For example, Sarraute was 38 years old when married women were granted legal majority, finally allowed to be adults under the law, and she was 65 years old when married women obtained the right to work without their husbands' consent (which, for Sarraute, meant having her husband sign off on her previous publishing contracts with Gallimard). With this in mind, we begin to get a sense of Sarraute's audacity in demanding that she be recognized not simply as a woman writer, but as a writer without qualification—a demand for an equality that simply did not exist in the society Sarraute lived in for the better part of her adult life (and that still exists only partially).

Sarraute began to write in the 1930s, nearly two decades before Simone de Beauvoir would drop a theoretical bombshell by declaring that women are made, not born. Wittig began writing after Beauvoir's *Le Deuxième sexe* [*The Second Sex*] (1949), and Garréta had access to feminist and queer theory—both were exposed to a sustained feminist critique and theorization of difference. For Sarraute, however, difference was something that was experienced in life but that could be transcended in writing. In her correspondence and interviews, when she evokes Russian proletarians reading Balzac, or a young man identifying with the elderly female character of Tante Berthe in *Le Planétarium*, she sees literature as being larger than the divisions brought about by class, sex, or age. In writing, she found a way of shedding her identity and the various forms of difference that that entailed, and this in a moment before thinkers gave lie to the seemingly essential nature of identity or difference in a way that had traction on society at large. Sarraute's writing may not have been informed by a theory of difference, but it itself theorizes against difference: this is the point of departure, chronologically and conceptually, for *Unbecoming Language*.

---

53. They would not be able to exercise their newly won right until the general elections the following year, when French women were able to cast a ballot for the first time on April 29, 1945.

WHICH STORY TO TELL?

In *Unbecoming Language*, I tell the story of these three writers and their hollowing out of difference and identity differently than you might expect. In this story of difference, subjectivity, identity, and doing things to them through language, neither French theory nor queer theory appear as characters, despite the centrality of difference and subjectivity to the poststructuralist French thought of the second half of the twentieth century that was taken up in the States as French Theory, and despite the centrality of identity (and its subversion) to queer theory. You may be wondering, why not?

Let's begin with French Theory. Since Descartes, French thought has been preoccupied with the question of subjectivity, and the French Theory of the 1960s on can be seen as attempting to account for subjectivity, be it to eliminate the subject or to recuperate and revitalize it.[54] To name a few key players, we have, for example, Althusser's conceptualization of the subject as constituted by ideology, Derrida's deconstruction of the subject through a rigorous critique of the metaphysics of subjectivity, and Lacan's theorization of the subject in structuralist, linguistic terms ("the unconscious is structured like a language").[55] And crucial to the French conceptualization of subjectivity has been difference, taken up famously in different ways by Derrida, Lacan, and Deleuze, such that French Theory's interrogation of subjectivity could be characterized as a project of conceiving difference as a constitutive element of subjectivity.[56] Moreover, Cixous, Kristeva, and Irigaray—the French Femi-

---

54. For a treatment of why subjectivity has been so central to French philosophy, see Williams, *Contemporary French Philosophy*. Even what's being called New French Philosophy or New French Theory (to distinguish it from the poststructuralism of the latter half of the twentieth century), which might be described as having moved away from its predecessor's linguistic turn to embrace a new materialist turn, is still concerned with the status and nature of human subjectivity, just from a more materialist as opposed to a discursive or linguistic perspective.

55. Althusser, "Ideology and Ideological State Apparatus (Notes Toward an Investigation)"; Derrida, *Of Spirit*; Derrida, *Of Grammatology*; Lacan, *The Four Fundamental Concepts of Psycho-Analysis*, 203.

56. Derrida came up with *différance*, which, in its difference from *différence*, and its play on *différer* (to defer), gestures toward how meaning is always deferred through an endless free-play of the signifiers, which is precisely the sort of free-play by which binaries can be deconstructed and thwarted; Lacan made sexual difference foundational to his theory of human subjectivation, where to become a subject and enter into the Symbolic order (the order of language, of the social) is to successfully sexually differentiate according to the Oedipal complex; Deleuze attempted to create a philosophy of difference wherein the relationship between difference and identity is inverted: no longer are two things, imbued with identity, compared and found to be different from each other so that difference follows from identity. Rather, difference is what constitutes those entities.

nists—are themselves deeply shaped by their engagement with these and other philosophers.

To read Sarraute, Wittig, and Garréta's treatment of subjectivity and difference through these theorists, however, would be to displace the center of conceptual gravity from their writing to that of the theorists, and to outsource the work of theorization. All three of our writers knew, to varying degrees, the work being done in French Theory. Sarraute, for instance, poked fun at Roland Barthes's arguments for the authority and agency of the text over that of the author, as theorized in his landmark essay "The Death of the Author," when she joked that his notion of the non-agential *scriptor*, who has no authorial authority over the text produced, just made her think of script-girls, or movie directors' female secretaries.[57] She also dismissed psychoanalysis as not having anything to say and as having invented an unconscious of which she has no knowledge.[58] Wittig had a career as an academic in addition to being a writer, and her critical essays demonstrate her knowledge of figures central to the intellectual landscape of post–1960s France: thinkers as diverse as Marx, Lacan, Lévi-Strauss, Benveniste, Saussure. And Garréta is perfectly at home engaging with any thinker, possessing a dizzyingly encyclopedic knowledge of philosophical and theoretical production from Plato to today. Sarraute, Wittig, and Garréta thus wrote concomitantly with these thinkers. They published novels that respond and contribute to the same urgent questions of subjectivity and difference as those being grappled with by Derrida, Deleuze, Lacan, et al. While surrounded by this intellectual, philosophical environment, Sarraute, Wittig, and Garréta's literary explorations were not written to participate in these other conversations—they were simultaneous but independent, firmly in the literary sphere.

But their novels are as much the site of theorization and thought as "pure" theory.[59] The literariness of Sarraute, Wittig, and Garréta's writing goes hand in hand with the conceptualization of unbecoming, of subjectivity without

---

57. See Sarraute, *Œuvres complètes*, 1694–95.

58. Halicks, "Interview with Nathalie Sarraute"; Rykner, *Nathalie Sarraute*, 168; Benmussa and Sarraute, *Entretiens avec Nathalie Sarraute*, 44.

59. As Timothy Bewes puts it: "The novel itself is a theorization [. . .] the novel cannot escape theoretical being; its discursive fabric is pontification, which is to say, theory." Didier Eribon bluntly states, "Great writers are often great theorists. [. . .] Literary works are often richer in existential, political, and theoretical insights than works published in philosophy or the social sciences." Anna Kornbluh makes the case for "the novel as critique." Bewes, "Reading with the Grain," 3; Eribon, *Théories de la littérature*, 5; Kornbluh, "Toward the Novel as Critique." And the 2018 Society for Novel Studies Conference is itself entitled "Novel Theory" and poses the question, "How do novels theorize?" (http://blogs.cornell.edu/sns2018/). Interestingly, this sort of collective engagement with the theoretical capacity of the novel appears to be largely Anglophone, perhaps because in the French and francophone tradition, theory is itself already

subjecthood. In her critical essays making up *The Straight Mind* and *Le Chantier littéraire*, Wittig insists on the fundamental importance of literature in the shaping and understanding of subjectivity, and she treats Sarraute's fiction as theory, as when she cites Sarraute's novels in these essays, according them the same (or more precisely, more) intellectual status as (or than) Lacan or Saussure, for instance. And Garréta, as we saw earlier, admires the lack of "disciplinary division between literature and philosophy, between narrativity and ideas" that eighteenth-century literature displays. We can see her writing, along with that of Wittig and Sarraute, as working to break down that division and present a narrativity that constitutes ideas. In this, they are actually joined by French Theory, itself composed of thinkers who wanted to wed philosophy to literature in a reenactment of the Enlightenment elision of the boundary between them. As Alain Badiou, himself a French philosopher who is often identified as part of the new generation of French Theory—even if his birthdate situates him chronologically more closely to Derrida and Deleuze's generation—has described it:

> Forty years on we have, perhaps, grown accustomed to the writing of Deleuze, Foucault, Lacan; we have lost the sense of what an extraordinary rupture with earlier philosophical styles it represented. All these thinkers were bent upon finding a style of their own, inventing a new way of creating prose; they wanted to be *writers*. Reading Deleuze or Foucault, one finds something quite unprecedented at the level of the sentence, a link between thought and phrasal movement that is completely original.[60]

Badiou's assertion is hardly a contentious one, and many readers of French Theory insist on the literary quality of these thinkers' writing—indeed, the literariness of their theoretical writing is an important part of what makes French Theory French.

Given our capacity to see these theorists' form as fundamental to their thought, it should be a simple matter to extend that same intimate linkage of form and thought to writers such as Sarraute, Wittig, and Garréta, who ceaselessly work and rework form. We've made the link between concept and form. I want to send it back in the other direction, and insist on the link between form and concept. My impression is that we more readily consent to dissolving the borders between theory and literature when theory is our starting point, our ground—when we know that a work was written with the express pur-

---

deeply literary and provides a much more visible convergence of the theoretical and the literary than does the novel.

60. Badiou, *The Adventure of French Philosophy*, lviii.

pose of theorizing—than we do to dissolving the borders between literature and theory, to attributing theoretical status or weight to a storyteller or writer, especially one of fiction. But if there were ever a set of writers who could be viewed as constituting a coherent theoretical project, it is Sarraute, Wittig, and Garréta. If Derrida, Deleuze, and Foucault are thought of as theorist-writers, I want us to think of Sarraute, Wittig, and Garréta as writer-theorists, and to attend to their writing so that we might be able to perceive their theoretical, conceptual projects. To do so, they must be read on their own terms, without the preemptive mediation of other theorists acting as an interpretive screen.

You may very well consent to refraining from reading Sarraute, Wittig, and Garréta through French Theory, and allow their corpus to put forth for itself a strong anti-identitarian vision that seeks to undermine difference. But, you might think, after having allowed their corpus to argue for such anti-identitarianism, why not then place their anti-identitarianism in conversation with what queer theory has to say on the subject, given that queer theory has become synonymous with anti-identitarianism?[61] Why not bring unbecoming into conversation with the sort of self-undoing that the conversation around queer negativity has invited for decades now? Given Wittig's lesbianism and Garréta's self-identification as queer, wouldn't reading them alongside and with queer theory be an obvious choice? Why not bring them into the queer conversation so that we can take them as anti-normative writers writing against the normativity of identity? While the language of dissolving subjecthood (or, as Robyn Wiegman calls it evocatively, self-decomposure)[62] and freeing subjectivity from the determinism of identity resonates strongly with the project of queer negativity, I abstain from a queer hermeneutics for both historical and conceptual reasons.

---

61. See Jagose, "Feminism's Queer Theory," 160; Wiegman and Wilson, "Introduction," 3. Queer theory can be seen as a critique of the identitarianism subtending feminism and gay and lesbian studies' attempts to cohere around the identity of woman, in the first case, and gay and lesbian, in the second, which led to a larger critique of identity itself, understood "as an artifact of the normalizing force of modern power," which then led to queerness's becoming "therefore characterizable not in terms of any positive substance but in oppositional relation to normativity," where identity is one of the most tenacious and consequential instances of normativity at work. Jagose, "The Trouble with Antinormativity," 31–32. While the anti-normativity that undergirds the multifarious and often conflictual project of queer theory has branched out beyond identity to critique other forms of normativity such as liberalism and nationalism, which are not so easily mapped onto the traditional repertoire of identity categories (sex, race, sexuality) associated with identity politics, anti-normativity can be seen as a form of anti-identitarianism insofar as normativity works to gather collectivities around its various iterations, where the shared norm can then be easily stabilized and fixed so as to become the foundation of a shared identity.

62. Wiegman, "Sex and Negativity," 219.

To read Sarraute, Wittig, and Garréta through the lens of queerness occludes the historical and cultural specificity of their configuration. To assimilate them into a queer genealogy would be to lose sight of how their writing, historically, does not have queer theory as its intellectual backdrop. It predates queer theory (Garréta's first novel, *Sphinx*, was published in 1986, several years before Teresa de Lauretis would introduce the term queer theory in a 1991 special issue of *differences*).[63] As evoked earlier, they were instead writing against the cultural and intellectual backdrop of a specifically French tradition of conceiving difference—e.g., the French appropriation of psychoanalysis, the French origins of poststructuralist thought, and a French, differentialist vision of emancipation for women—and abstaining from it: their literary production constituted an independent intellectual framework. Relatedly, the anti-identitarianism of Sarraute, Wittig, and Garréta's works isn't the anti-identitarianism of queer theory, which isn't so much anti-identity as it is pro-non-normative-identity, a non-normative stance that, as Robyn Wiegman and Elizabeth Wilson have shown, quickly solidifies into a normative anti-normativity.[64] Sarraute, Wittig, and Garréta are not anti-normative in the way that anti-normative queer theory is. Instead of saying *no* to the question of norms, or calling out identity and identitarian politics explicitly, they enact, literally, a project of indeterminism that has anti-identitarian effects. They simply construct an other-place, one where identity categories crumble, and difference, as the foundation upon which to build identity, becomes as unstable as sand. I see this anti-identitarian place as informed by a quintessentially French universalism, originating in the Enlightenment, to which each writer has a different relationship.[65] Reading these writers as queer would thus be to miss the way their corpus is itself a response to and a reworking of a distinctly French universalism. This isn't to say that queer readings of these

---

63. de Lauretis, "Queer Theory."

64. Wiegman and Wilson, eds., *Queer Theory without Antinormativity*. Special issue, *differences* 26.1 (2015). Lisa Duggan and Jack Halberstam, prominent figures in queer theory, critiqued Wiegman and Wilson's project, rejecting their characterization of queer theory and viewing it as intellectually disingenuous. See Duggan, "Queer Complacency without Empire"; Halberstam, "Straight Eye For the Queer Theorist."

65. Sarraute seems invested in the possibilities of French universalism as seen in her descriptions of the French school system in *Enfance*, which show her and her classmates acceding to a universal *citoyenneté*. Wittig and Garréta are both sensitive to the false universalism of Enlightenment French universalism, which elevates one type of subject (the white, straight, French male) as universal at the expense of all others, but they have different reactions. Wittig attempts to recuperate universalism while Garréta seems averse to the idea, finding more political potential in the American notion of queerness than in a French universality. Despite Garréta's aversion, the fact remains that she was shaped by the French idea and is a product of French culture, sociality, and schooling.

writers shouldn't be attempted, or that all readings must always historicize to be interesting. Far from it—one of my goals in writing *Unbecoming Language* and revealing these writers' interrelationship and shared influence is to encourage others to read and engage with them, to discover their own projects and desires for these texts. Those projects might be explicitly queer, but my own project here is not.

If my project distances itself from the label of queer and the concepts and vocabulary that come with it, it's primarily because the sort of unbecoming I see in Sarraute, Wittig, and Garréta's corpus does not map onto the theorizations of self-shattering and desubjectivation put forth by queer negativity and, in particular, the antisocial strand of queer theory that has been so influential in sustaining the debates and dissensus that have characterized queer theory since its inception.[66]

While there are clear resonances between my writers' project of unbecoming and that of queer theory's antisocial strand, queer theory is not the tool best suited for making sense of it for two reasons. First, queer theorizations of self-decomposure tie language too tightly to subjected subjectivity, and take subjectivity as already normed, already formed into a subject, by ceding as much ground and authority as it does to psychoanalytic models of conceiving the two. Unlike my theorization of unbecoming as the experience of subjectivity without subjecthood, Jack Halberstam, in an essay entitled "Unbecoming: Queer Negativity/Radical Passivity," grounds unbecoming in the psychoanalytic narrative of subjectivation through submission to the sym-

---

66. For some recent, metadisciplinary accounts of queer negativity that see queer negativity as fundamental to the shape and trajectory of queer theory, both past and present, see Wiegman, "Sex and Negativity"; Ruti, *The Ethics of Opting Out*.

Queer negativity has become a capacious term that refers to such distinct projects as Leo Bersani's call for a non-redemptive sexuality that, through shattering the self, renders collectivity and community impossible; Lee Edelman's rejection of reproductive futurity—of investment in the future, as exemplified by the elevation of the figure of the child—and its call for queers to identify with the death drive, embodying and embracing the homophobic narratives of queers as a dangerous threat to the social order; Heather Love's call to lean into loss and pain as a countermeasure to a problematic gay pride that would forget queer histories of exclusion; and Jack Halberstam's proposition that failure might serve as a non-normative means to create alternatives to stultifying, heteronormative conceptions of success. See Bersani, *Homos*; Edelman, *No Future*; Love, *Feeling Backward*; Halberstam, *The Queer Art of Failure*.

Queer negativity has dominated queer theory both in psychoanalytically driven ways, where negativity is not what destroys the social but rather what constitutes it, and in socially oriented ways, where negativity is constative rather than constitutive. In the latter, negativity is observed as it manifests itself in society (e.g., shame, suffering—these are produced by society but do not in themselves produce or structure society). What is pertinent here is the first kind of queer negativity, which has been most tightly woven around the term "antisocial thesis," first introduced to a broad audience by Caserio et al., "The Antisocial Thesis in Queer Theory."

bolic realm, to language and its norms.⁶⁷ Halberstam argues for a negative, queer feminist writing that foregrounds subjects who unbecome—who refuse to become subjects by refusing to speak and enter into a normative language. Here, what subjectivity remains after having foregone subjecthood is deprived of language, relegated to silence and passivity, which Halberstam identifies, correctly, as having powerful political consequences.

Sarraute, Wittig, and Garréta's unbecoming language, however, is one that does not ground subjectivity and the relinquishing of subjecthood in the giving up of language. Instead, they forego subjecthood through a vital experience of and relationship with language. Rather than abstain from language, they forge a different relationship to it. Halberstam's unbecoming subject "articulates itself in terms of evacuation, refusal, passivity, unbecoming, unbeing" tied to "negativity and negation."⁶⁸ The unbecoming subjectivity without subjecthood, by contrast, unbecomes not in order to experience non-agential passivity and unbeing, but in order to be more fully itself, to tap into a being that is richer and more vital than what the language of identity and difference provides. In other words, rather than relinquish language in order to accede to a state of subjectivity free from the subjection of subjecthood, Sarraute, Wittig, and Garréta bring the reader into their close encounter with a language that can rework our subjectivity and unchain it from the confines of subjecthood for as long as we are in contact with it.

Second, queer theory runs the risk of trapping Wittig and Garréta in identity, albeit a queer one, because of how neatly *queer* maps onto Wittig and Garréta's sexuality. In such a reading, Wittig's and Garréta's queer sexuality would be identified as the origin of their anti-identitarian writing, which would be unable to account for how Sarraute, as a heterosexual woman, is the origin of this collective corpus of unbecoming writing. Either Sarraute would be displaced as the starting point of this project, or Sarraute would be queered: a latent queer sexuality might be attributed to her, or other aspects of her biography might be pointed to in order to argue that she is queer for being non-normative, such as her being a Russian Jew. Her anti-identitarianism would thus be explained in identitarian terms, using a language her writing decidedly works against. In avoiding reading this poetics of unbecoming as a queer one, then, I am also trying to keep Garréta's and Wittig's sexuality from overdetermining our reading of this collective corpus and preventing us from having the sort of indeterminate and freeing encounter with language without which we cannot unbecome.

---

67. Halberstam, "Unbecoming."
68. Halberstam, 178.

At this point, I'd like to turn from these broader theoretical questions to more granular questions of vocabulary. As you've undoubtedly noticed, I've deployed the language of indeterminacy, anti-identitarianism, and anti-difference somewhat interchangeably, and I'd like to take the time now to explain why I do so. If I use all these terms, it's because none can represent adequately the nature of unbecoming. The project and poetics of unbecoming catches on all these terms without being fully caught by each one, and that is undoubtedly because the unbecoming language we find in Sarraute, Wittig, and Garréta's writing is experiential and provides us with an encounter with language that description cannot fully reproduce. Indeterminacy, anti-identitarianism, and anti-difference, together, however, can give an approximate idea of what unbecoming is.

I use indeterminacy to refer to a consequence of unbecoming. To be a subjectivity without subjecthood is to be a non-delineated subjectivity. With no contours, it's impossible to determine where and what such subjectivity is—it remains indeterminable and indeterminate, outside the demarcating, delineating identity categories that constitute subjecthood. It is in their resistance to these identity categories that Sarraute, Wittig, and Garréta's corpus is anti-identitarian. Their anti-identitarianism stands opposed to the identity of identity politics, to those identity categories that efficiently and invidiously contain and impose limits on our subjectivities, which, in the absence of social forces that would categorize us, feel unbounded. Finally, their corpus is anti-difference, which is a crude rendering of a more complex relationship to difference than a single prefix can indicate.

Etymologically speaking, identity and difference are at odds with each other: identity is derived from the Latin *idem* ("same") and denotes sameness. So why am I positing difference as what undergirds identity so that to be anti-identity is to be anti-difference? The way we use "identity" today, as a way of identifying which social categories we identify ourselves as belonging to, such as sex, race, class, and sexuality, applies a differentiating logic to sameness, or rather, builds sameness on difference. We identify these axes of difference and make them the basis of a feeling of sameness or similarity with other people who also embody this difference. Difference is mobilized into a sameness on which a collective identity can be built.

The social order has primed us to consent to being sorted into these different categories of sameness, and does not leave us with options for opting out: any positive affirmation of non-categorical identity turns into a new category,[69] and the only way out, as Sarraute, Wittig, and Garréta demonstrate

---

69. Consider how non-binary gender has itself become yet another site of categorization, as the proliferation of gender categories beyond male and female demonstrates.

in different ways, is to try to break down the material with which these categories are built—language. In other words, we've cut up difference to make categories, and have then claimed that those categories, which constitute identity, cohere through sameness. Given that these identity categories depend on their distinction from one other to function (a man is not a woman, black is not white, able-bodied is not disabled, gay is not straight), they are built on a reified difference. Sarraute, Wittig, and Garréta are anti-difference insofar as their writing demonstrates a sustained resistance to the way difference is used to imprison and (de)limit us, diminishing our sense of possibility for our subjectivities. They are anti-difference in the way that anti-difference feminists posit difference as a constructed concept. But they are not anti-difference in the sense that they are saying *no* to difference. To say *no* to difference would be to negate their very own existences.

They accept the pervasiveness and omnipresence of difference as something foundational to the way our society is currently ordered, and yet, rather than simply consent or resign themselves to a difference that would impose itself in every corner of intersubjective relation (the moment you encounter another person, you start the process of figuring out and establishing your difference), they use their writing to hollow out difference from within. By doing so, they reveal how malleable difference is, how it is in fact not impenetrable or impervious but instead, surprisingly fragile, contingent: a simple pronoun can put a deep crack in it, spoiling its integrity.[70] Within difference, while appearing for all intents and purposes as clearly visible and identifiable subjects, Sarraute, Wittig, and Garréta write their way into subjectless ways of being, hollowing out a space in which to be otherwise.

This hollowing out of difference constitutes a reworking of our subjectivity and has relational and political implications. By forcing us to have a different relationship to language than we normally do—to encounter a language that is indeterminate, working against identity and against the reification of difference into hierarchy—the relationship that is most profoundly transformed is not an inter-human relationship, but the relationship we have to the language that provides us with a way of connecting to the world and making sense of it and each other. Language is non-human even if it is intimately tied to the human. Its difference from the human becomes clear in Sarraute, Wittig, and Garréta's writing as they experience language as autonomous and material, possessing a body proper to it. This human-linguistic encounter replaces the identitarian sense of the world as it is with a non-sense that rejects categorization. Sarraute, Wittig, and Garréta lay the groundwork for a reworking of

---

70. As Chapters 1–3 show, the pronoun is important to all three writers' unbecoming writing.

sociality by creating the possibility for each of their readers to reenact their work of hollowing out difference, and, by showing us what it feels like to inhabit difference differently, to elude a subjecthood that is constantly rebuilt and reinforced day after day, interaction after interaction. Their texts create space within a world of difference to live without it. They hollow out difference and create pockets of unbecoming where we might be ourselves in our full plenitude.

How, if we experience this unbecoming, experience what such unbecoming language does to our subjectivity, can it not shift the way that we live with each other? If we experience our own boundedness as a contingent one, able to be undone by seeking out and relating to the unbecoming language we find in Sarraute, Wittig, and Garréta's texts, and others have the same experience, that means that beyond reworking our own subjectivities, we might rework the language that we use with each other, the language of our intersubjectivity. We might engage in a sociality of disarmament. Instead of reproducing the language that has produced us as identitarian others and sames, we might put that language down and opt for a language that works to keep our difference from congealing into a false and divisive sameness. Hollowing out difference collectively to make our extratextual world more like the textual ones we find in this book would mean making the burden of difference easier and lighter to bear, and it would create space in which to imagine a world with something other than difference as its gravity, as the force that holds things together in hierarchy.

This, I realize, is an undoubtedly utopian project, as identity is not something that we can do away with all of a sudden. I agree with the position famously dubbed "strategic essentialism"[71] by Gayatri Spivak and believe that, in our contemporary moment, we do not have the luxury as political actors of disinvesting in identity. It is precisely by embracing identity, albeit in a provisory manner, that we're able to engage in the coalitional politics that attend to our present and concrete lived realities, and to make progress toward hollowing out the categories that are the site of oppression until they are no more. The anti-difference French feminist Christine Delphy recognizes this and doesn't consider the project of abolishing an identity category such as gender to be incompatible with coalitional politics: "To try to abolish gender categories in no way contradicts the formation of gendered political communities—it would be absurd to say 'To get somewhere, let's act as if we're already there.'"[72] But to encounter the sort of unbecoming language that these writers

---

71. Spivak and Landry, *The Spivak Reader*, 214.
72. Delphy, *Classer, dominer*, 71.

deploy is to encounter a radical possibility, even if it is intermittent—a flash that momentarily lights up the sky of our lived lives.

I'd like to think that with enough readers experiencing a hollowing out of difference, this enterprise might coalesce, turning from a vague and nebulous ideal into a nebula of constant unbecoming, with and through a freed and freeing language. At the very least, however, this corpus serves as a reminder that the world of difference that we live in, and the kinds of difference that we necessarily take on in order to be a part of it, is as fictive (in the sense of fabricated) as the worlds we read. And even if it does nothing more than that, by making it possible for the selves we think we know ourselves to be to unbecome, this literature makes it possible to think or dream of what it might look like to travel beyond the horizons of a world marked and measured by difference, by constant delimitation and boundary-marking. This literature's unbecoming language acts as the most becoming of all of language's possibilities, and invites us to get to know it as a way of un-knowing all the things we thought we knew ourselves to be.

CHAPTER 1

Sarraute's Indeterminacy

A Universe without Contours

NATHALIE SARRAUTE. The name conjures up an image of an old woman's face whose deeply etched wrinkles and sharp features serve as a feminine counterpart to Samuel Beckett's—Sarraute, after all, did not become a renowned literary figure until she was well into her fifties, and she did not publish a bestseller until she was in her eighties. The name also conjures up an iconic photograph (fig.1): Sarraute, legs crossed, her toes in their leather pumps angled inwards toward each other in a typically feminine pose, stands demurely at the edge of a group of mostly younger men. These men, their legs uncrossed, are the avant-garde novelists who would make their fortunes under the name of the Nouveau Roman, or New Novel, the last literary avant-garde in France. And Sarraute's fortune, like theirs, would also get caught up with the New Novel, for better or worse.

With a career that spanned most of the twentieth century, Sarraute spent some seventy years exploring tropisms—a term she adopted from biology to describe the instinctive and involuntary reactions that take place in what she called *sous-conversation* [sub-conversation], under the surface of conversation—which are so small and rapid that they go unnoticed. In Sarraute's words, "They are indefinable movements that move very quickly at the limits of our consciousness; they are the origin of our acts, our words, the feelings we show, the ones we believe we feel and can define."[1] This obsession with the

---

1. Sarraute, *L'Ère du soupçon*, in *Œuvres complètes* (Paris: Gallimard, 1996; 2011), 1553. This quotation is taken from Sarraute's preface to the French edition of *L'Ère du soupçon*, which was not included in the English translation.

FIGURE 1. The New Novelists. Left to right: Alain Robbe-Grillet, Claude Simon, Claude Mauriac, Jérôme Lindon, Robert Pinget, Samuel Beckett, Nathalie Sarraute, Claude Ollier. Photo: Mario Dondero.

tropism would set Sarraute apart in most minds as a singular writer,[2] but this singularity did nothing to prevent her from being assimilated into the categories that make literary history and its developments intelligible.

Sarraute is most often placed in the categories of the New Novel and of the woman writer, both of which distort or obscure important aspects of her work and end up imposing a gendered writing with which she would disidentify. I want to draw Sarraute out of these categories in order to prevent them from serving as a *grille de lecture* [reading grid] that limits potential readings by providing us with a ready-made framework within which to think about the writer and her work. By removing Sarraute from these categories, we can read her instead with Monique Wittig and Anne Garréta, the three writers constitut-

---

A note on the complete works of Sarraute: Gallimard, in 1996, published a Pléiade edition of her then complete works. Unwilling to have the door closed on her career at the age of 96, she wrote and published her last novel, *Ouvrez*, in 1997. Gallimard, in 2011, published a new edition of the Pléiade that contains *Ouvrez* and thus truly constitutes Sarraute's complete works, but they did not issue this new edition a distinct ISBN. While the pagination for Sarraute's texts remains mostly the same, the section of critical materials is different as the commentary on Sarraute's critical reception in the press was excised to make room for *Ouvrez*. I will refer to the 2011 edition throughout; readers interested in checking my citations will have to make sure they are looking in the complete complete works of Sarraute.

2. Claude Mauriac wrote of Sarraute's singularity, "But what neither Balzac nor the most modern writers knew how to depict is what Nathalie Sarraute expresses." Mauriac, *L'Alittérature*, 321.

ing a collective corpus of anti-identitarian feminist writing that opens up new political possibilities for literature.

OUTSIDE CATEGORIES

It's difficult to disengage Sarraute from the New Novel, as she received much public attention through her identification as one of the New Novelists, achieving a level of success and recognition that she had not experienced for the first two and a half decades of her writing career, despite Jean-Paul Sartre's having supported and promoted her first novel, *Portrait d'un inconnu* (1948), for which he wrote the introduction. Even those scholars who are careful to insist on her difference from the New Novel still use the New Novel as a point of reference that helps to trace a clear definition of what Sarraute is not. Sarraute scholars, regardless of where they stand vis-à-vis the New Novel—whether they view it as a productive concept that helps to situate Sarraute and her work, or whether they view it as a distorting label that takes away from the singularity of her work—still feel compelled to contextualize Sarraute in relation to it.[3] The New Novel thus serves in some sense as the principal center of gravity for thinking about and situating Sarraute: not to actively disidentify Sarraute with the New Novel is to assent to her association with it and thus to accept the New Novel's avant-gardism as the primary or most relevant characterization of her experimental writing; and to disidentify Sarraute with the New Novel is to disavow the substantial impact the New Novel had on the reception of her work. My purpose here is neither to add to the scholarship on the New Novel nor to try to identify to what extent we can or should consider Sarraute to be a New Novelist. Rather, I am interested in examining the possibilities that open up if we read her not in relation to the New Novel, but completely outside of it.

Placing Sarraute within the category of the New Novel both effaces and emphasizes her genderedness: it assimilates her into this group of male modernist writers, insisting on the common cause shared by her and the other New Novelists, and it positions her, as in the photograph, as the odd woman out.[4] In the same way that Sarraute's disidentification with the New Novel in no way prevented her from being identified as a spearhead of the group, Sar-

---

3. Valerie Minogue and Arnaud Rykner, both major Sarraute scholars, represent these two positions, with Minogue taking the New Novel as a useful way of contextualizing Sarraute's quest for literary innovation, and with Rykner insisting on reading her against the New Novel. See Minogue, *Nathalie Sarraute*; Rykner, *Nathalie Sarraute*.

4. Marguerite Duras had been briefly associated with the New Novel, but that association did not stick the way it did in the case of Sarraute, and so Duras was able to construct herself according to the model of the singular writer.

raute's consistent disidentification with the category of woman writer has in no way prevented her from being identified as one. The idea of the woman writer has been used to compare Sarraute to other writers who are women—e.g., Marguerite Duras, Marguerite Yourcenar, Simone de Beauvoir, Maryse Condé, and Annie Ernaux—and has led to her autobiographical writing being tied to the specifically gendered stakes of writing as a woman, for instance, or to seeing her narratives as containing an anxiety symptomatic of being a woman writer working in a masculine field and transgressing social norms.[5]

Sarraute asserts unequivocally that her womanhood has nothing to do with her writing. The literary magazine *La Quinzaine littéraire* asked Sarraute and seventeen other French writers a set of three questions related to the larger question of whether writing can be sexed: "Is the writer at work aware of being specifically a man or woman? One is a man or woman and one writes: does this factor show up in the writing that is produced? If there is a difference, is it absorbed, removed, distanced, or, on the contrary, accentuated, utilized, exploited in writing?" Sarraute responded by saying, "I am convinced that there is no difference between men and women, as there is no difference between their respiratory or blood systems. [. . .] Consequently, I have never asked myself if there were qualities or faults that could be called masculine or feminine. I think these distinctions are founded on prejudices, on pure conventions."[6] Moreover, Sarraute has explicitly rejected the notion that women writers are connected to each other through a shared womanhood: "People always compare women to each other. I was asked once at a conference what similarity there was between Marguerite Yourcenar and Marguerite Duras. I said that there was an enormous similarity: they were both called Marguerite! Otherwise there is not an iota of connection between them."[7] Sarraute, in both instances, shows her aversion to having something contingent, like one's name or chromosomal configuration, turned into something foundational—a sentiment that informs her rejection of a deterministic sexual difference. Sexual difference, like characters and plot, are pure conventions and as such can be undone or overridden.

Despite Sarraute's resistance, she has continued to be identified as a woman writer, and in some sense, her resistance has itself sharpened the contours of the feminine writerly identity from which she tried to escape. Sarraute's absence, for example, from Alice Jardine and Anne Menke's *Shifting Scenes: Interviews on Women, Writing, and Politics in Post-68 France*, is framed as an abstention, a refusal to be anthologized or considered a woman writer.

---

5. See Hewitt, *Autobiographical Tightropes*; Willging, *Telling Anxiety*.
6. Sarraute, quoted in Hermann, "L'Écriture a-t-elle un sexe?," 29.
7. Weiss and Guppy, "Nathalie Sarraute."

However, by remarking on her absence from the ranks of the other women writers who consented to reflect on the relationship between being a woman and writing, attention is called to Sarraute as a woman writer in a way that simply omitting her wouldn't have.[8]

Neither the category of the New Novel nor the woman writer are able to represent Sarraute adequately. On the one hand, to place Sarraute in the New Novel, in the tradition of the avant-garde, is to put her in a masculine category and bind her to a masculinist and modernist resistance to literary conventions and norms. On the other hand, to identify Sarraute as a woman writer is to put her in a feminine category that binds her to a feminine form of resistance to masculinist literary culture, and, more broadly, to the patriarchy that subtends it. Both categorizations miss the larger point of Sarraute's writing, which is her commitment to indeterminacy and continual resistance to all categorization, seen in her ceaseless attempts to dissolve the contours of the identities that categorize us in order to open up our subjectivities to an immediate experience with a language that is *vivant*, alive. This language that Sarraute pursues knows no identity as such; it's a language that hasn't yet been killed through convention, disciplined by the social order into ratifying difference as the basis of the identity categories that fix us.

This isn't to say that Sarraute scholars haven't attended to her aversion to categorization—it is impossible to read Sarraute and not be struck by her resistance to fixity, her commitment to blurring or destroying the lines of demarcation that constitute categories. Rather, her anti-categorical writing hasn't been contextualized in such a way that we can see its full impact. By reading her outside both the masculine and feminine traditions constituted by the New Novel and the woman writer, it becomes possible to see the way Sarraute's writing elucidates the interface between the literary and the political.[9] By suspending Sarraute from these familiar categories, we can see how her anti-categorical writing has an inherently political dimension *because* it is produced from within the context of a quest for aesthetic, literary innovation.

---

8. Jardine and Menke, *Shifting Scenes*, 5.

9. This interface has been the subject of much debate, from Plato's polemics against poetry's corrupting powers, to Jacques Rancière's notion of literature's determining role in the distribution of the sensible. See Plato, *The Republic*, Book X, and Rancière, *Le Partage du sensible* and *La Parole muette*. By "distribution of the sensible," Rancière refers to how literature frames what subjects belonging to a certain collectivity or social order can see or not see, feel or not feel, sense or not sense—how literature configures a common sensorium. The interface that I am concerned with is not that of what impact literature has on politics, but rather the process by which it has that impact, or moves from the literary sphere into the political one. That is, I am interested in the literary processes that lead to a distribution of the sensible, a reconfiguration of how a collectivity experiences the world.

Sarraute did not see herself as a political writer and her interest in the tiny movements of tropisms, in unremarked psychological phenomena, would seem apolitical. For those familiar with Sarraute, it's probably surprising to see me assert that Sarraute's writing is political. While this may not be the most obvious reading of Sarraute, it's one that comes into focus when Sarraute is read alongside Wittig and Garréta. Their more obviously political writing serves as a backdrop that allows Sarraute's tiny, indeterminate tropisms to be seen in a political light and mobilized for a project of anti-identitarian writing that seeks to provide us with an encounter with unbecoming language. In the case of all three writers, it's precisely by pursuing the aesthetic and the literary that the political is produced, that an experience of subjectivity without subjecthood obtains. Let's turn now to what this experience looks like for Sarraute, which she would describe in terms of neutrality.

THE NEUTRAL: A UNIVERSE WITHOUT CONTOURS

Sarraute's commitment to indeterminacy, to undermining the fixity of difference and the proliferation of identity categories that difference produces, is rooted in her conviction of what she calls the neutrality of humankind. Sarraute's notion of neutrality takes the *being* of human being as a state free of difference, as a *being* without contours. As we saw in the Introduction, it is for her "this self-evident fact—or is it madness?—that each of us is an entire universe unto ourselves, that we feel infinite, without contours."[10] She would elaborate on her notion of the neutral in an interview, stating that "the human being for me is the neutral. There's a word for that in Russian, *tcheloviek*, and in German, *Der Mensch*—a human being, man or woman, regardless of age, regardless of sex."[11] She cites two differences that are used to categorize human beings into identity—age and sex—as examples of contours that for her do not exist in the neutral space of human existence. Later, in the same interview, she emphasizes that neutrality is not some balanced distribution of difference, where one difference is not allowed to have more purchase or influence than another, but the absence of difference altogether:

> *Talk to me about this neutral zone that is at the center of Man, taken in its broadest sense.*
> I am not thinking at all in terms of "androgyny." I work uniquely from what I feel myself. I don't place myself on the outside, I don't seek to analyze from

---
10. Sarraute, "Prière d'insérer" to *"disent les imbéciles."*
11. Benmussa and Sarraute, *Entretiens avec Nathalie Sarraute,* 184.

outside. Inside, where I am, sex doesn't exist. I never tell myself: that was felt by me, or a woman, or a man. [. . .] I am so much in what I am doing that I don't exist. I don't think it's a woman who's writing. That thing that I work on is in the middle of taking place somewhere where the feminine or masculine sex does not intervene.[12]

Sarraute's rejection of sexual difference may seem to be, at best, wishful thinking. As feminist theories of the social construction of gender from Beauvoir on have amply demonstrated, one's self-consciousness of oneself as a woman or one's active identification or disidentification as a woman does not matter. Being gendered is a social construction and position that is imposed from without regardless of whether one accepts it. Sarraute's conviction of neutrality is obviously limited or ineffectual against a greater social impetus to impose difference, as her being caught up in the category of woman writer, despite her repeated insistence otherwise, shows.

However, rather than focus on the limitations of Sarraute's claims, I want to focus on its possibilities. Sarraute experiences the space of writing, of her encounter with language, as one where the relentless imposition and reiterations of difference are no longer operative. Within this literary space, difference can be and is evacuated. While this may seem useless vis-à-vis the larger social sphere, it opens up the possibility for readers to also encounter language in Sarraute's texts as a similarly emancipatory experience, where one is freed, albeit momentarily, from the strictures of difference. And an experience once realized opens up the possibility and desire for a more sustained experience of difference-lessness. Just as the first light bulbs lasted only a few flickering moments but made concrete the possibility of sustained electric illumination, so too might these momentary experiences of identity-lessness make concrete the possibility of living without identity, and bring into greater

---

12. Benmussa and Sarraute, 184–85. Sarrautian neutrality is distinct from Maurice Blanchot's, for whom neutrality is the state of radical nonsubjectivity as manifest in the neuter (see Blanchot, *The Infinite Conversation*). Hers is an experience of radical subjectivity, one without subjecthood—the "I" that is so much in what it is doing is the "I" of subjectivity; it is not the "I" that doesn't exist, which is the "I" of subjecthood. Roland Barthes's notion of neutrality (developed at length in Barthes, *The Neutral*) posits the neutral as "everything that baffles the paradigm" (6), where the paradigm is embodied by the binary whose oppositions are the structuring and productive foundation of Western thought, and is driven by the desire to retreat from a hegemonic social order. It resonates with Sarraute's eschewing of the paradigm of sexual difference, but, for Sarraute, the neutral is a very real and accessible state, the affirmation of a truth about humankind, while such affirmation, in Barthes's view, would be a manifestation of arrogance, too close to dogma. For Barthes, the neutral is utopian, impossible to fully seize.

relief the manufacturedness and unnaturalness of the regime of identity we all live under.[13]

Sarraute's conception of neutrality is radical in its rejection of difference even when it has been neutralized, as seen in her rejection of androgyny, which is a state where neither masculinity nor femininity has the upper hand, rendering the sexual difference they manifest "neutral" in its effects. A neutralized difference, for Sarraute, is still a difference, and for her, true neutrality demands the dissolution of all difference, all contours, all identity. Language—the work she does with it, in it, on it, and the space she occupies when she does all those things—is the key to acceding to this neutrality: it is the mediation that enables her to be a universe without contours. Language is where one can have experience and subjectivity (Sarraute feels, she senses, and her texts are spaces where the reader gets to recreate those feelings and sensations herself) without the contours that make up such identities as "woman," "man," or the person behind "I." Sarraute writes, then, to free subjectivity from the contours that corral it into being a subject endowed with an identity into which subjectivity has been decanted. She writes to unbecome, and makes this experience available to her readers as well.

THE POLITICAL SARRAUTE

Sarraute's commitment to indeterminacy is political: her works enact the neutrality she believes is shared by all. In effect, she writes against the very foundation of a social order whose continued existence depends on maintaining the manifold differences issuing from the originary concept of difference that then coalesce into identity. What would modern polity be without the identitarian contours of nationality, immigration status, sexual orientation, sex, race, marriage and family status, age, language, economic power, disability, standardized test results, medical diagnoses, and all the other categories that

---

13. Here, I go further than Sarraute was willing to go, since she described the identity-less experience she writes of as an unsustainable one: "One couldn't live in my books or in tropisms. [. . .] One would go crazy. Social life and community would no longer be possible, nor action." Benmussa and Sarraute, *Entretiens avec Nathalie Sarraute*, 73. Sarraute thus cordons off her writing from lived life, but I believe experiencing her books can transform, rather than destroy, social life and action. In this, I read Sarraute generously, as Gary Wilder understands such reading, which entails thinking with a writer "to extend the logic of their propositions far beyond where they may have stopped." Wilder, *Freedom Time*, 13.

inhere in biopower and its establishment of the modern nation state?[14] Indeed, the polity divides in order to cohere.

Despite Sarraute's relentless attack on the contours that make the modern nation-state possible, she is not read or received as a political writer, and her work is not considered for its political stakes. Wittig, however, was able to detect the political force of Sarraute's work. She found something in Sarraute's writing that enabled her to produce her own work, which is unanimously recognized for its political program of combating patriarchy and its heterosexual regime of domination. Apart from Wittig, however, Sarraute's critics tend to replicate Sarraute's self-description as a non-political writer[15] and her insistence that when she writes, she has no identity: "When I write, I am neither man nor woman nor dog nor cat."[16] Such a statement, when used to distance her writing project from the political, reveals the underlying assumption that the political necessarily derives from or involves a subject in possession of an identity to whom interest can be ascribed.

While Sarraute describes her writerly self as emptied out with no one there—no one left to be political—it is difficult not to see in her own lived experience a political root to Sarraute's aversion to categories. During World War II, as a Jew in occupied France, Sarraute experienced firsthand the tyranny of categories and the terror they can produce. The consequences of being placed into the category of Jew were grave: she was disbarred as a lawyer and, after divorcing her husband to protect him, went into hiding after being

---

14. See *The History of Sexuality* for Foucault's now famous articulation of the interrelationship of knowledge and power as borne out in the modern nation-state's invention of biopower, which marshals scientific knowledge to control populations, or in his own words, designates "what brought life and its mechanisms into the realm of explicit calculations and made knowledge-power an agent of transformation of human life." Foucault, *The History of Sexuality*, 143.

15. Ann Jefferson, in her rich study of the central role of difference in Sarraute's work, reiterates Sarraute's aversion to being considered a political writer (e.g., her opposition to being considered a feminist writer) and tries to approach the question of Sarraute's political quality obliquely: "Without seeking to retrieve Sarraute for a reading of her work in terms of race or gender, an understanding of the ways in which theorists of these issues are confronted with questions of difference can be helpful in underscoring this dimension of Sarraute's own engagement with questions of difference." Jefferson, *Nathalie Sarraute*, 11. In other words, Jefferson wants to be able to mine the insights of explicitly political theory without having to assume the association with the political. By declining to read Sarraute as political against her self-characterization, however, Jefferson in effect depoliticizes theories of gender and race that set out to theorize from an explicitly political point of departure, and neutralizes their impact. Benoît Auclerc is a notable exception to this critical consensus about Sarraute's depoliticized writing, but he reads Sarraute in order to read Wittig. Where he's interested in the political quality of Sarraute insofar as it elucidates Wittig's work, I am interested in Sarraute's political qualities for what they have to say about Sarraute as well.

16. Rykiel, "Quand j'écris," 40.

denounced as the daughter of a Jew, leaving behind her husband and their eldest daughter.[17] Sarraute, who refused to wear the yellow star, had to assume false identities and was nearly arrested and deported following a close call with a zealous baker who was going to denounce her to the authorities. She lived under a regime marked by a politics of difference that obsessively identified and categorized the other in order to preserve the purity and dominance of the Aryan same. Sarraute scholars who are attentive to the ways in which Sarraute's biography can be read as informing her writing nonetheless take her insistence on her depoliticized writing project at face value and allow Sarraute her self-characterization as a depoliticized writer.[18] By reading Sarraute's work for the political, radically anti-identitarian force of her writing, however, we can see its rich interrelation with Wittig and Garréta's work. This interrelation in turn makes it possible to see how their collective corpus theorizes a new feminist poetics of unbecoming, which, unlike the more familiar poetics of écriture féminine, treats language as being inimical to difference.[19]

Wittig's critical intervention is to discern that what is political in Sarraute's work is language itself, not simply who wields it and against whom it is wielded (a view that attributes agency exclusively to the locutor and accordingly instrumentalizes language). As much as language is Sarraute's medium, Sarraute is language's. Wittig would consider Sarraute's will to empty herself of her self to let language speak and act through her to be a fundamental element of Sarraute's writing. She saw Sarraute shedding her identity to foreground language instead as a living and agential entity. Hence Wittig's description of Sarraute's œuvre in her posthumously published *ars poetica*, *Le Chantier littéraire* [*The Literary Worksite*] (2010), as "the first and only one of its kind to be written entirely from the side of language; everywhere, the referent you look for in life is here in the life of language."[20] Though Wittig never explicitly states the connection between living language and the category-shattering, indeterminate neutrality that Sarraute pursues, this Sarrautian experience of language as living is what drives Wittig to write against difference. For Sarraute, this living language is immanently inimical to the kind of difference that undergirds identity and leads to oppression—it cannot create these contours.

---

17. Sarraute's two younger daughters would eventually join her in a boarding school in Parmain, where she posed as a schoolteacher and her daughters posed as her nieces.

18. See Valerie Minogue's discussion of Sarraute's vocabulary in her last novel, *Ouvrez*, where Minogue draws attention to the recurrence of words like *blockhaus* and *prisonnier* that allude to the concentrationary universe. Minogue in Sarraute, *Œuvres complètes*, 2118. See also Jefferson, *Nathalie Sarraute*, 10–11.

19. See Chapter 4 for an elaboration of the poetics of unbecoming.

20. Wittig, *Le Chantier littéraire*, 69–70.

By examining first an early work, *Tropismes* (1939), then a mid-career work, *Les Fruits d'or* (1963), which was published at the height of the New Novel movement, and then a late-career work, *Tu ne t'aimes pas* (1989), which was published after the waning of the New Novel and Sarraute's and Robbe-Grillet's return to more traditional, conventional narrative forms through their autobiographical works,[21] we can see that her writing's dissolution of identity categories and hollowing out of difference become stronger over the course of her career. The more complete or explicit sort of blurring or removal of identity found in her later works shows her work becoming more explicitly anti-identitarian as her pursuit of the tropism becomes more refined and developed. However, if we take seriously Sarraute's affirmation that her entire corpus is a pursuit of the tropism, we should be able to find this political force starting in *Tropismes*. Let us take a look, then, at *Tropismes* to see what it is about this work that would make Wittig feel "blasted in the process" of reading it.[22]

TROPISMES: A DIFFERENT KIND OF LANGUAGE

It took Sarraute more than seven years to write *Tropismes*, a slim collection of 24 short prose pieces.[23] Sarraute was decidedly a writer of perspiration, not inspiration—it was normal for her to rewrite passages as many as fifty times.[24] The 24 pieces comprise a kaleidoscopic variety of voices, perspectives, genders, ages, and social positions. Each section is a discrete text that stands by itself and shows to the reader the tropisms that Sarraute claims we all experience but are unaware of because of how subtle and imperceptible they are. Recalling Sarraute's definition, tropisms are those movements that transpire just underneath the surface of conversation in response to another person's presence. Tropismic reality is the psychological material that sticks to words

---

21. Sarraute published *Enfance* [*Childhood*] in 1983, and Robbe-Grillet published *Le Miroir qui revient* [*Ghosts in the Mirror*], the first of an autobiographical trilogy, *Romanesques*, in 1984. *Enfance* is Sarraute's most conventionally narrative text, but it is still by no means a conventional one, as she splits the narrative voice into a masculine interlocutor and a feminine interlocutor in dialogue with each other. In Sarraute's work, greater narrative normativity does not correspond to greater identitarian normativity: she still manages to write against difference and identity in her more traditionally intelligible work.

22. Wittig, *The Straight Mind*, 45.

23. The first edition of *Tropismes*, published by Denoël in 1939, contained 19 Tropisms, and the 1957 Minuit edition, the one we know, contained 24—Sarraute added six new Tropisms between 1939 and 1941, and had one of the original Tropisms deleted. See Valerie Minogue's "Notice" to *Tropismes* in Sarraute, *Œuvres complètes*, 1717–19.

24. Sarraute, quoted in Rambures, *Comment travaillent les écrivains*, 153.

in the space between language and an unarticulated or inarticulable affective state. It is the space where sensation and language come together. The tropism is neither sensation nor language in and of themselves, but their union. There is no tropism without language, and there is no tropism without sensation, but the tropism is irreducible to each.

In this interstice between sensation and language, this synapse, Sarraute finds the substance and source of her writing. Sarraute operates in the interval between *sous-conversation* and *conversation*, or, as Dominique Rabaté conceives it, the interval between inside and outside: "Words are thus the indispensable agents of this delicate work of shuttling between inside and outside. They are the privileged vectors of this fragile passage. This preceding affirmation appears to me to be central in Sarraute. [. . .] The writer's work would consist, from then on, of returning words to their original movement and letting them float in this intermediary space that is their natural environment."[25] By operating in the interval between inside and outside, Sarraute places herself and the reader in an indeterminate, intermediary space where words can move outside the rigid boundaries of identity. Here, we can come into intimate contact with a subjectivity that is not and cannot be fixed, existing as it does in a space without contours.

Take the first tropism for instance, which sets the tone for the rest of the work, and is composed of a sequence of four short paragraphs. The tropism, and the book, opens with this sentence:

> Ils semblaient sourdre de partout, éclos dans la tiédeur un peu moite de l'air, ils s'écoulaient doucement comme s'ils suintaient des murs, des arbres grillagés, des bancs, des trottoirs sales, des squares.

> [They seemed to spring up from nowhere, blossoming out in the slightly moist tepidity of the air, they flowed gently along as though they were seeping from the walls, from the boxed trees, the benches, the dirty sidewalks, the public squares].[26]

We are placed in a situation of ignorance. We know that *ils* [they] are in an urban environment, as signaled by the walls, trees, benches, sidewalks, and squares. But we do not know who these *ils* are and the verbs Sarraute uses seem distinctly un-human in contrast to the human setting of the city: they seep or burst out from within this space, they hatch or bloom in the

---

25. Rabaté, *Poétiques de la voix*, 264.
26. Sarraute, *Tropismes*, in *Œuvres complètes*, 3; Sarraute, *Tropisms*, 1. I will occasionally emend Maria Jolas's translation. All subsequent citations will be made in-text.

wet warmth of the air, and they flow slowly as though they are seeping out from the various parts of the city. The verbs seem to be describing insects, plants, or spores—those life forms that lack animal sentience, self-awareness, and expressivity. The following paragraph depicts these *ils* as clustering into "longues grappes sombres entre les façades mortes des maisons" [long, dark clusters between the dead house fronts] (3; 1) and "devant les devantures des magasins, ils formaient des noyaux plus compacts, immobiles, occasionnant quelques remous, comme de légers engorgements" [before the shop windows, they formed more compact, motionless little kernels, giving rise to occasional eddies, slight cloggings] (3; 1). *Ils* are drawn to human buildings, for unknown reasons, and they are described as having some sort of collective or social existence, although it is unclear whether it is a conscious formation or a purely instinctual one.

At this point, halfway through the tropism, we are still ignorant as to what sort of creature or life-form is being narrated. Sarraute shifts direction and, in the third paragraph, she directs us toward and defamiliarizes the familiar trope of children who are enthralled by toys and storefront windows carefully dressed to whet their appetite:

> Une quiétude étrange, une sorte de satisfaction désespérée émanait d'eux. Ils regardaient attentivement les piles de linge de l'Exposition de Blanc, imitant habilement des montagnes de neige, ou bien une poupée dont les dents et les yeux, à intervalles réguliers, s'allumaient, s'éteignaient, s'allumaient, s'éteignaient, s'allumaient, s'éteignaient, toujours à intervalles identiques, s'allumaient de nouveau et de nouveau s'éteignaient. (3)

> [A strange quietude, a sort of desperate satisfaction emanated from them. They looked closely at the piles of linen in the White Sale display, clever imitations of snow-covered mountains, or at a doll with teeth and eyes that, at regular intervals, lighted up, went out, lighted up, went out, lighted up, went out, each time at the same interval, lighted up again and again went out.] (1)

Our previous uncertainty as to what was being narrated dissipates as the image of spores, plants, and insects is replaced by one of children transfixed before a store window and the fantastic world it stages for their puerile imaginations. The repetition of *s'allumaient, s'éteignaient* [lighted up, went out] reproduces the hypnotic effect the doll's blinking has on the children, and the language hypnotizes its readers as much as the action that is its referent hypnotizes the children. Sarraute, however, does not allow us to stay for long either in this state of knowing, of readerly certainty, or in the state of hypnosis.

In the last paragraph, Sarraute upends our expectations by revealing that the storefront display has hypnotized not a crowd of children, but rather, the adults who are their caretakers:

> Ils regardaient longtemps, sans bouger, ils restaient là, offerts, devant les vitrines, ils reportaient toujours à l'intervalle suivant le moment de s'éloigner. Et les petits enfants tranquilles qui leur donnaient la main, fatigués de regarder, distraits, patiemment, auprès d'eux, attendaient. (3)

> [They looked again for a long time, without moving, they remained there, in offering, before the shop window, they kept postponing until the next interval the moment of leaving. And the quiet little children, whose hands they held, weary of looking, listless, waited patiently beside them.] (1–2)

What had started to seem like a typical scene of childhood turns into something far uncannier, and the usual roles accorded to adults and to children are reversed.[27] Sarraute ends the tropism with the image of the children who are waiting because they are not caught up in the fictive world that the store has created for their consumption.

The tropism can be read as an allegory of reading, with the storefront display of the snow-covered mountain and the entrancing doll standing in for the sorts of fictive worlds created by the traditional Balzacian novel and its able mimetic narratives that produce what Roland Barthes has called the reality effect.[28] Sarraute, like the small children who are waiting for their grown-ups, is tired of this weary realism and tries instead to create the experience of reality for the reader. Her goal is not to describe reality but to make us experience the sensations that tropisms provoke in our mind. To prevent us from turning into readers hypnotized by mimesis and traditional realism, Sarraute makes a concerted effort to kick our feet out from under our various interpretative toeholds. As we move from sentence to sentence, each conclusion we draw comes undone. Each determination we make about who the *ils* are ends up the product of false clues that Sarraute plants in the text to lead us off course. Sarraute thwarts our attempts at drawing clear narrative contours and insists that our reading be marked by uncertainty and indeterminacy.

---

27. See Freed-Thall, *Spoiled Distinctions*, 135–38 for a discussion of Sarraute's creation of atmosphere in *Tropismes* and her depiction of a creepy domesticity. In her incisive analysis of *Tropismes* and a number of Sarraute's other works, Freed-Thall looks to Bourdieu to bring together the sociological and the aesthetic in order to theorize a distinctly Sarrautian aesthetics of the *douceâtre* [sweetish/bland].

28. Barthes, *The Rustle of Language*, 141–48.

But if I am to take Sarraute's conception of the tropism seriously, then I must relinquish this reading, which, as convinced as I am by it, is too certain, too sure of itself to be properly tropismic. Where Sarraute's tropism might be seen most effectively at work is in the way she compels me to let go of the *my* in my reading, to try not to hold on to it, to try not to pin the tropism down, but rather to let the tropism produce a sensation in me. To be in an interpretative mode is automatically to be outside the sensate mode. So, to be true to the tropismic spirit, let me cast doubt on my reading and try to dissolve the *my* by introducing other possibilities. Perhaps I've simply fallen into the very trap I'm trying to alert you to, and the *ils* is different in each paragraph, and the unity I've just read into the tropism a false one. In which case, Tropism I, rather than staging the unraveling of our reading of a unitary scene between children and adults that works against the usual parent/caretaker-child dynamic, stages our desire to create stable narratives, to fix the tropism rather than letting the tropism unfix us.

Tropismic language is language that moves between inside and outside, and we can see this dynamic at work in the metanarrative space of criticism and interpretation: I move constantly from being inside my reading, sure of it, to being outside it, regarding it with suspicion as just another instance of a pernicious instinct to fix language. Not only do I experience sensations while reading Tropism I, with the slippery language of oozing spores producing the sort of recoil that a word like *moist* also does, but I experience a sensation of confusion and a certain distress as I find the hermeneutical object I have created falling through my fingers despite my attempts to hold on. To read Sarraute's tropismic writing, then, is to be faced with the seemingly impossible imperative to maintain reading as a verb but reject it as a noun: to read without ever arriving at a reading. I will be the first to admit that I will fail, and what follows are readings that will undoubtedly fall into stability and fixity despite my desire to respect and convey the tropism in its movement and indeterminacy. However, I hope that these readings will gesture toward the indeterminacy and mobility that inspired them (which I am incapable of preserving in this critical mode), so that you may be able to find a way to pivot from critique to construction, the construction of a subjectivity unfettered by difference.

This first tropism speaks more to the unfixing of identity—the impossibility of fixing the *ils*—than the power of language. However, language's power is still gestured toward in its ability to recreate the sensations and situations it describes.[29] We see this in the repetition of *s'allumaient, s'éteignaient*; in the

---

29. For an excellent close reading of Tropism I that shows how Sarraute exploits the physicality of language to recreate experience, or sensation, rather than describe it, see Minogue, *Nathalie Sarraute*, 10–11.

long sentences of the first half reenacting the slow movements of the adults gravitating toward the storefront window; and in the final sentence with its many small, separated clauses mirroring the isolated children, who, unlike the adults that are clumped together in *grappes* [clusters], are separate from each other. And again, the *ils* in question might not be the adults at all but some other group. The uncertainty of the referent does not change, however, the emphasis in this tropism on the collective reaction to the storefront display, on the sensations and mental movements that lie just beneath the surface of their *quiétude étrange* [strange quietude], their *satisfaction désespérée* [desperate satisfaction]. In subsequent tropisms, Sarraute turns more to the crucial role language plays in creating and provoking these sensations such that *Tropismes*, taken in its entirety, points to the tropism as a sensation deeply intertwined with language.

Sarraute, in her essay "Le Langage dans l'art du roman" ["Language in the Art of the Novel"], articulates this interrelation by describing how tropismic language is different from ordinary language: "Words lose their ordinary meaning. They are words that are carriers of sensation. Of this sensation and none other. They make it emerge, certainly, but as integrated with them. They make it live and it, in turn, gives life."[30] Tropismic language isn't meant to signify or communicate a predetermined meaning. Rather, it is a language integrated with sensation, and this fusion between language and sensation brings both to life. Language enables the reader to experience the tropism, and the tropism prevents language from becoming the dead language of clichés and conventions. This dead language is the language of the traditional novel and its clear narrative—a language invested in clear referents to an intelligible reality, a language that keeps the reader at a certain remove. Dead or conventional language is akin to a snow globe, which represents a scene that can be observed and turned around from multiple angles—where the flurry of snow falling inside the globe can be seen in its totality. Living language, or Sarraute's tropismic language, strives to place the reader inside the snow globe, inside the movement of the snow, where a total vision and apprehension of the scene are sacrificed in order to enable sensation and experience in its stead.

For Sarraute, language and the sensation that constitute the tropism are inseparable, and this coextensivity is evoked strikingly in her second tropism. As with the first tropism, Sarraute thwarts our hermeneutic impulses by revealing how difficult it is to suspend our judgment, and puts pressure on the ease with which we jump to conclusions. At first glance, Tropism II seems to offer more information to the reader than the first tropism did. It begins

---

30. Sarraute, *Œuvres complètes*, 1691.

with a scene of *ils* who are torn away from their vanities in front of which they had been studying their own faces. A singular *elle* [she] is revealed as the reason their contemplation of their own faces is interrupted:

> "C'est servi, c'est servi," disait-elle. Elle rassemblait à table la famille, chacun caché dans son antre, solitaire, hargneux, épuisé. "Mais qu'ont-ils donc pour avoir l'air toujours vannés?" disait-elle quand elle parlait à la cuisinière." (4)
>
> ["Dinner is ready, dinner is ready," she said. She rounded up the family, each one hiding in his lair, lonely, ill-tempered, exhausted. "What on earth is the matter with them, for them always to look so worn out?" she said when she talked to the cook.] (3)

The tropism, for all intents and purposes, seems to be opening with a familiar scene of bourgeois family life: the task of getting an entire family to sit down for a meal, and the reluctance of the children to be loquacious around their parents. *Elle* reads as a figure of authority, the mistress of the house, the mother. The next paragraph seems to confirm this, as Sarraute describes *elle*'s many hours spent chatting with the cook: "préparant des potions pour eux ou des plats, elle parlait, critiquant les gens qui venaient à la maison, les amis" [preparing various medicines for them, or special dishes, she talked on and on, criticizing the people who came to the house, friends of theirs] (4; 3). With a single word, Sarraute undoes this reasonable conclusion as deftly as she did in the first tropism: "'Mademoiselle a de beaux cheveux,' disait la cuisinière, 'ils sont épais, ils sont beaux malgré qu'ils ne bouclent pas'" ["Mademoiselle has pretty hair," said the cook, "it's thick and pretty, even if it doesn't curl"] (4; 3). The *mademoiselle*, reserved for unmarried and young women, eliminates the initial narrative thread of the mother of the family gathering her children for dinner, and we are left instead with the more complicated and unexpected figure of a daughter, perhaps, or another relative, who spends most of her time gossiping with the cook, exchanging platitudes and passing judgment.[31] Their conversation is banal, peppered with such clichés as "ils ne l'emporteront pas avec eux" [they can't take it with them] in reference to a miserly family's wealth. But it's precisely beneath the surface of this conversation that tropismic energy can be detected and felt: something attaches to these seemingly insignificant words and is able to penetrate the psyche.

---

31. And, to add yet more uncertainty, rendering the referent of *elle* even more indeterminate, the *mademoiselle* could be referring not to the *elle* to whom the cook is speaking, but to the daughter of the house, who isn't present, in which case, the *elle* could be another domestic, like the cook, and their conversation one of gossiping about their employers.

Sarraute interrupts this conversation in the third paragraph with the sudden introduction of a solitary *il* [he], who seems to be one of the *ils* from before, but whose exact position in the family is indeterminable. This *il* is the site of tropismic sensation; through his sensations, we too wind up caught inside the tropism provoked by the preceding banalities:

> Et il se sentait filtrer de la cuisine la pensée humble et crasseuse, piétinante, piétinant toujours sur place, toujours sur place, tournant en rond, en rond, comme s'ils avaient le vertige mais ne pouvaient pas s'arrêter, comme s'ils avaient mal au cœur mais ne pouvaient pas s'arrêter, comme on se ronge les ongles, comme on arrache par morceaux sa peau quand on pèle, comme on se gratte quand on a de l'urticaire, comme on se retourne dans son lit pendant l'insomnie, pour se faire plaisir et pour se faire souffrir, à s'épuiser, à en avoir la respiration coupée...
>
> 'Mais peut-être que pour eux c'était autre chose.' C'était ce qu'il pensait, écoutant, étendu sur son lit, pendant que comme une sorte de bave poisseuse leur pensée s'infiltrait en lui, se collait à lui, le tapissait intérieurement. (4–5)
>
> [And he sensed percolating from the kitchen, humble, squalid, stamping thought, stamping in one spot, always in one spot, going round and round, in circles, as if they were dizzy but couldn't stop, as if they were nauseated but couldn't stop, the way we bite our nails, the way we tear off dead skin when we're peeling, the way we scratch ourselves when we have hives, the way we toss in our beds when we can't sleep, to give ourselves pleasure and make ourselves suffer, until we are exhausted, until we've taken our breath away...
>
> 'But perhaps for them it was something else.' This was what he thought, listening stretched out on his bed while, like some sort of sticky slobber, their thought infiltrated him, stuck to him, wallpapered him internally.] (4)

This sequence is extraordinarily complicated, and combines an articulation of the force of language with the sort of blurring of identities we saw in the previous tropism. On a narrative level, what is happening and being articulated is the *pensée humble et crasseuse* [humble and squalid thought] of the *elle* and cook's banal conversation as it takes on oppressive dimensions, overwhelming the *il* who is unable to avoid hearing it and winds up infiltrated by this language, covered in it both within and without. But this narrative clarity is disrupted by Sarraute's language, which makes it impossible to know who the subjects of this scene are, and what their relationship is with each other. The passage begins with the *il*, who could be a child in the family, or perhaps the father, and almost immediately the subject of the sentence shifts to that of the cook and *elle*'s conversation, the feminine *pensée humble et crasseuse* described as *piétinante* [stamping]. The adjectival *piétinante* then shifts to the verbal present participle *piétinant* whose subject is then revealed to be, not the *elles* [they] that had been described so far in the tropism as being the holders and articulators of such thought, but an *ils*.[32] The humble and grimy thought contained within the cook and *elle*'s conversation, the anthropomorphized thought whose stomping in the kitchen is heard by the *il* in his bedroom, is not limited to the cook or the *elle*, but belongs also to others, whose identities we do not know—a broad, general *ils*. These anonymous *ils* are seized by the same grimy thought that took over the cook and the *elle*, and the stomping initially attributed to the thought is then transferred onto these *ils*, who compulsively pronounce the same sort of banalities as had the cook and the *elle*. In the course of one sentence, the distinction between a human *il* and an abstract *pensée* is elided, and the feminine subject of *pensée* is then elided with a human *ils* who also contain the *elles* from the first part of the tropism and all these different subjects are then joined by an *on* [one/we/you] that interpellates the reader so that our experience of biting our nails and picking at our skin and turning about sleeplessly in bed ends up informing the oppressive compulsive utterances of this *ils*.

This reading could be mistaken, though, as Sarraute's use of many dependent clauses that follow one after another after another makes it difficult to isolate or identify which discrete subjects are being blurred together. It's just as possible that the *ils* who are stomping around in the kitchen are the combination of the *pensée* and of the *il*, caught up in a relentless repetition of moving around together, and that the site where this takes place is no longer even the kitchen but some other space. It is exceptionally difficult to do this sort of close reading of Sarraute at the sentence level because her words and clauses shift and move more quickly in our reading of them than is possible to articulate in writing.[33] But what I'm trying to show with this rather torturous breakdown of the sentence is that Sarraute sows confusion and uncertainty in her writing at the level of the individual word. To read this sentence normally is to be caught up in its whirlwind of movement, and Sarraute's repetition of

---

32. In French, *elles* and *ils* both mean *they* but *elles* is reserved for an exclusively feminine *they* whereas *ils* could refer to a group of all men or a group of both men and women.

33. Françoise Asso elegantly captures the difficulty of analyzing Sarraute's work: "To read according to the norms of a reading that analyzes 'naturally' is to always return to following a thread, to constructing a continuity by leaning on the logic of succession, which does not apply to the texts of Sarraute. If a writer can represent simultaneity, if the reader can perceive it holistically, the commentary then works against the natural movement of the text." Asso, *Nathalie Sarraute*, 50–51.

clauses and words creates a sentence that is so fast-paced that to read it, especially aloud, is both to feel disoriented and breathless.

Sarraute's repetitions and modulations relentlessly drive the sentence forward before we've even had time to process the clause we were in the middle of reading: the *piétinante* gives way to *piétinant* and the loss of that *e* creates an acceleration that is then continued by the repetition of *toujours sur place, toujours sur place* [always in the same spot], by the shift from *toujours* [always] to *tournant* [turning], which changes the tempo of the sentence, and by the repetition of *en rond, en rond* [round and round]. The sentence's frenzied careening forward comes to its peak with the last series of clauses whose emphatic, percussive repetition of *comme* [as] five times take us through to the end of the sentence, where we end not with a bang but with a whimper, as it trails off into ellipses whose silence and slowing down capture our own *respiration coupée* [cut off breath] and attempts to recover our breath. Through reading this sentence's fifteen clauses, we wind up sharing the experience of the *il* who experiences (or is part of) the *ils* who move about so frenetically with the humble, grimy thought of banality. This sharing is reinforced by the shift from *ils* to the more participatory *on*, which is a pronoun that works by inclusion, and interpellates the interlocutor, or in our case, the reader, by claiming us as part of that *on*.

In this passage, we doubly experience the force of language: we see language narrated as something that takes over the *il* and coats his insides and outsides, and we experience language as something that sweeps us up into an almost interminable sentence that sets us down in a state of confusion about which subjects were doing what verbs at which points. One of the strategies Sarraute has for dismantling identities is to use language to overpower and overwhelm the reader so that we can no longer keep anything straight or point to discrete identities with any sort of certainty. She adds layer of unknowing onto layer of unknowing. Already, we were unclear as to who was being described in the tropism—*elle* as mother then as daughter or perhaps an aunt or perhaps a live-in governess or domestic; *il* as a son or perhaps a father or perhaps an uncle or perhaps a live-in tutor or butler—and then Sarraute goes further and makes it impossible to tell which of these uncertain figures are the subjects of her sentence and if these subjects are even different from each other.

The tropism continues with *il*'s resignation to his situation and his conclusion that it is impossible to get away from the clichés and recycled formulas that constitute most of our social interactions:

Il n'y avait rien à faire. Rien à faire. Se soustraire était impossible. Partout, sous des formes innombrables, 'traîtres' ('c'est traître le soleil d'aujourd'hui, disait la concierge, c'est traître et on risque d'attraper du mal. Ainsi mon pauvre mari, pourtant il aimait se soigner . . . '), partout, sous les apparences de la vie elle-même, cela vous happait au passage, quand vous passiez en courant devant la loge de la concierge, quand vous répondiez au téléphone, déjeuniez en famille, invitiez des amis, adressiez la parole à qui que ce fût. (5)

[There was nothing to be done about it. Nothing to be done. To avoid it was impossible. Everywhere, in countless forms, 'traitorous' ('The sun is traitorous today,' the concierge said, 'it's traitorous and you risk catching your death. That was how my poor husband . . . and yet he liked to take care of himself . . . ') everywhere, in the guise of life itself, it caught hold of you as you went by, when you hurried past by the concierge's door, when you answered the telephone, lunched with the family, invited your friends, spoke to anybody, whoever it might be.] (5)

For him, this oppressive language is as omnipresent as the air. No matter the interlocutor, *qui que ce fût* [whoever it might be]—family, friend, acquaintance, or stranger—it emerges, passing itself off as life itself. After concluding the impossibility of escape, *il* proceeds to try to come up with a strategy for survival in this ineluctable situation. He considers the others—those who propagate this language without second thought and suffer no consequences—and how he should respond to them:

Il fallait leur répondre et les encourager avec douceur, et surtout, surtout ne pas leur faire sentir, ne pas leur faire sentir un seul instant qu'on se croyait différent. Se plier, se plier, s'effacer: 'Oui, oui, oui, oui, c'est vrai, bien sûr,' voilà ce qu'il fallait leur dire, et les regarder avec sympathie, avec tendresse, sans quoi un déchirement, un arrachement, quelque chose d'inattendu, de violent allait se produire, quelque chose qui jamais ne s'était produit et qui serait effrayant. (5)

[You had to answer them and encourage them gently, and above all, above everything, not make them feel, not make them feel a single second, that you think you're different. Be submissive, be submissive, be self-effacing: 'Yes, yes, yes, yes, that's true, of course that's true,' that's what you should say to them, and look at them warmly, affectionately, otherwise a rending, an uprooting, something unexpected, something violent would happen, something that had never happened before, and which would be frightful.] (5)

Il's social world is at stake in his response to them. If he pushes back against their language, he risks a complete rupture that would destroy any chance of connection. *Il* justifies his decision to submit to their language by imagining that if he were to pose any resistance and articulate his difference, he would destroy them: "il les secouerait comme de vieux chiffons sales, les tordrait, les déchirerait, les détruirait complètement" [he would shake them like old soiled rags, would wring them, tear them, destroy them completely] (5; 5–6). This fantasy of destruction, of power, quickly cedes to a darker fantasy of being destroyed, which ends Tropism II:

> Mais il savait aussi que c'était probablement une impression fausse. Avant qu'il ait le temps de se jeter sur eux—avec cet instinct sûr, cet instinct de défense, cette vitalité facile qui faisait leur force inquiétante, ils se retourneraient sur lui et, d'un coup, il ne savait comment, l'assommeraient. (5)

> [But he also knew that this was probably a false impression. Before he would have time to leap at them—with that sure instinct, that instinct for defense, that easy vitality that constituted their disturbing force, they would turn on him and, all at once, he did not know how, they would knock him out.] (6)

Sarraute, in this tropism, stages a dramatic confrontation between a monolithic *ils*, who are more properly represented by their language than who they are as individuals (their interchangeability strips them of any individual identity), and an *il* who is only an *il* by virtue of having a different experience of language than they. Tropism II is thus a confrontation between normative, dominant language and attempts to resist it.[34] And while the dominant language is narrated as completely overpowering and destroying non-normative language, this fantasy of obliteration is belied by the fact that the experience of language that we as readers are left with is from the perspective of the non-normative, which resists obliteration even as it fears it. A non-normative space is thus carved or hollowed out from within this normative language.

Sarraute's tropisms consistently stage this conflict between normative and non-normative languages and become apprehensible because of the gap between them.[35] Recalling Sarraute's description of the tropism as fused with

---

34. Over half a century before queer theory would develop its strong critique of normativity, Sarraute staged the invidiousness of normativity at the level of language.

35. Valerie Minogue qualifies this conflict as "the war between the petrifying power of words and the fluidity of experience." Minogue, *Nathalie Sarraute*, 1. I would nuance Minogue's description and characterize the war as being between the petrifying power of normative lan-

living language, we can define dead language as the normative language of formulas and clichés seen in Tropism II—fixed and ready-made language. Living language, in contrast, is mobile, non-normative language. It is not the product of molding oneself according to society's dictates and using the language it has prescribed. It is not the product of making ourselves legible by placing ourselves in preassigned categories and reading others and making sense of them by fixing them in their categories. In Tropism II, we witness the banality of gossip and social niceties, but let's not forget that the cliché often has grandiose ideas as its subject, and that banality is as sweeping as it is small. Clichés aspire to totalization, and there is an existential, ontological dimension to such hackneyed utterances as "It is what it is," which expresses a kind of Stoic or Zen response to the contingency of existence, or "Takes one to know one," which speaks to larger issues of subject formation, recognition, and intersubjectivity.

Normative language, for Sarraute, extends past the oft-repeated phrases that are most recognizable as clichés to also encompass single words that represent monolithic concepts we take for granted such as *Amour* [Love] and *Bonheur* [Happiness].[36] Sarraute applies her tropismic magnifying lens to them in order to reveal all the psychological movements that they provoke but obscure. This normative language is language that produces fixed ideas in people's minds, the way Love and Happiness (which get bandied about as if they were self-evident concepts) do. Normative language eliminates the gap between itself and what it represents, and claims to be entirely adequate to the task of conveying meaning. Françoise Asso remarks on the totalizing nature of the cliché, referring to it as language "that gives the illusion, all swollen with its own importance, of being big enough [. . .] to contain the real in its entirety."[37] Sartre recognized this dimension in his preface to Sarraute's first novel, when he wrote about the cliché, or *lieu commun*, saying:

> [. . .] this beautiful word has several meanings: undoubtedly it designates those worn out thoughts, but it means that those thoughts have become the community's meeting place. Each one finds him or herself there, finds the others there. The cliché, the commonplace, belongs to everyone and it

---

guage and the non-normative language that is able to accommodate and fuse with the fluidity of experience.

36. Sarraute reveals the tropisms produced by Amour in *L'Usage de la parole* and by Bonheur in *Enfance*. See *Œuvres complètes*, 946–54; 1024–25.

37. Asso, *Nathalie Sarraute*, 46.

belongs to me; it belongs in me to everyone, and it is the presence of everyone in me.[38]

The ready-made language that Sarraute diagnoses as dead language has the function of turning us into social beings and ordering us into relationships—into community, into citizens and subjects. This well-worn language is totalizing in its capacity to "say it all"; consequently, the cliché either brings an end to conversation so that nothing else can be said, or produces more clichés in response, since the only adequate response to the totality of the cliché is another cliché. Sarraute does neither. She responds to the cliché not with more clichés, but with the tropism and the living language it is a part of and that is a part of it.

In Tropisms I and II, Sarraute writes from an intermediary space, between inside and outside, in order to attempt to return words to their "natural," or neutral, environment. This is the space between the inside of a subjectivity without contours and the outside of the well-contoured subjecthood that is required to be part of a community—the space between solitude and sociality. Tropismic language thus does not dissolve identity categories in the outside world because it does not get rid of sociality. The voices that populate most of Sarraute's texts can be categorized according to age, gender, class, etc. *Tropismes* and Sarraute's subsequent works do not erase the well-defined roles and social structures that constitute the bourgeois world that serves as their setting. In *Tropismes*, we see how present familial and domestic structures are. *Martereau*'s principal dramatic action is centered around a real estate deal. *Le Planétarium* features conflicts that can occur during the seemingly banal task of decorating one's apartment, which becomes the stage for family drama. *Vous les entendez?* narrates a father's agony at having aesthetically insensible children who do not appreciate his Pre-Columbian statuette. And intergenerational conflict is a running theme in Sarraute's work. But Sarraute did not write of bourgeois life simply because she herself was bourgeoise and was writing what she knew. Rather, Sarraute zeroes in on the highly structured and coded system of the bourgeois family, which, in its codification, has reached the status of cliché and idealized normativity, in order to hollow it out and reveal it to be nothing more than a surface, devoid of substance.[39]

---

38. Sartre, Preface to *Portrait d'un inconnu*, in Sarraute, *Œuvres complètes*, 36. Sartre here imbues cliché with a potentially positive valence—it inspires collectivity and community—whereas for Sarraute it represents precisely the sort of language that is to be avoided at all costs. The solitary pursuit of the tropism entails eschewing community to privilege instead relationship with language.

39. I'm grateful to Olivier Wagner, the curator of Sarraute's papers at the BnF, for sharing with me his trenchant reading of Sarraute's corpus and observing that Sarraute targets the

But, to return to Rabaté's metaphor of the shuttle, the tropism, as mobilized by Sarraute, takes us from that outside world of sociality, and the difference and identity categories that it depends on, to the inside world of contourless subjectivity, where difference no longer has any purchase. To be in the indeterminate flux of tropismic language is to be in a non-identitarian elsewhere. Most of the time, the language we use and operate in is the dead language of convention and of sociality. But Sarraute sets out to give us an experience of the tropism, this other kind of language, which punctuates and perforates the otherwise smooth surface of sociality and reminds us that there is something else, that we can have subjectivity without subjecthood.[40]

In *Tropismes*, language becomes the most powerful force and reality present, and it is language's ability to shape reality that makes it so powerful. In the face of this language that exceeds the boundaries of sociality and various subjects' abilities to control it, identity falls away, and the categories upon which it depends are dissolved as we are taken from the outside world to an inside, tropismic, world. This is what would seize Wittig in her encounter with Sarraute, and what would drive Wittig's own work. As Wittig described Sarraute in an interview four months before Sarraute's death at the close of the twentieth century, "She is the genius of the century. Her work is beautiful literarily, philosophically, and it's also revolutionary; I don't know of any writer who can compare to her. She made us discover phenomena of living language that no linguist was able to bring to light."[41]

When Wittig calls Sarraute revolutionary, she means it in both the literary sense, in terms of writing in a new way, and the political sense, in terms of transforming reality. When we, as readers, join Sarraute and her tropisms in that intermediary, indeterminate space, we're positioned to experience language's force the way her anonymous subjectivities do and to have our own identities become erased, unfixed. We can unbecome, experiencing ourselves as a universe without contours. The tropism undoes the work that the social order does of imposing contours onto our subjectivities and decanting them into neatly demarcated and hierarchized identity categories. It creates for readers the experience of a reality that does not depend on socially constructed difference, which is revolutionary indeed.[42]

---

bourgeois family to politicize it as part of a strong anti-conformism that coexisted with her otherwise quite bourgeois life.

40. See Introduction for a discussion of subjectivity without subjecthood.

41. Devarrieux, "'J'ai connu la guillotine.'"

42. Benoît Auclerc articulates the importance of the political quality of Sarraute's work in Wittig's own work: "Hence the paradigmatic role Sarraute plays when Wittig tries to articulate in what way a literary work can become a war machine: the tropisms, in Sarraute's work, insofar

THE RUNAWAY TROPISM

Sarraute's belief in the living nature of tropismic language and its resistance to deadening normativity is not naïve, however. She makes it clear that language's liberation of subjectivity from the strictures of identity and categories is not an easy one. Her tropisms all tend toward an overwhelming negativity, as seen in Tropisms I and II. Paranoia, antagonism, oppression, aggression, and violence permeate her work, which speaks to the hegemony of the normative social order and its conventional, categorizing language—to the dangers of refusing to conform to that order. Sarraute's texts seem to negatively reinforce identity by making non-identitarian space seem terrible to occupy. To be a properly socialized subject would be to follow the path of least resistance and seemingly greatest reward, but Sarraute's narrative voices always opt for the harder path of staying with the tropism despite the alienation from the outside world that it entails. They always choose the life of language over the easy death of conformity.

We have all seen the costliness of resisting the dominant social order: people pay for being marginal with their very lives; political movements that seek to uproot oppressive regimes are met with violent repression. It's hardly surprising that Sarraute's staging of the tropism's indeterminate space, which is not bolstered by the sturdy structures of a dominant social order, would be framed as a frightening one. It's a risky venture to give up identity, to choose being a subjectivity alienated and isolated by its rejection of fixity over being a subject integrated into some external identity. Sarraute understands that liberation is frightening.

Wittig articulates the high stakes and risky nature of liberation with a problematic metaphor. In "One Is Not Born a Woman," one of the essays that make up *The Straight Mind*, Wittig's landmark work of feminist theory and criticism, Wittig takes the lesbian as an exemplary figure of resistance to heterosexuality as a figuration of patriarchy and develops the radical idea that "lesbians are not women."[43] She articulates the lesbian's role in dismantling this oppressive social order as being akin to that of the runaway slave, where the lesbian is effectively the person who flees from the difference that grounds heterosexuality:

> Lesbian is the only concept I know of which is **beyond the categories** of sex (woman and man), because the designated subject (lesbian) is *not* a woman,

as they resist all attempts at definition and leave behind all categorization, constitute the site of resistance to conformism, to identitarian assignments." Auclerc, "Wittig et Sarraute," 203.

43. Wittig, *The Straight Mind*, 32.

either economically, or politically, or ideologically. For what makes a woman is a specific social relation to a man, a relation that we have previously called servitude, a relation which implies personal and physical obligation as well as economic obligation [. . .], a relation which lesbians escape by refusing to become or to stay heterosexual. We are escapees from our class in the same way as the American runaway slaves were when escaping slavery and becoming free. For us this is an absolute necessity; our survival demands that we contribute all our strength to the destruction of the class of women within which men appropriate women. This can be accomplished only by the destruction of heterosexuality as a social system which is based on the oppression of women by men and which produces the doctrine of the difference between the sexes to justify this oppression.[44]

This metaphor is obviously problematic in the way it appropriates a racial identity—the American runaway slave is black—and uses it as an analogy for the seemingly unraced figure of the lesbian.[45] In what follows, I want to momentarily suspend my critique of the metaphor in order to see how the figure of the runaway slave, upon which Wittig models the lesbian—the key term for her political project—can be seen as describing the same dynamics present in the tropism, so that we can shift from a problematic analogy between the lesbian and the runaway slave as the key to freedom from a regime of difference to a more productive one between the lesbian and the tropism.

Given that she conceptualizes the woman as slave, put into servitude by the men who possess women as their property, Wittig views the lesbian as a fugitive from the heterosexual order who exists in a state of freedom, albeit a precarious one. In her thought, it is only by fleeing from one's class, be it the class of woman or of slave, that that class, and the social system which depends on it, can be destroyed, since there is no reason for the oppressors to put an end to the system otherwise. The metaphor of the runaway slave acknowledges the dangers of choosing to escape beyond categories and establish a space that exists outside the workings of the dominant social order: the runaway slave, if caught, had no protection in the justice system and faced grave retribution—amputation, whipping, branding, death.

The tropism functions in the same way as the runaway slave does. This living language, in its insistence on indeterminacy and being outside categories, is a fugitive from the dead, conventional language that dominates. This latter language is enslaved by ideology, in service to a social order that oppresses

---

44. Wittig, 20. My emphasis.
45. For a defense of Wittig's metaphor, see Crowder, "From the Straight Mind to Queer Theory," 494–95.

through its formulation of difference. In the same prière d'insérer to *"disent les imbéciles"* where Sarraute affirms that each person's subjectivity is a universe without contours, she discusses the tropism as developing through two oppositions. First is the opposition between feeling oneself to be without contours and knowing oneself to be viewed by others as bounded by contours and categories, reduced to being a character through a process of identification that necessarily produces "classifications, hierarchies: the 'supremely intelligent,' the 'imbeciles.' . . ." Second is the opposition between "the free, living, independent idea" and "the idea bound to characters who produce or support it, this idea petrified by contempt—'fools say'—or by religion, conformism, and terror." These questions of which language and ideas to choose (Sarraute elides the distinction between language and thought) have weighty consequences, as Sarraute develops further in the prière d'insérer: "What is twisting and turning before our eyes raises some of the most significant and consequential questions of our time." These consequences are so significant because an entire social order is at stake in the question of tropismic versus non-tropismic language. The tropism emerges as a response to intersubjective interaction, and it is precisely when we encounter an other that the question of difference and identification becomes central. What the tropism questions is sociality itself.

In *Entre la vie et la mort* (1968), Sarraute stages the psychic life of the writer faced with this choice between living and dead language.[46] One can either stay enslaved, operating within the dead language of categories and conventions and renouncing freedom and mobility for the sake of a costly stability, or one can join the fugitive, free language that is the tropism, and risk the various retributions that could follow. Sarraute's tropism, as a space and reality that exist outside the dominant social order, is the manifestation of a fugitive community whose precarity in no way diminishes the force of its freedom. This freedom may not be immediately or easily discernible in *Tropismes*, which represents tropisms somewhat indirectly, as embedded within an intelligible social world. However, in Sarraute's later works, she gives readers a more direct experience of the tropism. She moves the tropism away from being embedded within the outside world and instead embeds us in the tropism, in a direct experience of how its stubborn, desperate indeterminacy resists the overwhelming determinate order that would seek to reappropriate it and reimpose difference. Sarraute's tropism, like Wittig's runaway slave, is the powerful sign of a possibility made real, whose tenuous existence has profound political consequences.

---

46. I discuss *Entre la vie et la mort* at length in Chapter 4.

I thus propose to revise Wittig's elaboration of the lesbian as a radically anti-identitarian figure that abolishes the sexual difference that normally inheres in the usual definition of lesbian as a woman who loves women. Rather than likening the lesbian to the runaway slave, which reinforces the very identitarian logic that Wittig opposes by not addressing racial difference (thereby tacitly maintaining it), we should liken the lesbian to runaway language. Tropismic language is a better analogy for the lesbian in that it takes us out of identity, which is precisely what the lesbian is supposed to do. By doing so, we can read Wittig generously, taking her logic further than she did. Wittig's use of the runaway slave is problematic, certainly, and demonstrates the limits of the critical mode of writing, which cannot enact experience and create textual realities in the same way that fiction can. Wittig's literary writing is able to go further than her more theoretical essays can, to move beyond critique to the construction of something new in her literary worksite, which I discuss in the next chapter. If Wittig was able to build this worksite, it is because Sarraute's seemingly humble tropisms were, in the mind of a reader like Wittig, explosives that would clear the ground for her to do so. Let us turn now to Sarraute's later tropismic writing, which only increased in their anti-identitarian impact from the initial *Tropismes* that had already stunned Wittig.

THE TROPISM AFTER *TROPISMES*

Tropismes, as Sarraute's first work, was conservative in relation to the overall trajectory of her corpus. As Sarraute developed as a writer, her approach to the tropism would become more radical and experimental. Her writing, consequently, would become more explicitly anti-identitarian, increasingly destabilizing identity categories to the point of destroying them. At the beginning of her career, Sarraute was still uncertain of herself as a writer, an uncertainty evidenced in the modest length and format of *Tropismes*. The thought of writing novel-length tropismic works—of sustaining the tropism for so many pages—was out of the question: "I thought only of writing short texts like [*Tropismes*]. I couldn't imagine it possible to write a long novel."[47]

In its more conservative nature, *Tropismes* assumes an externalized view of the tropism. As readers, we're still in a concrete setting with recognizable markers that help us situate ourselves. Where Sarraute's language in *Tropismes* is still powerful and able to produce sensation, as seen in her deft deployment of clauses and her control of the rhythm and pacing of her sentences,

---

47. Weiss and Guppy, "Nathalie Sarraute."

it nonetheless operates in a largely descriptive mode—the tropisms are presented from outside the tropism, and the sensation we feel is an echo of the sensation experienced by the tropismic individual. From this vantage point, Sarraute used her first tropisms to map out the psychological and literary terrain that she would enter with subsequent works, taking her readers with her *inside* the tropism. In order to assure a firsthand experience of the tropism on the part of the reader, Sarraute gradually left behind external points of reference that mediate our experience of the tropism. She describes this process of bringing the reader inside the tropism:

> "To dispossess the reader and entice him, at all costs, into the author's territory. [. . .] Suddenly the reader is on the inside, exactly where the author is, at a depth where nothing remains of the convenient landmarks with which he constructs the characters. He is immersed and held under the surface until the end, in a substance as anonymous as blood, a magma without name or contours."[48]

We can see this trajectory toward greater interiority in the novels that follow *Tropismes*—*Portrait d'un inconnu* (1948), *Martereau* (1953), and *Le Planétarium* (1959)—which progressively eliminate the novelistic conventions of character and narrator to instead plunge the reader inside the anonymous, contourless, magma-like substance and experience of the tropism that is the substance of Sarraute's corpus. This increased interiority does not mean an erasure of all traces of exteriority—the sorts of familial and social structures that are present in *Tropismes* continue to be present in these and Sarraute's other novels—but in Sarraute's later writing of the tropism, we can see a will toward greater immediacy, toward taking the reader more deeply into tropismic interiority.

Sarraute's fourth novel, *Les Fruits d'or* [*The Golden Fruits*] (1963), is the first to apply the tropism's destabilizing power to gender, a category of difference that has been naturalized and essentialized through the capacity of females to bear offspring: in this text, gender loses its primacy as a principal mode of identifying people. In *Les Fruits d'or*, a novel about a novel entitled "Les Fruits d'or"[49] and the different reactions it provokes, Sarraute moves away from plot as it is traditionally understood—plot as what happens in a story, or the sequence of events that make up a story—and plunges the reader into a world

---

48. Sarraute, *The Age of Suspicion*, 71.

49. In scholarly discussions of *Les Fruits d'or*, the convention is to distinguish between Sarraute's novel and the novel-in-the-novel by referring to the former in italics and the latter in quotation marks. I follow this convention here.

of disembodied, anonymous voices. Very little can be said to "happen" in *Les Fruits d'or* even though the novel has a certain narrative coherence whose driving conflict or dramatic impetus is centered around the reception of "Les Fruits d'or" and its rise and fall in terms of literary glory. What could pass for a plot features human actors whom it is difficult to describe as characters, given the anonymity and fluidity of who is speaking at any given moment. *Le Planétarium* [*The Planetarium*] had also featured disembodied voices, but these had not been anonymous, since they were endowed with names and clearly articulated relationships fixed within the structure provided by a family unit. Here, however, Sarraute eliminates any indication of the relationships that connect the various voices to each other so that there is no way of confirming their relationship outside the individual interactions that arise around the aesthetic object of the novel, "Les Fruits d'or." Anonymity is a necessary step in bringing the reader into the interiority that is for Sarraute the realm of indeterminacy: a name is always imposed from the outside for the benefit of those on the outside. Even the act of self-naming necessarily places the self in an exteriorized relation to the self.

Les Fruits d'or begins with clearly gendered voices, male and female, that are discussing a visit to a male friend or acquaintance or relative who had circulated a postcard reproduction of a painting by Courbet to prove his aesthetic refinement. After this initial scene, which features a stable identificatory axis of gender, we are left awash in conversation, in a set of *je* [I], *tu* [you singular, informal], *il* [he], *elle* [she], *nous* [we], and *vous* [you singular formal, you plural] that are all responding to various works of art. This difficultly differentiated mass of aesthetic pronouncements culminates in an extended discussion of the novel "Les Fruits d'or." Whereas in a usual conversation, each pronoun serves to demarcate a specific subjectivity, Sarraute does not allow us to use the pronoun as we normally do: as a buoy we hold on to in order to orient ourselves. In *Les Fruits d'or*, the pronoun, instead of keeping us afloat in the narrative, throws us into it so that we are immersed in a sea of thoughts, sensations, and feelings, unable to easily make out one from the others: in the middle of a dialogue, after the em dash that sets off an interlocutor's speech, we slide without any warning from speech into their thoughts, or the thoughts of someone else. The writing moves from one thought to the other and back again so frequently that we are left wondering at any given moment who is saying or thinking what. The lack of differentiation is visually manifested in the proliferation of Sarraute's signature ellipses, and it is never clear whether one set of ellipses connects the thoughts and words of a single speaker or signifies instead a leap to someone else's.

From the beginning of the novel, Sarraute, as she does in *Tropismes*, wastes no time in having us lose our footing. Unlike in *Tropismes*, she makes it impossible for us to ever regain a new footing. In the following typical passages, Sarraute melds first-person, second-person, and third-person pronouns, and combines all possible points of view in just a few lines:

> Épinglée au mur sur le papier gris à grosses fleurs roses au-dessus du bureau pour capter l'inspiration, glissée dans la rainure entre l'encadrement et la glace au-dessus de la cheminée, tout à coup ... miracle ... la même ... Et leur air ... cet air qu'ils ont ... Pudique. Fier. Ma trouvaille. Ma création. Mon petit trésor secret. Ne me quitte jamais. Mais tenez, à vous, vous en êtes digne ... à vous je peux sans crainte: pas de profanation, aucune souillure. Avec vous, tenez, je partage. Un don. Mon bien le plus précieux ...
>
> [Tacked up on the wall, against the gray paper with the big pink flowers over the desk to receive inspiration, stuck in the crack between the frame and the mirror over the mantelpiece, all at once ... miracle ... the same ... And their look ... that look they have ... Shy. Proud. My find. My creation. My little secret treasure. Never leaves me. However, here, to you, you are worthy of it ... to you I can, with no fear: no profaning, no defiling. With you here, I'll share. A gift. My most precious possession ...]⁵⁰
>
> Je sens que moi aussi ça me gagne ... titillation exquise ... ça vient, ça me possède ... Incantations ... Extases ... Allons, tous ensemble, plus fort. Encore. Plus fort. Plus loin. Moi maintenant je m'avance, je franchis toutes les bornes, je lâche tous les freins ... Tout au bout ... rien ne m'arrête ... aucune crainte mesquine du ridicule, aucun souci glacé de pudeur. Encore. Jusqu'à l'extrême limite. Je m'abandonne ... Le voilà. Il tombe en transes, le Dieu le possède, il se convulsionne, les yeux révulsés, l'écume aux lèvres, il se roule par terre, arrachant ses vêtements ... Pour moi ... il se frappe la poitrine ... Pour moi, je ne crains pas de le dire ... Rien au-dessus. Courbet est le plus grand. Shakespeare. Dernier sursaut. Il se courbe en arc de cercle: Shakespeare et Courbet. (525–26)
>
> [I feel that I too am about to succumb ... exquisite titillation ... it's coming, it grips me ... Incantations ... Ecstasies ... Come now, all together,

---

50. Sarraute, *Les Fruits d'or*, in *Œuvres complètes*, 523–24; Sarraute, *The Golden Fruits*, 11. All subsequent citations will be made in-text.

stronger. Again. Stronger. Farther. Now I begin to move forward, I stride across all frontiers, I release all brakes . . . At the very end . . . nothing can hold me . . . no petty fear of ridicule, no chill concern with shyness. Again. To the very limit. I let myself go . . . Here he is. He falls into a trance, possessed by his god, he is in convulsions, his eyes bloodshot, foaming at the mouth, rolling on the ground, rending his garments . . . For me . . . he beats his chest . . . As for me, I'm not afraid to say it . . . Nothing greater. Courbet is the greatest. Shakespeare. Last twitch. He arches his body: Shakespeare and Courbet.] (12)

In the first passage, *ils* and *leur air* [their look] are described from an external point of view, but, almost immediately, Sarraute assumes an internal point of view, a move that leads to the first-person utterance, "Ma trouvaille. Ma création. Mon petit trésor secret" [My find. My creation. My little secret treasure]. *Ils* has turned into *je*: not only does the distinction between external and internal not hold, but neither does that between singular and plural.[51] After this moment of first-person enunciation, the perspective shifts again, this time toward the second person, so that the *je*, who had previously been viewed in the third person, is now being engaged with in the second person. The ambiguity between *vous* as singular and *vous* as plural places us in a state of indeterminacy, where the *vous* is not fixable—the interpellation that the second-person *vous* normally entails is incompletely operative here. In the second passage a similarly rapid shifting of perspectives also occurs. What starts off in the singular first person turns into the plural first person with "Allons, tous ensemble" [Come now, all together], and we are brusquely ejected from this interiorized perspective when Sarraute jumps from "Je m'abandonne . . ." [I let myself go . . .] to "Le voilà. Il tombe en transes" [Here he is. He falls into a trance], with the ellipses serving as the only form of transition. This oscillation between the external and the internal is restaged with the alternation at the end of the passage between *moi* [me] and *il*. Both these passages manifest Sarraute's will to undo any and all stable platforms of enunciation and pro-

---

51. Alternatively, the first-person statements could still be made from the perspective of the third-person observer, who is imagining each of the individuals who compose the collective *ils* to have the same internal monologue of "Ma trouvaille. . . ." Even in this scenario, distinctions are dissolved as this reading requires the third-person observer to place themselves wholly in the other person's perspective, which requires giving up their own. For all intents and purposes, they become the other person—the end result is the same as when the first-person utterances are considered to be made by that first person. Regardless of which reading one adheres to, Sarraute makes the various subjectivities and perspectives completely permeable, making sustained distinctions untenable.

duce instead a subjectivity that has no fixed base, one that cannot ossify into identity.

Because Sarraute combines subjectivities (and thus pronouns) with abandon, *ils* turning into *je* turning into *vous*, the distinctions between them are lost, and the pronoun no longer carries as much identificatory weight as usual—the pronoun no longer refers to an individual or a defined group of individuals. Since Sarraute tears down the divisions between pronouns, our tendency as readers to distinguish, identify, and bag and tag a novel's subjectivities as characters about whom things can be known, is thwarted.[52] As all three perspectives of the first-, second-, and third-persons are combined under the sign of a single em dash, this leveling of distinctions flattens that sacrosanct difference between one person's subjectivity and another's—the difference enabling you and me to wield the *I* that makes us feel like we exist. We can already see in this mid-career novel, with its melding of subjectivities, the sort of erasure of sexual difference that Wittig, influenced by Sarraute, would go on to target more specifically with her own work. Wittig's unorthodox use of the pronouns *on* and *elles* in *L'Opoponax* (1964) and *Les Guérillères* (1969), respectively, is preceded by Sarraute's attack on the rigidity with which pronouns are segregated from each other—a rigidity that shackles an individual to an identity—and by Sarraute's move away from traditional dialogue between two fixed, clearly separate, individual voices to something resembling Babel, an unfixed, amorphous exchange between plural voices.

One could argue that for all of Sarraute's dissolving of the usual boundaries between pronouns and the subjectivities they represent, she still privileges primarily masculine pronouns in the conversations that make up *Les Fruits d'or*, or the indefinite positive *on* or the indefinite negative *personne* [nobody], and that this represents a masculinization or de-feminization of the text. In this case, the kinds of identity-bending that occur in the text take masculine subjectivities as the privileged vectors for anti-identitarian work, with only occasional instances of clear gender-bending occurring where a feminine pronoun, and attendant narrative voice, loses its gendered specificity. This is all true, and Sarraute's justification for her use of the masculine pronoun as a way of creating not a masculine universe but a neutral one can sound like a concession to the phallocentric social conditions in which she writes, where the feminine is indeed more marked, and particular, than the masculine.[53] Indeed,

---

52. See Sarraute, "L'Ère du soupçon," where she describes the reader's (and the writer's) tendency to gravitate toward this sort of well-defined character.

53. See Minogue, "Notice" to *Portrait d'un inconnu*, in Sarraute, *Œuvres complètes*, 1741, and Jefferson, *Nathalie Sarraute*, 98, 110 for discussions of how assuming a masculine voice allows for greater neutrality. Elsewhere, Sarraute, in a series of interviews with Simone Benmussa,

Wittig's analysis in "The Mark of Gender" of the marked quality of femininity as it is inscribed and enacted in language would at first seem to support Sarraute's diagnosis of her situation as a writer who wants to create a neutral textual universe but cannot do so if she makes use of the marked language of feminine subjectivities. However, and this is where Sarraute's concession can be seen most clearly, Wittig takes this marked quality as a reason to revolt against language and destroy gender with language from within language, while Sarraute opts to avoid feminine pronouns and their marked nature and not take part in that battle. Rather than fault Sarraute for claiming to create a falsely neutral textual universe, or for reproducing the familiar cooptation of the universal by the masculine, we should see this first step toward exploring the tropism's capacity to destabilize identity, to the extent that pronoun distinctions no longer hold, as precisely that—a step toward the more visibly radical anti-identitarianism that characterizes her late career, as exemplified in the novel *Tu ne t'aimes pas* [*You Don't Love Yourself*] (1989).

Even Wittig, whose writing's political nature is uncontested, began more modestly, with her debut novel, *L'Opoponax* (1964), striking a different tone in its poignant revision of the *récit d'enfance* [narrative of childhood] than that of the programmatically lesbian works that would follow: it is with *Les Guérillères* (1969), Wittig's second novel, that we see her first explicitly political assault on phallocentric language. While Sarraute does not go so far in *Les Fruits d'or* as to divest the masculine pronouns of their universality, as Wittig would in *Les Guérillères*, where she strips *il* and *ils* of their longstanding status of representing all humanity, Sarraute still works with and against the pronoun in important ways and cuts loose the pronoun's strong connection to a certain enunciatory position. This work has enormous implications for subjectivity-formation, as seen in the linguist Émile Benveniste's assertion that the formation of subjectivity in language necessarily takes place through the creation and exercise of the pronoun.[54] In light of this, we could see Sarraute's inhabitation of the masculine-as-neutral voice as a refusal to have her subjectivity fixed by a femininity imputed to her as her official identity—as her anti-identitarian gesture as a writer, in keeping with her refusal to be considered a woman writer.

As Sarraute continued to write, following the tropism down its path toward greater and greater instability and indeterminacy, the sort of partial occlusion of gender that we see in *Les Fruits d'or* gives way to a complete eclipse of identity, as can be seen in her later work, *Tu ne t'aimes pas*. Sarraute's progression

---

describes the feminine voice as too marked to represent neutral experience. See Benmussa and Sarraute, *Entretiens avec Nathalie Sarraute*, 184–88.

54. Benveniste, *Problèmes de linguistique générale*, 2:263.

from *Tropismes* to *Tu ne t'aimes pas* is characterized by increasingly greater disembodiment, ambiguity, and lack—or rejection—of differentiation. Identity, or what is concretely identifiable, becomes less important while the tropism—sensation, as opposed to identification—and the language it is joined to become more so. *Tu ne t'aimes pas* is an exemplary text in its creation of a reality where the identity to which we tether our subjectivity is placed under extreme pressure: the experience of subjectivity becomes predicated on giving up identity altogether.

As opposed to the novels that precede it, *Tu ne t'aimes pas* strips away all indications of the outside world and withholds any sort of setting or context. All that remains is language and dialogue that are impossible to place in relation to some external situation. Even this dialogue is severed from the outside world, as it is not between two or more different people and their respective subjectivities, but, rather, takes place within a single mind. The subjectivity of an individual is divided into an uncountable number of constitutive subjectivities, all clamoring in response to the experience that the collective subjectivity—that is, the individual's subjectivity rendered as a collective—has of a declaration that some unknown person had addressed to them: "Vous ne vous aimez pas" [You don't love yourself].[55] All the subjectivities housed within the "person" targeted as the *vous* turn on and toward each other, eager to find out which voice or subjectivity in their ranks is implicated. Who, among their *nous*, is the *vous*? As Sarraute would describe the novel in an interview with Wittig:

> In *You Don't Love Yourself*, there was no *I*. There was nothing but us. Consciousness was still very much lacking any *I*, *I* being nothing "but a formless assemblage of unknown parts." There was nothing but multiple *nous* that represented he who did not love himself: he felt so tremendously complex that he did not know whom he could love in the middle of all that. What he sent outside, what he made appear on the outside, was one or several delegates who represented him.[56]

The self to which we attribute subjectivity turns out to no longer be the cohesive identity that it would normally be taken to be in a social situation: each *je* housed within that self represents a particular way of being in and reacting to

---

55. Sarraute, *Œuvres complètes*, 1149. This is the opening sentence of the novel. If the novel's title opts for the singular *tu* (*Tu ne t'aimes pas*) as opposed to the *vous*, it's to reinforce the idea that this collective *vous* is contained by a single person.

56. Wittig, "Le Déambulatoire," 7.

the world. Each delegate represents a certain configuration of sensation and affect, and is a fraction of the so-called individual's Being:

—"Vous ne vous aimez pas." Mais comment ça? Comment est-ce possible? Vous ne vous aimez pas? Qui n'aime pas qui?
—Toi, bien sûr . . . c'était un vous de politesse, un vous qui ne s'adressait qu'à toi.
—À moi? Moi seul? Pas à vous tous qui êtes moi . . . et nous sommes un si grand nombre . . . "une personnalité complexe" . . . comme toutes les autres . . . Alors qui doit aimer qui dans tout ça?
—Mais ils te l'ont dit: Tu ne t'aimes pas. Toi . . . Toi qui t'es montré à eux, toi qui t'es proposé, tu as voulu être de service . . . tu t'es avancé vers eux . . . comme si tu n'étais pas seulement une de nos incarnations possibles, une de nos virtualités . . . tu t'es séparé de nous, tu t'es mis en avant comme notre unique représentant . . . tu as dit "je" . . .
—Chacun de nous le fait à chaque instant. Comment faire autrement? Chaque fois que l'un de nous se montre au-dehors, il se désigne par "je, " par "moi" . . . comme s'il était seul, comme si vous n'existiez pas . . .

[—"You don't love yourself." But what does that mean? How is that possible? You don't love yourself? Who doesn't love whom?
—You, of course . . . you, the only one they were talking to.
—Me? Only me? Not all the rest of you who are me? . . . and there are so many of us . . . "a complex personality" . . . like every other . . . Who is supposed to love whom, then, in all this?
—But they told you: "You don't love yourself." You . . . The one who showed yourself to them, the one who volunteered, you wanted to be the one on duty . . . you went up to them . . . as if you were not merely one of our possible personifications, one of our virtualities . . . you broke away from us, you put yourself forward as our sole representative . . . you said "I" . . .
—We do that all the time. What else can we do? Every time one of us shows himself to the outside world he designates himself as "I," as "me" . . . as if he were the only one, as if you didn't exist . . .][57]

Sarraute recognizes that in our minds and the solitary space of our consciousness, emotions, and perceptions, we are not our identities or the labels, categories, and functions that we are for others, that we become in order to be seen by them. Instead, we are full of virtualities, an endless set of possibilities.

---

57. Sarraute, *Œuvres complètes*, 1149; Sarraute, *You Don't Love Yourself*, 1–2. All subsequent citations will be made in-text.

Sarraute's text opens onto a world of absolute interiority where, according to her, sex and other socially constructed differences and categories like it do not exist. While, early on in the novel, there's a brief moment where reference is made to being a middle-aged father of Irish origins (1155; 9), which would seem to fix this collectivity as a masculine one, Sarraute refuses to recognize this insertion of gender as an imposition of difference: she refuses to let subjectless subjectivity be marked by this trapping of subjecthood. As Sarraute writes later on in the novel:

—"Et nous ... Comment savoir si le respect nous manque ... Ici rien ne porte de nom. Personne n'exerce aucune fonction. Il n'y a ici ni père ni mère." (1245)

[—"And we ... How can we know whether we are lacking in respect ... Here, nothing has a name. No one has any function. Here there is neither father nor mother."] (156)

Names, functions, gendered roles—these are all fundamental to society and allow an individual to be recognized as part of it. In order to participate in the social order, an individual must allow herself to be categorized, situated, and ordered—she must consent to having all these identity-handles installed in her, or, to borrow Robyn Wiegman's metaphor, must consent to wearing all these identity clothes.[58]

In *Tu ne t'aimes pas*, Sarraute strips subjectivity of these externally imposed trappings of identity[59] in order to give the reader access to a truly interior interiority isolated from the social world outside—the world of difference and hierarchy. Again, Sarraute's tropismic entry into this interiority of contourlessness does not entail the destruction of the exterior world of contours and identities. The social world still exists: it provokes, with the statement "Tu ne t'aimes pas," the subjectivity's anguished collective response. But where the subjectivity is not a clearly delineated subject, as inside the tropismic magma of sensation, the difference that acts as the gravity of the exterior, social world—gravity insofar as difference makes the social order cohere and gives its various constitutive identities their weight—no longer holds. To put it

---

58. Wiegman, *Object Lessons*, 7.
59. Valerie Minogue comments on this removal of identity: "Everything has undergone scrutiny—names, roles, assigned functions, gender and number, and even verb tenses. The text removes, one by one, the labels of official language, and strips of their authority those names and adjectives that designate age, sex, familial and social roles." Minogue, "Notice" to *Tu ne t'aimes pas*, in Sarraute, *Œuvres complètes*, 1915.

another way, difference turns subjectivity into solid subjects, and the tropism transforms that solid subject into a gaseous subjectivity that has no contours.

If one of the subjectivities in this collective individual subjectivity were still to conceive of itself along some identificatory, differentiating axis such as name, function, gender, or sexuality, it would not truly be in a space of interiority but would still be reacting to and participating in some externality. In this text, for a voice to be heard, it must first be completely situated in the interior world of this anonymous person whose mind we are in. Any desire we might have to read these voices as being representative of a masculine subjectivity because the pronouns they occupy—*je, tu, nous, on, vous*—do not mark themselves as feminine, places an impassable distance between ourselves and the subjectivity that Sarraute offers up to us. Reading such identity into these unidentifiable voices, whose multiplicity signals a complexity that resists the simple unicity of identity and shows that subjectivity cannot be reduced to A, B, C, and D identities, is to place ourselves outside the conversation to which we have been invited as readers.

In order to experience what Sarraute experienced and be present with the voices in their space of sexless interiority where categories and distinctions are not yet operative—in order to read properly—we must leave that will to differentiate behind. We must stop going through the text with a fine-toothed comb, trying to find identity and difference where our host, Sarraute, has repeatedly told us that there is none. Granted, just because a writer says something is so does not make it so, and we could choose to read Sarraute against the grain of what she says, resisting how she, as a writer, attempts to control her texts' reception. We could read Sarraute as a woman writer and sound her works for glimpses of *écriture féminine*, or try to account for the impact her social situation as a woman, a Russian immigrant, a Jew, etc. has on her writing. Such a reading would make Sarraute's writing a simple reflection of Sarraute the subject.

I prefer to read Sarraute for what her writing can do, for its political potentiality, for the ways in which it works against identity and strives for the unbecoming experience of subjectivity without subjecthood. One could just as easily read her for those moments where she fails or does not completely succeed, and look for all the ways identity and difference are still intelligible and operative in her textual worlds. But rather than fault Sarraute for making exaggerated claims about the power of her writing, I would suggest that we look instead to the political quality of her conception of writing as an anti-identitarian space and for the ways her writing served for Wittig (and can continue to serve for us) as a catalyst to delve into literature for this political potential. I want to take Sarraute's writing as an opportunity to combine the aesthetic with the political, to see in language the material of an emancipation from the world as it is, and to see in fiction the possibility of realizing a different world.

Sarraute's corpus can thus be seen as an attempt to write into existence an experience of neutrality in French, a language in which there is no neuter, no neutrality built into the grammar that structures it. She resists the difference language enacts, naturalizes, and codifies, to place us in and make of us a universe without contours.[60] In *Tu ne t'aimes pas*, Sarraute delivers us this contourless, expansive universe, through a collective of infinite voices. To read contours of our own making—names, roles, functions, gender, sexuality—into a material whose formlessness she insists on would be to miss the radically new attempt at attaining the non-identity that makes her work so singular. It would be to make of Sarraute's writing simply a new realism rather than the making of a new reality.

Regarding such a durable identity category as that of sexual difference, Sarraute pushes further in *Tu ne t'aimes pas* than with previous works such as *Les Fruits d'or*. She undertakes, at eighty-nine years of age, with greater boldness than before, the work of making the category of sex obsolete, to cite Wittig,[61] or even impossible. By refusing to plot out human subjectivity onto preconceived axes of identity, Sarraute chooses to enact an experience that is outside both identity and society. Where *Les Fruits d'or* features voices that, though unidentifiable, still identifiably belong to different individuals, *Tu ne t'aimes pas* nullifies the difference between individuals by nullifying individuals altogether, and she stages intersubjectivity within the same subjectivity. Sarraute replaces the experience of an externalized social order with the chaotic disorder of an internal sociality that constitutes subjectivity: Sarraute's writing enacts the social without all the structures of difference and identity that society imposes on individuals as the price for entering into that symbolic order, for becoming one of many. Sarraute shows the many of one, the infinite complexity that makes identity a futile endeavor.

---

60. Even in an autobiographical work like *Enfance* (1983), which is the one text where we might expect concrete details and the recounting of particularities—it is, after all, her individual story, the story of her childhood—we can see the will to flatten and eliminate contours, in two notable ways. First, she splits the narrator into a masculine voice and a feminine one, so that the contour of sexual difference, of being a gendered individual, is attenuated. And second, she erases the contours of her Jewishness by refusing to mark herself as Jewish in the text, an erasure that mirrors her refusal to wear the yellow star during the Nazi occupation of France in World War II.

61. Wittig, commenting on *Les Guérillères*, explains: "The goal [. . .] is not to feminize the world but to make the categories of sex obsolete in language." Wittig, *The Straight Mind*, 85.

BEGINNINGS AND PROVOCATIONS

Sarraute, with her work on the tropism, on this neutral area of human subjectivity, and her ridding pronouns of concrete and differentiated referents that are tethered to identity, provides an important precedent for the profoundly political work Wittig would do in her combative texts, where pronouns are mobilized in the war against difference as weapons that attack gender, or sexual difference, where it first begins in language. We can see Sarraute and Wittig as both engaged in a struggle to undo the pernicious effects of socially constructed and reified identity, and as offering up alternative ways of being, even though they produce very distinct corpora that do not resemble each other stylistically. Nonetheless, their writing is driven by a shared impetus, and the differences in their œuvres can be conceived of in terms of scale. Where Sarraute condenses, Wittig expands. Sarraute's strategy is to attack difference through stripping the novel down to its bare bones: language and dialogue. Wittig's strategy is to create an alternative world: instead of distilling the universe we know into pure interiority, she creates a new one instead. Wittig's expansiveness goes so far as to create an alternative lexicon, as seen most clearly in her and Sande Zeig's *Brouillon pour un dictionnaire des amantes*, thereby creating a new language with which to rewrite history itself. Sarraute turns inward, away from expansion, and reduces her scope, removing the human, the social, and the historical altogether to leave behind just words. "Just words," however, sounds misleadingly small or reductive: language for Sarraute, after all, is at the heart of everything—at the heart of the real in which we live.

That Sarraute and Wittig would have a shared purpose is due to Wittig's literary debt to Sarraute, a debt that she acknowledges freely: it is Sarraute's work, unique for being written "entirely on the side of language," that inspires Wittig's conviction that language shapes reality, that "language molds the real," and prompts her to consider Sarraute the first to fully recognize how "language, far from being a reflection of 'things' and of social reality is in some manner what processes it [. . .] and even what creates it."[62] But influence does not have to be unidirectional. It's interesting to note that in later works like *Tu ne t'aimes pas*, we see a more complete or extreme example of Sarraute's removal of social categories such as sexual difference from the human universe that she is trying to make more apprehensible through writing.

It may be mere coincidence that *Tu ne t'aimes pas*, with its more radical erasure of difference, was written after Wittig's *Les Guérillères* and *Le Corps*

---

62. Wittig, *Le Chantier littéraire*, 69, 133, 140. See also Auclerc, "Le tropisme."

lesbien. However, I think we should consider the possibility of Wittig's influence on Sarraute, of Wittig's work on the real through language informing Sarraute's own work, especially given the two writers' long-standing friendship and their mutual support and admiration.[63] If we take Sarraute's and Wittig's œuvres side by side and observe how Sarraute's more radically anti-identitarian works come after Wittig begins producing her politically charged, defiantly lesbian works, a narrative emerges where Sarraute radicalizes Wittig who in turn radicalizes Sarraute. Together, they experiment with language to find ways to exploit its capacity to undo difference. In this labor they would eventually be joined by Garréta, who also works on language to shape the real, and whose writing is the present-day version of an anti-identitarian vision that can be traced back to the 1930s and Sarraute's first iterations of the tropism. This writing against difference is thus a collective endeavor, one whose continued existence sustains Sarraute's contemporariness and situates Sarraute at the beginning of a radically anti-identitarian corpus.

Reading Sarraute now is a provocation to imagine and experience neutrality and indeterminacy in a contemporary moment that continues—despite the lessons of queer theory's anti-identitarian subversions, the constructivist convictions of feminist theory, critical race theory's intersectional insights, and a turn in the humanities to the posthuman—to invest in the notion of difference and identity as a fundamental part of human existence. Queer theory wants identity, but wants it deconstructed; feminist theory continues to be vexed by the question of woman, or haunted, as it were, by the identity *woman* claims for itself; intersectionality, meant to undermine the monolithic quality of identity categories, has ended up producing a proliferation of localized identities that, for their specificity, are no less monolithic; and posthumanism, in attempting to work against the hubris of the humanist subject's ontological privilege, is unable to get out of the binary logic of opposition that shores up its dependence on the notion of a human identity even as it works to deconstruct it and reveal its blind spots. Sarraute, as we've seen, adopts the radical position of eschewing identity altogether, giving up the pleasures and privileges of being a subject for the sensations of subjectivity instead. Her writing aspires to be one where the human no longer exists as an identifiable, categorizable subject, but rather senses and lives as a boundless subjectivity that is, for Sarraute, the truth of who we are.

Let me end this chapter with a particularly evocative comment Sarraute made about her work and its reception in an interview with the French actress

---

63. See Hewitt, *Autobiographical Tightropes*, for the chapter on Sarraute, in which she discusses the camaraderie between Sarraute and Wittig.

Isabelle Huppert. Sarraute refuses to have her writing identified as an example of *écriture féminine*, as somehow fundamentally shaped and informed by her sexual difference as a woman, by speaking about her work's capacity to transcend such categories: "When *Le Planétarium* came out, I was interviewed by a young man who said to me: 'Ah! But Aunt Berthe is me, I just got married, I get up at night to look at the door handles . . .' That pleased me!"[64] Sarraute's pleasure is rooted in the young man's ability to identify with a female character, at her writing's ability to get him to take off his identity clothes of young masculinity and to strip Berthe of her identity clothes of elderly femininity, to dissolve both his and her identities, and the categories of age and sex that subtend them, and step into Berthe's subjectivity.[65] Sarraute takes pleasure in sharing this experience with her readers, in having us experience the kind of subjectivity and language that disrupts the current social order with its oppressive, compulsory designations of identity. She takes pleasure in having us experience the pleasure that comes from being in a language that allows such freedom and mobility, that allows us to move past identity. The most powerful part of exclaiming *Aunt Berthe is me!* is its assertion that, as Sarraute would put it, "we all resemble each other like two drops of water"[66]—that in our sameness, each of us is infinite, a universe without contours. This conviction makes Wittig and Garréta's writing possible, and, in the chapters that follow, we'll be able to see the ways in which both Wittig and Garréta, as writers of their respective moments, also work to erase the contours we think we cannot do without, to produce a contourlessness that Sarraute has shown to be a space of possibility made accessible through a living language.

---

64. Huppert, "Nathalie Sarraute," 10.

65. One might be tempted to see the young man's ability to identify with Berthe as due to their both being bourgeois, but Sarraute's letters contain instances of her asserting that despite her novels all speaking of a bourgeois world, she is convinced that the tropisms they contain are universal, so that a working-class reader would be able to read her work and experience tropisms without being hampered by class difference.

66. Finas, "Nathalie Sarraute," 4.

CHAPTER 2

Inside Wittig's *Chantier*

To Build a Trojan Horse

NATHALIE SARRAUTE was hardly a political firebrand or activist. While she embodied a radical resistance to the regime of identity in her writing, she led a quiet life as a bourgeois woman living in Paris's posh 16th arrondissement, writing in cafés, drinking whisky and sodas with friends, traveling around the world to speak at universities, and spending time at her country house in Chérence. Sarraute did lead a less than quiet life as Nicole Sauvage, her alias during the Second World War, when she lived in constant danger of denunciation, and her refusal to be identified as Nathalie Sarraute, Jew, was an act of resistance against the Vichy government and rule by the German occupiers. But after the war, Sarraute's political engagement primarily took the form of making donations to various organizations and causes,[1] and signing petitions and manifestos, as in *Le Manifeste des 121* [*Manifesto of the 121*], which was a statement signed by many prominent intellectuals and writers advocating for Algeria's right to self-determination.

Monique Wittig, on the other hand, was a revolutionary when it came to her politics. She was a young Marxist involved in the May '68 student movement, and the sexual discrimination she and other women experienced in it

---

1. For example, a donation of 100 francs to the Comité de Défense du Peuple Grec in 1967, when Sartre, representing the organization, called for donations to combat the dictatorship's repression and torture and help provide displaced Greek emigrants with housing, employment, and food. Fonds Sarraute.

led her to cofound the Mouvement de Libération des femmes.[2] Wittig protested in the streets, shouted down male chauvinist students at the Université de Vincennes, the radical left-wing university where the MLF had its first major collective meetings, and she was arrested by the police for her feminist actions, such as when she helped place a wreath on the Arc de Triomphe for the wife of the unknown soldier. She was involved in the publication of grassroots feminist magazines such as *Le Torchon brûle* [The Dishtowel Burns], as well as more academic feminist journals such as *Les Questions féministes*, headed in part by Simone de Beauvoir. We can see the impact of her activism on her writing: from *Les Guérillères* on, Wittig's writing seethed with an undeniably political, anti-patriarchal ethos that had been less explicitly present in her first novel, *L'Opoponax*, which had won the Prix Médicis, and been hailed as a work of genius. Here was a writer who had been poised to carry on the torch of the avant-garde modernism of the New Novel but had chosen instead to take up the torch of radical feminist, lesbian militancy.

Wittig's identification as a primarily political figure was complete once she published *The Straight Mind*, a collection of politico-theoretical essays that deconstructed the dominant heterosexual political, social, and economic regime as one that had invented the notion of difference in order to subjugate and oppress women and other categories of humanity. While the back cover of *The Straight Mind* describes Wittig as an "acclaimed novelist and French feminist writer" and explicitly identifies the essays as being not only political and philosophical, but also literary, including a blurb by Germaine Brée who writes that "Wittig most brilliantly analyzes certain transformations in the textures and structures of literary language," the predominant critical and popular reception of *The Straight Mind* ended up being that of Judith Butler, also featured on the back cover. Butler's blurb passes over Wittig's literary analysis to focus on the political and theoretical aspects of *The Straight Mind*: "Among the most provocative and compelling feminist political visions since *The Second Sex*. These essays represent the radical extension of de Beauvoir's theory, its unexpected lesbian future. Wittig's theoretical insights are both precise and far-reaching, and her theoretical style is bold, incisive, even shattering." Butler's engagement with Wittig as a political and theoretical figure is not surprising: two years prior, in *Gender Trouble* (1990), her landmark text

---

2. "Cofounded" is a bit of a misnomer in that the MLF and all the smaller groups that composed the movement were committed to collectivity, such that all the members or participants in these groups could be said to have founded it. The individual identity implied by the word "cofounded" says more about the larger public profile that individual activists such as Wittig, Christine Delphy, and Antoinette Fouque had than about their importance to the various groups they are associated with.

of feminist theory that has been recuperated by queer theory as a foundational work, Butler had engaged with Wittig's theoretical essays to read her alongside French theorists such as Foucault, Kristeva, and Irigaray. This characterization of Wittig as a political and theoretical figure has stuck, at least in the American academy, where on course syllabi, it is primarily her political essays from *The Straight Mind* that are assigned. A quick search of citations using search engines like Google Scholar or the MLA International Bibliography shows that *The Straight Mind* is disproportionately cited, demonstrating the extent to which Wittig has been taken up primarily as a theorist rather than as a novelist.[3]

Where Sarraute's bourgeois life and assimilation into the depoliticized New Novel have made it difficult for her to be read as a writer of political works, Wittig's visibility as a political figure and as a lesbian, feminist icon has made it difficult for her to be read as the writer of literary works. Even those who have read Wittig's novels, and accordingly are familiar with a Wittig beyond the feminist theorist of *The Straight Mind*, have a tendency to see Wittig's novels more for their political content and impact than for the literary process that created them. For these readers, these works' political program dominates over their literary one. The overwhelming weight of Wittig's reputation as a political figure may explain why, when it was published posthumously in 2010, her *Le Chantier littéraire* [*The Literary Worksite*],[4] came into the world with barely a whimper, in comparison to the resounding bang of *The Straight Mind*.

PUTTING WITTIG BACK TOGETHER AGAIN

What we have in place is a Wittig who has effectively been cleaved apart, so that Wittig the writer, the artist working with language as her material, is overshadowed, or perhaps a better word would be engulfed, by Wittig the

---

3. As of August 15, 2016, Google Scholar recorded 1536 citations of *The Straight Mind*, as opposed to 4 citations of *The Opoponax* (52 citations of *L'Opoponax*), 322 citations of *Les Guérillères* (49 citations of its two English translations), 221 citations of *The Lesbian Body* (169 citations of *Le Corps lesbien*), 18 citations of *Across the Acheron* (17 citations of *Virgile, non*), 63 citations of *Lesbian Peoples: Material for a Dictionary* (28 citations of *Brouillon pour un dictionnaire des amantes*), and only 7 citations of *Le Chantier littéraire*.

4. I translate *chantier* as *worksite* instead of *workshop*, as it was translated in the excerpt published in 2007 by *GLQ* (see Wittig, "The Literary Workshop"). This is because the French *chantier* carries connotations of labor that are lost in the English *workshop*, and labor is fundamental to Wittig's conception of literary creation.

feminist political figure.[5] As a result, Wittig's literary work comes to us always already assimilated into a political interpretation. This is not to say that Wittig's writing is not political—it is—but the problem is that her literariness, instead of being taken on its own terms, is seen as already political, so that we lose any sense of what is for Wittig the profoundly intimate relationship between the literary and the political. We can also frame this splitting in disciplinary terms. People who know Wittig from French literary studies tend to know the former Wittig, the author of *L'Opoponax*, which was lauded by such prominent literary figures as Sarraute, Marguerite Duras, and Claude Simon. People who are introduced to Wittig in feminist and queer studies tend to know the latter Wittig, the author of *The Straight Mind* and a figure seen by some as a protoqueer theorist.[6]

In order to put Wittig back together again, we need to consider *Le Chantier littéraire*, a crucial text for understanding Wittig, to be as important as *The Straight Mind*. *Le Chantier littéraire* makes clear the importance of Wittig's investment in literary work and takes the reader into Wittig's own literary worksite, which entails foregrounding Wittig's passionate relationship with Sarraute and her writing. In this text, we see Sarraute's writing described as political in the way it resists the use of language to reify difference, contra the dominant narrative that aestheticizes Sarraute's writing while depoliticizing it, and we can see Sarraute's profound influence on Wittig—the contiguity of their writing. Rather than the sort of continuity evoked by the linear metaphor of passing on one's torch, this contiguity has Wittig taking up a torch even as Sarraute continues to carry hers. Wittig lights her torch from Sarraute's. Where each writer goes with the torch she carries is different—Sarraute goes into the tropism, the psychological, while Wittig goes into the territory of mythologies, history, and utopia—but what enables each writer to explore the literary terrain she does is a shared fire, a shared conviction in language's capacity to do away with difference and create a radical experience of indifferentiation and indeterminacy, a capacity best seen in literature.

---

5. I am dealing here with the American reception of Wittig. Based on the relative paucity of critical work done in French on Wittig, and on conversations I have had with French Wittig scholars, who are few and far between, Wittig, both as a writer and as a political theorist, appears to have fallen into a state of relative obscurity in France.

6. See, for instance, Balén, "The Straight Mind at Work," which critiques Butler's treatment of Wittig in *Gender Trouble* and proposes that queer theory take up Wittig's materialist thought that "would not only move us toward developing a more radical theoretical framework for a queer studies that Wittig might have supported, but would offer creative frameworks for challenging oppression of all kinds." See also Crowder, "From the Straight Mind to Queer Theory," which discusses how and why Wittig is not assimilable to queer theory.

The two writers' contiguity is captured dramatically in *Le Chantier littéraire*, which is explicitly an extended homage to Sarraute. Though the work had been originally written and submitted, in 1986, as Wittig's doctoral thesis under Gérard Genette at the EHESS (École de Hautes Études en Sciences Sociales), Wittig continued to work on it long after she had received her doctorate, and planned to publish *Le Chantier littéraire* with P. O. L. in 1999. But 1999 was the year that Sarraute died, and following Sarraute's death in October, Wittig pulled out of her publication contract and returned to working on the text. Wittig returned *Le Chantier littéraire* to her own *chantier*, where she was still working on it at the time of her death, from a sudden heart attack, in 2003.[7]

Because Sarraute's death compelled Wittig to rework this text, we can see *Le Chantier littéraire* as a eulogy to Sarraute, bearing witness to Sarraute's life and work through a personal account of Wittig's own work and thought. *Le Chantier littéraire* is both an *ars poetica* and an explicitly literary revisiting of the political theory of *The Straight Mind*. This extended meditation on Sarraute's writing, which fuses these two projects—one literary, one political—together, is in effect Wittig's way of putting back together her cleaved self. Wittig takes the literary Wittig and the political Wittig and uses Sarraute to reassemble them.

Le Chantier littéraire is not only a testament to Sarraute—it can also be viewed as Wittig's last testament. It represents Wittig's most developed writing and thought as a text that remained present and current at the moment of Wittig's death, that was still in her *chantier*. As such, it represents Wittig's mature perspective on both her writing and political thought. With its panoramic perspective on four decades of work and thought, it gives us access to Wittig's goals and is a lens for viewing the entirety of her corpus, both creative and critical. *Le Chantier littéraire* enabled Wittig to keep Sarraute alive and present, her reflection and work on Sarraute extending her friend's life beyond the grave. And as a posthumous publication—its final form precisely not final, not yet declared finished by its creator—*Le Chantier littéraire* also enables Wittig to be present and in process even after death.

Le Chantier littéraire is important beyond the insights it provides on Sarraute and Wittig individually. It allows us to see who Wittig is and what she does as a writer, which, in turn, allows us to see the foundational role Sarraute played in Wittig's becoming Wittig and sheds light upon Garréta's own project, which takes up the stakes raised by these other two writers. As a

---

7. For more on the conditions surrounding *Le Chantier littéraire*'s publication, see Audrey Lasserre, "Histoire éditoriale," in Wittig, *Le Chantier littéraire*, 173–80.

commentary, manifesto, and a biography of sorts not of the writer as a person but of the writer as writer, *Le Chantier littéraire* enables us to bring together these three writers' works so that we are better able to see that all three are animated by a shared experience of language's potential to transform a reality marked by compulsory identification and seemingly inescapable difference. If *Le Chantier littéraire* is able to do so, it is because it brings together the political Wittig with the literary Wittig. This fusion lies at the heart of the argument I am making about these three writers and their projects, which are political because they are literary.

Given the importance of *Le Chantier littéraire* to understanding Wittig's work and the way it illuminates her writing's relationship to Sarraute's and Garréta's writing, its obscurity is that much more striking, especially when compared to the success that *The Straight Mind* enjoyed. *The Straight Mind* circulated in a wide number of intellectual spheres and disciplines and resonated with a broad audience, but *Le Chantier littéraire*, which takes up many of the same points as *The Straight Mind*—but from an explicitly and unequivocally literary perspective—aroused surprisingly little interest. Although *Le Chantier littéraire* was published quietly by a relatively small press, the Presses Universitaires de Lyon, in collaboration with the French press les Éditions iXe, part of it had nonetheless been made accessible to Anglophone readers through the publication of a translated excerpt in the 2007 special issue of *GLQ* on Wittig. This issue, featuring such prominent figures of feminist and queer studies as Alice Jardine, Judith Butler, and Robyn Wiegman, was undoubtedly widely read. Accordingly, the existence of *Le Chantier littéraire* was revealed to the broad readership *GLQ* commands as a top journal in queer studies, and to those who follow the work of the established scholars featured therein. However, a decade after the special issue on Wittig, *Le Chantier littéraire* has received virtually no critical attention. To date, there is only one review of the work, Renate Günther's review for *French Studies*, which gestures toward the significance of *Le Chantier littéraire* as "the first integral text to draw together the different strands of Wittig's work as a writer and theorist; as such it will prove an invaluable resource to students and researchers in contemporary literature, critical theory, and gender studies."[8] Günther's prediction has thus far proven false, and there has been practically no engagement with Wittig's posthumous work. This is not simply a question of translation, of Anglophones not having access to *Le Chantier littéraire* in the original French, as one might reasonably expect people interested in Wittig's last publication to refer to the

---

8. Günther, "Le Chantier Littéraire (Review)," 275.

GLQ excerpt.[9] Rather, it seems likely that the timing of the excerpt's publication had something to do with this failure to arouse interest. By 2007, the humanities had already begun to reject the linguistic turn and embrace the new materialist turn, with its privileging of materiality over and against an ostensibly immaterial language. Wittig's insistence on the literary must have appeared too stuck in the grand narratives of the twentieth century and their elevation of the textual.

We cannot definitively know why certain interpretations and narratives stick and others don't, or why certain texts inspire fierce devotion and enthusiasm and others do not. What the resounding silence surrounding *Le Chantier littéraire* seems to point to, however, is a reluctance on the part of feminist and queer theory scholars as well as literary scholars to engage with literature as theory, and a will to distinguish between literary and theoretical objects. And yet, Wittig's writing is striking precisely for how fiercely it claims an aesthetic, literary identity along with the function of critique.[10] For her, to theorize a language after and without gender—a language without the hierarchy imputed to gender by patriarchy—is to create literature in that same language. This is best seen in her theorization of innovative literary texts as Trojan horses, as war machines that have traction on reality and are capable of transforming it. Despite the so-called linguistic turn's privileging of language and the prestige that its prominent theorists—Foucault, Derrida, and Barthes—accorded to literature, literature and theory have diverged substantially. The notion that literature itself theorizes seems strangely radical today. The roots of Wittig's writing are in this radicality, and it is to these roots that I wish to turn—roots that connect Sarraute to Wittig to Garréta.

Because *Le Chantier littéraire* remains unknown to most people, even those familiar with Wittig, I want to begin by introducing the text, giving an account of its major claims and showing how its merging of the literary and the political entails a corrective rewriting of *The Straight Mind*. Once we have a working grasp of *Le Chantier littéraire*'s project, it becomes possible to examine Wittig's novels from this writerly perspective and better understand how they are constructed as Trojan horses containing a language capable of destroying identity and difference. These war machines, when admitted inside

---

9. According to Google Scholar, there are four citations of the excerpt in question, made by two people. The French reception of *Le Chantier littéraire* is nearly as nonexistent as the American one. At the time of writing, I have been able to find only two reviews of the work and six essays that cite it.

10. Theory and critique have come to stand for each other—"critical theory" is so often what is denoted by "theory," and it has become difficult to envision theory that doesn't function as critique.

the walls of the reader's mind, can transform the reader's conception and experience of language, and hence of reality. Where there is a fairly straight through-line in the other chapters (Chapters 1 and 3, on Sarraute and Garréta, perform readings of their corpora that show how their works enact an experience of unbecoming, of being a subjectivity without subjecthood; Chapter 4 works through a shared poetics that is founded in a relationship with language that treats it as having a body), this chapter twists and turns and doubles back on itself. This is because Wittig occupies a singular position as the fulcrum of this book, connecting Sarraute to Garréta, and because, in *Le Chantier littéraire*, she doubles herself, writing theoretically, in a critical mode and language, about what her fiction, her literary writing, itself conceptualizes. But by following the labyrinthine movement of this chapter, once you exit through the other side, you will be equipped to see how Wittig is what brings together Sarraute and Garréta, the political and the literary, the critical and the constructive, with her *chantier littéraire* providing a space in which unbecoming language can abide.

INFILTRATING THE ACADEMY: *LE CHANTIER LITTÉRAIRE* AS TROJAN HORSE

Le Chantier littéraire is an intimate work. While it bears a general resemblance to the format of a doctoral thesis, its tone, format, and relationship to knowledge production make it clear that what we have at hand is actually a parodic reinvention of the academic text that is consistent with Wittig's lifelong work of subverting generic norms and transforming genres from within.[11] Wittig hollows out this genre principally through her attack on the objectivity of academic writing and critical work and on the way this objectivity presumes to have a monopoly on rigor. *Le Chantier littéraire* is a work that does not seek to ventriloquize institutionalized academic language, but to invent a new kind. It is a Trojan horse that infiltrates the form of the thesis and its codified language in order to introduce foreign, new material.[12] What passes as a doctoral thesis—Wittig was rewarded a doctoral degree as a result of submitting it—does not actually observe most of the conventions and exigencies associated with

---

11. In *L'Opoponax*, Wittig rewrites the bildungsroman, in *Les Guérillères*, the epic, in *Le Corps lesbien*, the love poem, in *Brouillon*, the dictionary, in *Virgile, non*, the allegory, as iterated in Dante's *Divine Comedy*.

12. See Audrey Lasserre, "Histoire éditoriale," 174–75, where she develops the idea of *Le Chantier littéraire* as a Trojan horse that subverts the form of the *mémoire*, or thesis.

academic writing. *Le Chantier littéraire*, in this sense, infiltrated the institution of the academy.

Wittig's disregard for the standards of academic writing is perhaps most visible, literally, in her transformation of the footnote. The footnote is typically employed, liberally, to cite other scholars and indicate other works besides the author's own that engage with the issue at hand, or to indicate sources, in the form of documents or of people, which contributed to the author's thought process. It gestures toward a wider field of references that the reader might want to explore to gain a deeper understanding of the subject. It acts as a supplement, giving information that is interesting but does not necessarily directly develop the author's question. And it provides detail, which shows the author's familiarity with and knowledge of the object of the footnote, but would weigh down a larger, global understanding of the author's argument. In all these functions, the footnote asserts that its author is part of a larger conversation and serves as evidence of her erudition—it functions, in other words, to render the work to which the footnote belongs more authoritative and credible. It is a guarantee of the work's, as well as the author's, seriousness and respectability, and operates through the footnote's transparency: the actual existence of the references and citations given enables the reader to confirm the author's work and corroborate her line of reasoning, thus inviting the reader's participation in revisiting the sources and works that enabled the author to reach her conclusions. The footnote, then, is public: it is addressed for the reader's benefit.

In Wittig's case, however, she turns the footnote into a private instrument that is not used to guarantee the quality or reliability of the text. Precise, verifiable footnotes give way in *Le Chantier littéraire* to notes in the margins that provide only the vaguest indication of sources, and Wittig cites texts and authors in much the same way that Roland Barthes does in *Fragments d'un discours amoureux* [*A Lover's Discourse*].[13] Without titles, years, or page numbers, Wittig's footnotes, like Barthes's, often end up making the reader feel left out rather than clued in (unless, of course, the reader has the same reading history as Wittig), and they function on an intimate level, like notes by the author to herself that remind her of what she has already read and would easily know to return to. Wittig's text engages the reader—the text is a patient explanation to the reader of what transpires inside the literary worksite, on the writer's side of things—but is nonetheless liberally peppered throughout with these footnotes that seem to address Wittig herself more than the reader

---

13. Christine Planté, in her preface to *Le Chantier littéraire*, also makes note of Wittig's footnotes, and cites them as an illustration of Wittig's parodying of the form of the academic thesis. Wittig, *Le Chantier littéraire*, 16–17.

whose presence she is evidently aware of. Consequently, reading *Le Chantier littéraire* and experiencing the disjunction between the main text's public address and the footnotes' private address is much like having a conversation with a person who never meets your gaze.

The footnotes are a visual, immediately apprehensible subversion of the norms of academic writing, but where we can best experience Wittig's disregard for the exigencies of the academy is in the main text, where she draws upon her own experience as a writer as an authoritative form of evidence. She privileges the personal and anecdotal, which are outside the usual realm of sources deemed sufficiently rigorous or academic, and proposes to give the reader entry into a space—the literary worksite—that is usually only viewed critically from the outside. Wittig insists that the literary worksite can and must be viewed critically from the inside, as it is in assuming the writer's position at the intersection of the critical and the creative that Wittig's vision of language—and of the ways in which this language forms the literary and the political—becomes accessible.

For Wittig, the writer assumes both creative and critical functions because she is both writer and reader: the creative moment of writing is always followed by the critical moment of reading what has been written. Moreover, writers' conceptions of the literary possibilities of language are shaped by the texts they read, so that they never produce a work in a vacuum, but in conversation with the works that have come before and constitute a literary history that they are henceforth a part of. *Le Chantier littéraire* attempts to give us access to both modes by giving us access to Wittig as a critical reader of Sarraute's writing and to Wittig as a creative writer who responds to the inspiration Sarraute's writing provides for her. In doing so, Wittig explicitly targets what she considers to be the narrow vision that literary criticism and scholarship have of what counts as knowledge—a vision that leads to the dismissal of the experiential knowledge a writer can provide access to:

> Presque tous les courants de la critique littéraire moderne, pour autant que je les connaisse ont tendance à liquider le point de vue critique des écrivains comme non scientifique, comme pris à la glu dans sa propre intentionnalité. Mais c'est pour moi une erreur d'essayer d'éliminer ou au mieux d'en traiter avec condescendance. Je ne vois même pas comment on pourrait s'en passer. Car c'est un point de vue qui précède en quelque sorte le travail littéraire et qui nous donne un aperçu sur le faire, sur le procès d'écrire.[14]

---

14. Wittig, *Le Chantier littéraire*, 40. All subsequent references to *Le Chantier littéraire* will be made in-text.

[As far as I know, almost all strands of modern literary criticism have a tendency to dispose of the critical point of view of writers as being unscientific, caught up in the glue of its own intentionality. But I think it's a mistake to try to eliminate this perspective, or to, at best, treat it with condescension. I don't see how we could do without it. Because it is a point of view that, as it were, precedes literary work and gives us a glimpse of the act, the process of writing.]

Rather than cast aside writerly intention as subjective material that will lead critics and scholars astray from the straight and narrow path of objectivity and rational argumentation, Wittig instead advocates a demystification of the writing process, so that far from being a mysterious activity caught up in the transcendental language of inspiration or genius, writing is treated as the labor that writers such as Sarraute, Wittig, and Garréta know it to be.[15]

Wittig's statement challenges all who have a stake in interpreting literature to engage fully with the object of their study and to see that texts are material productions fabricated in a literary worksite by a writer. Wittig critiques literary criticism that treats texts as self-standing, self-made:

> Mais à force de s'en tenir à l'œuvre, au produit (d'un travail), on a fait place nette, on a éliminé l'écrivain de l'écriture. Des expressions comme "ce qui s'écrit," "ce qui se donne à lire," "l'écriture" sont des façons de dire qui rendent compte que le travail littéraire a évacué le travailleur (l'écrivain) tout comme la parole (le discours) a été vidée de son locuteur par les linguistes. À la fois écrivain et locuteur n'ont plus qu'une existence virtuelle. (41)

> [But by dint of holding on to the work, to the product (of a labor), we have made a clean sweep of things and eliminated the writer from writing. Expressions like "that which writes itself," "that which gives itself up to be read," "writing [*l'écriture*]," are ways of speaking that attest to how literary work has expelled the laborer (the writer) just as the word (discourse) has been emptied of its locutor by linguists. Both writer and locutor no longer have anything but a virtual existence.]

This does not mean the writer is supposed to have the last word about the texts that she produces, but that an essential part of accounting for a text is considering the writer's confrontation with a medium as infinite in its possibility

---

15. Garréta, in conversation with me, has described writing as sometimes akin to having teeth pulled, and, at other times, exhilarating, but in any case, as a lot of hard work with no guarantee that it will produce a functional novel.

as language, and as loaded—language bears the traces of all the significations that it has been used to create, and has had layers of meaning sedimented onto it. The text by itself is important, but it is not enough. The text's situation in history and the way a given historical moment influences the evolution of literary and aesthetic interests are important, but they are also not enough. Neither an ahistorical, purely hermeneutical approach that privileges the text nor a completely historicist approach that privileges context are able to take the place of an engagement with the writer's struggle with and work upon the material and medium of language.

At this point, it is worth pausing to define what Wittig means by materiality, as it is not entirely materiality in its Marxist sense of being part of the concrete, material base for human life from which abstract ideology follows, nor is it entirely synonymous with physicality, although Wittig does accord great importance to language's physicality. From the way Wittig uses the term throughout *Le Chantier littéraire*, materiality could be defined as the property of form. Language has a concrete form that literature is especially attentive to—one that makes it workable as a medium. This formal capacity derives from its physicality, from the fact that it can be heard and hence understood, seen and thus read. Simply stated, the materiality of language means that language is a material that can be worked upon. This emphasis on language as a material that can be worked upon—and on the text as the product of such labor—means that in addition to focusing on the text as a hermeneutical and historical object, we need to take seriously the process and labor by which said text is produced. I will be returning to the question of Wittig's writerly materialism later in order to distinguish it from the conception of materiality put forth by new materialisms, but let's first take a look inside her literary worksite.

INSIDE THE LITERARY WORKSITE

The literary cannot be contained within the field of literature as such, and exceeds the boundaries that demarcate literature from life, which is to say, from politics, taken in its broadest sense as signifying what pertains to the collective life of the *polis*, the city, in which *polites*, citizens, abide together. In this sense, politics encompasses the concrete fact of living together and its ensuing vicissitudes, the dynamics of power that inhere in living together, and the epistemes that determine how we live together and who has access to what power. In *Le Chantier littéraire*, Wittig writes to break down and render inoperative the distinctions between the literary and the political that *The Straight*

Mind, with its division into political and literary essays, unintentionally helped reinforce. This division did not take the form of the table of contents explicitly categorizing one set of essays as political and the other as literary. But if one looks at *The Straight Mind*'s table of contents, the essays are ordered not chronologically but thematically: the first five essays ("The Category of Sex"; "One Is Not Born a Woman"; "The Straight Mind"; "On the Social Contract"; "Homo Sum") constitute a political critique of gender that does not draw upon literature, and the last four essays ("The Point of View: Universal or Particular?"; "The Trojan Horse"; "The Mark of Gender"; "The Site of Action") all take literature as their starting point, and comment on specific literary texts by Sarraute, Proust, Djuna Barnes, and Wittig herself.

To be sure, we could see this artificial division as a simple consequence of the anthological nature of the work. After all, *The Straight Mind* was a collection of discrete essays that had been published in journals such as *Feminist Issues* and *Digraphe*, and "The Point of View: Universal or Particular?" had been the foreword to *La Passion* (1982), Wittig's translation into French of Djuna Barnes's short stories. The essays were gathered together and a structure was imposed on them after they'd already been written. *Le Chantier littéraire* proves to be that much more of an indispensable text in that Wittig takes up many of the concerns of *The Straight Mind*, but from a framework that brings them all together, privileging literature as a site capable of connecting such distinct issues as the social contract, the positioning of minoritarian perspectives vis-à-vis the universal, the category of sex, and language's production of gender. In short, Wittig undoes in *Le Chantier littéraire* the compartmentalization of her thought that was effected for and by the publication of *The Straight Mind*.

The reception of *The Straight Mind*, which privileges the political over the literary, is symptomatic of the sort of compartmentalization and violent cross-sectioning that critical analysis tends to perform on its objects. In *Le Chantier littéraire*, Wittig evokes, as a particularly vivid example of such analytic violence, what she claims linguists do to the body of language: transform the integral, solid body of language into "le grand corps de signes démembrés, démantelés, réduits, coupés, tel que nous l'ont légué les linguistes" (95) [the large body of dismembered, dismantled, reduced, cut up signs, as it has been bequeathed to us by linguists], a mutilated body that she describes elsewhere as "fragmentés, sans sens" (43) [fragmented, meaningless]. The implication is that the meaning and sense of language come not from being taken apart to be examined closely but from being considered as a whole. The writer, in her passionate and intimate relationship with language, has privileged access to this wholeness. *Le Chantier littéraire*, as a critical perspective that starts and ends with the integrity of language, seeks to restore to language's dissected body its vitality, and it constitutes a critical perspective that enables Wittig to restore life to her own work's dissected body.

Up to this point, I have articulated Wittig's view that it is necessary to take the writer's simultaneously critical and creative perspective and work into consideration—a necessity that derives from the writer serving as the one figure who respects and experiences the integrality and integrity of language as an irreducible and total entity. Examining the construction and the writing of *Le Chantier littéraire* will enable us to see Wittig's development of an original Wittigian exegesis, which we can then apply to Wittig's own work to reveal how the literary and the political come together to provide an experience of language's radically universalizing quality, in the Sarrautian sense of returning us to an experience of ourselves as a universe without contours.

Before reading *Le Chantier littéraire*, its structure already indicates the ambitious scope of Wittig's project and of her vision of a breathtakingly expansive and total language.[16] *Le Chantier littéraire* is composed of an introduction, five chapters, and a conclusion. The introduction is itself divided into four broad "propositions" or postulates concerning language: 1) *De l'hétérogénéité et de la versatilité des éléments en présence* [*On the heterogeneity and versatility of elements present [in language]*]; 2) *De la matérialité du langage* [*On the materiality of language*]; 3) *De l'effet des catégories philosophiques abstraites sur le réel social* [*On the effect of philosophical, abstract categories on social reality*]; 4) *Des effets divers du langage physique* [*On the diverse effects of physical language*]. The subsequent chapters treat, in the following order: *Le Chantier littéraire* [*The Literary Worksite*]; *Le Contrat social* [*The Social Contract*]; *Les Formes déjà-là: La littérature* [*Forms Already There: Literature*]; *Le Langage à travailler* [*The Language to Work On*]; *Les Catégories philosophiques: Un exemple, le genre* [*Philosophical Categories: One Example, Gender*]. The conclusion turns from the writer toward the reader's fundamental role in realizing an experience of literature's universality—its belonging to all.

Wittig conceptualizes and situates such vast concepts as the literary, the social, the political, and the philosophical over the course of *Le Chantier littéraire*. All these things are inflected through language, which, as she establishes in her introduction, is heterogeneous, versatile, and material: heterogeneous because language exists as both a concrete material signifier and an abstract signification; versatile because within language the concrete can become the abstract and vice versa; material because it is physically present and imbri-

---

16. While I see Wittig's language as total, it would be a mistake to describe it as totalizing, however. For Wittig, language doesn't appropriate reality because language already *is* reality.

cated in forming philosophical categories, which have an impact on social reality (44–45). In other words, the introduction treats language as constituting reality rather than being a mere construct. Before the real, the material, the social, or the philosophical has acted on language, language has already been involved in the creation of these things.

Language, in Wittig's estimation, has a particularly complex relationship to reality because its materiality, like that of light, is double. Just as light is both wave and particle, with both states having a real impact on the matter with which they interact, language is similarly double in its nature:

> De la même façon la nature du langage est double, participant à la fois de l'abstraction, de la pensée conceptuelle en tant qu'opposée au réel et au matériel, le signifié au signifiant, le figuré au propre, et de l'ordre matériel par les mots et leur espace géographique et sonore. C'est pourquoi il est possible d'affirmer que le langage participe du réel, qu'il est en fait tout aussi réel que le référent auquel on l'oppose, tout aussi réel que les relations sociales et que le réel physique puisqu'il participe des deux. (45–46)

> [In the same way, the nature of language is double, participating at the same time in abstraction, in conceptual thought insofar as it is opposed to the real and to the material, [acting as] the signified to the signifier, the figurative to the proper, and participating in the material order through words and their geographical and sonic space. This is why it is possible to affirm that language participates in the real, that it is in fact just as real as the referent to which one opposes it, just as real as social relations and as physical reality since it is part of both.]

In this compact summation of language's nature, Wittig articulates the foundational idea of *Le Chantier littéraire*. Language is no longer an abstract and less real thing that refers to the more real referent (more real in the sense of its existence preceding the existence of the signifier and serving as the condition of possibility for the signifier), which is readily accessible to the sensorium. Irreducible to a set of referents or signifiers, language is doubly real and has an existence that is richer than the one that referents or signifiers alone have because language is both abstract and concrete, conceptual and material at the same time.

Wittig unpacks this seemingly simple but dense assertion throughout *Le Chantier littéraire*. She turns her analytic gaze onto the concepts of the signifier and signified that have come to be taken for granted, and actually stops to think about what it means to claim that language exists as both signifier and signified, formal expression and conceptual content. In what follows, I take us through *Le Chantier littéraire*, chapter by chapter, showing how the entire text builds off this interplay between language's form and content, which is most clearly embodied in the metaphor of the Trojan horse, with which Wittig begins the text.

LITERATURE AS TROJAN HORSE

The introduction starts with a vivid narration of the Trojan horse and is Wittig's first evocation in the text of how a literary work can function as a war machine. The Trojan horse's form was what weaponized it, as its form's aesthetic appeal to the Trojans was what compelled them to open up their gates and let the enemy inside. After this, in the first chapter, "Le Chantier littéraire," Wittig turns to the idea of the literary worksite, where Trojan horses are made. As we've seen, Wittig conceptualizes the worksite as a space that resists academic discourse, which seeks to cut up language and isolate its content from its form. The literary worksite is a privileged space that respects and works with, rather than against, language's double nature. From this introduction of the literary worksite, Wittig then moves on to "Le Contrat social," showing what is at stake in the various productions of a literary worksite.

Here, Wittig develops a language-based notion of the social contract, in which language is itself the original social contract according to which every individual has equal access to and possession of language:

> Ce qu'on étouffe dans toutes les sortes de parleries qu'elles soient de la rue ou du cabinet philosophique, c'est le langage premier (dont le dictionnaire nous donne une idée approximative), celui où le sens n'est pas encore advenu, celui qui est de tous, appartient à tous, et que chacun à son tour peut prendre, utiliser, courber vers un sens. Car c'est cela le pacte social qui nous lie, le contrat exclusif, il n'y en a pas d'autre possible, un contrat social qui existe bien tel que Rousseau l'a imaginé et où le "droit du plus fort" est une contradiction dans les termes, là où il n'y a ni hommes ni femmes ni race ni oppression, ni rien que ce qui ne peut être nommé qu'à mesure, mot à mot, le langage. Ici on est tous égaux et libres, sans quoi il n'y aurait pas de pacte possible. On a tous appris à parler avec la conscience que les mots s'échangent, que le langage se forme dans un rapport de réciprocité absolue, sans quoi qui serait assez fou pour vouloir parler. Le pouvoir inouï, tel que les linguistes nous l'ont fait connaître, le pouvoir d'utiliser à partir de soi seul tout le langage avec ses mots au son et au sens éclatants appartient à tous. Le langage existe

comme le lieu commun où on peut s'ébattre en liberté et du même coup à travers les mots, tendre à bout de bras à autrui la même licence, sans quoi il n'y aurait pas de sens. (60–61)

[What one stifles in all sorts of chatter whether it's heard on the streets or in a philosophical salon, is original language (of which the dictionary gives us an approximate idea), language where meaning has not yet occurred, language that is everyone's, that belongs to all, and that each can in turn take, use, bend toward a meaning. Because that is the social pact that binds us, the exclusive contract, there is none other possible, a social contract that exists just as Rousseau imagined it, where "might makes right" is a contradiction in terms, where there are neither men nor women nor race nor oppression nor anything except that which can only be named as it occurs, word by word—language. Here we are all equal and free, and if we weren't there would be no pact possible. We all learned to speak with the awareness that words are exchanged, that language is forged within a relationship of absolute reciprocity, without which no one would be mad enough to want to speak. This incredible power that linguists have introduced to us, the power to use, starting with oneself, language, with its words and their dazzling sounds and meanings, which belongs to all. Language exists as the communal space where we can frolic freely and, in the same stroke, extend, through words, the same license to others—without this, there would be no meaning.]

As Wittig describes this situation lyrically, "Le langage existe comme un paradis fait de mots visibles, audibles, palpables, palatables" (61) [Language exists as a paradise made of words that are visible, audible, palpable, and savory]. Wittig evokes this social contract/paradise of language in language reminiscent of Sarraute's reflections on neutrality, as one where *men, women*, and *race* do not occur. They cannot, in this paradise of words, because they are not named *à mesure*, as they occur, but make sexual difference or race seem like originary, rather than constructed, concepts. These words determine rather than describe. Wittig's social contract surges out of the present as a result of an encounter with the present. It does not exist in the past to determine a future. Language, in its truest and most essential form, guarantees the full equality and freedom of all when it remains undeformed, not having lost its integrity through being sapped of its vitality and flexibility—its reactivity and malleability, its playfulness and its give—through *parleries*, or deadening uses of language.

In its reminder that language belongs to all, the chapter effectively universalizes the literary worksite, the space where "meaning has not yet occurred."

Wittig makes the claim that all people can, through engagement with a literary work that is a Trojan horse, learn to relate to language and its double nature the way a writer does. This new, writerly relationship to language is supposed to reveal language's liberatory nature, experienced as the original, egalitarian social contract that language is supposed to be. By having such an experience of language within literature, the reader might be empowered to return language in its everyday uses to that original, ideal language, as well.

From this declaration of the radical democratic nature of the literary worksite as one where language belongs to all, Wittig moves on to "Les Formes déjà-là: La Littérature," which turns to the question of how to relate to what is produced in other writers' literary worksites—other writers' works. At the beginning of this chapter, Wittig defines the Trojan horse as a literary work that is innovative and assumes new and unfamiliar forms:

> Tout travail littéraire important est au moment de sa production comme un Cheval de Troie, toujours il s'effectue en territoire hostile dans lequel il apparaît étrange, inassimilable, non conforme. Puis sa force (sa polysémie) et la beauté de ses formes l'emportent. La cité fait place à la machine dans ses murs. (73–74)

> [Any important work of literature is, at the moment of its production, like a Trojan horse; it is always carried out in a hostile territory where it appears to be strange, inassimilable, nonconformist. Then its force (its polysemy) and the beauty of its forms prevail. The city makes room for the machine within its walls.]

The rest of the chapter confronts the fact that all innovative literary works, once they have been acknowledged as important literary works that permanently alter the literary landscape and the set of possibilities for literary forms, become for all writers who come afterwards the old, pre-existing forms against which or by which new forms must be found and created. The process by which a new form becomes old is in effect the same process by which ready-made meanings are sedimented onto language. The effort to renew forms by breaking away from the old is mirrored by the writer's effort to engage with the material of language, as if for the first time, in order to remove it from its predictable or standard uses and do something new with it. The writer, in order to create the Trojan horse, must disrupt the seeming naturalness with which form and content are made to coincide, the repetition that would bind the signifier to a particular signified.

Wittig treats this problem in the following chapter, "Le Langage à travailler," where she addresses the primary problem that a writer faces in working with language as a medium. Unlike clay, stone, or sound, which, as materials to be shaped into an artistic product, carry no inherent signification in and of themselves, "ce qu'il est en écriture se complique du fait que le matériau utilisé pour le fabriquer, le matériau brut avant que toute forme en émerge, étant le langage, est bien de la matière, mais déjà aussi une forme" (93) [writing is complicated by the fact that the material used to make it, the raw material before any form has taken shape, being language, is indeed a material, but also already a form]. Here, Wittig points to the immediate slippage that occurs in language between form and content. Language already has a form, as manifested in all the different words, or signifiers, that exist as possible material for a writer to use, and this form already has a content, in that words already mean things and signifiers are already joined with their signification. Unlike other artistic media, language, the moment it has a form—which is to say, the moment it exists, as formless language is an impossibility—already has content. In "Le Langage à travailler," Wittig identifies literature as the space and writing as the process where this unquestioned fusion of form and content is troubled—where the writer is able to engage with language in its original state of materiality, when it has not yet had layers of meaning glued onto it.

Wittig sums up the central point of "Le Langage à travailler" as follows: "Tout écrivain doit prendre les mots et les mettre à nu" (97) [Every writer must take words and strip them bare].[17] Where the usual use or signification of a word acts as a uniform that it wears, which makes it and its function visible (the way a doctor's white coat or a firefighter's jacket signals its wearer's function), the writer's task is to remove that word of signifying clothing and "le dépouille de son sens conventionnel afin de le transformer en un matériau neutre, brut" (97) [strip it of its conventional meaning in order to transform it into a neutral, raw material]. The writer must do this so that the word can be deployed differently and used to create new forms—so that it can be part of a Trojan horse. Wittig is very clear that this work of stripping language down does not mean that the writer, in her engagement with language's materiality, can somehow stop it from signifying so that the reader can have as direct an apprehension of language's raw materiality as a viewer can have of the cool, smooth marble that makes a sculpture, or a listener of the different timbres produced by the different instruments playing in a concerto, for instance. As she writes, "Non que les efforts sur le langage en tant que matériel tendent à

---

17. For a development of this essential point, see Wittig, *Le Chantier littéraire*, 95–97.

évacuer le sens. Ils ne tendent qu'à évacuer le sens déjà-là, prévenu, vers une forme nouvelle, neuve, non encore advenu, d'où forcément se mettra en place un sens neuf non encore advenu" (115) [Not that efforts to work on language as a material aim to expel meaning. They only aim to expel the predictable meaning that is already there in order to move toward a new form that has not yet occurred, within which a new yet-to-occur meaning will be put into place]. The writer's work lies in enabling new meanings, and thus new realities, to be produced: this is the function of the Trojan horse as a literary war machine.

Wittig concludes "Le Langage à travailler" by asserting the inseparability of language's form and content (a fusion that Sarraute had insisted upon and developed all throughout her work)[18] to argue that language not only passively receives and replicates meaning but actively creates new meaning. Language is thus no transparent instrument that we use to describe the world that exists, but is itself what makes the self that lives in the world exist, what makes the world exist for the self:

> Il y a une dimension de soi qui vit dans le langage et qui implique la mobilisation de ses facultés intellectuelles: compréhension, appréhension, jugement, imagination, mémoire. Tous les faits de langage, les paroles, les écrits, les actions à tout moment forment et transforment le moi qui en même temps qu'il les agit est agi par eux. (122)

> [There is a dimension of the self that lives in language and implicates the mobilization of the self's intellectual faculties: comprehension, apprehension, judgment, imagination, memory. At all moments, all the acts of language in speech, writing, and actions form and transform the self, which is acted on by them at the same time as it acts upon them.]

Wittig moves from this assertion of the mutual traction that the self and language have on each other to her last chapter, "Les Catégories philosophiques: Un exemple, le genre," to consider another relationship between language and the world: that between language and a philosophical category such as gender, which obviously functions as a political category as well.

Here, Wittig revisits the arguments of her now classic essay "The Mark of Gender" (1985), which shows how the very existence of gendered language excludes women from that social contract of equality and freedom that language's inherent universality undergirds. In "Les Catégories philosophiques," Wittig takes up the questions found in this earlier essay and frames them within

---

18. Sarraute describes this fusion in her essay "Flaubert le précurseur." See Sarraute, *Œuvres complètes*, 1628.

a larger project of breaking down the artificial barrier between philosophy and literature by foregrounding language. She maintains that philosophical categories are not contained within the realm of philosophy, but instead "réside plus ou moins implicitement dans la langue, le discours de tous les jours, les disciplines des sciences sociales" (129) [reside more or less implicitly in language, in everyday discourse, the disciplines of the social sciences], that is, in language that deals with lived life, with concrete experience. It would follow that philosophical categories reside also in literature, which is made of language and rooted in human experience. Wittig uses her own novels, *L'Opoponax* and *Les Guérillères*, to show how those texts, as literary works, are able to work on the usual gendered logic of pronouns to wrest universality away from the masculine. "The Mark of Gender" in *The Straight Mind* also discusses her novels, but there are differences between "The Mark of Gender" and "Les Catégories philosophiques" that show that, in the latter, Wittig was making a concerted effort to commingle and imbricate the political with the literary.

In "The Mark of Gender," the essay is neatly divided into two numbered parts, where the first part addresses the way gender, and the oppression with which it is synonymous, is created and replicated through language, and the second draws upon her own writing to show how literature is the site for confronting such a philosophical and political issue. Through this division, "The Mark of Gender" recreates *The Straight Mind*'s cleaving of the political from the literary. In "Les Catégories philosophiques," however, Wittig does away with the numbered parts. While the development of her argument remains similar, having the "abstract" philosophical and political discussion and the "concrete" literary discussion occupy the same, undivided body of text establishes a visual continuity that implicitly affirms that the two subjects are coextensive.

In another departure from "The Mark of Gender," Wittig draws upon Sarraute to make the transition from the theoretical discussion of gender and its manifestation in and through language, to the literary argument made from the perspective of the writer inside her literary worksite:

> Un écrivain comme Sarraute est très conscient que le langage loin d'être un reflet "des choses" et de la réalité sociale, est en quelque sorte ce qui la traite ("bien sûr vous l'y trouvez dans la réalité puisque vous l'y avez mis") et même ce qui la crée. Toute son œuvre nous confronte à nos fabrications et ce qui s'écrit c'est ce qui y résiste. (140)

> [A writer like Sarraute is very aware that language, far from being a reflection of "things" and of social reality, is, as it were, what processes it ("of

course you find it in reality since you put it there") and even what creates it. All of her work confronts us with our fabrications and what is written is what resists those [fabrications].]

By using Sarraute to bring together gender and language, making Sarraute the thread that ties together this political object with a literary one, Wittig reiterates just how central Sarraute is to her work as both theorist and writer. For Wittig, Sarraute was the paragon of literature that theorizes the political—she was someone who wielded language in such a way as to render inoperative the distinction between the conceptual and the concrete, who understood language's double nature in being both these things at once.

And from this reaffirmation of the non-distinction between the literary and the political, Wittig concludes *Le Chantier littéraire* by interpellating the reader not as passive receiver or consumer of finished products but as the writer's equal partner in the literary worksite:

> Quels que soient d'ailleurs l'effort et le travail fournis par l'écrivain pour tendre à l'universalité, il ne peut aller qu'à mi-chemin. L'autre versant de l'effort et du travail appartient au lecteur sans lequel il n'y aurait jamais transformation complète et universalité réussie. (150–51)

> [Besides, whatever effort and work the writer puts in to reach universality, he can only go halfway. The other half of the effort and work belongs to the reader without whom there could never be complete transformation and the attainment of universality.]

Wittig charges the reader with the writerly task of engaging with language's double nature to make possible the literary and political project of the universalization of a particular point of view:[19] it is only when the reader is able to share the experience of the writer that they can each be brought from their respective particularity into an experience of the universal afforded by the paradise of words.

Le Chantier littéraire, from beginning to end, develops the idea of the double nature of language in order to articulate its most important consequence, that "il y a une plastie du langage sur le réel" (46) [there is a plasticity of language on the real]: language and reality shape and act on each other. The text's primary argument could be distilled as follows: literature is an art that uses language as its medium. Language as a medium is different from other artistic media because of its double nature, where it is both form and content,

---

19. For Wittig's elaboration of this idea, see Wittig, *The Straight Mind*, 59–67.

concrete and abstract, material and conceptual. Writers can and should exploit this specific quality to create innovative works of literature that function as Trojan horses to create new forms, and hence, new meanings. By doing so, language is used not simply to describe or reflect a preexisting reality, but to create and fashion a new one. Through this literary labor, which operates through the writer's passionate engagement with language, literature can resist received ideas of what should and does constitute reality, and work instead to create a new reality.

Literature's aesthetic drive toward new forms engages a political dimension that aspires to new realities, and it is in this double movement, which engages with language's double nature, that the aesthetic and the political are revealed to be co-constitutive. This has implications for how we are to read Wittig specifically and literature generally: we are to match the writer's labor with our own as readers and read for how the writer's work on language creates new forms, and for how those new forms create reality.

WITTIG'S MATERIALISM

One could criticize *Le Chantier littéraire* for being dated, fixed on a particular moment in literary criticism that does not describe literary criticism today (much literary scholarship today has moved beyond the structuralism and poststructuralism that Wittig critiques and responds to). However, such criticisms do not diminish the importance of this text insofar as it enables us to understand Wittig as she understood herself, that is, as a writer whose work on language through literature was also a political action that had real traction on social and philosophical, as well as aesthetic, reality. This belief in literature's traction on the real is rooted in Wittig's materialism—her singular and original perspective on the materiality of language.

Wittig's materialism cannot be assimilated either to the poststructuralist doxa about the discursive construction of reality, or to new materialisms' turn away from language in contemporary theory. Rather than affirm discourse as, in Foucault's words, "practices which systematically form the objects of which they speak,"[20] Wittig teases apart language from discourse and insists on language's, not discourse's, reality, and language's, not discourse's, giving reality its shape and form. If Wittig is able to distinguish language from discourse, it is because of the particular materiality that language has—its capacity to be a raw material ready to be worked on. This distinction is what enables Wittig's

---

20. Foucault, *The Archaeology of Knowledge*, 49.

materialism to resist new materialisms' concerted attack on poststructuralist affirmations of the discursive construction of reality and their theorists' desire to move beyond the human.

I use new materialisms in a broad sense to encompass such heterogeneous strands of thought as feminist science studies, object-oriented ontology, and speculative realism, all of which can be placed under the sign of a posthumanism interested in conceptualizing the non-human. They share the desire to move beyond an anthropocentric account of the world to return to "the real," understood as the matter that exists independently of or beyond the reach of human thought and its will to mastery. The real is thus matter that exists outside human mediation, and it critiques the exceptional status humanity has accorded itself by treating the human as a material thing: conceiving of the human as material, just like the rest of the world it inhabits, levels the difference between the human and non-human that anthropocentric types of thought would establish. Given the way language has been mapped onto the human—language distinguishing humans from non-human animals—as a way of standing in for the human, an important part of new materialism has been a strong anti-linguistic stance, a rejection of the primacy accorded to language by the poststructuralist thought that dominated during the years preceding the rise of new materialism, where language and discourse, and the human subjectivity tied so closely to them, constitute immaterial things from a new materialist vantage point.[21]

Wittig is decidedly not a posthumanist. Her writing, both critical and fictional, is the manifestation of a strong belief in human subjectivity and in the power of language. Wittig prevents the humanist baby of language from being thrown out with the discursive bathwater by holding on to the materiality of language as a way of resisting a human entrenchment in discourse, which deprives the lives we lead and the thoughts we think of a relationship to a vital, material language and the potentiality it holds. New materialisms, which do not make the distinction between language and discourse as Wittig does, have effectively relinquished both in order to turn to the real and the material. Wittig, on the other hand, says that to turn to language, as separate from and opposed to discourse, is to turn to the material. In other words, Wittig's materialism represents a radical kind of materialism, one

---

21. See Coole and Frost, *New Materialisms*; Huffer, "Foucault's Fossils" for succinct overviews of various new materialisms' critical stakes and of the diversity of this relatively new field whose outlines have not yet been firmly traced. See also Apter et al., "A Questionnaire on Materialisms" for reflections from over forty thinkers on the possibilities of new materialisms, in particular, as it relates to the arts.

that is built on language, rather than on that which exists outside it. It is an important counter to new materialisms' eagerness to move past language (and the human).

By holding on so strongly to language as a material thing, Wittig brings together the human and the material in a way that does not invalidate subjectivity. Material language is instead the key to a subjectivity without subjecthood, which we can reformulate as a subjectivity that has language, but that has not been petrified by discourse and the deadening, constrictive realities discourse would build. Neither poststructuralist nor posthuman, Wittig provides a politically vital alternative to both discursive realities and a materiality devoid of human subjectivity, and invites readers to join her in this alternative. *Le Chantier littéraire* reconceptualizes the role of the reader in a way that exceeds familiar narratives of readers who play a fundamental role in literature as a co-creator of texts: in Wittig's vision, what is at stake is no longer simply the constitution of the text, or the reader's vital role in enabling a text to come into being. Instead, Wittig demands that the reader separate language from discourse and from the socially sedimented meanings that it is assimilated with. Wittig insists that the reader be a laborer of language, because it is through this labor that language's materiality can be experienced.

Literature becomes the way for us, as readers, to engage with a language that does not simply exist as discourse and shape us as such, but impels us to be like writers and create new forms of language. This, in my view, is what makes *Le Chantier littéraire* so important, and it is a point to which I shall return. But before doing so, I want to read *L'Opoponax*, her first novel, through the exegetical model that *Le Chantier littéraire* provides. By doing so, we can see how Wittig goes about constructing a Trojan horse in her literary worksite in order to produce a literature that engages both the reader and language itself in a project of dismantling difference, and brings together the literary and the political such that they cannot be understood or experienced except along with and as each other. I focus primarily on *L'Opoponax* because it is considered less political and more aesthetic than the works that follow it, which have explicitly political plots and themes. *L'Opoponax* is a particularly good case study for seeing how fundamentally imbricated the literary and the political are in Wittig's work. While it lacks the bellicose language and overtly anti-patriarchal themes of *Les Guérillères* or *Virgile, non,* for example, or the explicit lesbian sexuality of *Le Corps lesbien*, in *L'Opoponax* Wittig still works on language to produce a form that combats the straight mind—a form whose political force derives from innovative work on and with language.

THE DEMANDS OF *L'OPOPONAX*

L'Opoponax was published in 1964 to great acclaim. Sarraute was on the jury of the Prix Médicis that year, and *L'Opoponax* took the prize. Nathalie Sarraute, Claude Simon, Alain Robbe-Grillet, and Marguerite Duras—the most prominent avant-garde writers of the moment—praised the novel. They considered it a masterpiece and an exemplar of the *récit d'enfance*, the narrative of childhood. This particular genre is a familiar one, which inspires certain expectations,[22] and it constitutes the form of this particular Trojan horse of a novel. Just as the original, mythic Trojan horse was recognizable as a horse but foreign to the Trojans in its form, *L'Opoponax* was recognizable to readers as a narration of childhood, but was foreign in its form: the novel is an account of childhood as written from the point of view of Catherine Legrand, a young girl growing up in the French countryside. As befits a bildungsroman, the novel presents a series of formative moments: the first experience of death, the acquisition of language through learning to read and write, the first day of school (the first time away from the familiarity and safety of one's home), the first experience of desire, which, in Legrand's case takes the form of a transition from the homosociality of her all-girls Catholic school to the homosexuality of her desire for a classmate.[23]

The novel's form, on the other hand, pushed, and continues to push, the limits of our expectation that a narrative of childhood should look like a traditional realist Balzacian novel, with conventions such as clear-cut characters and a decipherable plot, and correct punctuation and grammar. Even more avant-garde writers like Georges Perec or Raymond Queneau still produced largely readable works that retained most of the conventions of language and literature in their *récits d'enfance*, *W ou le souvenir d'enfance* and *Zazie dans le métro*, despite formal innovations such as Perec's use of the frame narrative, or double narrative, and Queneau's work on defamiliarizing language

---

22. The narration of childhood has a long history in French literature, treated most commonly from an autobiographical angle, as with Rousseau's *Confessions*, Georges Perec's *W ou le souvenir d'enfance*, or Violette Leduc's *La Bâtarde*, for example, or through the angle of the bildungsroman, as with Colette's *Claudine à l'école* or Raymond Queneau's *Zazie dans le métro*.

23. This homosexual desire is mediated by the Opoponax, an invention of Catherine Legrand's that, although it resonates with *opopanax*, which "refers to an acacia tree, a plant belonging to the parsley family, a fragrant gum resin or the extracted perfume of this resin" (Bourque, "Shattering the Gender Walls," 120), is something entirely other. The Opoponax shares with opopanax a multiplicity of forms—"On ne peut pas le décrire parce qu'il n'a jamais la même forme. Règne, ni animal, ni végétal, ni minéral, autrement dit indéterminé (*L'Opoponax* 179)—and is a shape-shifting, ungraspable creature that is used by Legrand to communicate with Valerie Borge, the object of her desire, and to forge an intimate relationship that Catherine Legrand by herself would have been unable to achieve.

through unusual orthography (recall his now famous phonetic transcription of "D'où qu'il pue donc tant?" [What's stinking up the place so much?] as *Douikipudonktan* [translated by Barbara Wright as *Howcanaystinksotho*]).

Queneau and Perec, for all their innovations, did not undermine conventions enough to make the structure of the traditional, Balzacian novel collapse, requiring a new structure to be built in its place.[24] But most importantly for a discussion of Wittig's formal innovations, their novels do not take on the task of reworking language to force the creation of a new reality. While both novels could be considered political in their content—with Perec's autobiographical novel constituting a reflection on the horrors of the Holocaust, and Queneau's whimsical tale portraying a nuanced and sympathetic portrait of marginalized members of society, such as homosexuals, single mothers, and, of course, children—neither novel tries to renovate language to get at the root of both the Final Solution and social inequality: the imputing of difference onto certain categories of human life. Wittig, on the other hand, in *L'Opoponax*, disrupted conventions in a sustained manner, such that at no point in the novel does she return to familiar forms for narrating childhood, and her rejection of the conventional *récit d'enfance* has form work in tandem with content to produce a text that contains, in a less immediately evident form, the radical universalizing quality that would be rendered explicit in the programmatically lesbian works to come.

That Wittig subverted the traditional form of the novel is apparent in *L'Opoponax* even before reading the text. Flipping through the pages, we can see a visible formal innovation in her rejection of division: the novel has no paragraph breaks, written instead as a solid block of text, divided seemingly arbitrarily into seven untitled and unnumbered chapters. The continuity of each chapter's block of text reflects the continuity of life as it is lived, as one's experience of childhood can hardly be neatly divided into discrete chapters and episodes in the moment of its living. These blocks of text contain sentences that run on, such as the following, from the novel's opening page, which narrates the experience of Catherine as a little girl going to school for the first time:

---

24. These remarks are specific to the *récits d'enfance* in question and are not meant as blanket statements about Perec and Queneau. Indeed, some of their other works could be pointed to as being revolutionary in the genesis of new forms such as Perec's intricately constructed *La Vie mode d'emploi*, or *La Disparition*, written entirely without the letter "E," or Queneau's *Exercices de style*, which tells the same story in 99 different styles, its perspectival multiplicity recalling that of cubism.

> Il y a beaucoup d'enfants qui jouent dans la cour de l'école mais pas du tout de grandes personnes seulement la mère de Catherine Legrand et il vaudrait mieux qu'elle ne rentre pas dans l'école c'est seulement les enfants, il faut lui dire, est-ce qu'il faut lui dire, et dedans l'école c'est très grand, il y a beaucoup de pupitres, il y a un gros poêle rond avec encore du grillage à losanges autour, on voit le tuyau qui monte presque jusqu'au plafond, par endroits il est en accordéon, ma sœur est sur une échelle contre la fenêtre, elle fait quelque chose, elle essaie de fermer la dernière vitre.
>
> [There are lots of children playing in the playground but not a single grown-up except for Catherine Legrand's mother and it would be better if she did not come again, school is only for children, she'd better tell her, should she tell her? Inside, the school is very big, there are lots of desks, there is a big pot-bellied stove with more of the diamond-shaped fencing around it, one can see the stovepipe which goes almost to the ceiling, it is pleated in places, Sister is standing on a ladder by the window, she is doing something, she is trying to close the top window.][25]

The run-on nature of the sentence conveys the atmosphere of childhood with remarkable immediacy, transmitting how sensorially and emotionally overwhelming it is to be a child exposed to so much newness. By the end of *L'Opoponax*, when Catherine has grown up and become an adolescent, the breathless cadence of childhood wonder has been replaced by the more measured cadence of a young woman who is able to negotiate her world with some sense of mastery, having consented to the rules and conventions of socialization. This conformity, which comes with age, can be seen in sentences that now resemble more the orderly sentences taught and enforced in school as the correct use of language:

> L'eau tout à l'heure transparente a maintenant le bleu céruléen du ciel, les arbres sont ocres orangés rose pâle. [...] Il faut faire pour demain une préparation latine. Catherine Legrand lit le passage des Géorgiques lentement d'un bout à l'autre. On ne comprend pas, quelque fois on a l'impression qu'un mot est familier ou un groupe de mots à cause de la racine qu'on rapproche de celle d'un ou de plusieurs mots français mais si on se reporte aux notes qui

---

25. Wittig, *L'Opoponax*, 7–8; Wittig, *The Opoponax*, 5–6. All subsequent citations will be made in-text. The English translation takes certain liberties that dampen the dramatic effects of Wittig's formal experimentation: it translates *on* as *you* rather than *one*, and, in this instance, this sentence has been divided into two shorter sentences. I replace the translator's *you* with *one* and otherwise occasionally modify the translation.

se trouvent au bas de la page on voit bien qu'on n'y a rien compris à moins qu'elles se trouvent là pour semer la confusion, pour tromper l'élève ennemi, pour donner une piste fausse. (250–51)

[The water which was transparent a little while ago is now the cerulean blue of the sky, the trees are ochre orange pale pink. [. . .] One has to do one's Latin homework for tomorrow. Catherine Legrand reads the passage from the *Georgics* slowly from beginning to end. One doesn't understand it, sometimes one thinks one recognizes a word or a group of words because the root is similar to one or more French words but if you look at the notes at the bottom of the page one finds that one hasn't understood a thing unless they are only there to create confusion, to deceive the pupil, to give a false scent.] (168)

We've gone from the simplicity of a description like "un gros poêle rond" [a big pot-bellied stove] to "le bleu céruléen du ciel" [the cerulean blue of the sky], from the straightforward anxiety of "il faut lui dire, est-ce qu'il faut lui dire" [she'd better tell her, should she tell her?] to the lyrical one of "pour semer la confusion, pour tromper l'élève ennemi, pour donner une piste fausse" [there to create confusion, to deceive the pupil, to give a false scent]. In other words, style has entered the picture. Communicating or conveying something matters less than how that something is communicated. Wittig is clearly mindful of language, attentive to both its quality and style, and to what the style communicates—here, the growth and maturation of Catherine. But this attentiveness to style, while certainly innovative, does not in and of itself make *L'Opoponax* a Trojan horse, and with these innovations alone, the novel would be at best an empty Trojan horse—an unmanned, deactivated war machine, whose unfamiliar and fascinating forms contain nothing transformative inside. Simply a sculpture . . .

What activates *L'Opoponax* as a Trojan horse and endows it with revolutionary substance is Wittig's pronoun work, seen in her unconventional use of *on* as the primary narrative pronoun.[26] The narrative takes place entirely from the perspective of the little girl Catherine and in her voice, but Wittig, instead of using the first-person pronoun *je*, the pronoun of interiority, uses (save in three exceptional instances) the third-person pronoun *elle*, which is singular and gendered. Most noticeably, she uses *on*, which is personal, but indefinite, able to stand in for an individual subject or a plural one, representing no fixed gender. Wittig makes good on the double nature of language through her pro-

---

26. For an extensive linguistic analysis of the pronoun *on* in *L'Opoponax*, see Chapter 5 of Livia, *Pronoun Envy*.

noun work, joining together form and content, her labor traversing both. The use of *on* has the consequence of transforming stylistic issues into political ones. The novel transforms an innovative description of childhood into the inscription of a new reality rendered possible through the creation of a new perspective, that of a subjectivity that exceeds difference—in this case, gender.

Wittig is able to do this and turn the pronoun into the material with which to build a Trojan horse by capitalizing on *on*'s capaciousness, which enables it to be both particular and general, concrete and abstract, singular and plural.[27] For example, *on* can stand for both Catherine and the group of children that she socializes with:

> Catherine Legrand se couche tout du long sur la vache, c'est doux, on tombe un peu mais on peut se retenir au cou de la vache c'est ferme chaud les flancs sur lesquels on roule ça sent bon la paille chaude, le fumier frais. Véronique Legrand a envie de se coucher sur la vache, Pierre-Marie Fromentin a envie de se coucher sur la vache, Pascale Fromentin a envie de se coucher sur la vache. On se couche tout du long sur la vache à tour de rôle qui se laisse faire en faisant de temps à autre un mugissement en tournant la tête du côté où on est. On est sur le toit des poudrières. (117)

> [Catherine Legrand lies down full length on the cow, it's nice, one slips a little but one can steady oneself against the cow's back it is solid and warm the flanks on which one rolls smell good of warm straw and fresh dung. Véronique Legrand wants to lie down on the cow, Pierre-Marie Fromentin wants to lie down on the cow, Pascale Fromentin wants to lie down on the cow. One takes turns lying down full length on the cow, who lets one do it mooing from time to time and turning her head towards one. One is on the roof of the powder mill.] (78–79)

In this passage we can see the progression from an *on* limited to the experience and sensations of Catherine Legrand to a larger *on* encompassing the experience of the other girls, Véronique and Pascale as well as that of the boy, Pierre-Marie. But *on* can also be deployed in such a way as to exclude Catherine, as when it is used to represent the experience of a subjectivity or subjectivities from which she is excluded:

> On se relève. On enlève les bouquets qu'on a dans la ceinture, les tiges sont écrasées et les fleurs têtes pendantes ne sont plus bonnes à rien. C'est au pied

---

27. See Écarnot, *L'Écriture de Monique Wittig*, 25–27, for more on the importance and capaciousness of *on*.

du hêtre que Catherine Legrand oublie le foulard de soie que la mère lui a prêté à condition qu'elle ne le perde pas. On est sous le préau. Il fait déjà complètement nuit sauf une vague clarté du côté du couchant. On entend que Catherine Legrand se souvient tout haut d'un coup du foulard sous le hêtre. Elle veut y retourner sur-le-champ. (89–90)

[One gets up. One throws away the posies one has in one's belt, the stems are broken and the flowers with their drooping heads are useless. Catherine Legrand leaves the silk scarf which her mother lent her on condition that she did not lose it at the foot of the beech tree. One is in the playground. It is already completely dark except for a dim glow where the sun went down. One hears that Catherine Legrand suddenly remembers that she left the scarf under the beech tree. She wants to go back right now.] (60–61)

Catherine is on an outing with her classmates, and the passage begins with *on* representing all of them together but quickly shifts to excluding her, since she stands out in the narrative as the only one to have forgotten something. The narrative shifts suddenly away from the permeability of the pronoun *on* to Catherine's impermeability and specificity, and the *elle* that is now used instead to represent her. The moment *on* and *Catherine Legrand* inhabit the same sentence, a splitting of subjectivity takes place: Catherine's person is contained exclusively within the signifier *Catherine Legrand*, the subjectivity of her classmates represented, then, in *on* without her. Catherine's separation from the others is accentuated in the last sentence of the passage: *elle* occupies the sentence by itself, and Catherine Legrand's subjectivity is thus further isolated, set apart. However, because *on* is also used to describe Catherine's subjectivity, tension is created between it and *elle*.

This tension that Wittig sets up is key, as it mirrors the tension that exists between the particular and the universal, and reenacts the way false universalism operates by isolating particularity as difference: *elle*, forced to bear the weight of gender as an exclusively particular pronoun, is excluded from the universality enjoyed by either the masculine *il* or indefinite *on*. Her project for pronouns in *L'Opoponax* is to resolve this tension between the *on* and *elle*. As the novel progresses, *elle* is eventually subsumed into the *on*. *On* renders inoperative the usual distinctions between particularity and generality in order to express, as universal, Catherine Legrand's childhood. Gone is the default male subject of the bildungsroman whose coming of age is taken to represent a universal coming of age.[28] In its place, Wittig installs a female subject whose

---

28. See Butler, "Wittig's Material Practice" for a commentary on this displacement of the bildungsroman's usual subject.

coming of age represents a universal coming of age whose gendered particularity is hollowed out through the process of being absorbed by *on*. This, in short, is precisely the universalization of the minority point of view that Wittig describes as being the purpose of her writing, the end goal of the Trojan horse's assault on the straight mind.

It is no coincidence that it's at the end of the novel, when *elle* has disappeared completely into the *on*, that *je* makes its only appearance as a pronoun that represents Catherine Legrand's subjectivity in all its fullness and radicality.[29] In the famous closing line of the novel, Wittig transitions from *on* to *je*: "On dit, tant je l'aimais qu'en elle encore je vis" (281) [One says, I loved her so much that in her I still live].[30] This *je*, after nearly 300 pages of *on* and *elle*, displaces the *on* that begins the last sentence and constitutes a stunning declaration and irruption of interiority in what was up to that point a text narrated from the outside. In Catherine's assumption of the first-person voice, two things occur: first, the splitting of her subjectivity into *on* and *elle* is reconciled, taken up and contained by the unity of the individual and the integral subjectivity expressed by *je*; second, Catherine, as a locutor, for the first time, appropriates all of language for herself, thus claiming for herself the freedom and the equality of the social contract that is language. As Wittig argues in *Le Chantier littéraire*, in a gloss on the linguist Emile Benveniste's theory of the connection between subjectivation and language:

> L'exercice du langage (entre autres la locution) fonde le sujet en tant que sujet, en tant que sujet absolu de son discours [. . .] Parler, dire *je*, se réapproprier tout le langage, ne peut se faire que par un *je* entier, total, universel, sans genre. Sans quoi il n'y a pas de parler possible. Un sujet relatif ne

---

29. *Je* occurs first at the beginning of the novel, when, in response to a question by a little girl named Josiane Fourmont, a voice that we take to be Catherine Legrand's responds with a "J'aime ma mère, oui j'aime ma mère" (23) [I love my mother, yes I love my mother]. The other time *je* appears is in the middle of the novel, but as a *je* of free indirect discourse, attributed to the Opoponax that is Catherine Legrand's invention. The first instance of *je* represents an immature Catherine Legrand who has not come to internalize and fully own her lesbian resistance to a patriarchal social order—this *je* thus lacks the depth and force of the novel's final *je*. And this final *je* at the end of the novel is a more direct representation of Catherine Legrand's subjectivity and interiority than the *je* of the Opoponax who, like the pronoun *on*, represents Catherine Legrand as well as the other girls who are suspected of being the Opoponax. See Wittig, *L'Opoponax*, 247–48. For more on the implications of why so many critics of the novel (including Wittig herself) efface these other instances of the *je* in their discussions, see Livia, *Pronoun Envy*, 104–5.

30. My translation: Weaver's translation leaves *tant je l'aimais qu'en elle encore je vis* untranslated.

pourrait pas parler du tout sauf à se faire l'écho, à pratiquer un langage de perroquet, emprunté. (138)

[The exercise of language (among other things, locution) creates the subject as a subject, as an absolute subject of her discourse. [. . .] To speak, to say *I*, to reappropriate for oneself all of language, can only be accomplished by an *I* that is whole, complete, universal, genderless. Otherwise there is no speech possible. A relative subject would not be able to speak at all except to become an echo, to speak a parroted, borrowed language.][31]

It is significant that Catherine is able to found herself as "an absolute subject of her discourse" by borrowing *tant je l'aimais qu'en elle encore je vis* from the sixteenth-century French poet Maurice Scève. This would at first appear to be the epitome of speaking a borrowed language and being a relative subject, but it is instead the manifestation of Wittig's description in Le Chantier littéraire of the writerly imperative to strip words bare and expel the predictable meaning that is already there in order to be able to make new forms.

For readers trained in French literature, this appropriation and others of lines borrowed from sources as varied as Baudelaire, Flaubert, Malherbe, Louise Labé (and also non-French sources such as Virgil and Giacomo Leopardi), reveal the way Wittig's writerly method is one of cannibalization, where she writes with language that has come from elsewhere.[32] Wittig's borrowings are more than just echoes or parroting of the canon. She hollows out this familiar language, founded in sexual difference and used to tell heterosexual narratives, and invalidates their predictably straight meaning in order to create a lesbian meaning and attendant form instead. She shows, through Catherine Legrand's navigation of her own literary education, how to use literature differently to carve out a lesbian subjectivity (and the language with which to express it) from language that was never meant to be used in this way. This lesbian interiority, instantiated by Catherine Legrand's assumption of Scève's *je*, thus shows how new forms and new realities arise not from the creation of new language, but from reinventing language—doing things to the language we already have. And for readers who are completely oblivious to the novel's intertextuality, the main point of Catherine's assumption of the first person still obtains: while they miss the novel's subversive intertextuality, they are still

---

31. This seems to respond to Benveniste's assertion, "It is in and through language that man constitutes himself as a *subject*, because language alone establishes the concept of 'ego' in reality, in *its* reality which is that of the being." Benveniste, *Problems in General Linguistics*, 224.

32. For more on the intertextuality of *L'Opoponax*, see Duffy, "Rereading 'L'Opoponax'"; Lebovici, "La Bonne," 189.

able to feel the impact of Catherine's fully taking hold of her lesbian subjectivity through the shift to the first person.

Through Catherine's appropriation of language and all its possibilities, Wittig ends *L'Opoponax* by bringing Catherine out of the exteriority of both *on* and *elle* into the possibilities opened up by occupying *je*, which she describes as follows: "La possibilité de dire *je* c'est pour tous les individus la possibilité de se parler, de se concevoir au-delà des genres" (139) [The possibility of saying *I* is for all individuals the possibility of speaking, of being conceived beyond genders]. Wittig isn't talking simply about the first person as a grammatical concept, in which case a woman who assumes the first person in French is decidedly not beyond gender when she has to feminize past participles in writing a sentence like "Je suis allée" [I went]. Instead, Wittig is acknowledging the way one's experience of interiority does not operate in gendered or differentiated terms when one is a *je*. Taking a cue from Sarraute's insistence on the indeterminacy of subjectivity, Wittig sets up *je* as a pronominal space where one does not experience oneself either as a *tu*, interpellated by another person who reduces one to identity categories, or as an *il* or *elle*, where one's subjectivity is effectively evacuated so that one is no longer present as an interlocutor, a participatory presence in a scene of language. The *je*, for Wittig, is the pronoun that indicates that its wielder is present in the use and exchange of language, and irreducible to difference and the categories it creates.

The irruption of the *je* at the end of the novel is thus a declaration of the completion of the process of universalization of a minority point of view, where the task of destroying gender is achieved: unfettered by sexual difference, Catherine is able to represent the universal. This is the final destination of a journey made through pronouns: Catherine's subjectivity, which began inscribed within the fixed particularity of *elle*, was progressively detached from this pronoun's definite genderedness and placed under the sign of *on* instead. Then, *on*, whose lack of loyalty to any given point of view renders it less fixed and less particular than its definite pronominal counterparts, was taken over by *je*, with its appropriation of language and its existence beyond and outside the limits of an externally, socially imposed difference and particularity.

Wittig, in evaluating the success of *L'Opoponax*'s universalizing enterprise in *Le Chantier littéraire*, demurs and gives the last word to Claude Simon, the acclaimed Nobel laureate and New Novelist:

> Si j'en crois ce que Claude Simon a écrit de *L'Opoponax*, la tentative d'universalisation, à partir d'un groupe marqué, au moyen d'un pronom personnel indéfini (plutôt que de dire qu'il s'agit d'un genre masculin) a réussi. Il a écrit

en parlant du caractère principal de *L'Opoponax*, une petite fille: "Je regarde, je respire, je mâche à travers ses yeux, sa bouche, ses mains, sa peau . . . Je deviens l'enfance."

[If I believe what Claude Simon wrote about *L'Opoponax*, the attempt to universalize a marked group through a pronoun that is personal and indefinite (rather than say that it is the masculine gender) succeeded. He wrote in speaking of the main character of *L'Opoponax*, a little girl: "I look, I breathe, I chew through her eyes, her mouth, her hands, her skin . . . I become childhood."][33]

Wittig draws on Simon's praise to support her claim that *L'Opoponax* was about universalizing a marked group, that is, about degendering femininity (not to be confused with masculinizing the feminine),[34] through a concerted labor on and with pronouns as a part of language particularly imbricated with subjectivity.

Moreover, by showing how Catherine appropriates Maurice Scève for herself, making it mean something new for her and Valerie, Wittig presents us with the same opportunity to appropriate *L'Opoponax* as readers and use its language for ourselves to have the same experience of universalization. This act of appropriation is what Wittig refers to when she describes the purpose of the pronoun *on* in the novel and why she opted for this particular pronoun: "*One, on*, lends itself to the unique experience of all locutors who, when saying I, can reappropriate the whole language and reorganize the world from their point of view."[35] That is, just as *on*, in its capaciousness and its resistance to definition, enabled Wittig to detach Catherine from the particularity of *elle* by taking her into itself, so too does *on* take us in as locutors who also experience language the way Catherine does: we can claim for ourselves the universality that Wittig sees within the pronoun *je*. To return to the framing metaphor of the Trojan horse, the goal of *L'Opoponax* as a war machine is to unleash a reality in which difference, as gender, for example, is inoperative.

---

33. Wittig, *Le Chantier littéraire*, 143.

34. This degendering of femininity means degendering masculinity as well. Wittig argues explicitly against masculinizing the feminine or feminizing the world: "The direction I was striving toward [. . .] wasn't toward the feminization of the world (something as horrifying as its masculinization) but toward trying to render categories of sex obsolete in language." Wittig, *La Pensée straight*, 123. This passage, while published in the French translation/reworking of "The Mark of Gender," is not present in the original English version. Dominique Bourque conceives of this project under the interesting rubric of *démarquage*, or unmarking. See Bourque, *Ecrire l'inter-dit*.

35. Wittig, *The Straight Mind*, 84.

The innovative use of *on* constitutes the material and form of this particular Trojan horse. What it contains, the substance that it lets out once it has gained entry into the minds of readers through the process of reading, is this *je* that guarantees full participation in the social contract, acting as the gateway to a paradise of words that provides full freedom and equality to all within it.

L'Opoponax is exemplary in bringing together the aesthetic with the political. The work on pronouns, it must be remembered, was motivated by Wittig's desire to create a new literary—that is, aesthetic—form: Wittig was able to work on language in this way because she was inside the literary worksite, not outside it as a socialized individual trying to use pronouns in a way that would be incomprehensible in social situations and normal conversation. In this text, whose full political import was lost on many readers, who saw in it nothing but a virtuosic continuation of the depoliticized, modernist New Novel movement, there is a concerted effort to take hold of pronouns and force *elle* to pass through *on* and be transformed by it into an integral and universal *je*. This transformation of subjectivity through pronouns is a stunning installation of a reality that operates outside the parameters of the straight mind, or reality as we know it. It isn't Wittig's fault that critics saw *L'Opoponax* as simply an experimental *récit d'enfance*,[36] restricting the universalizing power of language to the retrospective recollection or reenactment of a universal childhood (Mary McCarthy titled her review of the novel, "Everybody's Childhood"), instead of seeing it as a war machine that directs its universalizing power to a present (not past) reality and personhood. Beyond a writing of childhood, *L'Opoponax* is a restoration of individual subjectivity not yet interpellated by the ideology of the straight mind into assuming an identity.

Through the exegetical model that *Le Chantier littéraire* provides, it becomes clear that *L'Opoponax* is in fact more ambitious than the texts that follow. *Les Guérillères, Le Corps lesbien,* and *Brouillon pour un dictionnaire des amantes,* for example, employ lesbianism as a provisory concept,[37] a sort

---

36. For example, Mary McCarthy recognizes its literary innovations as constituting a "discovery in the laboratory of the novel," Albert Sonnenfield deems the novel a dull (because experimental) "autobiographical novel of childhood," and Duras considers the novel "the first modern book on childhood." See McCarthy, "Everybody's Childhood"; Sonnenfield, "Review of The Opoponax"; Duras, "Une œuvre éclatante."

37. Wittig theorizes *lesbian* as a concept, writing that "Lesbian is the only concept I know of which is beyond the categories of sex (woman and man)." Wittig, *The Straight Mind,* 20. In other words, *lesbian* is the only concept that exists outside the straight mind. It is provisory insofar as the goal isn't to establish *lesbian* as a dominant or privileged identity, itself a site of difference, but to deploy *lesbian* against the straight mind's categories of sex. *Le Chantier littéraire* does not mention *lesbian* as a concept, which speaks to a more confident articulation of literature's capacity to take us to universality immediately.

of stepping-stone to the universality in which *L'Opoponax* places us directly, without the conceptual support and relative concreteness of lesbianism serving as an intermediary. Granted, *L'Opoponax*, if thematized, could be characterized as the account of a first experience of lesbianism, but unlike Wittig's subsequent novels, it does not foreground lesbianism as the principal material of the novel, even if it is the culminating experience and the means through which Catherine assumes the liberatory pronoun and perspective *je*. Applying *Le Chantier littéraire*, Wittig's last work, to *L'Opoponax*, her first work, brings her writing full circle, returning us to her conviction, lost because of her own success as a theorist, that the political and the literary come from the same *material*—language.

As I have argued, because *L'Opoponax* is the least immediately and explicitly political novel in Wittig's corpus, it provides a better case study of Wittig's bringing together of the literary and the political, of the double nature of language, than her other novels, whose bold, anti-patriarchal, lesbian content delivers their political impact without the reader's having to do as much work to recreate the writer's work of inhabiting her *chantier* and experimenting on language. Because the novel seems to describe a familiar reality rather than create a new one, *L'Opoponax*'s political impact is not as readily visible. Without fantastical narratives such as that of Amazonian women warriors, as in *Les Guérillères*, or of lovers tearing each other apart only to put each other back together with their saliva, as in *Le Corps lesbien*, the new reality experienced by the reader of *L'Opoponax* resembles the extratextual reality of the reader's world (even with fifty years' distance, the novel, apart from a few dated details, such as the extraordinary nature of Catherine Legrand's wearing pants, reads as surprisingly present). In order to release the political content contained deep within this Trojan horse's pronominal material, the reader is required to fully recreate the writer's work in order to achieve the process of universalizing a minority point of view. Granted, this outcome is not a guaranteed one, as it would be easy, for a reader who does not fully engage with the new use of language in the way Wittig herself did in order to create it, to see nothing new about this other reality that the novel creates, to see *L'Opoponax* as simply another narrative of childhood. As becomes clear in *Le Chantier littéraire*, however, with her explicit appeal to readers to do the same work on language that writers do, Wittig wagers that those readers who do see how language can transform reality into something new will be equipped to take that transformative experience of language from the literary worksite into the extraliterary space of the world to turn social space, and its language, into its own *chantier*. Wittig's commitment to literature is inseparable from her political commitment. For her, both literature and activism are ways of responding to and reshaping reality, of effecting a revolution. This revolution, as we shall see, is a Sarrautian one.

WITTIG'S SARRAUTIAN REVOLUTION

For Wittig, Sarraute was a revolutionary. In a letter, Wittig told her that if the world were made up of Sarrautes, or if everyone contained even just a little bit of Sarraute in them, then the revolution would already have taken place.[38] The recent uprisings of May '68, although De Gaulle's militaristic police had ultimately suppressed them, had made revolution on a large scale seem possible,[39] and the MLF, carrying on that revolutionary spirit, was at its peak in agitating for a fundamental change in the place of women and the ways in which they were perceived. Given Sarraute's distance from the sort of political activity Wittig and her feminist comrades were engaged in, such a statement of Sarraute's revolutionary credentials seems surprising. What could Wittig possibly mean by saying Sarraute was the ultimate model for revolution?

Wittig's conviction that literary work can and does have an impact on society, and her insistence on the relationship between language and reality, have their antecedent in Sarraute's own convictions. Wittig's notion of an immanently political literature has its roots in Sarraute, who approaches the question of the political obliquely. Sarraute, in 1960—the year she signed the controversial *Manifeste des 121*, and at a time when Sartre was the French left's dominant intellectual force, and committed literature claimed for itself the privilege of being the only socially engaged and responsible form of writing—responded to a questionnaire sent out by the Marxist journal, *La Nouvelle critique*, asking about the political role of the writer. Sarraute responded by claiming that a literary work's political or revolutionary impact was an unintended but fortuitous consequence of a writer's commitment to literary innovation:

> Sometimes, a writer, in expressing, with the most sincerity possible, the reality that gives itself up to his investigations, has the fortune of also being a writer who contributes directly to the transformation of society. Take Brecht, for example. But those who don't have this fortune are also, albeit in the long

---

38. Fonds Nathalie Sarraute, letter dated August 8, labeled "Après 1970s."
39. See Ross, *May '68 and Its Afterlives*, for an account of May '68 that attends to how radical, subversive, and politically potent this event was, unlike the youth revolt and non-event that May '68 was eventually reframed as.

run, in a more deferred and diverted way, revolutionary writers. Because their works, in unveiling unknown aspects of reality, pierce appearances, sweep away received ideas, make all conventions shatter. All true literature has the opportunity to also be revolutionary, in the social meaning of the word. Look at the literature of reactionary writers: that of Balzac who was a monarchist; that of Dostoyevsky, a passionate tsarist.[40]

For Sarraute, revolutionary impact, rather than serving as a conscious goal, is the inevitable result of literary innovation, of the writer's sincere efforts to make something new, but with the caveat that the temporality of such political impact may very well be deferred to some unknown future. The political, in literature, is an accidental by-product that can only be obtained through an aesthetic engagement with form. Sarraute's description of the political potential for literature closely resembles Wittig's own language in *Le Chantier littéraire* when, for example, Sarraute describes how literary works that sincerely seek to innovate by treating some new or undiscovered aspect of reality destroy conventions.

Sarraute, in her response to *La Nouvelle critique*, essentially articulates the same sorts of ideas that Wittig would go on to theorize through the figure of the Trojan horse. However, Sarraute displaces the political as the primary subject of interest, in contrast to Wittig. Or rather, she displaces the temporality of the political presence of writing, where a literary work is revolutionary in an aesthetic manner in its present moment, while it is revolutionary in a political manner in a future moment, as a sort of afterlife of the work. Sarraute frames the political impact of literature as automatic and unchosen, outside the realm of intention, and as usually occurring outside the writer's own time. By placing the writer and the political in a relationship of non-coincidence, she is able to maintain her own narrative of being an apolitical writer, who, while not opposed to the idea of her writing possessing a political afterlife, in no way seeks it out.

Rather than wanting to have her (political) cake and eat it, too, Sarraute instead refuses to eat it, so that it is up to others to find and experience the political quality of her works. Her most explicit avowal of her writing's political purchase is rather underwhelming: "I believe that my books, which describe movements observed in the bourgeois (but I'll say it again, one finds movements of the same order in everyone), constitute, indirectly, a critique of the bourgeoisie."[41] Rather than claim her writing's self-critical dynamic (Sarraute, in the same response, identifies both herself and all other French writers as

---

40. Sarraute, in "À quoi servez-vous?," 86.
41. "À quoi servez-vous?," 87.

belonging to the bourgeoisie, so that any critique is necessarily a self-reflexive one), Sarraute qualifies her statement: her critique of the bourgeoisie isn't specific but universal, applying to everyone, the proletariat along with the bourgeoisie, and it's indirect. The political project of Sarraute's writing, then, is far removed from and watered down in comparison to that of Brecht, whom she evokes as an exemplar of revolutionary writing. Far from seeking to foment revolution through her writing, Sarraute saw the writer's principal obligation as the pursuit of new forms that enable the expression of new or hitherto unknown realities, a task she did not see as inherently political.[42]

How do we get, then, from Sarraute's tepid acknowledgment of literature's potential political life and her decidedly non-activist literary sensibilities to Wittig's energetic revolutionary project and a conception of literature as a war machine? And is it fair to characterize Wittig's deep, uncompromising political drive as deriving from Sarraute and her corpus of unrelenting interiority? I would argue that it is indeed fair, despite the unlikeliness of Wittig's obtaining a political education from Sarraute. What is at work here is not simply a matter of Wittig taking the indirect nature of Sarraute's critique—where the action of description itself has the function of critique if its object and the form it takes is new[43]—and proceeding to transform it, through the force of her activist temperament, into a blisteringly direct critique of difference that would compel the temporality of the work's impact to coincide with the present moment of its publication. Wittig's vision of revolutionary literature goes beyond critique to combine it with the construction of a different reality, and it obtains directly from her reading of Sarraute's fiction and the impact of Sarraute's theorization of language and its relationship to reality.

In her essay "Roman et réalité" [The Novel and Reality], Sarraute develops the idea of reality and its coextensivity with language as follows:

> What is this invisible thing that literature renders visible, which is not the obvious, banal, already revealed reality that is known, mined from all directions, and that each person can perceive effortlessly?
>
> It is something that is made of scattered elements that we guess at and sense very vaguely, of amorphous elements that lie there deprived of existence, lost in the infinite mass of possibilities, virtualities, which are melted into a magma, imprisoned in the gangue of the visible, suffocated underneath the already-seen, banality and convention. [. . .]

---

42. Sarraute, "L'Ère du soupçon," in *Œuvres complètes*, 1587; Sarraute, "Roman et réalité," in *Œuvres complètes*, 1644.

43. That is, if, as Sarraute puts it, the writer attains "a morsel of unknown reality and the discovery of a form in which this reality can be captured." "À quoi servez-vous?," 85.

> In the absence of a form that creates them, it is obvious that these elements would have stayed invisible. Only form makes them exist. Without form, they are nothing. But—and here is the important point—the reverse is true: form is nothing without them.[44]

Reality cannot be experienced as reality unless it has a form, and for Sarraute, this form is made of language. Reality exists through language and language exists through reality—to try to separate the two into distinct concepts or experiences is impossible for Sarraute, for whom to have the one is necessarily to have the other. As Sarraute would say in an interview, "Form and content [are] one and the same."[45] This coextensivity informs Wittig's assertion that language shapes the real, that to shape the one is to shape the other, and that language, in its double nature, is both form and content, both what shapes and is shaped.

Wittig's revolution is thus a Sarrautian one. But where Sarraute is interested in making visible and apprehensible a present but as yet unexplored or unknown reality, Wittig is interested in creating a reality that does not yet exist. Her reality is a future one—we aren't yet in a world beyond the straight mind—that breaches the present through the literary work's ability to bring textual temporality together with our extratextual one. Sarraute's writing, as she conceives of it, reveals what is already there—the fundamental sameness of people that exists before any creation of difference—and acts like an X-ray to show what is beneath these layers of socialization and categorization. Wittig uses her writing not as an X-ray but as a high-pressured power washer that works to scrape off these sedimented, exterior layers, so that we might be able to get to that foundational bedrock of equality upon which we might build—it is preparatory, anticipatory. Sarraute's writing places us immediately in tropismic space—characterized, as we saw in Chapter 1, by indeterminacy and a rejection of socially constructed categories—and moves inwards, reacting to menacing categorizing external forces by retreating to the surer space of a difference-less interiority in which to unbecome. Wittig, firmly planted in the outside world, uses her writing to attack social conventions directly.

For Sarraute, conventional, non-tropismic reality exists through the banal, categorizing, normative language that she writes against, and the universal tropism exists through the disorienting, indeterminable, and shifting language that is the substance of all her works. For Wittig, a world outside the straight mind becomes possible through her creation and use of a language that eschews gender and linguistic inscriptions and replications of dif-

---

44. Sarraute, Œuvres complètes, 1644–45.
45. Sarraute, 1660.

ference and particularity. Both Sarraute and Wittig are writing a new reality into being, whether already present or situated in the future. They work on language to resist the language of the old reality, which can be best described as discourse—language that has been used to form utterances that, through repetition, acquire meaning intelligible to the social order that created that meaning to begin with. What are banalities and clichés, received ideas and imposed categories, if not discourse? Sarraute, by pitting discourse against tropismic language in her writing, paves the way for Wittig to launch a full-out war against the discourse of the straight mind with the arsenal at her disposal in the *chantier littéraire*, where language can be stripped of its discursive habits and made to signify and create something else other than the well-worn narratives of difference. Wittig takes seriously Sarraute's steady assertion that form and content, signifier and signified, cannot be cleaved apart, and turns it into the foundation for her writing, upon which everything else is built.

BEYOND DISCOURSE

As we saw earlier, Wittig takes a radical stance by insisting that it is language, and not discourse, that constructs or shapes reality. For Wittig, language, in its raw materiality and concrete, physical existence, already participates in and is part of reality before its realness has had the opportunity to be interpreted and processed into socially intelligible terms—before language has turned into discourse. For Wittig, that is where the importance of the literary worksite and the work of literature lies: literature is precisely where the writer (and reader) can experience the reality of language before it has been pressured into becoming discourse. Here again, we can see Sarraute's influence, as Sarraute also wants to take the reader back to what she calls a living language, which, for her, is a language that resists the deadening power of discourse. In the interiority that Sarraute's language inhabits and imposes, even though the tropism and the language that captures it exist in response to social interactions, Sarraute effectively cuts language off from the exterior social space in order to contain it in the polyphonic interiority of an indeterminate human subjectivity: she replaces society with the sociality of our own individual subjectivities, as seen most dramatically in *Tu ne t'aimes pas*.

In both writers' cases, the transformative experience that one can have of language is a distinctively individual one, framed as interiority by Sarraute, and by Wittig as the absolute appropriation of the universality that the first-person point of view and pronoun provides. No question of a "we" or a "you" or a "them" and much less a "s/he" encountering a vital language in this way: it must happen through the "I," through the immediate and intimate experience that literature can provide, which gives the reader an opportunity to experience language in its materiality—the sort of materiality that a writer must confront if she is to create a new form and reality. The individual appropriates language absolutely, as opposed to receiving a social and contingent distribution or allocation of language (e.g., the gendered language to which women are constrained). This is a different way of relating to language and has profound political ramifications. This radical vision of language is the vision of the absolute equality of all before and through language.

If Wittig insists on language's relationship to reality rather than discourse's, which is what most thinkers of the relation between language and reality focus on from both poststructuralist and new materialist perspectives, it isn't because discourse cannot be worked on—obviously it can, as discourses evolve—but because it isn't engaged with primarily as a medium. Discourse, while it has a form, isn't engaged with in its form. Instead, the essence of discourse lies in its content and the impact that this ideological content has on the social spaces in which it circulates. As a consequence, discourse is less material than language in that it isn't treated as a form, but as an effective method of communicating a message. Discourse is as concrete as language because it is made up of words, which are physical, but discourse, being dead and deadening language, in the Sarrautian sense, is not material in the Wittigian sense because it can no longer be worked upon while it is caught up in its signifying. Discourse thus circulates in social reality defining bodies, norms, concepts, etc., working on subjectivities to turn them into subjects.[46]

Let us turn to Wittig's description of the relation among language, discourse, literature, reality, writing, and reading, with which she concludes "Le Contrat social":

> One of the effects of Sarraute's work is to strip down the social pact (language), to show it for what it is (discourse) when it has been domesticated, enslaved like the subject who speaks it, and to show it for what it can be in reality (as in literature), powerful and liberatory, if the locutor (all locutors) did in her acts of speaking the same work as the writer who writes. (72)

---

46. A new materialist like Karen Barad has a very different conception of discourse, and rejects the idea of discourse as a linguistic or signifying phenomenon, characterizing such an approach to discourse as a "mistake of representationalist thinking." Barad, *Meeting the Universe Halfway*, 147. For Barad, discourse is material because it isn't a "human-based practice" (149). Her conception of discourse is obviously at odds with Wittig's, but where Baradian and Wittigian conceptions of discourse converge is in the idea that discourse produces boundaries, e.g., the way discourse produces the boundaries of identity.

While activism and explicitly political action and discourse are necessary insofar as they make visible the need for change, they are not in and of themselves enough to realize it. They might make space for change, but are unable to fill that space with a new and unbecoming subjectivity, which, through a new experience of itself, has effected a radical reconceptualization of reality. For Wittig's powerful and liberatory reality to be realized, language is required, and hence literature, as it is literature that demonstrates the way language is material that can be worked on to build up or dismantle the reality of the categories that subject us—it is literature that shows the locutor, or reader, how to work the way a writer works.

Wittig's metaphor of the Trojan horse explains how literature can act on us to subtly but thoroughly rework our subjectivity so that we can rework, as writers do, the language that built up our subjecthood: contained within the seemingly familiar form of the text, waiting to spring out, is the experience of language in its fullness, a language that has been stripped down and freed of predictable, sedimented, conventional meaning. This is the language that emancipates and makes possible a truly absolute *je*. Literature, for Wittig, is a revolution that happens in interiority, through an encounter with language. It is not the spectacular revolution of a politics that takes to the street: it works on people one by one, changing each individual's reality and reworking their subjectivity so that they can unbecome, breaking loose from the difference that has mired them in particularity and subjecthood in order to experience the paradise of the free and equitable exchange of language between two absolute *je*s described earlier in "Le Contrat social." It spreads the word that a different reality, a different social contract, a different language is possible.

I want to return to another passage I cited earlier, zeroing in on the section that imagines what a collectivity formed of such *je*s might look like:

> Here we are all equal and free, and if we weren't there would be no pact possible. We all learned to speak with the awareness that words are exchanged, that language is forged within a relationship of absolute reciprocity, without which no one would be mad enough to want to speak. This incredible power that linguists have introduced to us, the power to use, starting with oneself, language, with its words and their dazzling sounds and meanings, which belongs to all. Language exists as the communal space where we can frolic freely and, in the same stroke, extend, through words, the same license to others—without this, there would be no meaning. (61)

This is not simply a utopian vision of what life could look like. It is the affirmation of a space that is already open to us—the space of literature—as seen in Wittig's use of the present tense ("here we are all equal and free"; "language exists"), and it is the expression of a desire for what life together might look like were we to live outside literature the way we can in it. This is a political statement that lays out how we are to live together so that language, and the power that inheres in its use, rather than subject us, is the ground for equality and freedom. This language, which is conceived of as a communal space, begins first with the self, originating thus in the sort of experience of subjectivity that literature, as created by Sarraute and Wittig, provides, where the writerly experience of language is taken up by the reader as her own.

When readers and regular locutors become writers in their use of language, their new relationship to language is the foundation for a new interlocution, a sociality of absolute reciprocity where the determining aspect of personhood is not an identity category always already embedded in hierarchy, but rather, the exchange of a language that is free and for all, not partitioned or owned. These lessons in using language differently, in being used by language differently, are ones that *Le Chantier littéraire* teaches us through the Trojan horses it produces. The Trojan horse follows its course, becoming dismantled and losing its form (the horse that has been broken out of is no longer the horse it was) in order to create something new, and this is a lesson in reverse engineering for the reader who becomes a writer—someone who experiences language in its materiality and works with it to make something new. The *chantier* is not only where weapons are built, but also where one rebuilds what its Trojan horses destroy. The Trojan horse produced by the *chantier littéraire* destroys preexisting forms, yes, but only in order to create new ones in a constant renewal of form, so that nothing can ever become fixed, conventional. As Wittig describes the *chantier*, "le chantier littéraire pour vaste qu'il soit n'a pas d'espace propre excepté dans la page blanche" (78) [the literary worksite, as vast as it is, does not have a space of its own save the blank page]. The *chantier* is, at its core, a space of creation, and the blank page, an emblem of the infinite potential of a form perpetually renewed.

Reading *Le Chantier littéraire*, and reading Wittig's fiction through this overlooked text, demonstrates that Sarraute's work provides the blueprints for Wittig's *chantier*. Sarraute's insights into language, discourse, and reality compelled Wittig to build this *chantier* from which she would attack the foundation of the straight mind and its seeming universality in order to replace it, bit by bit, with the original social contract, the paradise of freed language. Wittig's commitment to such writing would not go unnoticed and was taken up by Garréta, born sixty-two years after Sarraute and twenty-seven years after Wittig. Coming of age after May '68 and having her formative years inflected through postmodernism seem to render the collective impossible for Garréta, whose sense of the political consequently does not resemble either Sarraute's or Wittig's: Sarraute hollowed out the depoliticized modernism of the New Novel to fill it with the contourless, indeterminate experience of a subjectivity not subject to categories; Wittig transformed the Marxist feminist materialism that was a driving force of the MLF, and at the same time that the personal was discovered to be political, she made the literary political; Garréta appropriates queer theory and queer models of resistance.

Profoundly affected by her encounter with Wittig's Trojan horses, Garréta builds her own *chantier*, and, with materials and tools shaped by her particular historical and social situation, takes up the project of writing against difference and refusing to submit to costly identity categories. Sarraute provided Wittig with the material with which to make her writing political; Wittig provides Garréta with the ability to access the revolutionary in a postmodern moment, if fleetingly, by giving her the experience of the literary political, the political literary.

CHAPTER 3

Garréta

No Subject Here

WE'VE SEEN HOW the political nature of Sarraute's writing and the aesthetic, literary nature of Wittig's writing have been occluded by the categories used to account for them. Garréta's literary project has been similarly occluded by categorization. In Garréta's case, her membership in the Oulipo has come to dominate characterizations of her so that she is primarily introduced and known as an Oulipian. This handle has stuck to her as tenaciously as that of New Novelist stuck to Sarraute, and, like Sarraute, Garréta is the lone female novelist in a group of experimental male writers.[1] As in Sarraute's case, the categorization of Garréta is productive to a certain degree: examining Garréta through the lens of the Oulipo draws attention to the fundamental role the constraint plays in her construction of her texts, demonstrating the impressively intentional and motivated nature of her formal choices. And the group's commitment to the idea of literature's potential inflects Garréta's writing with an interesting positivity—an investment in the capacity of language to constantly renew itself through a literature whose production will never be exhausted—that complicates the otherwise pessimistic, melancholic negativity that permeates her novels.

---

1. While Garréta is not the only female member of the Oulipo, she is its only female novelist. The English translation of *Sphinx*, published in 2015, takes up both categories to market the book on its back cover, lauding it as "a landmark literary event: the first novel by a female member of the Oulipo in English."

What the category of the Oulipo does not do, however, is make visible the political dimension of Garréta's writing. The Oulipo enjoys a level of media attention and popularity that is rare for literary figures (it's difficult to imagine any other writer or group of writers, who, month after month, would draw in a public large enough to fill the auditorium of the Bibliothèque nationale de France as the Oulipo is able to do with *Les jeudis de l'Oulipo*), but their reputation is decidedly apolitical—their political commitment resembles Sarraute's declaration of *engagement* as a citizen, not a writer, more than it resembles Wittig's conceptualization of literature as war machine.[2] Through her association with a group known primarily for the both ludic and impersonal effects of its members' constraint-driven experimentation, Garréta also falls under the depoliticized light cast upon the rest of the Oulipo. The constraint turns the reader's attention toward facture without provoking, as with Wittig's writing, an examination of how a text's construction can be used toward political ends. The Oulipo's self-consciousness about form does not produce the same political consciousness as Wittig's because their concern with form is limited to the way language works within the confines of a single given text—the constraints in operation in one text do not have a direct impact on the form of another text—whereas Wittig's concern with form is expansive, coming to bear upon the entire operation of language not just within the text, within that instance of textual reality, but within social reality. Identifying Garréta as an Oulipian is a convenient way of making her writerly identity intelligible by reducing it to the constraint, a narrative that's occluded that of Garréta's debt to Wittig and her literary, political vision.[3]

There is another category that Garréta is placed into, which has the opposite effect of politicizing Garréta, but, I would argue, misses the more radical political dimension of her writing to be found in its formal innovations. It politicizes Garréta without attending to how the literary is political in its literariness. This category is the category of *queer*. In the overwhelmingly straight

---

2. Jean-Jacques Poucel comments on Oulipo's reputation as an apolitical group: "Among certain orders of contemporary vanguards, there is one criticism that seems never to tire: namely that the Oulipo as a group insistently refuses to align its research with an explicit ideological or political platform." Poucel, "Family Vocation" (paper presented at *Oulipo@50/ L'Oulipo à 50 ans*, Buffalo, New York, October 5–8, 2011), http://vimeopro.com/user10120706/ methodigital-1/video/35599044). This doesn't mean that Oulipians haven't been political: for example, Jacques Jouet, Jacques Roubaud, Michelle Grangaud, and Hervé Le Tellier made a public declaration explaining they were holding a reading in Strasbourg on March 27, 1997 to protest the extreme-right Front National's assembling there that day. Nonetheless, the apolitical reputation still holds.

3. A rare example of scholarship that treats Wittig's influence on Garréta can be found in Feole, "Le déchaînement littéraire," which compares Garréta's *Sphinx* to Wittig's *Le Corps lesbien*.

French literary field, Garréta is a rare explicitly, visibly queer figure. She was the plenary speaker for Sciences Po's[4] Queer Week in 2013; the 2015 English translation of *Sphinx* was marketed and lauded as a landmark work of queer literature; and *Pas un jour*, a novel recounting lesbian love affairs or encounters, was motivated by the desire to write against the silence that lesbian sexuality is relegated to in the French literary landscape.[5]

Similar to the category of the Oulipo, however, the category of *queer* is also reductive when it comes to examining Garréta's writing, and obscures the political project of writing against difference: *queer* leads people to read Garréta through an identity politics that focuses on her biographical self. The fact that she writes as an identifiably queer person about explicitly queer things places what she does with language under the sign of queerness. This results in Garréta's political impact being situated in her subjecthood, which is to miss the anti-identitarian core of her writing. While the category of the Oulipo places *Ciels liquides* and *La Décomposition*—her novels that don't seem to treat recognizably queer subject material—under the sign of the apolitical, the category of *queer* appropriates texts like *Sphinx* and *Pas un jour* for an identitarian politics.[6] *Pas un jour* and *Sphinx* become political as a result of their anti-heteronormative avowal of queer sexuality, their performance of the literary equivalent of Queer Nation's battle cry: "We're here, we're queer, get used to it!" Garréta's decision to be out not simply in her personal or social life but in her writing is undoubtedly political, but that is not where her deepest political impact lies.

If we keep Garréta within this frame, the political-because-literary quality of her writing retreats from view, and the political impact that remains visible operates on a purely thematic level. Similar to the way Wittig's imbrication of the literary with the political is more recognizable in her post–1968 works, which are all set in a utopian lesbian universe, than in *L'Opoponax*, Garréta's *Sphinx* and *Pas un jour* are also easier to take up as having a political project because they feature protagonists who reject conventional notions of gender and heteronormativity.[7] That is, Garréta's writing is seen as political in propor-

---

4. Sciences Po is the nickname for the Institut d'études politiques de Paris (Paris Institute of Political Studies), a prestigious French university that has produced many leading French political and business figures.

5. Lucille Cairns has described *Pas un jour* as a "decidedly queer text." Cairns, "Queer Paradox/Paradoxical Queer," 71.

6. While *queer* as a concept was meant to destabilize identity, it arguably functions as an identity, despite the anti-identitarianism it has become identified with.

7. For examples of such readings of *Sphinx* and *Pas un jour*, see Feole, "Le déchaînement littéraire"; Rye, "Uncertain Readings and Meaningful Dialogues"; Kosnick, "Reading Contemporary Narratives as Revolutionaries." Much Garréta scholarship passes over an explicitly

tion to how lesbian or queer its subject matter is. This sort of reading seeks to find in these undoubtedly queer novels subjects who can be identified as queer, in direct disregard of the admonitions we find in her writing not to take her novels as sites from which a subject can be excavated. In *Pas un jour,* where she explicitly disavows the subject and its possession of identity, Garréta addresses her seemingly autobiographical narrator in the second person: "[T]u n'as pas le cœur de leur dire (d'ailleurs, [les lecteurs] refuseraient de te croire, car cela est une effrayante nouvelle tant que nous n'aurons pas fini de cuver l'ivre-mort de notre petit moi) que nul sujet ne s'exprime jamais dans nulle narration" [You don't have the heart to tell them that no subject ever expresses herself in any narration. And besides, [readers] would refuse to believe this terrifying bit of news—we're still punch drunk on our little selves].[8] In Garréta's mind, or at least, in the mind of Garréta's authorial presence, as readers and writers, we've yet to come fully to our senses as long as we're invested in the idea that a subject can be found within literature.

If, instead of looking at Garréta through the categories of the Oulipo and queerness, we look to Sarraute and Wittig instead, it becomes clear that the political dimension of her writing, like Sarraute's and Wittig's, exists as part and parcel of the aesthetic or literary dimension. It operates not through recuperating a subject to whom (or which) we can ascribe political capital—the lesbian, the queer, the gender-nonconforming, etc.—but by leading the reader away from identity and its determinism toward indeterminate, identity-less subjectivity in all its potential, toward unbecoming.

While the easiest and most obvious way to read Garréta for the political is through the lens of identity politics, the less obvious but, I would contend, more productive way to read her is for a poetics that turns away from a politics of representation (the politics of a queer voice or perspective). Instead, we ought to apprehend an aesthetics of language whose formal possibilities point not to how humans use language to become subjects endowed with political agency, but to how language can act on humans to erode subjecthood. Where Wittig conceives of the novel as a space in which to use language to bring us back to an originary, egalitarian social contract, Garréta constructs the novel through constraints in order to free the reader from the constraint of identity and create an experience of a subjectivity without subjecthood.

---

political consideration of her work, despite its self-conscious queerness, and instead examines formal concerns such as the constraint and intertextuality (e.g., O'Meara, "Georges Perec and Anne Garréta"; Andrews, "Intertextuality and Murder") or thematic concerns such as the role of technology (e.g., Durand, *Un monde techno*).

8. Garréta, *Pas un jour,* 10; Garréta, *Not One Day,* 3.

In what follows, I undertake readings of two of Garréta's novels, *Sphinx* and *La Décomposition*, which draws her out of the usual categories of the Oulipo and of the queer under whose signs she is placed, to align her instead with Wittig, and through Wittig, Sarraute. By understanding the influence of Wittig, the bridge between these two writers who come from opposite ends of the twentieth century, we can see that Garréta adds her own distinctive postmodern twist to a Wittigian politics that finds its origins in Sarraute. I begin with *Sphinx*, Garréta's first novel, as it is the novel for which Garréta explicitly acknowledges Wittig's influence.

SPHINX: DIFFERENCE IS NEVER THE ANSWER

In April 2015, with the publication of the English translation of *Sphinx*, the French novelist Anne Garréta became accessible for the first time to an Anglophone readership. When it was first published in 1986, this love story irrupted onto the French literary scene. The novel, which tells of the tragic encounter between a nameless young theology student turned DJ and A***, an African American cabaret dancer, astonished its readers through the virtuosic feat of keeping its protagonists' genders completely indeterminable. Garréta, then a twenty-three-year-old *normalienne*, had scrubbed the French text of all marks of gender.[9] Critics, both then and now, have marveled at this complete erasure of gender, even as they have overlooked Garréta's other treatment of difference—the emphasis on racial difference that accompanies her systematic effacement of sexual difference in the novel.

The love story is traditionally understood as requiring difference, in the broadest sense of the term, given that the whole point is that love joins two (or more) individuals. In Garréta's iteration of the love story, however, she erases sexual difference and presents race as the difference that love can then reconcile or traverse: her love story features the relationship between a white European and a black American. This raises the question of why erasing sexual difference should either produce or expose racial difference when the novel was written to express the principle of "fuck difference," as Garréta shared

---

9. This elimination of gender indicators applies only to the protagonists, who constitute an indeterminate duo in the midst of the other gendered characters. Jeanette Winterson published her own version of an indeterminate love story with *Written on the Body* (1992), written in English, which is a less gendered language than French. It is unclear whether Winterson was aware of Garréta's work, and *Written on the Body* is different in its experiment with sexual indeterminacy in that only the narrator's gender is indeterminate, while the love object is identified as a married woman.

with me in a March 2013 interview in Paris.[10] While the difference Garréta denounces is sexual difference, which she considers to be fetishized dogma, and not racial difference, it seems inconsistent and politically incoherent to decry one form of fetishized difference while promoting another when the problem surrounding difference is precisely the process by which it assumes the status of a concept around which an entire social order can be organized. I thus see "fuck difference" as applying more broadly to all fetishized difference that has been solidified into identity even if the original statement was narrower in its scope. Accordingly, a careful examination of what may be read as a caricatural treatment of racial difference will show that Garréta's seeming instrumentalization and exploitation of race for the purposes of destroying sex, or gender, are actually consonant with what I see as her larger project of writing against difference tout court, an investment that we can trace to the major influence of Wittig on her own writing and thought. In other words, if Garréta seems to build up racial difference in *Sphinx*, it is only to tear it down after having shown how such difference is built up through language in the first place.

Michel Foucault has taught us that discourse has the power to create identity. His *La Volonté de savoir* [*The Will to Knowledge*], the first volume of his unfinished *Histoire de la sexualité* [*The History of Sexuality*], argues that the homosexual did not exist as such until the category of the homosexual was created by sexologists and began to circulate in discourse. This and other identity categories were thus effects of discourse rather than its cause. Thanks in large part to feminist and queer theories informed by Foucault's insights, the idea that identity is discursively constructed with nothing natural about it is now commonplace. While we are quick to recognize the force of discourse, it is not so clear how it comes to have that force—the power to ossify difference and create categories such as sex and race. Discourse is language that has been fixed into a function, but as we saw in Chapter 2, Wittig insists that it also be unfixed, that language can be teased apart from discourse. To put it another

---

10. Garréta pronounced these strong words in English in reaction to the celebration of sexual difference that dominated both the literary and intellectual landscape of France in the 1970s and 1980s by means of *écriture féminine* and the codification of a body of thought that came to be known as "French Feminism" in the Anglo-American academy, both of which advocate combatting phallogocentrism through attending to and giving voice to the feminine that has been repressed by patriarchy. (Evidence of the artificial nature of the construct "French Feminism" can be seen in the way Monique Wittig, a fiercely anti-difference feminist, is frequently grouped and cited along with Hélène Cixous, Julia Kristeva, and Luce Irigaray, all three philosophers of difference.) For a polemical account of the origins of French Feminism, see Delphy, "The Invention of French Feminism." For a more measured account, see Moses, "Made in America." See Chapter 4 for more on *écriture féminine* and French Feminism.

way, discourse can be returned to language. But how does language become discourse in the first place? How does it become fixed?

As a mode of writing that programmatically claims to reflect the world it describes, literary realism often does little to strip discourse down to language in a way that would allow readers to question the gendered norms that have become thoroughly embedded into social practice.[11] In the conventional realist novel, language only exists in an already socialized form and is thus unfit to do the work that Wittig describes in *Le Chantier littéraire* of stripping words of the social significations that have sedimented onto them. Language must be stripped of the history of its social usage, thus allowing words to return to their pure materiality, to language in its raw, pre-signifying state, before it has been mobilized around some ideological or conceptual purpose.[12] Wittig teases language apart from discourse in order to tap into the radical political potential to be found in turning to language, rather than discourse, as a site for new meaning. Precisely for this reason, Garréta, like Wittig before her, treats the experimental (as opposed to the conventional) novel as a cultural form where discourse and language can be played against each other.[13] The self-awareness of the experimental novel's literary language calls attention to the materiality of language. Because the novel must also reference the world outside itself in order to make good on its promise of a textual simulation of lived reality, or a textual experience of an unlived reality, it also calls attention to itself as discourse. This double function gives the novel an advantage over theoretical texts as the means for working with, on, and against language to work against identity and the difference that undergirds it.[14] It is the novel that has the potential to effect change, reader by reader, by undoing those categories that seem to make sense of reality and order the world in a necessary way. In short, it is the novel, and not theory, that functions as a Trojan horse, the figure Wittig uses to explain how a literary text such as *Sphinx* "can oper-

---

11. There are some notable exceptions, such as Charles Dickens's *Dombey and Son*, where the "son" is actually a daughter, or Balzac's *La Cousine Bette*, where a masculine Bette takes advantage of her feminine position in order to achieve a masculine position of domination. In both cases, though, these individual aberrations only prove the rule, and the structures of social norms are preserved. I am grateful to Nancy Armstrong for drawing my attention to these examples.

12. Wittig, *Le Chantier littéraire*, 92–102.

13. Because of their political investments in the novel, Garréta and Wittig tease apart language from discourse to come up with new ways of using language much more than other writers who do not resist the gendered machinery of the French language.

14. Wittig, *Le Chantier littéraire*, 44.

ate as a war machine upon its epoch," an epoch marked then, in the 1980s, as it is now, by difference.¹⁵

Garréta sees herself writing "after" Wittig in a double sense—after Wittig chronologically and after her in the sense of deriving inspiration from Wittig's writing:

> Monique Wittig is an extremely important writer to me. In a way, she made it possible for me to write my first novel, *Sphinx*, which attempted to take literally what she means when she says that it is necessary to eliminate and destroy the mark of gender in language, and that this can only happen through exercising language itself.
>
> I thus have a debt that is not a debt but that obligates me nonetheless—it isn't that I owe something to Monique Wittig, but that she opened up a possibility for me. So it is important to me that I continue to pass on something that I think she offered to me, that I have not found except in her. I am absolutely committed to this.¹⁶

In this homage to Wittig, Garréta offers up a paradoxical characterization of her debt as "not a debt," but something that still has the weight of an obligation, even if she does not think of the obligation in terms of owing anything, but of compelling a new possibility. In this, Garréta reconceptualizes debt as something that no longer puts the debtor in a position of having to give up something of herself in proportion to the value of what she has received, giving the creditor influence over the debtor. Garréta understands her debt to Wittig as a liberating possibility that is conceived of in terms of something that can be passed on to others to do with as they please. Her obligation does not mean hewing to Wittig's way of experiencing this possibility; rather, it obligates Garréta to become Garréta. This debt demands creativity rather than conformity.

Garréta's obligation is to do something with this possibility of using language to undo difference, to attempt to free others from the categories of identity that are embedded in language—and that are made of and by language. As Wittig explains, rather than having language do things to you, you must begin doing things to language:

> The ontological farce that consists of trying to divide a being in language by imposing a mark on her, the conceptual maneuver that wrests away

---

15. Wittig, *The Straight Mind*, 69.
16. Garréta, "Wittig, la langue-le-politique," 25.

from marked individuals what rightfully belongs to them—language—must cease. It is necessary to destroy gender entirely. This endeavor can be entirely accomplished through the use of language.[17]

The same language that genders women and marks them as particular can also destroy that mark of particularity, provided one knows how to make it do so. Wittig uses the lesbian subject to displace the universal male subject implied by the unmarked term through her work on pronouns as we see in her revisions of various literary genres. In *L'Opoponax* (1964), Wittig exploits the indeterminate nature of the pronoun *on* to dismantle the gendered bildungsroman and universalize a young lesbian's point of view. She reworks the epic in *Les Guérillères* (1969), by expanding the feminine third-person plural *elles* to represent all humanity instead of the specificity of groups of women. Reworking lyric love poetry in *Le Corps lesbien* (1973, *The Lesbian Body*), she works upon and breaks down the *je* and *tu* to establish a relationship of intersubjectivity and interlocution that is based on an absolute reciprocity and interchangeability between the first- and second-person pronouns that are normally distinct. In *Brouillon pour un dictionnaire des amantes* (1976, *Lesbian Peoples: Material for a Dictionary*) and *Virgile, non* (1985, *Across the Acheron*), she defamiliarizes such familiar texts as the standard dictionary and Dante's *Divine Comedy* by overturning their androcentric perspectives.

Through these works, Wittig demonstrates that genre as literary *genre* has been built on genre as *gender*. Garréta similarly defamiliarizes genre by taking the traditional love story, the seemingly ageless articulation of heterosexual desire, and removing gender from the equation. She works with the possibility opened up by Wittig and makes it hers by replacing Wittig's lesbianized subject with her own project of rendering the subject indeterminable and undifferentiated. But, as we will see, Garréta experiments not only with sex but also with race, and the project of indeterminability is brought to bear on both categories. It is precisely Garréta's experimentation with sex *and* race—where the first is somewhat expected when it comes to deconstructing difference through language, while the latter is unexpected—that makes the novel so important. Let us turn now to *Sphinx* to see the kind of work Garréta does on and to language—work that shows race to be as unnatural a category as sex and makes the text's racial differentiation ultimately serve her project of indifferentiation and indeterminacy.

Sphinx was written and published well before Garréta was inducted into the Oulipo in 2000 and before she became known in academic circles for

---

17. Wittig, *Le Chantier littéraire*, 138–39.

her familiarity with American approaches to queer and gender studies. Nonetheless, *Sphinx* anticipates what was to become Garréta's investment in writing within the constraints for which the Oulipo is known, and it exposes the discursive formation of identities that would become a key insight of queer theory.

Garréta's future intellectual positions are already apparent in *Sphinx*. The language of the novel does away with sexual difference by refusing to reveal the sexes of the protagonists. The reader is given no clues as to whether the relationship is between two men, two women, or a man and a woman. Were she writing in English, she would be writing a novel without using *he* or *she*, *him* or *her* to describe the main characters. In French, subject pronouns, adjectives, compound past tense verbs, and direct object pronouns can all indicate gender, so Garréta carefully avoids these parts of speech and privileges the infinitive, imperfect, and preterit *passé simple* over compound tenses, indirect objects over direct objects, and impersonal, passive constructions in place of the gendered subject pronouns *il* and *elle*.

If the result is surprising in English translation, it is even more so in French. Writing against what seems to be the naturally gendered grain of French, Garréta also resists the naturalness of bodies and their sexed nature. This carefully wrought withholding of deterministic language exposes the constructed nature of identity, or what Judith Butler describes as performative identity,[18] a notion that would be popularized by queer theory. It seems hardly a coincidence that A***—who calls to mind Josephine Baker, another African American cabaret dancer who was a master of turning identity into a performance on Parisian stages—and the narrator, as a DJ, both inhabit the novel as part of the performance industry. From the very beginning, Garréta keeps her protagonists' identities indeterminate when it comes to their sex and sexuality, thus setting her readers up to think of identity as something performed, not something fixed that can be ascertained.

Garréta refuses to let her protagonists' bodies bear the mark of sexual difference. A sexual encounter would be the ultimate occasion for either ascertaining sexual difference, in the case of heterosexual encounters, or for disavowing it, as in the case of homosexual ones.[19] In *Sphinx*, however, the body remains stubbornly illegible in terms of its sex:

---

18. Butler, *Gender Trouble*. See particularly Chapter 3, "Subversive Bodily Acts."

19. This reading is necessarily reductive in its generality and does not account for the possibility of experiencing sexual difference in homosexual relationships, a question Judith Butler poses provocatively in Butler, "Critically Queer."

J'ai dans la bouche, encore, le goût d'une peau, de la sueur sur cette peau. Contre mes mains l'impression tactile que me firent et cette peau et le modelé de cette chair [. . .]. Je ne saurais raconter précisément ce qui advint, non plus que décrire ou même faire mention de ce que je fis ou de ce dont je fus l'objet [. . .]. Sexes mêlés, je ne sus plus rien distinguer.

[I have in my mouth, still, the taste of skin, of the sweat on that skin; against my hands, the tactile impression of skin and the shape of that flesh [. . .]. I don't know how to recount precisely what happened, or how to describe or even attest to what I did, what was done to me [. . .]. Our sexes mingled, I no longer knew how to tell anything apart.][20]

The sexed nature of bodies in sexual encounters is occluded by treating the body as unspecific skin, flesh, and sweat, and by disregarding genital specificity to articulate instead the confused nature of the coupling. Unintelligible in terms of its sex, the indeterminate and protean body can reflect whatever the reader desires it to be. The title *Sphinx* evokes this indeterminacy by referencing the impossibility of knowing, or in this case, the impossibility of figuring (out) the body and assigning it an identity. Falling into an identitarian trap, reviewers have tended to read the relationship in *Sphinx* as heterosexual or homosexual depending on their own sensibilities. Finding it difficult to suspend certainty and commit to indeterminacy, they have assumed there must be some form of sexual difference (or identity) that Garréta had intended to write into being.[21]

This striking feat of her sustained refusal of sexed bodies is accompanied by a less spectacular, perhaps, but equally significant recoding of the bodies in question in terms of race. The novel identifies the narrator as white and A*** as black: "J'appris qu'une peau noire telle celle de A*** exigeait un maquillage d'une tout autre teinte et d'un tout autre dessin qu'une peau blanche" [I learned that black skin like A***'s demands makeup of a completely different hue and variety than white skin] (22; 9). In the absence of sexual difference, racial difference is introduced, as if bodies still have to be differentiated one way or another for their connection to be meaningful. In *Sphinx*, A***'s black body signals both racial difference and cultural difference. A*** is not simply

---

20. Garréta, *Sphinx*, 1986, 78; Garréta, *Sphinx*, 2015, 54–55. The translation is slightly modified here and elsewhere. All subsequent citations will be made in-text.

21. See, for example, Savigneau, "Un genre énigmatique." For an account of more instances of willful gendering, see also Livia, *Pronoun Envy*, 52–54. Garréta has described *Sphinx* to me as a way of holding up a mirror to readers and revealing their own desires, showing how these desires shape the experience of reading.

given a black body as a black iteration of the French citizen. The character is not French or Francophone but foreign, which, in this context, means American. A*** and the narrator therefore have different languages as well as different skin tones, and they come from different places. While removing sexual difference, then, Garréta has nonetheless doubled difference. She has inscribed the bodies of both A*** and the narrator with the category of race, a difference embedded in a narrative of biological essentialism that translates greater or lesser levels of melanin and pigment into the concepts of blackness or whiteness. She has also inscribed their bodies with the purely cultural difference of nationality. A body does not announce its Frenchness any more than it announces its Americanness, but in *Sphinx* Garréta has tied this cultural difference to racial difference. However, these categories of identity do not carry equal semiotic weight in the novel.

In the second half of the novel, the cultural difference manifest in the language and customs of A***'s American family, which stands in for black America at large, assumes principal importance. Once they become lovers, the narrator and A*** go to Harlem and then visit A***'s extended family somewhere in either Long Island or New Jersey. The narrator describes the experience of conversing and eating soul food with this family as a profound experience of feeling at home:

> Il me semblait être là chez moi, tant ils surent me donner l'impression d'appartenir à leur famille, oubliant sans effort la différence de race, de couleur, de civilisation, de classe et tout ce que l'on voudra bien pointer et accentuer parmi les traits possibles d'altérité. Il me semblait avoir toujours entendu cette langue qu'ils parlaient entre eux, avoir depuis toujours mangé de cette même nourriture qu'ils m'offrirent.
>
> Et les vieilles mammas noires riaient de plaisir à me voir manifester un tel appétit. A***, qui toujours me vit, à l'endroit des nourritures terrestres, faire montre d'ennui ou d'indifférence, s'étonnait et se réjouissait. Il semblait que j'oubliais de dépérir, que je goûtais enfin à la vie, que j'y mordais sans l'entremâcher de paroles, propos de table qui, en Europe assez généralement et en France en particulier, constituent la substance essentielle des dîners. (88)

> [I felt at home there, so much did they make me feel like a part of their family, effortlessly forgetting our differences in race, color, culture, class—everything that one might cite as possible traits of alterity. It was as if the language they were speaking and the food they were cooking had always been familiar to me.

And the old black mammas laughed with delight to see that I had such an appetite. A***, who was used to seeing me bored or indifferent when faced with earthly sustenance, was astonished and overjoyed. It seemed that I was forgetting to waste away, that I was finally tasting life, that I was biting into it without words getting in the way, those tableside conversations that, in Europe generally and France in particular, constitute the essential substance of meals.] (63)

Here, Garréta's narrator figures the alterity of African Americanness as able to do away with all alterity. Black America's culture and dialect—which the narrator finds as familiar as French—is the means of forgetting or transcending alterity and tasting the freedom to be oneself regardless of color, creed, class, etc. The narrator casts black language as naturally resistant to difference in a way that French is not. I contend that it is no accident or contradiction that in her attempt to erase difference, Garréta, through her narrator, appears to shore up African American difference as somehow exemplary and salvific.

This turn toward black America shifts the focus away from biological expressions of racial difference, emphasizing instead cultural and especially linguistic expressions. It would appear that Garréta has bundled the biological with the cultural in order to approach the question of racial difference through language and, in this way, to insist that this other difference, like sexual difference, also be approached in terms of language. Where Garréta deploys language as a means to undo sexual difference in French, the narrator privileges black language as the site where the desire for hybridity, for a fluid identity liberated from the strictures of fixed difference, is best realized. In the description of eating soul food with A***'s family, what comes to the fore is not the difference between cuisines so much as the difference in languages. For the narrator, meals centered around soul food do not require the sort of conversation—i.e., language—that a French meal does; in the narrator's telling, conversation around the French dinner table invariably diminishes one's appetite for life. The primary difference between the two cultures represented by the pair of lovers is thus linguistic, and language will consequently be the means of turning the categorical oppressiveness of French, and its embedded difference, against itself.

However, we have to question Garréta's use of a caricatural image of black America in a novel dedicated to blurring identity and destroying the foundational difference of identity categories. Why does she perpetuate any stereotypes of racial alterity, even if to combat other stereotypes? Indeed, Garréta's use of a worn-out stereotype such as the "old black mamma," uncomfortably close to the mammy figure, would seem to legitimate an unquestionably crude form of difference. This is especially remarkable coming from a feminist who uncompromisingly rejects the notion of essential difference. Garréta's call to "fuck difference" is most powerful if it is not a watered-down version of feminism that objects to one form of difference but tolerates another.

It is completely possible that Garréta's anti-difference ethos, which aspires to the universal in the absoluteness of its declaration, in fact depends on a fetishization and instrumentalization of blackness—universalism, as we know all too well, often turns out to be an oppressive, supremacist particularism. It may be that *Sphinx* is in fact very much a text of its time: the 1980s was a moment when the inconsistencies and racist blind spots of second-wave feminism—i.e., "white" feminism—became all too apparent (as seen in the necessary critique performed by intersectionality).[22] It is possible that Garréta's anti-difference ethos has itself evolved over the decades from one that targeted gender and sexuality at the expense of race to one that is more explicitly anti-racist.[23] All these interpretations are possible, but I intend to posit another one, which makes *Sphinx* politically potent today, so that the novel is not simply an artifact of less enlightened times.

From an apparent fetishization of blackness, coupled with the caricatures and stereotypes that pop up throughout the novel, it would be easy to cast Garréta as a writer insensitive to matters of race, but such a reading conflates Garréta with the narrator. Given that Garréta is undeniably behind the scrubbing of gender difference in the novel, it's tempting to confuse Garréta with the narrator and, when it comes to race, attribute that same intentionality to Garréta rather than to the problematic character of the narrator. If I insist on distinguishing between Garréta and her narrator—as I did in my discussion of the family dinner—to attribute the problematic treatment of race to the latter, it isn't merely to perform a recuperative reading of or to offer an apology for Garréta. On a number of fronts, I believe it makes the most sense and results in the most productive reading to distinguish Garréta's narrator from Garréta herself. First, if we take seriously Garréta's debt to Wittig, it is logical to treat the novel as a hollow text, a Trojan horse, instead of adopting the perhaps more obvious reading, in which Garréta's twenty-three-year-old self's feminist politics turn out to be not particularly developed, as evinced by

---

22. While intersectional, or third-wave, feminism is often credited with calling out second-wave feminism's inattention to matters of race, the need for a feminism attentive to race and class was already being voiced by black feminists in the 1970s. See, for example, the Combahee River Collective Statement, which explicitly called attention to "the fact that the major systems of oppression are interlocking." Smith, "Combahee River Collective Statement," 264.

23. The 1980s are often evoked as a racist decade, but it is worth noting that it was also the decade in which France began to develop a collective consciousness regarding matters of race, as seen in the founding of the NGO *SOS Racisme* in 1984.

a deeply problematic conceptualization of race. This reading, which requires no interpretation because of its obviousness, turns the text into a solid rather than a hollow object. Second, the less facile reading, beyond being consonant with the Wittigian mode of writing a literary text as a Trojan horse that contains something very different from what its equine form promises, integrates *Sphinx* into the rest of Garréta's anti-identitarian corpus. Garréta's first novel can thus be read with the novels that follow rather than as a one-off that doesn't belong with the rest of her literary production. And finally, Garréta's entire corpus demonstrates that she is anything but an easy or transparent writer. Her novels are meticulously constructed, and reading them requires work—they are not beach reading, easily consumed.[24] A simplistic reading of *Sphinx*—without the necessary labor to attend to Garréta's own labor in creating the novel—will miss the revelation that the novel is anything but racist: it grapples directly with the problem of racism in order to enjoin the reader to dismantle both racial difference and sexual difference.

Before proceeding with an analysis of the complex construction of Garréta's deconstructive work, I want to first address the enormous riskiness of Garréta's Trojan horse venture. I am making a case for seeing Garréta's deployment and construction of racial difference as a means to tear it down, but such a reading requires labor. The astounding blindness to race that *Sphinx*'s readers have demonstrated is a perfect example of what happens when you don't read laboriously. Instead of a powerful "fuck difference" ethos that articulates a radical political vision of a new sociality unordered and unfettered by any form of difference, an effortless reading may lead to a celebration of the dissolution of sexual difference at the cost of tacit acceptance of racial difference, and not just any form of racial difference, but a racist one. In other words, this reading results in a "white feminist" text that does more harm than good in promoting the idea that some invidious forms of difference must be tolerated for the sake of abolishing another. These are the high stakes of Garréta's novel, and we can certainly debate whether or not it's worth the risk. In what follows, however, I will show what happens if we do put in the work to activate the Trojan horse of *Sphinx*.

To read *Sphinx* laboriously is to read Garréta's deployment of racial stereotypes critically, to see it as the means of ironically calling attention to the way the narrator turns cultural differences into natural differences as they are attached to certain bodies. Following this line of thinking, we could say

---

24. For example, Garréta explained to me that her 1999 novel *La Décomposition* was written according to multiple principles of construction, such as "a systematic transduction algorithm applied to chunks of *À la recherche du temps perdu*" in the text of the novel, and that many of the structuring principles of her novels are opaque and go unperceived by readers.

that Garréta uses fiction in much the same way Étienne Balibar uses political theory, to argue that "biological or genetic naturalism is not the only means of naturalizing human behaviour and social affinities [. . .]. *[C]ulture can also function like a nature*, and it can in particular function as a way of locking individuals and groups a priori into a genealogy, into a determination that is immutable and intangible in origin."[25]

In other words, Garréta's apparent investment in racial difference is an ironic one, and the reinforcement of racial difference that accompanies the radical destruction of sexual difference serves as a decoy for difference that reveals itself as hollowed out. This irony, which is hardly obvious or self-evident, can be seen in the narrator's description of black American dialect:

> L'anglais que je parle a gardé les stigmates de cette fréquentation presque exclusive des Noirs. Imperceptiblement, des expressions, des incorrections caractéristiques de leur parler se sont glissées dans le tissu de langue académique qu'on m'avait enseignée au lycée. Cela, depuis, m'a été un trouble dans mes conversations: cette langue que je parle est un hybride monstrueux; j'ai mêlé Oxford et Harlem, Byron et le gospel. (89)

> [My English still bears the stigmata of keeping company almost exclusively with black people. Imperceptibly, the expressions and characteristic improprieties of their speech slipped into the tissue of the academic English I had been taught in high school. This has disrupted my conversations: the language I speak is a monstrous hybrid, mingling Oxford and Harlem, Byron and gospel.] (64)

Garréta here doles out the clichés: of course, black American English is riddled with ungrammatical variations on standard English, of which the most correct iteration is to be found at Oxford; of course, the most obviously black idiom is gospel music, and it goes without saying that Harlem is the purest iteration of black American culture. This characterization is disturbing in its racial insensitivity and caricatural treatment of American black culture, but I would argue that Garréta does so in order to parody facile caricatures, rather than to reproduce them uncritically.

The obvious reading of Garréta that takes this passage at face value reproduces a fetishistic view of blackness. Black American language—the sign that turns racial difference into cultural difference and naturalizes the distinction between them—is the guarantor of hybridity and subversion. It undoes Eng-

---

25. Balibar, "Is There a 'Neo-Racism'?," 22.

lish by undermining the correctness of white, Anglo-Saxon, Puritan English. According to this reading, Garréta's grounding of the novel's anti-difference enterprise in an essential black language is a concession made in the name of eliminating sexual difference, the seemingly universal difference that cuts through other differences such as race and class. The marginal status of black English leads directly to the fetishization of black culture and desire for the black body. Following this logic, the narrator sees in blackness the perfect medium for breaking up fixed categories of identity, but the price for such destabilization is the fixing of blackness.

While the French language fixes difference with its gendered grammar, black African American language counteracts that fixity through soul. The narrator claims: "Mon Amérique à moi est noire: sa musique, ses voix, sa nourriture. Noires, il y a un terme pour cela, *soul: soul music, soul food*" [My America is black: its music, its voices, its food. These black things have a name, *soul: soul music, soul food*] (87; 62). Black culture, refracted through soul, provides Garréta with the possibility of a language that is not beholden to the subordinating logic of French. Blackness comes to stand in for an identity that is more American than the soulless, sanitized Americanness of what the narrator describes as "l'Amérique blanche, anglo-saxonne et puritaine" [white, Anglo-Saxon, Puritan America] (87; 62). Black Americanness consequently permits a greater distance from French and from France, whose "universal" citizen is configured as white, heterosexual, and male. By contrast, black skin, black language, and black culture exemplify a language that offers a promised land of freedom and equality. The narrator's desire for a differently racialized body is not so much the desire for a different kind of body as it is the desire for a language and culture less dependent on difference than French language and culture. Black language provides a model for what Garréta is trying to do with French, that is, to undo its gendered and gendering operations. While this racializing might be positive in its valence of a certain black superiority, it remains grounded in an essentializing difference. One form of difference is swapped out for another, and we wind up right where we began, stuck in difference.

The true allegory of *Sphinx* is not the allegory of black alterity as a difference that might create more fluid ways of being human; it is an allegory for the invidiousness of all forms of difference. To read *Sphinx* laboriously, to read it as a complex text, we have to reject the narrator's reading of race as the allegorical production of a better kind of alterity. Rather than be taken in by a difference that promises to transcend other differences, Garréta rejects racial difference as the lure that would lead the reader back into the trap of difference. Garréta's polarized stereotypes and the caricatures they form offer parodic representations of black language that are not meant to be swallowed whole, taken as they are. A necessary condition of the Trojan horse is that it resembles closely enough the object it claims to be—a statue of a horse, in the Trojans' case, a racist and reductive rendering of blackness, in Garréta's—in order to be let inside the city walls (the reader's mind) to launch its attack. For Garréta to reject racial difference as the lure that would lead the reader back into the trap of difference, it must first be able to pass as an alluring difference.

Garréta's attention to the language of black difference, which assumes a more important role than black skin, points to the crucial role language plays in creating and reifying forms of difference. When she places language that eliminates sexual difference in relation to language that shores up racial difference, Garréta exposes the equally constructed nature of both these differences. By bundling racial difference with cultural difference, she shows how easy it is for us to slide from the cultural, to the biological, to the essential. The social order has primed us to identify difference and then compels us to perform it. Once the reader sees Garréta's use of stereotypes for what it is, it becomes difficult if not impossible to accept her construction of blackness. This leads us to examine the tendency to bundle differences, as if we could impute a more complex identity to individuals by doing so. Why, she forces us to ask, must we insist on transforming bodies into signs? According to this reading, in distinction from her narrator, Garréta is saying that bodies are not simply meant to be read and identified so much as to be lived in. In a Foucauldian gesture, she invites us to consider her novel as the site for new "bodies and pleasures."[26]

Garréta challenges her reader to resist the instrumentalization of bodies that occurs when we inscribe them with difference through signifiers of identity. Rather than giving us access to richer, fuller subjectivity, difference deadens our subjectivity, quite literally, in *Sphinx*: A*** dies tragically, as does A***'s mother, and with them, the kinship structure based on the redemptive difference ironically described in the novel, and the salvific relationality it contained. In a nod to the seventeenth- and eighteenth-century novels that are Garréta's academic specialty, she ends this novel by also murdering her narrator, as if to say that the narrator must pay for the knowledge that may have been gained.[27] Reading Garréta, the early modern specialist, with these eighteenth-century heroines in mind, her killing of both the narrator and the narrator's love object can be read as a repudiation of knowledge and a warn-

---

26. Foucault, *The History of Sexuality*, 159.

27. I imagine that Jean-Jacques Rousseau's Julie, from *La Nouvelle Héloïse* [*Julie, or the New Heloise*] and Denis Diderot's Sapphic Suzanne (along with the various abbesses Suzanne left in her wake), from *La Religieuse* [*The Nun*], were at the back of Garréta's mind when she killed off her narrator.

ing against the kind of misleading knowledge that identity, founded in difference, is mistakenly thought to provide. Both race and gender exemplify such a promise of knowledge, where a person is known or at least knowable—where being identifiably something makes you identifiably someone. In *Sphinx*, the spectacular removal of gender and the display of race work together simultaneously to make clear the extent to which we, as socialized subjects, equate knowledge with identity. Indeterminacy, as enacted in the novel, is preferable to the fatal determinacy of presuming to know. For the anti-identitarian Garréta, literature is the site of not knowing rather than the site of revelation.

We can also view the death of the narrator as an inevitable consequence of a writerly commitment to a certain vision of the aesthetics of literature, which is what the philosopher Jacques Rancière argues in his essay "Why Emma Bovary Had to Be Killed."[28] In Rancière's analysis of the relation between Flaubert and Emma, Emma must die because she betrays the novelist's aesthetic by trying to translate the pure sensations captured by literature into a concretely pretty, pedestrian life. Because Emma tries to concretize the aesthetic experience she finds in literature and incorporate it into her life by buying trinkets, furniture, and dresses, thereby missing the point of literature, she must be killed to teach the reader a lesson about literature. In Garréta's case, the aesthetic stakes concern difference, not literariness. Garréta's narrator's death reprises Emma's death at Flaubert's hands, insofar as it serves as a warning to the reader. The narrator of *Sphinx* is shown to be invested in the aesthetics of difference, retaining racial difference in the narrative despite getting rid of sexual difference. In this, the narrator betrays Garréta's literary vision of freeing experience and sensation from the identitarian categories through which they are understood and processed, and has to be killed.

Perhaps it is no coincidence that Garréta, like Wittig, chooses a sculptural figure as her operative metaphor: the mythical sphinx is best known to us through its sculptural representations, and the Trojan horse was able to

---

28. I invoke Rancière not merely as someone who theorizes the authorial need to kill off a character, but as an intellectual touchstone for Garréta, who is interested in his philosophy of radical egalitarianism. If Garréta's work displays an affinity for Rancière's thought, it is no surprise, given her debt to Wittig. More than a decade before Rancière coined *littérarité* [literarity] as a way of connecting the literary and the political, Wittig, in her 1986 PhD thesis, was already articulating a radical conception of living language as language freed, through a writerly action on and with the materiality of language, from the social meanings attached to it. This living language is theorized as the original social contract in which absolute reciprocity and equality found intersubjective relations, as seen in Chapter 2. Wittig thus articulates the political potentiality of literature from a practitioner/artist's perspective, while Rancière approaches the question from a more abstract, philosophical point of view. See Rancière, *The Flesh of Words*, 103, 108. Wittig, *Le Chantier littéraire*, 55–72. For more on literarity as a political operation, see Chambers, "The Politics of Literarity."

function as a war machine because it was received as a wooden sculpture, as a work with aesthetic qualities. Existing in three dimensions, the sculpture's form and materiality are apprehended immediately, while the medium, be it stone, or wood, or metal, is recognized as raw material, or "matériau brut" as Wittig puts it, that has been worked.[29] Through a title associated with the sculptural, Garréta insists on the importance of form for literature, an idea foundational to Wittig's theorization of the literary text as a Trojan horse, a war machine that "pulverize[s] the old forms and formal conventions."[30] Wittig's logic and literary practice manifest her conviction that the pulverization of old forms and formal conventions can lead to the pulverization of social forms and conventions as well. This coming together of the political with the aesthetic, or literary, can be seen in *Sphinx,* in Garréta's work against difference and in her stance of "fuck difference." Garréta's mobilization of the novel to engage in literary formal experimentation that does this political work of dismantling identity follows Wittig's interpretation of Marcel Proust.

Wittig characterizes *À la recherche du temps perdu* [*In Search of Lost Time*] as a Trojan horse that infiltrated a straight Parisian society and homosexualized it; the act of reading forced Proust's readers to acknowledge that despite themselves, the novel was constituting a homosexual subject as undeniably real. In order to read the *Recherche*, they had to assume Proust's homosexual point of view as their own and enter fully into the work's homosexualized textual reality. Through literature, Proust was able to alter the terms through which an entire social order viewed itself, making the straight world and the straight mind interpellated by Proust no longer quite so straight. If Proust had this effect, Wittig maintains, it is only because he used his artistry to universalize his particular, homosexual point of view and present it so that it could take the place traditionally occupied by the universal straight white male. Wittig explains what it took for Proust to get his Trojan horse past the walls of Parisian society:

> History, I believe, intervenes at the individual and subjective level and manifests itself in the particular point of view of the writer. It is then one of the most vital and strategic parts of the writer's task to universalize this point of view. But to carry out a literary work one must be modest and know that being gay or anything else is not enough. For reality cannot be directly

---

29. Wittig, *Le Chantier littéraire*, 93. Wittig treats the Trojan horse as a sculpture and aligns it with the work of the writer precisely because the sculpture results from the sculptor's brute force and labor on its materials. Wittig sees the writer as undertaking the same work on a similarly resistant material, language. See Wittig, 93–98.

30. Wittig, *The Straight Mind*, 69.

transferred from the consciousness to the book. The universalization of each point of view demands a particular attention to the formal elements that can be open to history, such as themes, subjects of narratives, as well as the global form of the work. It is the attempted universalization of the point of view that turns or does not turn a literary work into a war machine.[31]

For Wittig, the literary work emerges through the particularity of the writer's point of view. For the work to shape the world, however, to "operate as a war machine upon its epoch," it cannot stay particularized: the literary work must open up onto something larger.

Ultimately, Garréta's novelistic experiment in indeterminability operates more as a Trojan horse than as a sphinx, which serves as the guardian of thresholds, determining who can or cannot pass. Instead of drawing in certain readers and ignoring and blocking others, Garréta's literary language constructs the novel as a universalizing war machine. Rather than homosexualize the reader, as Proust does, or lesbianize the reader, as Wittig does, Garréta's novel confronts the reader with an indeterminable identity. At first, there appears to be a difference to rally around—racial difference—but that difference functions as a Trojan horse. Just as the original Trojan horse is a wooden sculpture that announces its facture, its materiality, Garréta's novelistic Trojan horse shows that it is made of language. If Garréta demonstrates that language creates difference as it becomes discourse, she then asserts that discourse, and hence difference, can be returned to language by destroying sexual difference and hollowing out racial difference. In doing so, she gestures toward a Wittigian vision of literary language as the means by which the writer might "tear open the closely woven material of the commonplaces, and [. . .] continually prevent their organization into a system of compulsory meaning."[32]

Sphinx rejects the idea of insurmountable difference or differences and supersedes individual identity in order to create new forms of indeterminacy that address everyone and no one in particular. As Wittig sees it, if a novel is to have political impact and staying power as literature, it must be able to speak to all readers: it cannot screen readers for whatever configuration of differences would constitute an ideal reader—it cannot be a gay novel, or a feminine novel, or a black novel. For Garréta, as for Wittig, this universalization is able to come about in the novel precisely as it permits readers to reenact the writer's task of separating language from discourse. Through the act of reading a Trojan horse, the reader is able to break open the particular categories discourse creates and circulates, to access language as language, in all its

---

31. Wittig, 74–75.
32. Wittig, *The Straight Mind*, 100.

potential. *Sphinx* invites us to disallow identity as a valid concept despite how costly it may be to do so. It overdetermines racial identity to show the reader that the inability to determine identity is preferable to fixing it.

Sphinx is a dark novel of loss and punishment, where the protagonists' sexual indeterminateness is not able to eradicate the sexed and raced nature of society. The scene of their sexual encounter stands out, however, as a rare, utopian suspension of the compulsory difference of the social order. As the narrator describes the combining of bodies, seeking to recall the feeling of indeterminate flesh pressed against indeterminate flesh, not only is sexual difference rejected, but—so subtle as to be easily overlooked—racial difference disappears as well.[33] In this sexual encounter where the narrator and A*** are rendered equal, where both act and are acted upon ("ce que je fis [. . .] ce dont je fus l'objet"), Garréta, who first evokes the protagonists' skins in racialized terms, refrains from doing so in describing this contact of black skin against white skin. This places the scene firmly under the sign of "fuck difference," driven by a vision where race, far from being fetishized or reified, is also to be dismantled.

This scene gives us a glimpse of a world in which we do not consent to difference, where we are able to experience and encounter the other without structuring that experience through ready-made concepts. Where Foucault's utopian gesture in *The History of Sexuality* imagined bodies and pleasures that operate outside the "austere monarchy of sex,"[34] Garréta's gesture is even more expansive, envisioning the overthrow of that other austere monarchy, the monarchy of race. The hope is that we will not consent to be subjects of a monarchy that does not serve us, and instead refuse familiar scripts for identities that limit us to a predetermined set of possibilities. Just as Foucault does not offer a blueprint for how to overthrow the monarchy of sex, Garréta does not offer instructions for how to overthrow sex and race. She instead creates a horizon of possibility and shows us that, however we get there, if we ever get there, it will have to be through language, through working to break down and let go of the well-worn language that has made us who we are so that we might become who we've never been.

LA DÉCOMPOSITION: DECOMPOSING IDENTITY

In my discussion of *Sphinx*, I focused primarily on the way Garréta hollows out identity by setting up racial difference as a straw man. In the novel, the

---

33. I thank Hannah Frydman for calling my attention to this absence.
34. Foucault, *The History of Sexuality*, 159.

pronoun is also important as a tool for compelling the reader to relinquish identity, or at least, to pay attention to how tightly we hold on to identity, despite the ways in which identity binds and oppresses us. In *Sphinx,* Garréta sets up *je* as a pronoun that refuses to let gender stick to it, to be determined. If we read the narrator as being male, we are compelled to reveal the processes by which we take the seemingly neutral absence of the mark of gender and perform precisely what Wittig describes as the default universalization of masculinity, where the masculine gender is taken as that which operates outside or without gender. And if we read *je* as being female, we reveal our tendency to conflate the author and the narrator in addition to our instinctive assignment of identity to people. *Sphinx,* in its relentless identification of our own processes of categorization, makes it impossible for us, in good faith, to naturalize difference in its various iterations. Though *Sphinx* targets racial difference as well as sexual difference, Garréta's choice to exploit the ambiguity and indeterminacy of *je* as a pronoun most clearly serves the purpose of dismantling gender in her skillful avoidance of gender-marked language and is more obvious than the subtler work against the naturalization of racial difference.[35]

In *La Décomposition* (1999), Garréta's third novel, her work on pronouns shifts away from a frontal assault on gender to a more subtle attack on the subject as a self-contained, distinct entity whose integrity and clear boundaries are concretized in the boundaries of pronouns, where a pronoun serves as both the means by which the human subject is constituted and as proof of the subject. Émile Benveniste, the French linguist who was an important influence on Wittig's own thinking about the pronoun and its political potential, comments on the relation between the pronoun and the constitution of human subjectivity:

> It is in and through language that man constitutes himself as a *subject,* because language alone establishes the concept of "ego" in reality, in *its* reality which is that of the being.
>
> The "subjectivity" we are discussing here is the capacity of the speaker to posit himself as "subject." [...] Now we hold that that "subjectivity," whether it is placed in phenomenology or in psychology, as one may wish, is only the emergence in the being of a fundamental property of language. "Ego" is he who *says* "ego."[36]

For Benveniste, the subject as an "ego" that can posit its subjectivity by proclaiming its fully realized selfhood is as unproblematic as his taking man as

---

35. For a more critical take on Garréta's pronoun use, see Chapter 2 of Livia, *Pronoun Envy.*
36. Benveniste, *Problems in General Linguistics,* 224.

the universal human subject. Garréta cannot consent to such a bundling. She teases apart the subject and subjectivity Benveniste views as a unity: her retention of subjectivity is built upon a resounding rejection of the subject. However, in doing so, Garréta, like Benveniste, Wittig, and Sarraute before her, still takes up the pronoun as playing a particularly important role in constructing identity and making subjectivity intelligible. In *La Décomposition*, she strips the pronoun of its tendency to shore up subjecthood, of the identity that accompanies the subject like a faithful shadow. As we'll see, she performs this by severing the naturalized connection between proper names and bodies, and between pronouns and their antecedents, which calls attention to how fragile referentiality is and how easily it can be diverted or thwarted. By cutting the thread that sutures subjectivity to subjecthood, Garréta transforms the pronoun. No longer does the pronoun, which stands in for the name, shore up identity and the well-defined subjects that it takes under its wing. The pronoun, in Garréta's novel, constitutes an anti-identitarian shore: there is no clear line of demarcation between water and land, between our subjectivity and the world we live in, but a constantly shifting shoreline that's stable only in its mobility and mutability.

La Décomposition is a 244-page pastiche of Proust that does Proust at the same time as it undoes, or decomposes, him, turning the Proustian cathedral of *À la recherche du temps perdu* into a veritable bloodbath, the site and cause of serial murder.[37] The premise of the novel is simple: the narrator, an aspiring serial killer, turns to Proust's magnum opus as a literary model for his murderous opus. The narrator looks to Proust's characters to determine which random people are the objects of his depopulating enterprise. For example, the thirty-seventh sentence of the *Recherche* contains the first mention of Mme de Saint-Loup. The narrator is to then go to some public space, such as a metro station or a café terrace, and count the passersby. If the thirty-seventh passerby has the same gender as the Proustian character of reference—in this case, if she's a woman like Mme de Saint-Loup—they are elected as the nar-

---

37. The novel is filled with references to and rewritings of Proust: "Longtemps je me suis consumé de bonheur aux récits de duels, de massacres, de tueries" [For a longtime, I was consumed by happiness from stories of duels, massacres, and slaughter], riffs on Proust's famous incipit, "Longtemps je me suis couché de bonne heure" [For a longtime, I went to bed early]. Garréta, *La Décomposition*, 35. All subsequent citations will be made in-text. The mythical, romantic images of the magical lantern from Marcel's childhood are replaced by criminal, violent ones, and the lover conjured up during sleep is replaced by a fraternal assassin. The madeleine's ability to conjure up memories long gone is restaged, this mnemonic power housed, in Garréta's version, in a crime scene's chalk outline announcing a once-present body. For an interesting analysis of the novel that focuses on the Oulipian constraint and on intertextuality, see Andrews, "Intertextuality and Murder."

rator's victim. If the passerby has the wrong gender, then the narrator is not to murder that day (28–29).[38] Once the murder is successfully accomplished, the narrator is to delete all mentions of that character from a digital version of the *Recherche*, the idea being that eventually, the narrator will be able to completely decompose Proust's novel and evacuate it of the characters that give the work its meaning:

> Il s'agit par cet alliage sanglant d'un nom et d'un corps, d'un personnage de roman et d'une personne réelle que forgera le meurtre, de faire coup double, et double grâce. D'une part, dépeupler le monde selon un principe formel, impersonnel; d'autre part, décomposer un trop long roman en en effaçant les personnages. (27–28)

> [Murder will forge this bloody alloy of a name and a body, of a character in a novel and a real person, by which it will realize two blows that are also acts of grace. On the one hand, depopulate the world according to a formal, impersonal principle; on the other, decompose a novel that's too long by erasing its characters.]

Coupling murder with erasure—redacting "real" living human beings with the same precision that goes into redacting text—provides the material for the narrator's own novel, from which we readers will hopefully learn to divest literature of real subjects, and more broadly, recognize identity for the pipe dream it is.

While the novel's plot is certainly singular, of an erudition that we do not expect of a crime novel or *polar*, *La Décomposition* is also singular for its anachronistic return to an eighteenth-century non-distinction between philosophical writing and literature—the majority of the novel is filled with the narrator's expounding on the baselessness of identity and personhood and hence, the subject and self, as concepts. Garréta describes the dual nature of *La Décomposition* as a philosophical treatise in a novel:

> We mustn't forget that in the eighteenth century, the separation between literature and the *belles lettres*, ideas and philosophy, was an inoperative distinction. The separation between fiction and the intellect produced two mon-

---

38. Making the murders contingent on gender agreement reprises *Sphinx*'s targeting of gender as a pernicious form of difference. Garréta writes, "Cette règle d'accord sera ma loi, le principe, la focale de mes meurtres" (28) [This rule of agreement will be my law, the principle, the focus of my murders]. In *Sphinx*, gender is what is destroyed; in *La Décomposition*, gender—or rather, submitting to and upholding the rule of gender—is dramatized as leading to destruction.

sters: the didactic novel (read, Zola, whom I abhor); and the dumbing-down of average fiction, which has resulted in there no longer being anything but didactic novels or brainless ones. Yet the novel enables us to process ideas with all the necessary irony, and destabilize a corpus of doctrines."[39]

The novel, in Garréta's view, processes ideas and can reconceptualize the world. Fiction doesn't have to be the vehicle for either the handing down of knowledge or mere entertainment. In Garréta's hands, the novel becomes a tool for challenging the usual boundaries of our thought, the received ideas and categories by which we navigate a world that we take for granted or submit to unthinkingly.

La Décomposition is able to attempt a decomposition of its readers' investment in identity and subjects on two levels: first, through the philosophical statements made by the pedantic narrator who feels the need to lay out in painstaking detail his murderous method, in the academic sense of the term; second, through Garréta's unconventional use of second-person pronouns, which uproots the stability that makes pronouns such reliable receptacles for and indicators of subjects. We can see that *La Décomposition* sets out to decompose identity through both discourse and language: through the philosophical arguments that comprise a discursive anti-identitarianism, and through the medium of language, exploiting the pronoun, à la Wittig and Sarraute, as a material to be worked on and with to make pronominal form deform rather than reaffirm identity.

I begin my analysis with the philosophical arguments against identity because they are the most straightforward iterations of anti-identitarianism in the novel. These arguments, as with the erasure of the mark of gender in *Sphinx*, stand out as the most visible attack on difference. At the crux of the narrator's project is a joining together of murder and aesthetics, of (the creation of) death and literature, where perfection in crime and perfection in literature are each marked by a certain impersonality. Toward the novel's beginning, Garréta's narrator proclaims this quest for impersonal criminal and aesthetic perfection:

> Il nous faut donc raisonner nos raisons et assurer à nos meurtres l'impersonnalité rigoureuse d'une contrainte. Le meurtre est un processus gouverné par des règles: l'art réside dans l'invention concertée et systématique de règles nouvelles, et non dans notre soumission à un code ordinaire des passions ou de l'imitation qui a nom vulgaire "inspiration" et n'excède jamais le degré

---

39. Garréta, interview with Lindon, "À quoi ça sert?"

de subtilité d'une simple signalétique. [. . .] Mais quelle difficulté à fonder un art du meurtre qui fasse l'économie de la notion de motivation! La loi incarne depuis son origine ou plutôt depuis l'origine de la réflexion sur la loi, la croyance en des sujets plus ou moins constants. (23)

[We must thus think through our reasons and ensure that our murders have the rigorous impersonality of a constraint. Murder is a process governed by rules: art resides in the concerted and systematic invention of new rules, not in our submission to an ordinary code of passions or to the imitation that goes by the vulgar name of "inspiration" and never surpasses the subtlety of a simple system of signs. [. . .] But how difficult it is to make murder an art that does without the notion of motivation! The law, from its beginning, or rather, the beginning of reflection about the law, embodies belief in subjects that are more or less constant.]

Referring to the aesthetic principles of the constraint-driven Oulipo that she would be inducted into in 2000, the year following *La Décomposition*'s publication, Garréta articulates an aesthetic project that takes the eradication of the personal as its goal. The impersonal is conceived of as aesthetically superior to the expression of the personal, to works that codify a subject. In the world of *La Décomposition,* the narrator turns on its head the usual narrative of real subjects who exist outside and in distinction from fiction. Subjects do not exist, identities are destroyed, and fiction is taken as facticity:

Hors la fiction, il ne se trouve point de crime parfait? Loin de conclure de cette maxime à la fictivité (et donc à l'inexistence) du crime parfait, je l'entends littéralement comme l'aveu de sa facticité. (26)

[There's no such thing as a perfect crime outside fiction? Far from concluding from this maxim that the perfect crime is fictional (and thus nonexistent), I understand it literally as a confession of its facticity.]

The literal and the literary converge in a disturbing, murderous vision of reality, where the literary has the power to literalize and the distinction between reality and fiction no longer holds.

Garréta insists on distinguishing between fictionalization and falsification, where the former participates in the real in a way that the latter does not. She takes the example of autofiction, a genre of writing especially popular in contemporary French literature, characterized as fictionalized autobiography, in order to make this point:

Enfin, n'y avait-il pas de l'obscénité, de la facilité (et une facilité dangereuse pour celui qui s'y abandonne) [...] pour un auteur à raconter et faire passer sous couvert de roman le rebut de son journal intime? C'est là confondre fiction et falsification. (207)

[Finally, isn't there something obscene, facile (a dangerous facility for whoever abandons himself to it) [...] about an author recounting and having pass as a novel the dregs of his diary? That's confusing fiction with falsification].

For Garréta, there is more integrity and truth in "pure" fiction than in the adulterated fiction of autofiction, which derives literary capital from the allure of knowing that part of what you are reading is "real"—from peddling the distinction between fiction and reality that *La Décomposition* is trying to do away with.[40]

But returning to murder, why tie it to aesthetics, and in particular, to literature? Garréta comments on this combination of objects by explaining how what's at stake in the novel is the "forging of a necessary link between fiction and reality" and the collision of aesthetics with ethics—an aesth-ethics.[41] The traditional character, alive and well in contemporary fiction despite Sarraute's systematic attempt to destroy it, is taken up by Garréta as the ideal site for bringing together fiction and reality, and eliminating a boundary that continues to be zealously guarded today. In choosing Proust, Garréta's narrator has taken as his target a literary monument that exemplifies the use of literature to shore up identity through identification. He speaks disparagingly of the way Proust's characters have been mobilized by "real" people living outside the novel to reinforce the identities of friends and acquaintances:

[Ils] s'amusent à dire de tel de leurs amis, assidu au bordel comme au musée, "mais c'est un vrai Swann!" (tout comme du médecin qui leur révèle, pauvres poulets crédules, la vérité de leurs entrailles, "notre Du Boulbon"; ou encore du vieil oncle homosexuel qui dissipe l'héritage auprès de gigolos, "ce Charlus au petit pied"). (26)

[They have fun saying that a friend who visits brothels as diligently as he does museums "is a real Swann!" (just as they call the doctor who reveals the truth of their entrails to them, poor credulous fools, "our Du Boulbon";

---

40. Autofiction, even as it claims to blur the boundaries between fiction and reality by bringing the two together so that one can't know where fiction ends and reality begins, still relies on the cachet of the "real" as distinct from pure fiction. For more on Garréta's critique of autofiction, see my "Autofiction Infiltrated."

41. Frédéric Grolleau, Interview for *Paru.com*, September 1, 1999, archived at http://cosmogonie.free.fr/paru.html.

or the old homosexual uncle who squanders his inheritance on gigolos, "this little Charlus").]

In other words, readers already elide the boundary between the fictional and the real by identifying real people with and as fictional characters, the same sort of elision we see in everyday speech where "literally" stands for "figuratively." Garréta takes this casual link that's already made between fiction and reality and treats it seriously, turning it into a causal link instead, where what happens in fiction has a direct impact on the real, and vice versa. In a gesture that has an oddly moralizing quality to it, Garréta makes our casual use of literature have consequences. Forcing and forging a connection between fiction and reality sends us back to Wittig's theorization of literary language's traction on the real. Where Wittig theorizes this necessary connection in *Le Chantier littéraire*, Garréta does so in the novel itself, but couched in ironic terms, as irony is a quality that she seems to consider crucial to being able to process ideas.

In the "method" chapter ironically entitled "Œdipe & Amok" (a barb at psychoanalysis's psychologizing and subject-driven language and the importance it attributes to the Oedipal complex), Garréta's narrator, having announced his intentions to bring together fiction and reality, clearly articulates the novel's anti-identitarian project. Anticipating his reader's possible objections and questions as to his method, which could lead to a real person being murdered as that character without bearing any resemblance to the Proustian character that he or she is identified as, the narrator glosses the fictive nature of identity:

> "Madame de Saint-Loup" ne présente aucun des traits que le roman prête à Mme de Saint-Loup? C'est bien là le clou! L'identité s'opère en vertu non pas d'une ressemblance mais d'un baptême résultant d'un calcul. (29–30)

> ["Madame de Saint-Loup" doesn't have any of the traits that the novel assigns to Mme de Saint-Loup? There's the rub! Identity operates not through resemblance but rather through a baptism resulting from a calculation.]

Because the narrator tries to maintain, or at least, to not resist, the discrepancy between the fictional Proustian character and the corresponding real person, the connection between fiction and reality is revealed as operating not through resemblance or identification—the qualities that drive the casual collapsing of fiction with reality, which Garréta is punishing—but rather, through calculation, being planned so that fiction has traction on reality, the one coextensive and consubstantial with the other.

According to the narrator's philosophy, identity—this powerful motor of the vehicle of the subject in which the social order traffics—is neither natural nor motivated. Maintaining the interval between "Mme de Saint-Loup" and Mme de Saint-Loup proves that point, and is meant to render visible the process by which identity is created and conferred onto someone, a process that's invisible in those instances when the gap between the idea of the identity (Proust's Mme de Saint-Loup) and the person to whom that identity is attributed (the person in real life whom one refers to as a Mme de Saint-Loup) is minimal—when the identity seems to fit, in other words. The narrator, by targeting victims who do not seem to fit the identity he assigns to them—who do not resemble the characters they're taken as—does so to prove that identification is not a natural process, but one that's constructed and ritualized: just as baptism is a ritual that serves to induct its object into the church and make the baptized person a member of an institution that seeks to shape the course of their life, so too is identity the consequence of a ritual that serves to induct its objects into a social order whose ideology, the narrator argues, is as deliberately formulated, or calculated, and far-reaching as theology. From here, it's not a particularly far leap to connect the identity that Proust's characters stand in for to the sorts of identity at stake in identity politics. Garréta seems to be arguing that other identities such as race, gender, and sexuality operate through the same logic of correspondence or resemblance, where raced, sexed, and sexualized persons are considered such because they seem to fit with the idea of the race, sex, and sexuality they're thought of as embodying. *La Décomposition* has a stake in denaturalizing identity.

Here, though, is the rub for us as readers of *La Décomposition*. The novel is like a laboratory in which factors have been carefully controlled to enable the theory to play out according to Garréta's own anti-identitarian terms. Of course, it's possible, with enough assiduity, to write a novel that both sets the starting premises and ensures an ending that follows from them—to prove one's point tautologically. Garréta, by writing a novel that corresponds to the narrator's ideology, would seem to be committing the same circular error that Wittig attributes to psychoanalysis when she writes that Lacan, rather than making any real discoveries, simply invented the psychoanalytic concepts that he proposed to have found.[42] *La Décomposition* would seem, then, to be a case of Garréta discovering non-identity because she put it there.

This potential tautology is why the second-person pronoun plays such an important role in the novel: Garréta's use of it takes the anti-identitarianism

---

42. "Who gave the psychoanalysts their knowledge? For example, for Lacan, what he calls the 'psychoanalytic discourse,' or the 'analytical experience,' both 'teach' him what he already knows. [...] In my opinion, there is no doubt that Lacan found in the Unconscious the structures he said he found there, since he had previously put them there." Wittig, *The Straight Mind*, 23.

outside the laboratory and enacts it in the space of lived experience, in the reader's encounter with the text. Through the pronoun, the reader can confirm that the novel's anti-identitarian results have not been falsified—that the anti-identitarianism that the narrator is gunning so hard for can and does exist in the real world of the reader. The pronoun bridges the world of the novel and the world of the reader (whose situation in the world is molded by the pronouns that place people in relation to each other) so that by being addressed in the second person, the reader's relationship to the narrator is put into sharp relief. It is no longer a matter of a novel's character behaving the way he or she ought to because that is the writer's will. Instead, a real person—the reader as the person behind the pronoun—is the locus of experience.

The novel, by making the anti-identitarian experience it contains transcend the seemingly evident boundary between the fictional world and the real world, collapses the distinction between them. This was the narrator's goal all along. At one point he apostrophizes the reader, evoking the idea that a book is limited to its pages, that by closing a book we can exit the textual world, only to deny us that possibility by denying that these two spaces are distinct:

> Lecteur, sais-tu seulement par où tu es entré et où se trouve la porte, et s'il y en a même une? Tu peux certes sortir de ce récit par effraction, en refermant maintenant le livre. Mais la chambre noire ne s'en évanouira pas pour autant. Dans cette chambre noire, pour toute éternité, et quand bien même tu en condamnerais la porte, je t'attends, lâche lecteur.
>
> Car cette chambre, et telle est l'énigme inscrite au front de la chimère ou du golem qui en garde l'invisible seuil, tu y étais déjà avant que d'y entrer et tu y seras encore quand tu en sortiras. (159)

> [Reader, do you know where you entered and where the door is and if there even is one? You can certainly leave this narrative by force, by shutting the book now. But nonetheless, the darkroom will not vanish. In this dark room, for all eternity and even if you should seal off the door, I am waiting for you, cowardly reader.
>
> Because in this room, and such is the riddle inscribed on the forehead of the chimera or the golem who watches over the invisible threshold, you were already there before entering and you will still be there when you leave it.]

This room that Garréta evokes is *la chambre noire*, the darkroom that she describes in the novel as the space where reader and writer meet. This space is the text: "Nous revoilà lecteur, vous et moi, dans la chambre noire, sans portes ni fenêtres, du texte" (155) [Here we are again, reader, you and me, in the darkroom, without any doors or windows, of the text]. *Chambre noire* evokes the *camera obscura*[43] [literally, dark room] as a space where reader and writer join to figure an image. However, both are invisible to the other—unfigurable: "Je ne puis vous voir, vous ne pouvez me figurer" (155) [I cannot see you, you cannot depict me]. In the text, reader and writer are caught up together in the act of representing and looking at something, and the surface upon which this representation is projected is the wall of the mind—the reader's mind as she reads, and the writer's mind as she writes, with the medium of language constituting this shared surface. The narrative is both what contains the space and what is figured inside it. To be more precise, the text constitutes this camera obscura's shape and contours, and the narrative is what fills it, what is projected—conjured up, represented—inside it. The narrator's challenge to the reader to figure where and how she found herself in the text functions as a rhetorical question. I would wager, however, that there is an actual answer, and that the point of entry, despite the absence of doors and windows, is the pronoun as that which lets us inside but does not let us out. We're challenged to try to seal off a passageway ("condamner une porte") while Garréta uses the pronoun in such destabilizing ways that the pronoun becomes impossible to seal off, or perhaps, in.

Before I examine Garréta's unsettling deployment of second-person pronouns, let me turn your attention to a passage from *La Décomposition* that's particularly useful both in its disdain for our investment in the idea of subjecthood and individual identity, and in the way it signals that these things are embedded pronominally, particularly in the first-person pronoun *je*:

> Qui vous croyez-vous? Une âme immortelle, substance et principe éternels, jetée ici-bas pour son malheur et sa repentance? Un fantôme de conscience, statue intérieure perchée, comme sur des échasses, au sommet de l'altière colonne de mémoire carottée dans le riche tuf du temps passé et perdu? Un enchevêtrement unique et original de fibres subtiles, chacune empreinte du chiffre, de la signature en code exprimable, de votre individuelle identité? Et tapie au centre, là-haut dans la boîte noire derrière vos yeux, Sa Majesté le Je? (228)

> [Who do you think you are? An immortal soul, eternal in substance and principle, cast down here to be unhappy and repent? A ghost of consciousness, an interior statue perched, as if on stilts, on top of the stately column

---

43. The *Oxford English Dictionary* defines *camera obscura* as "an instrument comprising a darkened room or box with a convex lens or a pinhole on one side, used for projecting an image of an external object on to a surface inside the instrument so that it can be viewed, drawn, or (in later use) reproduced on a light-sensitive surface."

of memory, sampled out of the rich tuff of past and lost time? A unique and original entanglement of subtle fibers, each imprinted with the figure, the signature—in an expressible code—of your individual identity? And crouching at the center, up high in the black box behind your eyes, Their Majesty the I?]

Garréta assembles all the usual trappings of identity and of belief in our unique subjecthood: interiority, consciousness, soul, memory, a singular genome and the genetic identity that comes with it, a mind—that black box behind our eyes—in which reigns the all-powerful I. The reference to *Their Majesty the I* ties all these assertions about human identity and subjecthood (which Garréta would characterize as fictions, but, as is borne out all too clearly in life, fictions with very real consequences) to the self, the very idea of which is made possible by and depends on the first-person pronoun *Je* that names it and acts as a guarantor of its existence. It's because of a simple pronoun that all these other ideas—consciousness, soul, memory, etc.—are able to cohere into the subject they serve to define and prove. The pronoun, in other words, is not merely a simple component of language that neatly signals an antecedent, but actually serves to bring that antecedent into being. The antecedent of the pronoun—the subject—is not anterior to the pronoun that seems to come after it.

Garréta's narrator makes very clear his disdain for the work that the first-person pronoun does, and all the concepts and meaning that get decanted into *je*, but it's actually in Garréta's use of the second-person pronouns, *tu* and *vous*, that we can see the writerly work Wittig theorizes in *Le Chantier littéraire* of stripping language of its conventional signification, of playing discourse as a socially codified form of language against language as a medium full of potential. In Garréta's second-person pronouns, we can see the way her formal experimentation—and refusal to abide by the rules of linguistic sociability, where the pronouns have their proper place and get along together—leads to the decomposition of identity as we know and live it. Garréta's drawing and quartering of *Their Majesty the I*, while compelling and polemical, still maintains the conventional use, form, and function of the first-person pronoun. The pronoun and what it stands for might be reviled and abused, but the pronoun maintains its integrity unlike in the case of Garréta's use of *tu* and *vous*, which is triply transgressive: she uses *tu* when we might expect a *vous* to be more suitable, *vous* where we might expect *tu* normally, and she uses the second person to refer to the actions and feelings of a person who better corresponds to the narrator than to the addressed reader.[44] All these things undermine those pronouns' usual functions.

---

44. This anticipates Garréta's use of *tu* as the narrative pronoun in *Pas un jour*.

As readers familiar with French know, *tu* and *vous* have different functions, and their distinction is invested with much social capital (take, for example, the anxiety of figuring out which pronoun to use).[45] *Tu* is the pronoun of informality, close relation, and familiarity—it implies either the equal or superior social status of the locutor—and it's singular. *Vous* is the pronoun of formality, a certain relational and affective distance, social transactions, and respect—it implies either equal or inferior social status—and it can be either singular or plural. In *La Décomposition,* however, Garréta turns these uses of the pronoun on their head, and, through a disturbingly canny combination of transgressing and observing pronominal norms, upends the hierarchy they maintain. It isn't a full-on frontal assault against the pronoun, but an eating away of it from the inside, similar to the way termites eat away at a house's wooden beams until the structure has completely lost its integrity.

Garréta's constant shifting between *tutoiement* and *vouvoiement* begins early on in the text, before any of the murders has been narrated. As the narrator lays out his project and complicated method, he speaks directly to the reader in familiar tones: "Lecteur, tu me trouves obscure encore? Faut-il vraiment tout t'expliquer?" (27) [Reader, do you still find me obscure? Do I really have to explain everything to you?] only to retreat, on the very next page from the informal *tu* to the honorific *vous*: "Mais pourquoi ce roman-là? Parce que, l'avez-vous assez soupiré, frivole lecteur, la vie est trop courte et Proust est trop long" (28) [But why this novel? Because, and you've sighed about this enough, frivolous reader, life is too short and Proust is too long]. Garréta's tone shifts, from the exasperation we express toward people with whom we're close to one of arch irony. This sort of shifting between *tu* and *vous* continues throughout the text, and is most striking when the reader is placed at the scene of the murder with the narrator. For example, in a chapter dedicated to the murder of a woman who's been baptized Françoise, after the faithful servant and cook in Combray, the narrator addresses the reader in a solicitous tone:

> Aujourd'hui, jour de marché, mon lecteur je vous emmène. Où? Devant une pyramide des plus belles asperges. Quoi faire? Attendre que paraisse notre prochaine victime. (109)

---

45. On the vicissitudes of navigating the second-person pronoun in French, see Haget, "On se tutoie?"

[Today, market day, I am taking you, my reader, somewhere. Where? In front of a pyramid of the most beautiful asparaguses. To do what? Wait for our next victim to appear.]

The narrator shifts tone dramatically as he narrates following Françoise home to her apartment from the market and slitting her throat by posing as an expected dinner guest. He insults the reader and drops the honorific, returning to *tu*: "car poli je suis, au-delà de toute mesure, grossier lecteur qui n'essuies pas même tes pieds au paillasson" (115) [because I am polite, beyond all measure, you vulgar reader who doesn't even wipe your feet on the doormat]. The narrator withdraws the generosity with which he'd initially shared his victim and brought the reader into a complicitous *nous* [we], the *tu* distancing him from the reader.

The vacillation is constant between *tu* and *vous*, between being a maligned reader and a respected one. As readers, we never know where we stand in the narrator's estimation, and this uncertainty is an indication of the ambivalence that he himself feels toward us. The narrator cannot help but be ambivalent as we occupy a position of paramount importance: it's our readerly presence that enables the narrator to speak, to relive his past crimes and re-experience his pleasure in the present. The narrator's murderous project, which targets the connection between human life and the representation of such life in language, depends on the reader: "Il suffit d'un lecteur et d'un seul, d'une victime et d'une seule, pour que mon projet s'achève et que l'infinie et transsubstantiative réversibilité de la prose en crime, du crime en prose s'opère" (150) [A single reader and only one, a single victim and only one, is sufficient for my project to be accomplished and for the infinite and transubstantiative reversibility of prose into crime, of crime into prose, to be effected].

The narrator's ambivalence toward the reader presents us with an uncomfortable alternative between a *tu* and a *vous* that have both lost their positive potential. We can either identify with a *tu* that does not signal a reciprocal intimacy but is used to insult us as being slow-witted or ill-mannered—an alienating *tu*—or with a *vous* that, rather than indicate unfamiliarity, distance, or respect, accuses us and implicates us as the narrator's accomplices—a criminal *vous*. But what's ultimately more unnerving than having intimacy joined with insults, or respect tied to criminal complicity, is the way, by the end of the novel, Garréta has somehow pulled off a pronominal sleight of hand so that the *vous*—the reader brought in from the outside to witness the narrator's criminal exploits—has become the narrator himself, and the distinction between the *je* and the *vous* has been effaced. No longer are we mere accessories to a murderous project we don't think represents our desires,[46] but we're forced by the second-person pronoun into inhabiting a subjectivity that we'd like to reject but are not allowed to, if we are to keep reading. Garréta accomplishes this quite subtly by eventually eliminating the addressing of the reader as reader—*mon lecteur, lecteur frivole, grossier lecteur,* etc.—that initially accompanies all these second-person pronouncements, so that there are sentences featuring *vous* where the distance that the explicit identification "mon lecteur" provides is no longer there, leaving us with the unsettling question of who is who and who is doing what.

This indistinction and the ambiguity of the referent for Garréta's *vous* are represented effectively in the novel's last chapter, which features the narrator in a sleeping car of a train shooting at a mirror (or similarly reflective surface), mistaking the victim's image for the victim. The scene is completely ambiguous and difficult to decipher, putting our ability to identify and distinguish one identity from another into crisis: it's unclear whether the mirror the narrator shoots at is in his train or a different train or even how it would be possible to shoot into another sleeper compartment from one's own, which leads to the possibility that the mirror that the narrator shoots at is in fact in his own compartment, and is in fact his own image, which puts the gender of the narrator, who has up to this point used masculine adjectives and verbal constructions to refer to himself, into doubt, as the victim targeted is Albertine, a woman. Perhaps he mistook his own image for that of another person? Perhaps he's a woman and mistook her own image for that of another woman's?[47]

The novel's ending gives no clarity as to what actually happens. The novel draws to an indeterminate close in which distinction, which is crucial to

---

46. Allow me to address you directly, reader. Would you really identify with a desire to depopulate the world, slit throats, push bodies over a highway overpass into oncoming traffic, shoot someone in the back of the head at the movie theater—desires that our narrator realizes?

47. In an earlier chapter, "À l'éditeur" [To the Editor], which takes the form of the narrator's letter to his publisher, such a deliberate masking of gender is suggested when the narrator claims that the editor prefers the narrator to be a man: "Vous serez, je n'en doute pas, du parti de préférer un sujet masculin. Il faut que puisse en effet planer, comme un parfum diffus et quelque peu écœurant, le soupçon d'une identification possible entre notre sujet et la matière de mon récit. Or, vous le savez, le meurtre—et le meurtre violent plutôt que feutré—est province presque exclusive de la moitié mâle de l'espèce: les statistiques le prouvent, l'opinion commune le croit, la vraisemblance et l'homophonie l'exigent" (140) [You will undoubtedly side with those who prefer a masculine subject. It's necessary that, like a diffuse and slightly sickening perfume, a hint of a possible identification between our subject and the material of my narrative might linger. Now, as you know, murder—and violent, rather than muted, murder—is the domain almost exclusively of the male half of the species: the statistics prove it, popular opinion believes it, plausibility and homophony require it]. This suggestion of the falsification of the narrator's gender, at the demands of the well-socialized reader's expectations, is rendered more trenchant with our knowledge that the voice behind the narrator is that of a woman, Anne Garréta.

asserting identity, and the originary identity of the novel—the narrator's—are called into question. The question of what's fiction and what's "real" emerges within the boundaries of the text, only to have the distinction between the two crumble upon contact. What the narrator proclaims, Garréta effects through her writing. This is precisely the reversibility of prose into crime, of fiction into reality. This reversibility, the collapsing of fiction and reality, is able to occur because of the indeterminability imposed by the feedback loop of a hermeneutic instinct in crisis. Garréta's deployment of the second-person pronouns mobilizes the reader, with or against her will, into serving as the agent of this reversibility: through Garréta's use of *tu* and *vous*, the narrator claims us as fully with him in his world, and we can no longer skulk on the sidelines with one foot in our world and one foot in the novel's, getting to have our fiction and our reality, too, as separate things. Because of *La Décomposition*'s pronominal instability, the distinction between narrator/writer and reader collapses, which resonates with Wittig's vision in *Le Chantier littéraire* of a readerly writer and a writerly reader.

Garréta has said, "I think one of the things that works in the book is the *je* that addresses the *tu* and the *vous* that are the reader, and that constantly displaces the point of view," and she draws attention to the impact this pronoun trouble creates, when, in the same interview, she likens *La Décomposition* to "a videogame from a first person point of view, but sometimes you find yourself the target."[48] Pronouns, these seemingly small elements of language, can have outsize consequences, and Garréta's use of them is not only unsettling, but violent, targeting identity and subjecthood. The novel effectively places our identitarian desires in the line of fire, and it's with marked aggression that Garréta attacks the way we use pronouns to solidify and corroborate identity, where pronouns house our identity the way a hermit crab uses shells to house its fragile body. Not only does Garréta, by putting into place a constantly shifting point of view that makes it impossible to properly situate and locate ourselves, make it impossible for us to use pronouns to contain our subjectivity within a reassuringly solid and stable identity, but she also has those pronouns correspond to subjectivities we would rather not inhabit—the murderer, the idiot, the victim. We are left exposed as a subjectivity that has not yet been assimilated into deterministic categories, and that is exactly where Garréta wants us.

The underlying moral of *La Décomposition*, beneath the narrator's moral of depopulating the world, is that we need to get out of the subject-hood.[49]

---

48. Garréta, quoted in Axelle Le Dauphin, "Gare à Garréta."
49. The last chapter's mirror scene can be seen as a metaphor for the way subjecthood, or identity, is not so much fiction as it is false. It's an image that fakes us out, representing something that isn't actually there.

Assailed by pronouns we don't want, having our pronouns taken away from us just as we get used to them, the novel effectively works to drive us out of our pronouns, which house our identities as discrete subjects. But this leaves us with the question of where we go from here. After hundreds of pages of a hostile, deranged, and sociopathic narrator doing his best to destroy identity from both sides of the fiction/reality divide that the novel reveals is not a divide at all, after this bloody trail of death and destruction, where do we go? The novel ends on an ambiguous and negative note, with the narrator's destination uncertain and the narrator in a state of terror, his heart skipping a beat—*failing* is the word Garréta uses (*défaillir*)—with every gun-like sound of the train rattling against the rails, each sound a potential bullet targeting the narrator. And that is where the reader is left as well—unsure of where we are, and terrorized. The logical, or at least, the most obvious response to this question of "where to now?" would seem to be, well, elsewhere. If we cannot stay in subjecthood, in identity, then we must move on to a place without these things. Garréta seems to realize that this is a frightening venture. It involves not simply relinquishing the identification of others—a difficult enough task—but, more difficultly, letting go of our own identity. *La Décomposition*'s ending, as unresolved as it is, acknowledges the gaping distance that exists between a reality built on the subject and its manifold identities and the reality that has been not so much depopulated as de-identified (which amounts to the same thing insofar as the idea of population is built on the idea of demography, the biopolitical ordering and categorization of human life).

Garréta doesn't take us to this other place, unlike her narrator, who takes the reader all over his city in pursuit of his victims, and unlike Sarraute, whose writing plunges us immediately into an experience of subjectivity without contours, and unlike Wittig, whose utopian spaces of universalized particularity place the reader in a different place that's already-here even though it's nowhere. What Garréta does, unlike Sarraute and Wittig, is to put the reader through the painful process of being stripped of identity. She makes it impossible for us to turn back to identity. The idea is that we will move forward because the alternative has been destroyed—nothing is left, identity has been revealed to be a false image in a shattered mirror that can no longer represent that image. We can be like Narcissus, caught up in an image, albeit a broken one, or we can turn away from this image of ourselves that we've been so seduced by, and be in the world in all its and our unknown-ness. The world she proposes to bring us into is one that's real because it's joined together with fiction but stripped of the falsity that characterizes what's taken as a reality severed from fiction. Garréta confronts the reader with the choice and possibility of venturing into fiction that posits non-identity as facticity, but leaves it up to us as to how we clear that difficult path from identity to non-identity, from subjecthood to unbecoming.

QUEERER THAN QUEER

Where *Sphinx* clearly bears the influence of Wittig's vision for turning the pronoun into a war machine, *La Décomposition* displays a Garréta whose pronoun-work more closely resembles Sarraute's. Her use of the pronouns *tu* and *vous* destabilize the reader's pronominal position and turn the reader's subjectivity into a site that's always changing, thwarting whatever will the reader might have to enter the text as a stable, identity-laden subject. Garréta, similarly to Sarraute, uses pronouns to force us to undo our own identities and take off our identity clothes to enter the text. In the shifting pronouns we encounter in *La Décomposition,* however, we can see the mark of the queer 1990s, and Garréta's work bears this influence in a way that Sarraute's does not.

La Décomposition was published in 1999, at the close of a decade that saw the conception of queer theory and the publication of foundational texts of queer theory such as Judith Butler's *Gender Trouble* (1990), Eve Sedgwick's *Epistemology of the Closet* (1990), Michael Warner's edited volume *Fear of a Queer Planet* (1993), and the special "Queer Theory" issue of *differences* (1991) that introduced the term into academic discourse. The 1990s saw the explosive entry of queer theory into the intellectual and cultural domain, and the dissemination of ideas that have since become synonymous with queer theory—in particular, the idea of identity as performative and queer theory's imperative to erode identity and make it fluid and unstable by transgressing the rigidity of categories such as homosexual and heterosexual, thwarting such binary thinking through queerness's refusal to respect such boundaries. Queer acts of subversion, such as drag, which Butler discusses at length in *Gender Trouble*, are taken as destabilizing existing structures of oppression. But for all of queer theory's impact in promoting a radically subversive notion of identity, for which it has been dubbed anti-identitarian, its destabilization has failed to destroy and bring down these structures even as it has made them more porous. Queer theory has introduced the notion of movement and fluidity, so that rather than being trapped by these identity categories, we can circulate freely within and through them.[50] But for Garréta, a wider range of movement

---

50. While queer theory tends to celebrate the destabilization of identity as politically salutary, one could argue that destabilizing identities actually reinforces them by turning them into something around which to mobilize. For example, in *Sexing the Citizen,* Judith Surkis demonstrates how masculinity became stronger in Third Republic France for being seen as in crisis.

isn't enough. She pushes queer destabilization to its limit, imbuing her acts of destabilization with so much forceful, consistent pressure that they actually break down identity completely, rather than simply create openings within it. Garréta's queer project, in other words, can be considered to be queerer than queer in its outdoing of queerness—it actually reaches the non-identity that serves as queer theory's asymptote or that queer theory finds, intermittently, in the orgasmic interval of *jouissance*.

When the novel comes to a close, the reader, after a sort of death by a thousand destabilizations, is left with either a radically different experience and conception of identity that lead to its rejection, or with the uncomfortable knowledge that she'll return to an identity that's been voided of substance. Garréta isn't a particularly optimistic writer (her corpus is marked by morbidity, melancholy, and violence), but I would submit that in this textual blowing up of our identitarian present, Garréta demonstrates an investment in the future, a gesturing toward a non-identitarian horizon that crystallizes a dire alternative between staying inside a decomposed cadaver of an identity or moving into a life whose form has yet to be discovered.

Garréta's texts compel us to confront identity and demand that we destroy it using the weapons that Garréta herself puts at our disposal: these queerer than queer Trojan horses of the *chantier littéraire* she shares with Sarraute and Wittig. To have access to one writer's war machines is to have access to the others', which is to have access to language as a living and creative material that can exceed discourse's stultifying and oppressive constructions of reality. It's to have as intimate a relationship to language as Sarraute, Wittig, and Garréta do—to take on the same debt that is not a debt but a gift, an obligation, an imperative.

CHAPTER 4

Toward a Poetics of Unbecoming; or, Language Has a Body

AS WE'VE SEEN in the last three chapters, in Sarraute, Wittig, and Garréta's works, language, rather than being co-opted almost immediately by discourse, is prevented from being used to discursively construct and reinforce categories of difference that trap us in identity. What I'd like to do in this chapter is move beyond the anti-identitarian processes and operations of each writer's corpus to examine their poetics—what animates their writing. The anti-difference feminist theory and practice of those materialist feminists—e.g., Monique Wittig, Christine Delphy, Colette Guillaumin, Nicole-Claude Mathieu—who followed Simone de Beauvoir in rejecting femininity as a pernicious social construct created to always put women in a position of alterity and immanence, has been largely forgotten in our historical accounts of French feminism. Particularly in the American context, when we think of French feminist thinkers and writers, we tend to jump straight from Simone de Beauvoir to Hélène Cixous, Luce Irigaray, and Julia Kristeva, her poststructuralist successors. In a literary context, the absence of a visible corpus of anti-difference writers has made it harder to theorize a feminist poetics that has literary language bypass, rather than embrace, difference.[1] But we've had a corpus of writers against difference all along. With the benefit of hindsight, we can see Sarraute, Wittig, and Garréta's collective corpus as enabling a poetics

---

1. Simone de Beauvoir was a brilliant, key philosopher of the twentieth-century, but Beauvoir's innovation was more apparent in her philosophy than in her fiction, which hardly bucked formal conventions.

against difference to be conceived and articulated, whose political stakes Wittig articulated in her theoretical writing.

French Feminism, as mentioned in the Introduction, is now a historical term referring to the American academy's codification of Cixous, Kristeva, and Irigaray as the vanguard of feminist literary criticism in the 1970s and 1980s. It was American feminist academics' way of responding to the importation *en masse* of the French male theorists of French Theory with female theorists of their own.[2] If American feminist literary critics invented French Feminism and placed its literature under the loaded sign of difference, we can correct this, not by inventing a new French Feminism, but by looking to the literature that's already there—Sarraute, Wittig, and Garréta—to show how there's been a literature against difference all along, just as there's been an anti-difference French feminism as well. Because of the strong chain of influence that connects these three writers to each other, theirs is a cohesive corpus, which makes their poetics—a poetics of unbecoming—strong enough to stand on its own against *écriture féminine* and the monopoly it's enjoyed when it comes to feminist poetics. However artificial the grouping of Cixous, Kristeva, and Irigaray is, and however little resemblance it bore to the reality of French feminisms on the ground,[3] their codification as the thinkers of French Feminism did have one particularly important consequence: *écriture féminine*'s visibility as an emancipatory feminist poetics grounded in the body, which can thus serve as a foil for the poetics of unbecoming, which is also an emancipatory feminist poetics grounded in the body.

Cixous coined the term *écriture féminine* in her 1975 manifesto, "Le Rire de la Médusa" ["The Laugh of the Medusa"], where she joyously calls for women to harness their feminine difference and libido, and translate them into writing and cultural production, turning their bodies into texts, thereby producing radical political and social change.[4] While Kristeva and Irigaray do not specifically use the term, as thinkers of sexual difference who each see emancipatory potential in femininity, they have also been placed under the sign of

---

2. See Moses, "Made in America"; Braidotti, "Thinking with an Accent." Now that we've moved on from the heyday of French Theory, the members of this trio have been able to be taken up in other ways: Irigaray and Kristeva are taken up more in feminist philosophy than in feminist literary scholarship, and Cixous is a celebrated novelist and playwright. French feminisms nowadays have branched out considerably beyond Cixous, Kristeva, and Irigaray, but are quite diffuse and not very well taken up by the American academy. See Descarries, "Language Is Not Neutral" for a critique of the way the hegemony of the English language in contemporary feminist work isolates French-speaking feminists and prevents them from being better known.

3. See Winter, "(Mis)Representations" for an indictment of French Feminism's disconnection from the reality of French feminist activism and thought.

4. Cixous, Cohen, and Cohen, "The Laugh of the Medusa."

écriture féminine.[5] Cixous, Kristeva, and Irigaray are all strongly influenced by psychoanalysis, and they see women as having been repressed by patriarchal culture and a phallocentric language that has excluded them. *Écriture féminine* describes what happens when women have been liberated from repression by turning to the feminine body as the source of a new, non-alienated language and discourse. For all three, they espouse the feminine not in order to simply invert patriarchy—none of them advocate replacing the cult of the phallus with the cult of the feminine at the price of oppressing the masculine. Rather, their recuperation of the feminine is in pursuit of a deconstructive transcending of the binaries of masculine/feminine, man/woman. They pursue a mode of relation—what Irigaray would call an ethics of sexual difference[6]—that would put them not in a relationship of opposition or hierarchy but in a relationship of difference, one not co-opted by patriarchy or by matriarchy.

Cixous, Kristeva, and Irigaray formulated complex theoretical responses to the problem of language and oppression and grappled with the difficulties of thinking (about) language with/in language itself. But their poetics of difference acts as an apology for something—difference—that we might just be better without. Thinkers of difference like them may try to set up difference as something distinct from opposition (the logic of A *and* B as opposed to the logic of A and not-A), where opposition is at the heart of the sorts of binarizing logic that have been so invidious. Wittig, however, rejects the notion of difference as non-oppositional because, in the world we inhabit, difference, even if it's conceived of as not being in the service of opposition, inevitably winds up being co-opted by political and social forces that tether difference to hierarchy—difference cannot maintain a pure existence in the world as simply difference. Wittig puts it succinctly: "Thought based on the primacy of difference is the thought of domination."[7] Non-oppositional, non-hierarchical difference cannot exist in lived reality.[8] The theoretical space in which differ-

---

5. Kristeva sees revolutionary writing such as Lautréamont's and Mallarmé's as registering the repressed, unconscious *jouissance* of femininity on the symbolic order through illogical construction and unconventional grammar and syntax, disrupting the symbolic order's will to mastery. Irigaray sees feminine auto-eroticism as inherently multiple, as manifested in the way the vulva's lips are always touching themselves, and models a *parler-femme* (translated by Toril Moi as *womanspeak* in *Sexual/Textual Politics*) on this auto-eroticism as a language uniquely feminine in its difference from the usual phallocentric language. See Kristeva, *Revolution in Poetic Language*; Irigaray, *This Sex Which Is Not One*.

6. Irigaray, *An Ethics of Sexual Difference*.

7. Wittig, *The Straight Mind*, 2.

8. Even seemingly innocuous differences such as hair color aren't preserved from hierarchical valuation as seen in the statement, "Blondes have more fun." Granted, this type of hierarchy may seem anodyne or trivial, but it still shows the automatic way humans use hierarchy to process difference or plurality.

ence can be something other than opposition is so short-lived as to be nonexistent: difference, assuming the stance of the always-already, always devolves into domination. Sarraute, Wittig, and Garréta maintain a suspicious view of difference, and difference, once removed from the psychoanalytic grounding they reject, has no redemptive value. Their writing takes us away from the glistening architectures of difference that difference promises to produce if we were just able to tap into a language proper to it. Instead, their writing takes us to unbecoming, to subjectivity without subjecthood.

We need an anti-differentialist poetics that can mobilize positivity the way *écriture féminine* does, with its vision of a transcendent, libidinal feminine body. In Sarraute, Wittig, and Garréta's writing, we can find such a poetics—a poetics of unbecoming. Like *écriture féminine*, this poetics is also founded on the body, one very different from the feminine body: the body of language. There is still a difference in place; however, it isn't the difference of sexual difference, but rather the difference between human and language, a difference akin to Saussurean difference—the interval or space in which signification can take place. *Écriture féminine* is characterized by desire—the unleashing of desire, of feminine libido, according to Cixous, and the recognition of the multiplicity of feminine desire, according to Irigaray—and the poetics of unbecoming is too. But the poetics of unbecoming houses a desire that draws the human out of the bounds of the human body. In what follows, I look to some of Sarraute, Wittig, and Garréta's novels to see how they enact this poetics of unbecoming—how their desire, as writers and as humans, transcends the boundaries and the strictures of a strictly human body to be desire for the body of language, for language as a body, but one that is not human. Theirs is a poetics of desire, not desire in language[9]—where language is the structure of desire, where desire animates language and makes it exceed speech, communication, and meaning—but desire *for* language. And not just any desire for language, but one that desires language outside the psychoanalytic frame that would presume to contain and explain both language and desire.[10]

---

9. I'm alluding to the collection of essays by Kristeva translated and published in English under the title *Desire in Language: A Semiotic Approach to Literature and Art* (1980).

10. This is where the poetics of unbecoming departs from what could appear at first to be the closely aligned position of Barthes, who, in works such as *The Pleasure of the Text*, calls for an embodied, desiring relationship to language and sees the writerly text (*le texte scriptible*) as one that necessitates the active effort and engagement of the reader, which results in *jouissance*. This text of *jouissance* resists ideology and doxa, and takes the reader outside sociality and subjecthood. The emphasis on *jouissance*, which shows the influence of Lacan, stands at odds with the anti-psychoanalytic grounding of the poetics of unbecoming, which does not operate through *jouissance*'s interruption and loss of consciousness and signification. Unbecoming is not a transgressive violation of boundaries—the sort of limit experience that *jouissance* entails—but rather, an emancipatory reworking of subjectivity, a shedding of the ill-fitting

CORPS-À-CORPS WITH LANGUAGE

"Un écrivain se trouve situé, confronté, corps à corps, avec ce panorama du langage [. . .]."

A writer finds herself situated, confronted, body to body, with this panorama of language [. . .].
—Wittig, *Le Chantier littéraire*, 51–52

Before discussing Sarraute, Wittig, and Garréta's writing and the ways in which they treat language as a corporeal, autonomous, non-human entity that can be interacted with and desired, it seems worthwhile to first consider the question of the body. The body is a peculiar term: it seems to be self-evident and universal so as to need no explanation or gloss (surely everyone has a general sense of what *body* refers to when it's deployed to shore up a distinction from the mind or the immaterial, or to elucidate phenomena that are taken to be embodied such as desire, sexuality, materiality, sensation, affect, etc.), but it also needs constant explanation and glossing (the body is material, yes, but it is also discursive; what comes first, the body or our idea of the body, etc.). The ease with which *body* takes a definite article—The Body—is a testament to how naturalized and seemingly self-evident its existence as a thing is, and to how we take for granted the body's epistemic accessibility and a certain democratization of experience (the body—now here's something that everyone has and experiences).[11] We think we know our bodies, we think we know what our body is in our inhabiting it—we know it to be different from all those other bodies around us that we don't inhabit but come into contact with, and yet we know it to also be very like those other bodies. We want conflicting things from the body: we want it to be treatable in material terms and to exceed materiality.[12] We want the body to be both immanence and transcendence, signifier and signified, to be us and to be separate from us. The body seems completely contingent, and yet we deploy it as if it were somehow a stable thing, and the many metaphorized uses of the body—the body politic, the social body, a literary or artistic body of work, a body of water—speaks to

---

identity clothes we wear. Rather than lose ourselves, we become more ourselves as unbounded subjectivities; rather than stop meaning, we mean more.

11. We can see this in scholarly work on the body that foregrounds the body in titles, as with Bordo, *Feminism, Western Culture, and the Body*; Suleiman, ed., *The Female Body in Western Culture*; Fausto-Sterling, *Sexing the Body*; and Canning, *Historical Perspectives on Bodies, Class, and Citizenship*, to name just a few. The body is never accompanied by a question mark in the title but is taken as a graspable object of examination.

12. A now classic case of this desire to reconcile the body as materiality with the body as a discursive site is Judith Butler, *Bodies that Matter* (New York: Routledge, 1993).

its ability to be treated as stable even if it is anything but. If we can reach any sort of consensus about our conceptualization of the body, it would seem to be that the body is a contested site for signification, but one that, despite the proliferation of discourses of, on, and around the body, takes the body as an experiential site of sensation.

To use mathematical terms, we treat the body with precision but not with accuracy. We complicate the body in myriad ways, but do so after appending *the* before it to pin it down so that we might be able to complicate it, unable to do so without that act of fixing it. And in fixing it, we theorize the body's effects and its operations, but not what it is.[13] The body, because of our inability to separate ourselves from it, because of its constant presence in all our activities, whether welcome or not, frustrates our attempts at analysis and critique. Thankfully, for my purposes, I'm not trying to come up with yet another theorization of the body, nor to weigh in on the various theoretical models we have, but rather, to show how a new poetics comes to light when we allow language to get in on *body* as well, when we take *body of language* not as metaphor but as description.

We can compare the non-human body of language that founds the poetics of unbecoming with other approaches to language's corporeality, which tend to take corporeality metaphorically or anthropocentrically: in the Christian tenet of holding that Christ is the Word made Flesh, the Word takes on human flesh, so that it doesn't have a body proper to it. In Derrida's reflections on language as prosthesis in *Monolinguisme de l'autre, ou, la prothèse d'origine* [*Monolingualism of the Other, or, The Prosthesis of Origin*], the idea of prosthesis takes the human body as its point of reference, thus mapping language onto the human. The Canadian poet Daphne Marlatt treats language as a body to striking effect in her essay "Musings with Mothertongue," and writes that language is "a living body we enter at birth, [which] sustains and contains us. it does not stand in place of anything else, it does not replace the bodies around us. [. . .] it is both place (where we are situated) and body (that contains us), that body of language we speak, our mothertongue. it bears us as we are born into it, into cognition."[14] This body, even as it is described as not standing in place of anything else, or replacing the human bodies around us, is still described in maternal terms, which has the effect of maintaining the anthropocentric angle and attributing human functions and relational forms

---

13. In this respect, we treat the body much as the linguistic turn treats language. That is, primarily through its effects: the linguistic turn attends to discourse, which is certainly a form and a use of language, one that emphasizes how language circulates in society and the effects it has in socializing humans, while passing over language in its non-discursive forms.

14. Marlatt, "Musings with Mothertongue," 53.

to it. The French Symbolist poet, Stéphane Mallarmé, came up with the idea of *écriture corporelle* [corporeal writing], as embodied by dance, which takes the human body in movement as a kind of writing, or language, a notion that's been taken up by other writers, such as the American poet Paul Auster.[15] But in this line of thought, the body replaces the usual signifiers of language, and such a replacement is antithetical to the autonomy and distinctness that Sarraute, Wittig, and Garréta attribute to language in their writing, where language cannot be replaced by anything: it is only ever itself. Marie-Ève Mathieu proposes that when we read, the human body becomes language, *corps langagier*, roughly translatable to linguistic (language-y) body, which is what makes a relationship between reader and writer mediated by the text possible.[16] This inverts the expected dynamic, decentering the human, but this vision of a human-language effaces the difference between human and language.

Postcolonial writing has also provided much rich material on the role and operation of language, as its writers have had to contend with an imposed, obligatory multilingualism, which often results in considerations of the relationship between body and language, as both are caught up in colonialism. Abdelkebir Khatibi, for instance, attends to the intimate imbrication of body and language, when he writes, "But the mother tongue, which is opened [*qui est entamé*], cannot disappear from the body's syntax."[17] But here again, the human body is the primary focus, and despite the inextricability of the one from the other, the human body remains the point of reference, and language's corporeality is integrated into human corporeality.

More recently, new materialisms, animated by a potent posthumanism, have turned away from language as the ultimate form of anthropocentrism to take up instead the material and the real, eschewing epistemology in favor of ontology, knowledge and representation in favor of existence and experience. Even a new materialist who is interested in language, as is Mel Chen, trained as a cognitive linguist, stops short of according language the sort of vital body that Sarraute, Wittig, and Garréta do. Chen seeks to counter new materialist "moves to evacuate substance from language, for instance, the notion that language is simply dematerialized"[18] and treats sign language as an exemplary case of language's materiality, where the body, in all its materiality, is language. In language reminiscent of Wittig's, Chen writes:

---

15. See Abecassis, "Montaigne in Brooklyn."
16. Mathieu, "Des corps textuels," 118.
17. Khatibi, *Maghreb pluriel*, 199.
18. Chen, *Animacies*, 51.

> Language is as much alive as it is dead, and it is certainly material. For humans and others, spoken and signed speech can involve the tongue, vocal tract, breath, lips, hands, eyes, and shoulders. It is a corporeal, sensual, embodied act. It is, by definition, animated. [. . .] Words more than signify, they affect and effect. Whether read or heard, they complexly pulse through bodies (live or dead), rendering their effects in feeling and active response.[19]

The only body that is recognized in Chen's description of an alive language is a human or animal one. Language is accorded materiality, vitality, and agency, but it lacks a body proper to it, and it is not recognized as an entity with which humans can enter into a relationship. That is, Chen is concerned with the way language can affect and effect, but not so much with the way language is itself affected and effected. But it is precisely this reciprocity that exists between language's non-human body and ours that is at the core of the poetics of unbecoming.

In looking at Sarraute, Wittig, and Garréta's writing, what emerges are scenes of writing that are confrontations between the writer—necessarily embodied even if that body loses its fleshly materiality when we as readers access the writer through the words on the page—and language as similarly endowed with a body, albeit a body that is not a human body, but a body that is a body insofar as it is responsive, a material manifestation that constitutes a site of experience and a point of contact and interface with the human bodies of the writer (and of the reader, who comes afterward). At this point, one may wonder why I insist on language's corporeality over and beyond its materiality, given that there are non-corporeal materials that can respond to stimuli and serve as stimuli. I do so partly because Sarraute, Wittig, and Garréta use the language of corporeality to write of language, and I want to take that seriously, as being more than just a rhetorical device, and partly because of the deeply affective dimension of these writers' relationship to language, which is experienced as reciprocal. And affect, as affect theorists have convincingly argued, belongs to the realm of the somatic.[20]

The body of language with which Sarraute, Wittig, and Garréta enter into a passionate *corps-à-corps*[21] is not as easily apprehensible as the bodies of those writers: we've seen their bodies in photos, heard their voices in person or in

---

19. Chen, 53–54.
20. See Reber, *Coming to Our Senses*, in particular, the introduction, "Headless Capitalism," for a complex and wide-ranging account and interrogation of affect as soma and the consequences thereof for and in capitalism.
21. *Corps-à-corps* is difficult to translate into English: literally, it means *body-to-body*, and it signifies both hand-to-hand combat and lovemaking. In either case, what we have are bodies in close contact with one another.

recordings. We don't question their embodiment because it takes the same form as ours in our mortal fleshliness. In reading Sarraute, Wittig, and Garréta, we gain access to the body of language through hearsay (or rather, readsay). That is, the confrontation these writers have with the body of language takes place offstage, and even the writers themselves can only attest to the confrontation after the fact. In this sense, the writers love and desire language in a situation of asymmetrical revelation akin to the relationship between Cupid and Psyche, where Psyche loved and was loved by Cupid, but with the condition of being unable to look upon or identify him through anything but physical contact. If we are to experience the body of language ourselves, it will only be through undertaking the difficult task of entering *le chantier littéraire.*

One final caveat: as with most theoretical proposals, the final truth-value of a claim cannot be readily proved or disproved. As with difference, the claim that language has or is a body is disputable. Some may find language's embodiedness persuasive, and others not at all. However, what's clear is that in their writing, Sarraute, Wittig, and Garréta articulate a relationship to language that treats language as if it has a body, and take that body as something other than a human or animal body—language's body turns out to be proper to language. This stance of *as if* is what's interesting and theoretically productive. In the end, it doesn't matter whether language has or doesn't have a body—that isn't what's really at stake. What's at stake is that when one writes, as do Sarraute, Wittig, and Garréta, in relationship to and with a language that's experienced as corporeal, autonomous, vital, and alive, it creates a space for a feminist poetics of unbecoming, for a writing that can forego difference while still holding on to desire as the motor for all creation.

SARRAUTE: THE TROPISM'S *SUBSTANCE VIVANTE*

Sarraute kept writing the same thing throughout her long career of nearly seven decades. Each of the works that comprise her corpus pursues the tropism, which she has described as a *substance vivante* [living substance]. This immediately implicates corporeality, as to qualify as alive is, in our current understandings of biology, to have a body. Though she never explicitly states that tropismic language is endowed with a body, the body of Sarraute's *substance vivante* is something we encounter, again, as in the case of Cupid and Psyche, through its effects on the human body of the writer. For Sarraute, the tropism and the reality that it constitutes are invisible, like the invisible bodies of the microorganisms that inhabit the world around us, and while Sarraute may not be able to show us the body of this substance that exists outside our perceptive capacities, she works to enable us to ascertain its presence through its acting upon us.

In her essay "Roman et réalité" ["The Novel and Reality"], Sarraute describes tropismic reality as follows:

> For the novelist, reality is the unknown, the invisible. It's what he feels he is the first and the only one to see; what doesn't allow itself to be expressed by forms that are known and already in use. But that requires, in order to come to light, a new mode of expression, new forms. [. . .]
>
> It's something made up of scattered elements—which we perceive and sense very vaguely—of amorphous elements that lie there, deprived of existence, lost in the infinite mass of possibilities, of virtualities, melted into a magma, imprisoned in the crust of the visible, suffocated under the already seen, under banality and convention.[22]

Sarraute conceives her writing practice here as seeking to bring back to life this unknown reality, this tropismic language that's been killed by the conventional forms of language that proliferate as its most visible manifestation. The tropism, and the reality that it undergirds, is like a species that has been endangered and whose very existence has been occluded by the overpopulation of conventional, banal language that dominates this ecosystem of signification and experience. The writer must make space for this species of *substance vivante* through the construction of a new form. Sarraute's writing, then, can be thought of as an act of linguistic habitat creation and preservation.

Sarraute sees the tropism as a mass of infinite possibility that is trapped by social conventions—by the more easily accessed, dead and deadening language of the immediate world, which immobilizes it. She further elaborates the crucial role that form plays in liberating the tropism from the tyranny of the regime of the visible, the goes-without-saying, the self-evident, the already signified, the conventional: "Only form makes them exist. Without form, [the tropism's elements] are nothing. But—and here's the important point—the reverse is true: form is nothing without them."[23] The tropism is thus composite, like lichen, which is a single entity created from the joining of algae and fungus, or the human body, which is the site of populations of incredible biodiversity such as the bacteria that occupy our gastrointestinal tracts.[24]

---

22. Sarraute, *Œuvres complètes*, 1644.
23. Sarraute, 1645.
24. Obviously, this metaphor has its limits, as form is not a living entity, but the point is that two different entities can fuse together to constitute another entity, that one life-form can be more than one, or, as Irigaray might put it, a life that is not one.

The tropism, though irreducible to language, cannot be experienced separately from language and is caught up in an automatic and necessary relationship similar to the one we as humans have with our bodies. We're more than just our bodies—a dissection or analysis of our body, hormones, brain chemistry, or histological constitution cannot fully account for the emotions and thoughts that drive us to make our lives and our persons what they are—but we cannot experience life except as embodied beings. Similarly, the tropismic reality that is the *raison d'être* of her writing is not itself language, although it's what animates and constitutes language. Sarraute's description of the tropism as *sous-conversation*, existing in a layer of psychic reality just beneath conversation, is instructive. Conversation, as an inherently intersubjective and communicative deployment of language, is in the realm of speech. To have a conversation with someone is to experience language as speech. The tropism, as it exists beneath or before conversation, and as it's experienced instinctually—before thought, before cognitive processes of understanding—can be thought of as a becoming-language, caught before it has become transformed, through a social and intersubjective interaction, into speech, into language meant for others. The tropism is an about-to-be-language that arises in response to the social, to being treated as a subject, but it's experienced internally by a subjectivity without contours, which is how Sarraute figures the subjective site of tropismic activity.

In text after text, Sarraute painstakingly and meticulously tracks the tropism to show that we cannot experience the tropism outside its incarnation in language, which is immanently physical, possessing texture, weight, and tone. Sarraute's œuvre attests that language, if it is to transmit sensation and experience to us, as Sarraute would have her writing do, cannot bypass our physical senses. In an essay on the language memoir, Alice Kaplan speaks to the power that language has to shape us: "Language is the place where our bodies and minds collide, where our groundedness in place and time and our capacity for fantasy and invention must come to terms."[25] To experience language in its transformative potential, the body must be as fully mobilized as the mind. Sarraute goes one step further in asserting the importance of the body, however. For her, not only the human body, but the body of language as well, must be mobilized.

Sarraute's texts all bear witness to the corporeal dimension of human encounters with language, and her autobiographical novel, *Enfance* (1983), is exemplary in this regard. With its vivid accounts of multilingualism, which stage her movement between Russian and French, *Enfance* treats the different way each language acts upon the body. In a passage where Sarraute compares

---

25. Kaplan, "On Language Memoir," 64.

her French to her father's French, her accent-less French "r" and his Russian-inflected one, and her Russian to his, she describes the physical requirements for being able to produce this Russian "R": "Il me rend la pareille en me faisant prononcer comme il faut le 'r' russe, je dois appuyer contre mon palais puis déplier le bout retroussé de ma langue . . ." [He gets his own back when he teaches me to pronounce the Russian "r" properly, I must curl up the tip of my tongue and press it against my palate, then uncurl it . . .].[26] The difference between *langue* as *language* and as *tongue* is elided as Sarraute stages language as a positioning and an action of the tongue: *langue* coincides with *langue*, and language appears to inhabit the human body as its own.

Sarraute plays with the coincidence of language and tongue in a particularly poignant episode where Natacha (Nathalie's Russian name), just eight years old, is on the train from her mother's home in St. Petersburg to her father's home in Paris. Natacha is distressed by this departure, which would end up being her last, with Sarraute's mother abandoning her daughter to her ex-husband's custody. To console herself and manage the emotional pain of this rupture, Natacha plays with the two languages at her disposal, French and Russian, and Sarraute describes the respective corporeal configurations each entails:

> Par moments ma détresse s'apaise, je m'endors. Ou bien je m'amuse à scander sur le bruit des roues toujours les mêmes deux mots . . . venus sans doute des plaines ensoleillées que je voyais par la fenêtre . . . le mot français *soleil* et le même mot russe *solntze* où le *l* se prononce à peine, tantôt je dis sol-ntze, en ramassant et en avançant les lèvres, le bout de ma langue incurvée s'appuyant contre les dents de devant, tantôt so-leil en étirant les lèvres, la langue effleurant à peine les dents. Et de nouveau sol-ntze. Et de nouveau so-leil. Un jeu abrutissant que je ne peux pas arrêter. Il s'arrête tout seul et les larmes coulent. (1048)

[Now and then my distress abates, I fall asleep. Or else, I amuse myself by chanting the same two words in time with the sound of the wheels . . . always the same two words which came, no doubt, from the sunlit plains I could see out of the window . . . the French word *soleil* and the same word in Russian, *solntze*, in which the 'l' is hardly pronounced, sometimes I say sol-ntze, pulling back and pushing out my lips, with the tip of my curled-up tongue pressing against my front teeth, and sometimes, so-leil, stretching my lips, my tongue barely touching my teeth. And then again, sol-ntze. And then

---

26. Sarraute, *Œuvres complètes*, 1012; Sarraute, *Childhood*, 36. All subsequent references will be made in-text.

again, so-leil. A mind-destroying game which I can't stop. It stops of its own accord, and the tears flow.] (94–95)

The alternation between *solntze* and *soleil* entails physical configurations of contact and absence, of the tongue pushed up against the front teeth (contact) and the tongue barely touching them (absence), of the lips gathered together (contact) and the lips stretched out, apart from each other (absence). For Sarraute, what starts off as an exercise in referentiality—Natacha looks outside her window, sees the sun on the fields, and begins to pronounce the words *solntze* and *soleil* that seem to index the light hitting the snow outside—winds up an exercise in creation, in the transmission of sensation that is at the heart of her literary project. No longer do the words for sun refer to the sun, but they create the sensations of contact and absence—language uses the body, which produces it, to figure contact and absence.

Natacha's multiple languages constitute different ways of inhabiting her body, and these different physical postures in turn indicate different affective registers of connection and disconnection, contact and absence. In pairing *solntze* and *soleil*, Russian and French, Sarraute is able to bring together body and mind, fully mobilizing each to permit a negotiation of a painful reality: it's no coincidence that it's Russian, Natacha's mother tongue, that brings the parts of her mouth together and models contact and presence, while French, this foreign tongue in a foreign place that imposes distance between her and her mother, separates her lips and the parts of her mouth in a configuration of absence. I would wager that if the demands *soltnze* and *soleil* made on the body were different, such that the Russian would enact absence while French enacted presence, that this episode would not be part of *Enfance*.[27]

My examination of *Enfance* thus far would seem fairly basic in its treatment of language's corporeality. No one would dispute that language is corporeal: speaking is a physical process that involves our lungs, tongue, and teeth; reading is a physical process where we use our eyes (or our fingers, in the case of Braille) to make out words; writing is a physical process where we use our hands to grasp the pen or type at our computers. Thus far we've seen language as a product of human corporeality, but Sarraute goes further: her corpus demonstrates the way language has its own corporeality. Here, the analogy of the human body and its relationship to the microorganisms who

---

27. While this passage might readily evoke the famous account of Freud's grandson's game of *fort-da*, where he throws a spool and pulls it back in an attempt to cope with the trauma of maternal absence, I don't want to impose a psychoanalytic reading on her, as both the unconscious and the difference that are foundational to psychoanalysis are concepts that I'm working without and against.

inhabit it reemerges as a useful one, demonstrating how a body can be part of another body while still having its own body. Sarraute doesn't conceive of language's autonomy as meaning that it can have an existence apart from that of the human that is its source,[28] but she treats language's having a body as a necessary condition for its being able to enter into contact with our embodied selves. The logic goes something like this: since the transmission, or rather, re-creation, of sensation is the goal of her writing, and because sensation is necessarily somatic, for language to operate on the level of sensation, it must also be somatic, corporeal.

We can see this idea of the necessarily embodied encounter between language and the human in Sarraute's reflection on writing as the process of listening to language: "Because when I write, I listen. I always listen to each word and the same goes for when I say things. Everything I say, I hear, I always hear words, I always hear them internally, I hear the rhythm, I hear the words—besides, it's like that when I read, I always read while hearing the text."[29] For Sarraute, dealing with the written word means taking it off the two-dimensional page and into the three-dimensional space of her body. To produce or receive language is to feel the way a word sounds—its rhythm, weight, timbre, and tone. If reading is the way we can see language, hearing (and speaking) is a way we can touch language, our body entering into contact with its body. Sarraute speaks in general terms here of what Wittig articulates specifically in *Le Chantier littéraire* as the mutual imbrication of human and linguistic corporeality:

> Pour en revenir aux métaphores qui sont utilisées pour la parole: il y a des verbes comme toucher, frapper, choquer, fracasser, commotionner [. . .]. La métaphore de l'action de ces verbes concernant les paroles peut qualifier les mots écrits aussi bien, tels qu'on peut se les imaginer toucher la vue. Le plan visuel se prête aussi bien que l'espace sonore à l'actualisation du langage où il lui permet de se réverbérer à la fois sur la page et derrière l'œil dans le cerveau et ses agents, à l'infini, sous les formes cryptiques, les plus emblématiques, les plus abstraites, dans un échange obscur et secret avec la conscience. C'est sans doute cette dimension de leur réalité qui est la moins connue. C'est-à-dire ce qu'un mot accomplit dans la conscience par sa forme

---

28. *Ouvrez* (1997), Sarraute's last published work, does come close, however, by erasing the human and social context for language as much as possible to stage the myriad dramas and conflicts that exist between words. Individual words are the primary actors, but the human is not completely eliminated, simply moved off stage, similar to the way adults are removed from the world of Charlie Brown in the comic strip *Peanuts*, a removal that in no way means that adults are nonexistent.

29. Sarraute, *Lecture*.

matérielle, la plus brute, la plus dénuée de sens, la plus concrète et la plus abstraite à la fois (chaque mot en soi un Cheval de Troie) [. . .].

[To return to those metaphors used for spoken words: there are verbs like touch, hit, shock, smash, disconcert, rattle [. . .]. The metaphor of the action of these verbs about words can apply to written words as well, as one can imagine them impacting one's sight. The visual field lends itself as well as the acoustic field does to actualizing language: each permits language to reverberate endlessly, at once on the page and behind the eye in the brain and its agents, in an obscure and secret exchange with consciousness in the most cryptic, emblematic, abstract forms. It is undoubtedly the least known aspect of their reality. That is, it is what a word accomplishes in the consciousness through its material form, which is at the same time the most crude, the most meaningless, the most concrete and abstract (each word in itself a Trojan horse).][30]

Wittig's reference to the dark and secretive exchange that language has with consciousness (which brings us back to Kaplan's assertion that language is where body meets mind), makes the point that human physicality enables language to be meaningful (without our bodies, we cannot read, write, hear, or speak—activities necessary to experiencing language as meaningful). Conversely, language's physicality enables human physicality to become meaningful—to attain consciousness. When we make sense of language, either from having read or heard it, the words enter our bodies and have an impact on our minds before the latter imbues them with meaning: the physicality of language does work on us before we do work on it. Having a physical encounter with language isn't optional, something we can opt out of. It is thus incumbent on us to make sense of the implications of that physical encounter.

At this point, one might concede the point about language's physicality and materiality, but still not consent to the idea of language having a body. Sure, language can act on our bodies because it's material, but isn't it unreasonable to impute to language a body and agency? Or, in a slightly different vein, one might consent to language's body and agency, but only in metaphorical and figurative terms, where language is consigned to a relationship of similarity or analogy to corporeality and never allowed to have it. This is where Sarraute's novel, *Entre la vie et la mort* [*Between Life and Death*], can show the importance of language's being granted a body and agency, above and beyond its physical and material reality. In this novel, Sarraute writes from a position

---

30. Wittig, *Le Chantier littéraire*, 107–8.

of dead seriousness about language as a living thing, as it is through language's life that the tropism, and Sarraute's entire corpus, is validated.

Entre la vie et la mort (1968), Sarraute's fifth novel, takes up the question of what's at stake in writing, where the life and death evoked in the title is that of language. At this point in her career, Sarraute had already ascended to a position of literary influence and legitimacy after the publication of *L'Ère du soupçon* in 1956 and her incorporation into the New Novel. Between then and *Entre la vie et la mort*, she had published *Le Planétarium* (1959) and *Les Fruits d'or* (1963), and branched out into theater with two plays written for radio, *Le Silence* (1964) and *Le Mensonge* (1966), published together by Gallimard in 1967. In 1968, Sarraute enjoyed critical acclaim. In *Entre la vie et la mort*, however, she casts a critical eye on the position a writer occupies in society, and deconstructs literary success and fame. In the face of her own success, Sarraute reiterates her first loyalty to writing and language above all. *Entre la vie et la mort* pushes the limits of genre by presenting as a novel what reads as an *ars poetica*. Because of how un-novelistic the novel appears to be, Sarraute has to remind her reader in the "Prière d'insérer" that *Entre la vie et la mort* is in fact a novel and "n'est nullement [. . .] un art poétique" [is in no way an *ars poetica*][31] despite the extended reflections on writing and language that characterize it. Eschewing events, actions, and characters, Sarraute helps us understand the writing process as she envisions it by dramatizing the two possible paths a writer can take.

One path is characterized by a torturous solitude that leads to being received with incomprehension or derision by both readers and other writers who don't understand or believe in living tropismic language. It's a path where the writer must be their own reader in order to be understood, alienated from others but able to participate in the life of the text and interact with the words that are its living bodies. The other is a path of empty sociality, paved with the cadavers of a lifeless text—"un champ jonché de cadavres" [a field littered with cadavers][32]—whose language has been killed through conventional forms, clichés, and facile aesthetic conformity. But it's a path that can lead to acclaim by readers and entry into the society of Writers—into a Literary Life based not on working with language to create a living text but on performing Writerly-ness, fulfilling the public's expectations and preconceived notions of what a Writer is. It's the path of a writer motivated not by his relationship to language but rather by human sociality and status.

---

31. Sarraute, *Œuvres complètes*, 1831.
32. Sarraute, 729.

In *Entre la vie et la mort*, Sarraute depicts the writer's task and the process of literary creation, and what an enormous burden it is. In Sarraute's case, this burden is also a privilege: critics and writers, then as now, recognize Sarraute's singular ability to delve into this area of reality where language and the innermost parts of the human psyche commingle and form each other.[33] Sarraute is a pioneer, a tropism whisperer who has privileged access to this living substance that she discovered, able to interact with, perceive, and represent it unlike any other writer before or after her.[34] Poised between language's life and death, Sarraute stays with the tropism, and through her careful working and reworking of language, serves as an intermediary. She turns herself into a medium for the tropism, between life (the tropism) and death (conventional language), working to render the former accessible to readers.

Sarraute takes the question of literary and aesthetic creation (treated from the reader's perspective six years earlier in *Les Fruits d'or*) and approaches it from the writer's side. She depicts the writer's experience of writing, the writer's consciousness as it is situated in language not yet written, not yet fixed into sentences on the printed page. Throughout the novel, Sarraute features scenes of writing, which are not to be confused with images of a writer. She isn't interested in drawing up a portrait of The Writer at Work, and the monolithic identity that the definite article implies, nor is she interested in drawing a portrait of a writer, and the particular and concrete identity that the indefinite article implies. Instead, she presents contradictory narratives of writing so that the reader cannot give in to the temptation to create a character out of the experiences being presented by assigning them to one individual history or person. The focus of the novel is not the story of a writer, but rather, the dynamic, affectively fraught relationship that exists between writer and living language.

In *Entre la vie et la mort*, Sarraute characterizes language in a dizzying number of ways, moving from one mode of sensation to another to keep up with language's movements. We could characterize Sarraute's distinction between living language and dead language as follows: living language is made up of the *substance vivante* of the tropism and as such is always in movement, and if it's to be experienced as living, it must be apprehended sensorially in the moment, not conceptually after the fact. This mobility makes such language resistant to conventional narration, which flattens (and thus kills)

---

33. See Mauriac, *L'Allitérature*, 321; Ann Jefferson, "Notice" to *Entre la vie et la mort* in Sarraute, *Œuvres complètes*, 1830; Wittig, *Le Chantier littéraire*, 69–70.

34. To paraphrase Wittig's critique of psychoanalysis, one could say Sarraute finds the tropism because she invents and puts it there, but that in no way lessens the fact that Sarraute remains the foremost—indeed, the only—writer of the tropism.

language, turning it into a medium that can convey experience after the fact, or narrate, by being converted from a sensorial experience of the present into bits of textual data that speak of a moment already passed.[35] Another distinction we could make is that living language eludes mastery—it has agency and autonomy—while dead language has been domesticated by the human, and killed in the process.

In the earlier parts of the novel, Sarraute emphasizes language's mobility and materiality by treating it as a germ, microbe, and virus—something microscopic, vaporous, or unseen—that works its way into your body; as a growing plant that needs to be transplanted into fertile soil; as an animal that needs to be captured alive:

> Des mots surgis de n'importe où, poussière flottant dans l'air que nous respirons, microbes, virus . . . on est tous menacés. [. . .] Des mots très ordinaires, si je vous les répétais vous vous moqueriez de moi, et pourtant ils ont pénétré en moi, ils se sont incrustés, je ne peux plus m'en débarrasser, ils enflent, ils appuient . . .

> [Words sprung from just anywhere, dust floating in the air we breathe, microbes, viruses . . . we're all threatened. Very ordinary words, if I repeated them to you, you would laugh at me, and yet they entered into me, they became encrusted, I can't get rid of them, they are swelling, pressing . . .][36]

> Il faut capter cela, ce mouvement, l'isoler, chercher . . . n'est-il pas possible pour qu'il se reproduise avec plus de netteté et se développe de créer ces conditions plus favorables? . . . le faire passer ailleurs, dans d'autres images mieux assemblées, d'autres paroles ou intonations, comme on transplante une pousse sauvage dans un terrain amélioré, enrichi de terreau, nourri d'engrais, dans un lieu bien clos, une serre où sera maintenue constamment une température appropriée? . . . (666–67)

> [This movement must be caught, we must isolate it, try . . . wouldn't it be possible in order for it to recur more clearly and evolve, to create more favorable conditions? . . . to insert it elsewhere, among other, better assembled images, other words or intonations, the way we transplant a wild shoot in improved

---

35. Sarraute refers elsewhere to her work as akin to that of a slow-motion effect in cinema, where she, rather than pinning down the tropism, which would kill it, is able to slow it down enough to allow the lay reader to perceive it. Sarraute, *Œuvres complètes*, 1554.

36. Sarraute, *Œuvres completes*, 654; Sarraute, *Between Life and Death*, 52. All subsequent references will be made in-text.

earth, enriched with loam, fortified with fertilizer, in an enclosed spot, a hothouse in which the appropriate temperature is constantly maintained? . . .] (72)

C'est là, comme une bête vivante, lovée sur elle-même, chaude, qui respire, palpite doucement, l'œil mi-clos, prête à se dérouler . . . ils vont s'en approcher, surpris, inquiets . . . ils vont la toucher . . . (678)

[It's there, like a live animal curled up to itself, which breathes, gently pulsates, eyes half-closed, about to uncurl . . . they are going to touch it . . .] (92)

Sarraute uses these metaphors to convey, in as many different ways as possible, that language is not just material but alive, or at least, to be treated as such. The categories that we have for classifying biological life are inadequate to the task of classifying language's living-ness, hence Sarraute's moving from the microbiological to the vegetal to the animal, leaving each behind in a restless attempt to find ways of expressing what sort of life language has. While Sarraute might succeed in conveying language's vitality by enabling readers to experience the sensations that living, tropismic language provokes, she doesn't come up with a new category of life to account for a language she cannot treat as anything but alive. In these iterations of language's materiality, which occur toward the novel's beginning, Sarraute emphasizes the effects language has on the (human) body to insist on the foreignness of language. She defamiliarizes this thing that, through its assimilation with the act of human communication, has become so completely subordinated to the human that it's thought of as an immanently human thing, an extension of our human selves. Sarraute pushes against this overly familiar relationship with language by asserting that language isn't merely an instrument of communication but something completely other. While Sarraute might not come up with a category that seems adequate to describe language (and why would she, when her work is anti-categorical and her evocations of these other categories of life results in placing language outside them?), she maintains that language, far from being simply a human invention, is so different as to be of an entirely different species.

In much the same way that humans can master and manipulate life on the cellular level with innovations in biomedical technology, dominate animal life through hunting, and control and cultivate plant life through botanical and horticultural knowledge, they can also exercise some degree of control over the foreign substance of language. But, just as there are microbes and viruses against which humans are helpless, wild animals that remain outside the purview of animal husbandry, and plants that grow against our will or in no relation to it, language can never be fully tamed or possessed by humans. If anything, language winds up having the last word in the novel. By setting up language as so other, Sarraute is better able to convey that language's life is its own, and not a reflection or a projection of our human life. She must first make this rupture between language, the defining quality of humanity,[37] and humanness, to ensure that we understand language's autonomy. Once she makes this rupture, she's able to move on in the later parts of the novel to treating language in terms that are less antagonistic and more passionate, and do not depend on a dynamic of possession or subjugation, although she will give plenty of examples of this sort of use of language in order to demonstrate what *not* to do. Sarraute strives not only to show how language is living, but also to show how writers can kill language, reducing it to static and lifeless forms.

Later in the novel, after having made the case for language's alterity, Sarraute begins to refer to language in anthropomorphic ways, which promotes the idea of a relationship with language even in its foreignness. She accords language a consciousness that enables it not just to act on humans as a foreign body but to relate to them. In the earlier instances of this anthropomorphization, the relationship is never conceived of as one of reciprocity or equality but one of writerly subservience to language:

[L'écrivain] est derrière les mots pareil à la vieille servante au visage gris, aux yeux, aux mains usés, qui tapote un pli de la robe aux lourdes broderies, redresse un nœud de moire, pique sur le corsage une fleur toute simple, tandis que ses jeunes maîtresses s'impatientent, s'arrachent à ses mains, prennent leur envol pour le bal. [. . .]

Les mots sont ses souverains. Leur humble sujet se sent trop honoré de leur céder sa maison. Qu'ils soient chez eux, tout est à eux ici, ils sont les seuls maîtres . . . Qu'ils s'abandonnent à leurs fantaisies de grands seigneurs, qu'ils étalent partout pour sa joie, pour sa fierté, leur désinvolture, leur insolence savamment concertée. (663)

[[The writer] stands behind the words like an old servant, gray of face, with worn eyes and hands, who pats the pleats of a heavily embroidered gown,

---

37. Language is widely held to demarcate the human from the nonhuman, as articulated by linguists like Émile Benveniste (see Benveniste, *Problèmes de linguistique générale*, 1:62, 259–60 and philosophers like Martin Heidegger (in "Letter on Humanism," he refers to the "human being as not only a living creature who possesses language along with other capacities. Rather, language is the house of being in which the human being ek-sists by dwelling, in that he belongs to the truth of being, guarding it." *Pathmarks*, ed. William McNeill, 254.

arranges a knot of moire ribbon, pins a single flower on a corsage, while her young mistresses grow impatient, escape from her hands, take their flight for the ball. [...]

Words are his sovereigns. Their humble subject feels only too honored to give up his home to them. They should make themselves at home, everything is theirs, they are the only masters ... Let them give free rein to their lordly imaginations, let them display elsewhere, to his joy, his pride, their off-handedness, their sophisticatedly concerted impertinence.] (67)

In each depiction of language here, as young mistresses whose beauty and energy stand in sharp contrast to the gray face and worn hands of the old servant woman representing the writer, and as a haughty feudal lord who can displace the writer and take over his home, language's will and agency are cast as completely subsuming the writer's. In each case, this submission is cast as positive, enabling the writer to derive joy from seeing language's power and energy in action, from being chosen to provide language with what it wants. The writer here is satisfied with letting language take center stage.

As the novel progresses, however, the characterizations of language as sovereign and writer as subservient fall away. These later descriptions are imbued with passion, and Sarraute writes about language in terms of love. For example, after a particularly unpleasant interaction with other writers who deride the writer when they simply don't understand the tropismic substance he's pursuing, the writer sheds his former servility, replaced now by a protective, passionate, paternal indignation mixed with shame and humiliation:

Une fureur, une haine qu'enfle la souffrance, l'amour humilié—celle d'un père qui voit sa fille chérie, qu'il a amenée au bal, dédaignée de tous, faire tapisserie—le pousse à faire sortir d'ici, allons, ça suffit, il faut rentrer, la fête a assez duré ... à trainer loin de leurs regards l'objet dérisoire de tant de soins, le porteur indigne de tant d'espoirs ... à le dissimuler, qu'il disparaisse, surtout qu'on n'y pense plus, qu'on oublie. (679–80)

[Fury, hatred swollen by suffering, by humiliated love—the hatred of a father who sees his darling daughter whom he has brought to the dance, slighted by everybody, a wall-flower—impels him to remove from here, come now, that will do, we must go, the party has lasted long enough ... to take far from their sight the absurd object of such solicitous care, the unworthy bearer of such fervent hope ... to hide it, may it disappear, above all, they should not give it another thought, forget it.] (94)

Language is no longer the writer's master. Instead, a filial language is depicted as an extension of the humiliated progenitor: its success is his success, its failure falls equally on him. The relationship here is still not one of equality, as paternity entails authority over the (female) child, but unlike the previous relationships, this one isn't founded exclusively on domination. We find an element of mutuality, derived from shared origins and kinships, that's absent from those other hierarchical relationships. With the familial metaphor, Sarraute introduces the notion of commonality, which works to attenuate the absolute otherness invoked by her first metaphors of microbial, plant, and animal life-forms. Language is still other, just as a child is a separate person from their parent, but there's reciprocity, an ability to see oneself in the other. Before, language simply acted on the writer, their relationship reduced to one of cause and effect, marked by disposability and interchangeability (a servant's function can be carried out by another servant, a subject can be replaced with another subject). Now, the writer is able to identify with language and feel part of his own subjectivity caught up in how language is received by others. He's imbricated with language, his life caught up with its.

As the novel progresses, Sarraute shifts terms again, this time replacing the familial metaphor with that of language as a friend or lover with whom the writer has fallen out of touch. This metaphor places language and the writer on equal footing, unlike the hierarchy of the father-daughter relationship:

> Et tout d'un coup, c'est comme si dans la salle de bains tiède recouverte d'émail étincelant où il se détendait, trempant toujours plus amolli, plus affaibli dans l'eau mousseuse et parfumée, une petite fenêtre s'était entrouverte . . . Il perçoit, il reconnaît, montant d'une ruelle par-derrière, d'une arrière-cour, des odeurs, des bruits familiers . . . relents de linge humide, de détritus . . . tumulte assourdi des disputes, injures, cris, taloches, rires, chants . . . cela monte vers lui de là-bas . . . où tout s'agite, foisonne, s'épand, s'abandonne, désordonné, informe, impur, innocent . . . Il faut s'arracher d'ici, courir, revenir vers cela . . . Vers elle qui se tient là avec en elle ce vacillement, ce louche flageolement . . . il sent, tandis qu'il s'approche d'elle, cette avidité d'autrefois, cette humilité, cette tendresse . . . "Il y a des éternités . . . Je suis si content . . . Pourquoi ne se voit-on plus jamais? Quand pourrait-on se revoir? Bavarder un peu, comme on faisait dans le temps, dîner ensemble?" (721–22)

> [And suddenly, in the warm, gleaming enameled bathroom, where he was relaxing, soaking away, getting limper, weaker every moment in the foamy, perfumed water, a little window had opened . . . It's as though he recognized, rising from a little back street, from an inside courtyard, familiar odors,

sounds . . . whiffs of damp linen, garbage . . . a sort of muffled tumult of quarrels, insults, shouts, blows, laughter, singing . . . in which everything is in movement, swarming, it spreads out, lets itself go, disordered, formless, impure, innocent . . . He must tear himself away from here, hurry, return to that . . . To the thing that is waiting there, bearing in itself that wavering, that ambiguous trembling . . . he feels, as he approaches it, the old avidity, the humility, the affection . . . "It's been ages . . . I'm so glad . . . Why do we never see each other anymore? When shall we meet again? To talk, the way we used to do, dine together?"] (163)[38]

The writer's subjectivity, in isolation from living language, is deadened, overcome by lassitude, such as one feels when soaking in a hot bath. Language, as it exists outside his subjectivity, represents the world, the energy and movement (and conflict) that make up life. If the writer is to get out of the lulling warmth or security of his self-contained subjectivity and create, he must move toward language and engage with it in a relationship. Language is conceived of as a person who has a life of their own, and any interaction—seeing, speaking, dining—that takes place does so because of a concerted effort to make time and space for it. In this scene, the writer recognizes that language is not an ever-present medium or material that can be taken for granted, at the disposal of his whims and rhythms. Language will not come to or wait on him; he must go to it. Above all, language provokes a deep emotional response in the writer—tenderness, desire, humility—that is at the heart of his reaching out to it. This latest metaphor for language emphasizes affectivity and affinity as the foundation for the writer's relationship with it, treating language not as some thing but someone.

Finally, at the end of the novel, after having taken the reader from language as foreign life-form or body, to language as dominator, then ward, then friend or lover, Sarraute comes full circle and returns to the role of language in writing. After having communicated language's alterity, power, vulnerability, and desirability, Sarraute returns to the question of how language operates in the *chantier littéraire*, and the last pages of the novel confront the reader with the decision the writer, and hence Sarraute, is constantly confronted with: to choose between living or dead language—the *entre la vie et la mort* of the novel's title. The choice between two different kinds of writing is cast as a choice between two different kinds of bodies. In an illustration of what sort of body dead language has, Sarraute shows the writer betraying language and its

---

38. Jolas translates *elle* as "it," but it could just as easily refer to a "she."

fragile vitality by starving it to make it fit into the clothes literary convention would have it wear:

> [. . .] cette petite chose impalpable, timide, tremblante, qui chemine, progresse doucement, propulsant les mots, les faisant vibrer . . . qu'elle daigne juste se montrer . . . tout sera mis en œuvre pour la servir . . . et il a essayé de la dresser, veiller sa ligne, à se faire toute mince pour bien porter ces modèles de grand couturier, ces phrases qu'avec tant de soins, d'efforts il a dessinées, sobrement élégantes ou savamment désordonnées, ou brochées et chamarrées de mots somptueux . . . il lui a appris, lui aussi, comme tant d'autres, à s'effacer pour mieux les présenter, les mettre en valeur, et elle doit maintenant . . . il préfère ne pas aller regarder, il ne veut pas s'en assurer . . . d'ailleurs lui-même probablement ne verrait rien . . . elle doit avoir fini par acquérir la grâce anonyme et grêle, la désinvolture appliquée des mannequins . . . (721)

> [. . .] that little intangible, timid, trembling thing, the thing that plods steadily along, progresses gently, propelling the words, making them vibrate . . . may her ladyship deign to make an appearance . . . everything will be done to serve her . . . and he had tried to train her, to teach her good manners, he made her watch her figure, become very slender so as to look good in the models of the big dressmakers, in these sentences he designed with such care, such effort, soberly elegant or cleverly disordered, or brocaded and embroidered with sumptuous words . . . he also taught her, like so many others, to be self-effacing, the better to present them, to show them off, and now she must have . . . he prefers not to go and look, he doesn't want to make sure of it . . . he himself, moreover, would probably see nothing . . . she must have ended by acquiring the anonymous, high-pitched grace, the studied offhandedness of mannequins . . .] (161–62)

The writer has violated the integrity of language's body, turning it into an anorexic one, abusing it in the name of literary fashion and subduing its agency. Instead of respecting its will and desire, he has reduced language's body to that of a beautiful, anonymous, and ultimately lifeless mannequin's in order to dress it up in well-cut but unoriginal sentences.[39] Sarraute, in a

---

39. French *mannequin* means both *model* and *mannequin* in English, but, given that a human model's function is to be a walking mannequin, a walking object, the characterization of the *mannequin* as lifeless—and Jolas's choice of the English mannequin over model—seems fair.

moment of something resembling optimism, stops short of pronouncing that language dead, and proposes instead to resuscitate it:

> Juste peut-être ici, on dirait qu'il y a comme une vibration, une pulsation ... un pouls à peine perceptible bat ... il faut se dépêcher avant qu'il soit trop tard, sinon il sait maintenant ce qui va arriver ... les belles phrases vont s'assembler en une forme qui aura un jour l'aspect lugubre d'un champ jonché de cadavres où ceux qui viendront retrouveront partout des visages qui leur sont connus, où chacun pourra sans peine identifier ses morts ...
>
> Mais rien n'est encore perdu, et c'est encore là, encore tiède, vivant, il faut le dégager, l'arracher d'ici, faire éclater ces phrases rigides, briser ces formes parfaitement modelées ... le ranimer, que cela se redresse, se déploie librement, rejetant tout ce qui l'entrave, sauf juste ici et là quelques fragments ... (729–30)
>
> [Just here, perhaps, there would seem to be a sort of vibration, a pulsation ... a barely perceptible pulse is beating ... he will have to hurry before it's too late, if not, he knows now what will happen ... the fine sentences are going to gather together in a form that one of these days will take on the lugubrious aspect of a field strewn with corpses, where at every turn the people who come there will find faces that are known to them, where everyone will be able to identify with no trouble his own dead ...
>
> But nothing is lost yet, it's still there, still warm, alive, it must be extricated, torn away from here, those rigid sentences must be exploded, those perfectly modeled forms must be broken up ... revive it, let it rise up, spread out freely, rejecting everything that impedes it, except just these few fragments here and there ... .] (176)

Sarraute sets up a striking contrast between the wan, weak body of language as model, objectified and stripped of the tropism,[40] and the warm, animated bodies of a language allowed freedom and agency. The life of language is based in its capacity to move, in both senses of the word, and its beauty comes not from how it measures up to literary trends or is received by the critical community of readers and writers, but from the relationship, necessarily intimate and private, that the writer can have with it.

---

40. Elsewhere in the novel, Sarraute describes the deleterious effects of trying to separate or extract the tropism from language: "Il est impossible d'en arracher une parcelle sans que cela se vide de sa sève, de son sang" [It's impossible to tear off a scrap of it without its losing its sap, its lifeblood] (678; 92).

The writer's choice *entre la vie et la mort* is this: does the writer go along with literary fashion, with what's easily and widely received as a beautiful use of language, and instrumentalize language for his gain, or does he take the body of language, starved for the sake of "beauty," and resuscitate it, bringing it back to health? Which is more important: being able to negotiate society as a Writer who is part of the *confrérie* of Writers who perform that identity and please the reader-consumers who buy (into) that identity when they buy books? Or exploring tropisms with and through a language that is a *substance vivante*, as equal partners in the quest for the life and reality found at the limits of what human and language together are able to reach?

For Sarraute, in her dogged dedication to the tropism, there is only one choice: one must choose the language of life instead of leaving lifeless bodies in one's wake as victims to a culture of literary consumption. The closing paragraphs of *Entre la vie et la mort* act as a sort of vow of fidelity that the writer makes to language:

> Il faut avoir la force de m'arracher à eux [the atropismic Writers], de me réveiller, de revenir à moi, il faut me boucher les oreilles, me pincer . . .
>
> La suivre où elle voudra . . . Elle qui ne se laisse pas nommer . . . ce que je sens . . . moi seul . . . cette chose intacte, vivante . . . Je ne sais pas ce qu'elle est. Tout ce que je sais c'est que rien au monde ne peut me faire douter de sa présence. Bien que par les moments je la perde de vue si longtemps que je suis sur le point de flancher, de me laisser persuader qu'elle n'existe pas.
>
> Je la cherche, agité, anxieux, partout où il est possible qu'elle se montre, qu'elle me fasse signe . . . de ces petits signes entre nous que personne d'autre, semble-t-il, ne perçoit. [. . .] Heureusement elle est là, elle le seul garant, le seul guide . . . elle s'impatiente, nous n'avons pas de temps à perdre . . . (733–74)
>
> [I must have the strength to tear myself from them, to wake up, come to myself, I must stop my ears, pinch myself . . .
>
> Follow it wherever it will . . . It, the unnameable . . . what I feel . . . this untouched, living thing . . . I don't know what it is. All I know is that nothing in the world can make me doubt its presence. Although at times I lose sight of it for so long that I am on the point of giving in, of letting myself be persuaded that it doesn't exist.

I look for it, upset, distressed, everywhere it might possibly appear, make me a sign . . . those little signs between us that no one else apparently, perceives. [. . .] Fortunately it's there, the only guarantor, the only guide . . . it is growing impatient, we have no time to lose . . .] (181–83)

While there is only one choice to be made, it's a difficult one, and Sarraute acknowledges the relative facility of choosing the other path to fame and success, despite the costs to language. The writer who chooses to write because of language, and not such extraliterary objects, writes ultimately for himself. He does not turn his relationship with language into a spectacle to be consumed, thus objectifying and instrumentalizing it. Rather, he seeks out language, waits on it, follows it. Language here is akin to Dante's Beatrice, a guide who, unlike the poet Virgil—the writer—can enter into Paradise. With this allusion, language is cast as someone the writer must respect and love in order to reap the rich fruits of their complicity.

Despite staging the relationship between the writer and language as an intimate one, as a *tête-à-tête* (or, in Wittig's terms, a *corps-à-corps*), Sarraute doesn't want to limit the *we* in "we have no time to lose" to that dyad. The *we* here opens up onto other possible configurations of collectivity, as Sarraute ends the novel by directly invoking "vous mon double, mon témoin" (734) [you my double, my witness] (183) in an invitation to join the writer. Ann Jefferson sees this *we* as a splitting of the writer into reader and writer, a division that ensures the authenticity of Sarraute's writing.[41] Sarraute often splits the writer's subjectivity, which we can see most clearly and dramatically in *Enfance*, where Sarraute sets up a masculine interlocutor alongside her narrating *je*, who questions her decisions and memories to ensure that the writer remains truthful. What's important about the *we* in this particular instance is the way it breaks open, through its polysemy, the dyadic relationship of writer to language to allow for and even require a third party. While the reader modeled here is a part of the writer himself, Sarraute creates the possibility for a truly third party—the outside reader—to join the writer in his attempt to hold on to language and follow it wherever its tropismic life takes it. Sarraute, after all, does not write *Entre la vie et la mort* and keep it secret. She publishes it and makes it available to a public and unknown set of readers. The intent isn't to perform a privileged relationship with language to the exclusion of the reader, but to enable readers to have a writerly relationship with language (as Wittig theorizes in *Le Chantier littéraire*).

---

41. Jefferson, "Notice" to *Entre la vie et la mort*, in Sarraute, *Œuvres complètes*, 1828.

Even though Sarraute criticizes insensitive and insensible readers within the novel itself, she has a certain faith that her readers, regardless of how much or how little they resemble what we imagine to be the expected consumer of modernist literature, will understand what she's doing when they have their own encounter with tropismic language. Sarraute wants to expand the number of people who experience language as living, as she does. The novel thus confronts its readers with the same choice as the writer's: it asks us either to choose living language and seek out the tropism, or to choose dead language and settle for a ready-made and readily available aesthetic experience of literature that has been deemed beautiful or worthwhile by the market and the commentariat. The journalist Martine de Rabaudy describes Sarraute's desire to reach out to readers as "[preferring] to conquer readers over a public."[42] The writer's observation of "those little signs between us that no one else, apparently, perceives" doesn't express a will to exclude all other readers and set up the tropismic writer (and hence Sarraute) as the only individual who can know tropismic language. By showing the process through which the writer navigates between the life and death of language to choose the former, Sarraute guides us in our own navigation of the language we're immersed in as human beings living in the social realm. *Entre la vie et la mort* is an invitation to readers to experience language as Sarraute does—tropismic and alive.[43]

To convey to readers what such an experience entails, Sarraute proceeds carefully in *Entre la vie et la mort*, using each successive metaphor to bring us closer to a radical notion of language's equality with us, of our relationship with language as one of mutuality that preserves our respective autonomy. It's unsurprising that in her metaphors staging our relationship to language, Sarraute likens language's body to that of a human's, endowed with a pulse and a human kind of mobility, as our conception of relationality remains anthropocentric.[44] And it follows that Sarraute would use metaphors of other species to stage language's full autonomy and alterity. But the point is not to take these metaphors at face value—if we did, we would be stuck in contradiction.

---

42. Rabaudy, "Nathalie Sarraute."

43. For a reading that sees Sarraute coercing rather than inviting readers into becoming tropismic readers, see Courson, *Nathalie Sarraute*, 124. Courson takes the reader and writer to be in an antagonistic relationship with each other, such that the reader is forced to submit to the writer the way the writer is forced to submit to language. This characterization strikes me as too harsh, however, and overlooks the reader's agency as well as that of the writer (who chooses whether to follow language).

44. Certainly, there's been a vigorous theoretical movement to dethrone the human from its place at the top of the ontological hierarchy (e.g., new materialisms), and plenty of pet owners refer to their animals as having human emotions and being related to them (e.g., having granddogs), but that seems less like an affirmation of real ontological equality and more like projection—the fact remains that anthropocentrism is difficult to shake off.

Rather, the proliferation of metaphors serves to approximate, using the vocabulary available, how language functions as a body—as a life-form that can act and be acted upon—and how it functions relationally, endowed with an affective capacity.[45] They show how language is inadequate for capturing language's body and vitality. The only adequate language in this case is an experience of such language itself, rather than the use of representational language. To return to the novel's ending, "I don't know what it is. All I know is that nothing in the world can make me doubt its presence." All the metaphors deployed by Sarraute are not meant to capture for us what living language is, but rather, to testify to Sarraute's experience of having been present with it, and guided by it—a testimony that invites us to also choose a life with living language.

WITTIG: AN OFFERING TO A GODDESS

Wittig, as one of Sarraute's most faithful readers, responds to Sarraute's invitation with a resounding *yes*. In Wittig's case, allowing a living language to guide her leads not to a project of tropismic writing, as it does for Sarraute, but to a program of political lesbian writing—to her Trojan horses. Thus far, I've privileged *Le Chantier littéraire* as a text that elucidates Wittig's literary practice as well as Sarraute's and Garréta's. As discussed in Chapter 2, *Le Chantier littéraire* proposes a deeply materialist conception of language, and it's in that text that Wittig explicitly declares that to be a writer is to be caught up in a *corps-à-corps* with language, in a passionate, corporeal encounter. As with any critical and theoretical text, *Le Chantier littéraire* makes claims and offers explanations, but it cannot enact those claims the way fiction can. *Le Chantier littéraire* describes the writer's worksite, but it's only within the fictional text itself that readers can enter into the *chantier* as more than observers. Thus, to track how Wittig relates to language as an embodied and autonomous entity, I turn from *Le Chantier littéraire* to *Le Corps lesbien* (1973), where her political utopianism intersects with a singular vision and experience of language's corporeality that is enacted textually in a way unlike what is found in the rest of Wittig's works. It is an exemplar of Wittig's conception of the corporeality, desirability, and vitality of language as a very real body.

Le Corps lesbien, in both its content—the novel recounts the repeated passionate and mutual dismemberment and reconstitution of the lesbian lovers'

---

45. As you've undoubtedly noticed, Sarraute's work focuses more on how language makes the writer feel than on how the writer makes language feel, and one could accuse Sarraute of anthropocentrism, or one could reframe that in generous terms to suggest that Sarraute is simply avoiding the arrogance and hubris of speaking for another.

bodies—and its title, foregrounds human corporeality. The female body and its viscera provide the material for both the plot and the pages of lists of body parts (in all capital letters) interspersed throughout the text. It's thus no surprise that critics and readers have privileged human corporeality in their discussions of the text—that corporeality is what hits the reader over the head on every page. While Wittig's innovative use of language and her unorthodox syntax do not go unremarked, these readings of the novel examine how Wittig acts upon language in order to upend our notion of the universal human body: they take the female body as the point of reference rather than the male body that serves as the standard bearer for ideal human embodiment, à la Leonardo Da Vinci's Vitruvian Man. In these readings, the female body is a powerful tool that dethrones the phallus and introduces a new regime of signification that, unlike *écriture féminine*, would be unsexed.[46] While these readings speak powerfully of the political potentiality of Wittig's writing, their focus on human corporeality comes at the expense of leaving language's corporeality unexamined, privileging human over linguistic agency.[47]

In what follows, I use *Le Corps lesbien* to examine how the human, figured through the body, is a way to see through to language's own body. Focusing less on what the human lovers do to each other, I concentrate on how Wittig makes room in the text for language's agency, for the way an embodied language acts upon her as the writer. By concentrating on language's corporeality as opposed to that of the human lovers, I work to strip away the illusory transparency and passivity of language as medium and material to show the body of language that lies beneath—this body cannot be possessed or mastered by the human, but only experienced and sensed. In order to see how language is embodied in this text, we need to first see what the text *is* and does, and

---

46. Karin Cope, in "Plastic Actions," focuses on the lesbianization of language, examining how Wittig continues the demasculinization and unsexing of textual space begun in *L'Opoponax* and *Les Guérillères*. Namascar Shaktini, the first American to work on Wittig, also focuses on the lesbianization of language, on how "her restructuring of meaning establishes the lesbian body in its place as a new primary signifier in a new nonphallocentric Symbolic order" (Shaktini, "Monique Wittig's New Language," 90), and, in "Displacing the Phallic Subject," she devotes much attention to Wittig's rewriting of phallocentric myths such as those of the *Odyssey* and Orpheus and Eurydice and to her lesbianization of ancient gods by turning them into goddesses—the canon equivalent of stripping the masculine pronoun of universality.

More recent work on *Le Corps lesbien* continues to focus on lesbianizing language and subverting the Western tradition. See Bourque, *Ecrire l'inter-dit*; Brooks, "The Body in the Text"; Davis, *Beautiful War*.

47. Or, if language's corporeality is examined, as in Lynn Higgins's reading of the novel, it's treated as a metaphor that can elucidate the human body, thus maintaining language as something that belongs to the human or is in service to it. See Higgins, "Nouvelle Nouvelle Autobiographie."

what its agenda is. Doing so will allow us to see through to the body that is then revealed.

According to Wittig, *Le Corps lesbien*'s political motives are as follows: to reappropriate pornographic language, severing it from its objectification of the female body; to effect a similar rupture with the language of love and erotic literature, which serves to reify the female body as the quintessential love object; and, most broadly, to give a voice to lesbians and create a lesbian text that severs all relations with masculine culture and literature and the phallocentric history that they represent:

> The wager [in *Le Corps lesbien*] was to triumph over the very captivating words of pornography.[48]

> This anatomical vocabulary is cold and distant and I used it as a tool to cut off the mass of texts devoted to love.[49]

> *Le Corps lesbien* has lesbianism as its theme, that is, a theme that we can't even describe as being taboo since it doesn't have any real existence in the history of literature. Male homosexual literature has a past and a present. Lesbians, they're mute—like all women are as women on all levels.[50]

Wittig uses one form of language (anatomical vocabulary) to counter an ideologically charged language (pornography, love literature), using the clinical language of the former to neutralize the highly charged and motivated language of the latter. With this neutralized language, Wittig sets out to start a new tradition of lesbian literature that doesn't borrow from or refer to any of the literature devoted to masculine sexuality—literature tout court, as we've known it through the canon. Wittig's *Corps lesbien* is an attempt to build a lesbian corpus.

Le Corps lesbien consists of 110 poetic vignettes that are set on islands that, as Wittig explains in her preface to the English translation, "allude to the Amazons, to the islands of women, the domains of women, which formerly existed in their own culture. They also allude to the Amazons of the present and the future."[51] In the utopian space of this virtual, transhistorical Lesbos, Wittig stages the passionate relationship between two *amantes*: a j/e that's bro-

---

48. Wittig, *Le Chantier littéraire*, 108.
49. Wittig, "Some Remarks on The Lesbian Body," 46.
50. Wittig, online catalogue for the *Éditions de Minuit*, "Le Corps lesbien."
51. Wittig, "Author's Note," 9. There is no author's note to the original French edition of the novel. This addition to her project is likely because of the English translation's inability to represent the split nature of the *j/e* in the English *I*, which has only one letter, and for the way

ken, cut in two by a slash, who constantly addresses a *tu* that's whole, the object of *j/e*'s love and desire. They are surrounded by a society of *elles* who are at turns both antagonistic and sympathetic, but always a third party to their union, which is never peaceful, but piece-full, consisting of a continuous tearing apart of each other's bodies. C. J. Rawson succinctly summarizes the novel as he enumerates the myriad forms of its constant violence:

> Here, bodily violation is itself love. The heroines of Wittig's Sapphic utopia spend nearly two hundred pages mutilating, dismembering, eviscerating one another, chewing each other's sinews and vitals, vomiting, decomposing, penetrating and being penetrated through every orifice and to the depths of every vital organ. Innards are fondled. Bits of lung are spat out, chewed, pressed against the lover and given to her to swallow. Gentle tendernesses of love-biting turn to the crunching and the tearing apart of the beloved, piece by piece, muscle by muscle and vein by vein.[52]

In its repetitiveness and unrelenting explicitness, the violence recalls pornography, where there is nowhere to hide from the bodies on display. There is no respite from this constant mutual destruction of each other's bodies save the irruption of an alternative text every ten to fifteen pages.

This other body of text is composed of line after line of anatomical vocabulary printed in large capital letters (at least three or four times larger than the typeface used for the lovers' narrative), and weaves in and out of the text with no apparent logic and reason (fig. 2). Each intervention takes up two full pages—the visible surface of the open book—so that the narrative it interrupts is hidden. In this text's layout on the page, there are no page numbers present to situate the reader;[53] this second text exists outside the narrative text's logic. Although part of *Le Corps lesbien*, it refuses to be organized by or in relation to the narrative. It thus exists separately, self-contained and unaware of the tumultuous narrative taking place around it. At every irruption of this blaring stream of anatomical language, the reader is hit with a sudden block of meaninglessness. Like words in a dictionary, which mean nothing by themselves, these very large and in-your-face body parts are not connected to each other through syntax—Wittig isn't using them to communicate in the usual way. In

---

the English translation is unable to render the feminine specificity of such forms of address as *ma douce, ma bien-aimée, ma très belle* that are scattered throughout the text.

52. Rawson, "Cannibalism and Fiction," 285.

53. Since the pages are themselves unnumbered, in order to find these pages, one must turn to the pages either before or after to situate oneself. In the English translation, this anatomical text only ever occupies one page and remains numbered, diminishing its impact somewhat.

DORSAUX LES ILIA-
QUES LES RONDS LES
CARRÉS LES TRIAN-
GULAIRES LES PYRA-
MIDAUX LES ABDO-
MINAUX LES FES-
SIERS LES BICEPS LES
TRICEPS LES TEN-
DONS D'ACHILLEA
LES SUPINATEURS
LES JAMBIERS LES
SUBLIMES LES DÉ-
DAIGNEUX LES SU-
PERBES LES COM-
PLEXES LE DIA-
PHRAGME LE VAGIN
L'ANUS LE VOILE DU
PALAIS LE TISSU
CONJONCTIF LE MÉ-
NINGES LA DURE-
MÈRE L'ARACHNOI-
DE LA PIE-MÈRE LA
SCLÉROTIQUE LA
CORNÉE LA RÉTINE
LA CHOROIDE LES
GENCIVES LA PLÈ-
VRE LA PÉRITOINE
L'ÉPIPLOON LES

FIGURE 2. An example of interrupting text from Wittig, *Le Corps lesbien*, 112–13.

this sense, this anatomical vocabulary and its manifestations throughout the text constitute a sort of lexicon akin to the dictionary, which Wittig describes in *Le Chantier littéraire* as follows:

> Mais il y a le dictionnaire cet alter ego des écrivains. Là est la carrière du chantier où les mots gisent comme matériau. [. . .] Cependant le dictionnaire est différent de toutes les autres formes où se manifeste le langage en ce sens qu'il le fournit comme global, un corps global, dans un ordre (l'ordre alphabétique) qui n'est pas producteur de sens et qui expose de ce fait les mots fournis un à un dans leur matérialité (scripturale, graphique), ne serait-ce que dans son énumération, et en ce sens qu'il offre à l'appréhension une diachronie, un ordre discontinu dans lequel le langage ne s'offre jamais dans son utilisation puisque pour devenir actuel il obéit à une syntaxe (à un ordre synchronique).

> [But there's the dictionary, this alter ego of writers. There's the worksite's quarry where words lie still as material. [. . .] However, the dictionary is different from all other forms where language manifests itself insofar as the dictionary produces language as global, a global body, in an order (alphabetical)

that doesn't produce meaning and that, through this fact, exposes words in their materiality (scriptural, graphic), even just through its enumeration. In this sense it offers up for our apprehension a diachrony, a discontinuous order in which language never offers itself up in its utilization since to become present it obeys syntax (a synchronic order).][54]

Wittig returns the language used to describe bodies—in particular, the female body (the text lists non-sexually differentiated organs, such as the lungs, but also female reproductive organs, as opposed to male ones)—to a place before meaning, as it is when words are ordered syntactically into sentences that they start to signify. By doing so, she attempts to give readers access to a language that exists before ideology, unlike words that are sentenced to produce meaning. Wittig describes this language as "le langage premier (dont le dictionnaire nous donne une idée approximative), celui où le sens n'est pas encore advenu, celui qui est de tous, appartient à tous, et que chacun à son tour peut prendre, utiliser, courber vers un sens" [the first language (of which language now gives us an approximate idea), language where meaning has not yet occurred, language that is everyone's, that belongs to all, and that each can in turn take, use, bend toward a meaning].[55] But even though language before syntax is ostensibly devoid of meaning in its potential form as a collection of words waiting to be used, Wittig, in her modification of words (e.g., "LES TENDONS D'ACHILLEA," which feminizes Achilles), shows that her raw language is not phallocentric, and has already appropriated the universal for the feminine. *Le Corps lesbien*'s anatomical pages act as a dictionary, a writerly alter ego existing in a utopian time—that of the *guérillères* after their victorious appropriation of the universal.

As Wittig commented, she intends for this lexical mass to purify pornographic language, to strip the words used to describe women's bodies of their ideological charge and inject a clinical distance between them and the reader. Wittig acknowledges that even this so-called scientific, objective language is still ideologically charged: for example, *vagin* [vagina] derives from the Latin word for *sheath*, defining this organ in relation to what it's supposed to contain—the penis. Nonetheless, she still sees this language as being less ideologically loaded than non-scientific language and sees it as able to "réduire à néant (pendant la durée du livre) cet autre 'langage' institutionnalisé" [reduce to nothing (during the book's duration) this other, institutionalized 'language'].[56] The mouth, breasts, genitals, hair, buttocks, anus—body parts and orifices

---

54. Wittig, *Le Chantier littéraire*, 98.
55. Wittig, 60.
56. Wittig, 108.

typically possessed by men in pornography and literature—are removed from their usual sexualized context. No longer ordered by a syntax commanded by a hegemonic, phallocratic sexuality, they've stopped being objects of a man's action. Instead, they lie fallow alongside a legion of other body parts that are not usually thought, much less named (e.g., *la duremère* [dura mater], *la piemère* [pia mater], *la plèvre* [pleura]), but are here articulated with care and precision. Their absorption into this desexualized language neutralizes them.

The anatomical text not only neutralizes: it also confronts us with a language stripped of a narrator, of a human voice. It's a language not beholden to some human will or subjectivity that animates and orders it into meaning. Beyond the obvious fact that Wittig chose these terms herself, the text comes as close to existing in and of itself as possible, and because of its asyntactical quality, it asserts a certain autonomy. Looking at the large characters and feeling the visual impact of these words, we process them first as a block of text, a visual object consisting of black marks on white paper, before we make them out as discrete words. Because of these words' separation from communication, their un-instrumentalized nature (they're not visibly in the service of some authorial or narrative power) translates to autonomy. Where Sarraute turns to complex metaphors to try to persuade us of language's autonomy, Wittig takes a much more direct route that takes advantage of the page's physicality and the typography's visual impact.

Wittig insists that this anatomical vocabulary cuts off and frees language from masculinist ideology and phallocentric influence, thus imparting its autonomy to this other language. This raises the question, however, of why she takes up an ostensibly liberatory (though clinical and cold) vocabulary to recreate and reproduce what appears to be a pornographic, sadistic violence. Why would she found the lesbian love she narrates on what looks like the very same violence it's supposed to be counteracting? Take a typical passage like this one:

> M/on clitoris l'ensemble de m/es lèvres sont touchés par tes mains. A travers m/on vagin et m/on utérus tu t'introduis jusqu'à m/es intestins en crevant la membrane. Tu mets autour de ton cou m/on duodénum rose pâle assez veiné de bleu. Tu déroules m/on intestin grêle jaune. Ce faisant tu parles de l'odeur de m/es organes mouillés, tu parles de leur consistance, tu parles de leur mouvement, tu parles de leur température. Tu essaies à ce point d'arracher m/es reins. Ils te résistent. Tu touches m/a vésicule verte. J/e m/e morfonds, j/e m/e plains, j/e m/e tombe dans un gouffre, ma tête est entraînée, m/on cœur m/e vient au bord de m/es dents, il m/e semble que m/on sang s'est tout figé dans m/es artères. Tu dis néanmoins que tu le reçois en quantité énorme sur

tes mains. Tu parles de la couleur de m/es organes. J/e ne peux pas les voir. J//entends ta voix siffler dans m/es oreilles. J/e m/e concentre pour t'écouter. J/e m/e vois étendue, toutes m/es entrailles sont déroulées. J//ouvre la bouche pour chanter une cantate à la déesse m/a mère. Par cet effort le cœur m/e faut. J//ouvre la bouche, j/e reçois ta langue tes lèvres ton palais, par toi monstre adoré j/e m/e mets à mourir tandis que tu ne cesses pas de crier autour de m/es oreilles.

M/y clitoris m/y labia are touched by your hands. Through m/y vagina and m/y uterus you insert yourself breaking the membrane up to m/y intestines. Round your neck you place m/y duodenum pale-pink well-veined with blue. You unwind m/y yellow small intestine. So doing you speak of the odour of m/y damp organs, you speak of their consistence, you speak of their movements, you speak of their temperature. At this point you attempt to wrench out m/y kidneys. They resist you. You touch m/y green gallbladder. *I* have a deathly chill, *I* moan, *I* fall into an abyss, m/y head is awhirl, m/y heart is in m/y mouth, it feels as if m/y blood is all congealed in m/y arteries. You say nevertheless that you receive an enormous quantity of it on your hands. You speak of the colour of m/y organs. *I* cannot see them. *I* hear your voice hissing in m/y ears, *I* concentrate on listening to you. *I* see m/yself stretched out, all m/y entrails are unwound. *I* open m/y mouth to sing a cantata to the goddess m/y mother. M/y heart fails in this effort. *I* open m/y mouth, *I* admit your lips your tongue your palate, *I* prepare to die by your side adored monster while you cry incessantly about m/y ears.[57]

What starts off as a description of a seemingly typical sexual encounter quickly turns, by the end of the second sentence, into something else as *tu* penetrates *j/e* with a totality exceeding the usual bounds of human sexuality. Their lovemaking turns into a vivisection. The exposed organs turn into the site of union, displacing the more predictable and usual erogenous zones as the place to feel the other's body. *Tu* violates *j/e*'s body in that she violates its wholeness, reducing *j/e* from a unitary body to its constitutive organs. *Tu* guts *j/e* and removes her vital organs so that she is at the point of death. This reads less as *une petite mort* that we would associate with orgasm, but *une grande mort* from which there is no return to the body. Why does Wittig make recourse to this violence when her goal is to counteract the violence done to women throughout the ages in the name of a naturalized phallocentrism? The violence, while it might seem to reproduce the very violence Wittig repudiates, is different in three fundamental ways.

---

57. Wittig, *Le Corps lesbien*, 33–34; Wittig, *The Lesbian Body*, 37–38.

First, unlike patriarchal violence, which has silenced women and lesbians, this violence produces speech: *j/e* speaks constantly, addressing both her lover *tu* and the *elles* that surround them. She is never silent, and as readers, we are confronted with her voice as much and as constantly as we are with the lovers' bleeding and dismembered bodies. *Tu* is also not silent, and she sings and speaks and responds to *j/e*. Although we don't have direct access to the content of her speech, we know that she speaks, as she discusses the smell, temperature, and color of *j/e*'s organs. This incredible violence pushes the lovers further into language rather than into silence or language-less sounds of pain.

Second, the violence is completely mutual, which is perhaps the most surprising element of the text. The patriarchal violence Wittig is responding to is unidirectional and founds a heterosexual society that depends on the domination of women. In *Le Corps lesbien*, however, the violence is marked by mutuality, as *j/e* kills *tu* as often as *tu* kills *j/e*. These killings do not result in a permanent death: the lovers are always restored to life in the next vignette, ready to kill and be killed again. In their commitment to a wholly reciprocal violence, the lovers appropriate dying and resignify it. *J/e* and *tu*'s deadly lovemaking is figured as a representational act, where what is represented is a truly radical egalitarianism—no organ is too insignificant or significant to be spared, no one ever has the upper hand. The text is one of equal dismemberment, where each lover gets to consume the other's organs as much as she gets to have her own organs consumed. *J/e* does not possess *tu* more than she is herself possessed. She does not destroy more than she is herself destroyed. She does not dominate more than she is herself dominated. The relationship between *j/e* and *tu* is one of absolute reciprocity, indicated by the constant role reversal the lovers perform between dominance and submission. Their relationship enacts a state of equilibrium, that point at which roles, in their fluidity, never become fixed, never set.

Wittig's violence is thus used to represent an unbounded relationality whose reciprocity and equality are based in endless mobility—there can be no inequality and hierarchy if there is no way to fix subjectivities long enough to be able to assign relative value to them. This mobility is reinforced metaphorically throughout the text as the lovers give up even their human embodiment to assume the bodies of different species of life: spores, protozoa, horses, sharks, fish, butterflies, microscopic cells, to name a few.[58] These lovers reject roles and cannot be confined by them—how can they when they are not even anchored within human corporeality? Bodies, in *Le Corps lesbien*, do not confine; they do not contain and house and preserve the autonomous individual.

---

58. Wittig, *Le Corps lesbien*, 24, 42, 57, 67, 101, 172, 173; Wittig, *The Lesbian Body*, 29, 45, 56, 64, 91, 152, 154. All subsequent references will be made in-text.

The continual breaking down of the lovers' bodies enables them to experience the other with a fullness that they couldn't were they to remain sealed hermetically, human *being*s contained within skin bags.

Finally, this violence, which results in death (albeit one that lacks finality), is transcendent, leading to resurrection. The Egyptian myth of Isis and Osiris, with its focus on dismemberment and resurrection, mirrors *Le Corps lesbien*'s structure.[59] Through rewriting the myth, Wittig writes death as life. The following passage, where the lovers assume the roles of Isis and Osiris, frames their violence as mutual, as a gift of sorts that provides *j/e* with the opportunity to resurrect the body it has killed:

> [. . .] elles m/e demandent où te faire une sépulture dans quel ordre ramasser tes fragments ce qui fait que j/e m/e redresse hurlante, j/e prononce l'interdiction d'enregistrer ta mort, que la traîtresse responsable de ton déchiquètement ne soit pas inquiétée, j/e prononce que tu es là vivante quoique tronçonnée, j/e cherche en toute hâte tes morceaux dans la boue, m/es ongles raclent les menues pierres et les cailloux, j/e trouve ton nez une partie de ta vulve tes nymphes ton clitoris, j/e trouve tes oreilles un tibia puis l'autre, j/e te rassemble bout à bout, j/e te reconstitue, j/e remets en place les yeux, j/e rapproche bords à bords les peaux séparées, j/e produis avec empressement des larmes de la cyprine de la salive en quantité voulue, j/e t'en enduis à toutes tes déchirures, j/e mets m/on souffle dans ta bouche, j/e réchauffe tes oreilles tes mains tes seins j//introduis tout m/on air dans tes poumons, j/e m/e redresse pour chanter, [. . .] m/oi Isis la très puissante j/e décrète que comme par le passé tu vis Osiris m/a très chérie m/a très affaiblie [. . .] (86–87)

> [They ask m/e where you should be interred in what order to collect your fragments which makes m/e recoil shrieking, *I* pronounce a ban on the recording of your death so that the traitress responsible for your being torn to pieces may not be alerted. *I* announce that you are here alive though cut to pieces, *I* search hastily for your fragments in the mud, m/y nails scrabble at the small stones and pebbles, *I* find your nose a part of your vulva your labia your clitoris, *I* find your ears one tibia than the other, *I* assemble you part by part, *I* reconstruct you, *I* put your eyes back in place, *I* appose the separated skin edge to edge, *I* hurriedly produce tears vaginal juice saliva in the requisite amount, *I* smear you with them in all your lacerations, *I* put m/y breath in your mouth, *I* warm your ears your hands your breasts,

---

59. See Higgins, "Nouvelle Nouvelle Autobiographie," 160; Cope, "Plastic Actions," 87–88.

I introduce all m/y air into your lungs, *I* stand erect to sing [. . .] *I* Isis the all-powerful *I* decree that you live as in the past Osiris m/y most cherished m/y most enfeebled.] (80)

Wittig takes the transcendence of the body's usual boundaries—represented elsewhere as the metamorphosis into other species—to a radical end. Death, and the resurrection that it produces, is the necessary condition for a union that's as complete as it is imaginable: the resurrection and the reconstruction of the lover's broken body is realized through and by *j/e*'s own body, who, in re-integrating and re-membering *tu*, integrates her body with *tu*'s. *J/e* uses her tears, saliva, and *cyprine* (the neologism Wittig coins to refer to vaginal secretion) to put *tu* back together. *Tu*'s new breath comes from *j/e*'s breath and *tu*'s warmth comes from *j/e*'s. *Tu*'s life is thus bound up with *j/e*'s, a one becoming two that's reminiscent of childbirth while rejecting maternity.[60] To reinforce this theme of death and resurrection, of death as a necessary means to enter into true life, taken to mean complete union with the lover, Wittig casts the narrator *j/e* as a feminized Jesus Christ—"Christa la très crucifiée" (30) [Christa the very crucified] (35). In this rewriting of a grand narrative, *j/e*'s body is mortified and brought back to life.

Despite these differences between Wittig's vision of violence and the patriarchal violence and dominance she's reacting against, the question of what makes this violence necessary remains. In writing a lesbian text and beginning a new type of literature, free from masculine influence, couldn't a narrative of tenderness (instead of tenderized flesh) have been written instead? Couldn't Wittig have opted to recount an eternal passion that knows no death? What could motivate this violence? I submit that the driving force for this violence is the desire to make language's body emerge, to make it visible and perceptible to the reader.

Just as the mortification of the lovers' bodies leads to their resurrection, a process that renders their vitality that much more urgent and evident, Wittig's mortification of language throughout the novel serves to render its body and vitality that much more urgent and evident as well. Wittig's violence toward language, however, registers as less stunning than her more spectacular violence toward human bodies. And yet, the violence depicted toward the female bodies in the novel, as shocking as it may be, is a secondary, or later violence. Wittig's violence acts first upon language before it's mobilized by narrative

---

60. Elsewhere, in the anatomical text, there's an extraordinary moment where Wittig diverges from the enumeration of organs to slip in the formula, XX + XX = XX (144; 128). Wittig's most explicit rejection of maternity is in the entry "Mère" in *Brouillon pour un dictionnaire des amantes*.

to act upon fictional human bodies: before we consume the narrative, before our piecing together of the story results in the tearing apart of the lovers. The moment we open the book and turn to any page, before we read words and the sentences they form and the narrative woven from those sentences, we see the slashes that aggressively attack the language connected to *j/e*'s narrative subjectivity. We see the singular first person's pronouns, possessive adjectives, and objects cut up and fragmented: *je* cut into *j/e*, *me* into *m/e*, *moi* into *m/oi*, *j*' separated from verbs that began with vowels with a double slash (//), as with *me* when it is an object before verbs that also begin with vowels. On every page, we see the visible signs of a *je* cut off from language and a language that's maimed to realize that rupture. Language is visibly violated. Normal syntax, grammar, and orthography come undone[61] and instead of an orderly subject and a well-ordered language, we get a fragmented, disruptive because disrupted *j/e*. Wittig explains the use of this *j/e*:

> The fascination for writing the never previously written and the fascination for the unattained body proceed from the same desire. The desire to bring the real body violently to life in the words of the book (everything that is written exists), the desire to do violence by writing to the language which I [*j/e*] can only enter by force. 'I' [*j/e*] as a generic feminine subject can *only* enter by force into a language which is foreign to it, for all that is human (masculine) is foreign to it, the human not being feminine grammatically speaking but he [*il*] or they [*ils*]. [. . .] *J/e* is the symbol of the lived, rending experience which is m/y writing, of this cutting into two which throughout literature is the exercise of a language which does not constitute m/e as a subject. *J/e* poses the ideological and historical question of feminine subjects. [. . .] If I [*J/e*] examine m/y specific situation as subject in the language, I [*J/e*] am physically incapable of writing 'I' [*Je*], I [*J/e*] have no desire to do so.[62]

Two things stand out for me in this text: first, the emphasis on the body as the object of writing, and second, Wittig's situating the writer as being confronted with a choice between two types of language, as with Sarraute in *Entre la vie et la mort*.

Wittig brings together as analogous the desire for an unattained lover's body (the thrill of the pursuit, the distance that drives courtly love, etc.) and the desire to write the new (which, for Wittig, as a good student of the New

---

61. For more on this subversion of language, see Bourque, "On dirait une revolution."
62. Wittig, "Author's Note," 10–11. Le Vay renders this broken *j/e* in the English as an italicized *I*, which has the unfortunate effect of accentuating *I*'s wholeness rather than its brokenness.

Novel, amounts to being a real writer). She identifies desiring a human body and desiring to do things with language as both proceeding from the same desire. This desire for a *corps-à-corps* with language animates Wittig's entire corpus and is shared by Sarraute and Garréta. While we might assume that the "real body" here refers to a human body, it's instructive to read it instead as the body of language. It's important to note that Wittig sees the bringing to life of this real body as taking place through violence. If we take this real body to be that of language, we begin to realize how we normalize that violence to language: our shock or disturbed sensibilities end up being provoked instead by the violence recounted in the narrative. In privileging human corporeality over the visibly maimed body of language, which we don't normally consider to be corporeal, we opt to respond to the violence of content over the violence of form. Wittig, however, attempts to force us to pay attention to the forgotten material—language—and see it as a real body.

Now, Wittig, as a woman, a minority subject, sees writing as forcing a choice between two situations: one, use language "normally" and consent to a language that represents alienation, domination, and oppression, thus perpetuating those very things by collaborating with and participating in it, and two, resist language's normal use and disrupt language's reproduction of oppression, cutting off this masculinist language's ties to the universal through violence upon the material of language. Obviously, Wittig opts for the latter, which corresponds to Sarraute's writer's choosing life. For Wittig, you can either do violence to language or let language do violence to you. In the latter case, that violence doesn't lead to a joyous resurrection but rather oppression under patriarchy. In the former case, that violence leads to a new life for language.

To do violence to language, then, is the prerequisite to writing a lesbian text, and moreover, to writing a text whose language retains its autonomy and vitality. Wittig recuperates the minority subjectivity of lesbians from silence and gives it a voice in *j/e*, who, as a wielder of language and discourse, is not monolithic (already, the slash that cuts it into two prevents *j/e* from coalescing into any sort of hegemonic subject position), the way the masculine universal subject of phallocentric language—the *je*—is. *J/e* embodies the minority subject, which, as Wittig articulates in *La Pensée straight*, isn't whole, even as it attains the universal, as all great literature does in her estimation:

> [Historically,] the minority subject is not self-centered as is the [logocentric] subject. Its extension into space could be described as being like Pascal's circle, whose center is everywhere and whose circumference is nowhere.

[The minority subject can disperse itself into many centers, it is forcibly de-centered, a-centered.][63]

The minority subject, the feminine subject, the lesbian subject—none can attain universality the way the heterosexual masculine subject does by taking itself to be the center, the stable point of reference. The minority subject operates by always moving away from a center. This self-dispersal and deconstructive creation of multiple centers (seen in *Le Corps lesbien* in the lovers' transformation into various goddesses and species) necessitate fragmentation and proliferation. By breaking the *je* into *j/e*, the minority subject is universal without being monolithic. It is universal without inscribing itself inside a clearly delineated circumference that determines who's in and who's out (as with the boundaries between species, sexes, races, etc.). *J/e*'s minority subjectivity, in its movement, breaks language in order to open it so that women are no longer on the outside of a language from which they are estranged.

This linguistic violence, taken as necessary given Wittig's political aims, still doesn't explain the need for violence on the narrative level. To make sense of this second violence, we need to allow language to be a real body, maimed by Wittig in order to enter into it: a body that rises up and strikes back—the *tu* to Wittig's narrating, authorial *j/e*. When we shift our framework to allow the language of *Le Corps lesbien* to be a body—but not a human body, despite the descriptions of *tu*'s entrails and genitals and secretions—then the violence's motivation becomes clear, and the resonance between *j/e* and *tu*'s violent relationship and the violent breaking open of language in order to enter into it and be unalienated from it is more than coincidental: it's a deliberate, conceptual coinciding.

When we look past *tu*'s seemingly human body—the narrated body—to see it as a linguistic body, then the violence wrought upon this lover stops testing our limits as readers for how much guts, vomit, and pus we can take in, stops being provocative to the point of obscenity. By undoing and dismembering language's body, we can come to think of it as truly alive. It's through its undoing and unbecoming that language can assume its body. In the dynamic of this reciprocal violence, language's body is given space to act upon and be acted upon—to become something we can *experience*, with which we can be in relationship, as *j/e* and *tu* are in relationship. This violence, rather than seeking to test the reader, is a generous gesture toward the reader: it's a metaphorization of how Wittig renders language's body concrete and visible in the

---

63. Wittig, *La Pensée straight*, 101. More or less the same passage is found in *The Straight Mind*, 61–62. I've bracketed where the two texts differ: e.g., *logocentric subject* is called the *straight subject* in *The Straight Mind*.

anatomical text—a long narrative gloss that explains what we are to do with language's body. As with Sarraute, Wittig thus invites the reader to join this experience of the relationship between writer and language.

We've seen that the cycle of dismemberment, death, and resurrection ultimately works to bring the lovers closer, integrating the body of one with the other while still maintaining each one's autonomy. This integration—this passion and fusion—is what Wittig feels as a writer for language: she finds herself "situé, confronté, corps à corps, avec ce panorama du langage" [situated, confronted, body to body, with this panorama of language], where the *corps-à-corps* consists of "cette étreinte mortelle avec ses mots violents, véhéments, passionnés" [this mortal embrace with its violent, vehement, passionate words].[64] The passion Wittig writes is a literary, linguistic passion between her body and language's body, more so than between two human bodies. Wittig's comments on the genesis of *Le Corps lesbien* support this reading:

> So let's go back to my literary workshop, where I am with fire between my teeth and still nothing but my blank page. Suddenly giving me a big laugh (for one can laugh even in anguish) two words came in: *Lesbian Body.* Can you realize how hilarious it was for me? That is how the book started to exist: in irony. The body, a word whose gender is masculine in French with the word *lesbian* qualifying it. In other words "lesbian" by its proximity to "body" seemed to me to destabilize the general notion of the body.[65]

The *corps lesbien* in question does not take a lesbian's physical body as its referent—it cannot, because for Wittig, lesbianism is not a sexual orientation, defined by physical acts or drives, but a political identity. Wittig's lesbian is a defector from the heterosexual social contract, someone who creates and seeks out her (or his) own society by refusing to be defined in relationship to a man economically, politically, and ideologically—a refusal that places her outside the categories of sex, beyond the concepts of man and woman:

> Lesbianism is much more than homosexuality (the conceptual homologue of heterosexuality). Lesbianism is much more than sexuality. Lesbianism opens onto another dimension of the human (insofar as its definition is not founded on the "difference" of the sexes). Today, lesbians discover this dimension that is outside of what is masculine and feminine.[66]

---

64. Wittig, *Le Chantier littéraire*, 51–52.
65. Wittig, "Some Remarks on The Lesbian Body," 46.
66. Wittig, *La Pensée straight,* 93. An earlier version can be found in Wittig's essay "Paradigms," originally published in English in Stambolian and Marks, eds., *Homosexualities and French Literature.*

Wittig's definition does not take woman or women as its foundation (in contrast to the "woman-identified woman"[67] at the heart of American radical lesbianism), thus allowing for the possibility of those we call males, as well as females, to be part of lesbian society (although the bodies of *j/e* and *tu* are female).[68]

In *Le Corps lesbien*, the ostensibly human lesbian body pointed to in the title is in fact a foil for the body of language, which emerges (or rather, is submerged) as the actual lesbian body. For Wittig, the idea of a lesbian body is laughable and impossible, as it sets up lesbian as an essential identity. If we follow her logic, which rejects femininity and the ways it does patriarchy's work by attaching itself to ideas and activities through the adjective *feminine*, then we must also reject the idea of a *lesbian body*, where *lesbian* ends up doing the same essentializing work. While no one would contest that lesbians have bodies—one could refer to a lesbian's body—*lesbian body* is a non-starter. Wittig's point in *Le Corps lesbien* is to show the impossibility of there being a lesbian body save in language, save through the assembly and ordering of words. Language is thus a lesbian in *Le Corps lesbien*, as it should be, since it does not exist in relation to masculine, phallocentric language and culture. The body not only exists as a function of language, it *is* language. Before, there was no lesbian body (lesbian in the Wittigian sense), but after Wittig's mind put those two words together, a lesbian body began to exist. Because of its linguistic origins, the only "real" lesbian body is a textual one. It's to this lesbian corpus, this textual body, that Wittig ascribes all the workings of a physical woman, of an *amante*, in a metaphorization of Wittig's desire for language's *étreinte mortelle*. Whatever the *j/e* does to *tu*, Wittig as writer does to language.

Let's return to Wittig's rewriting of the Isis and Osiris myth to read it as the literary, fictional site of all the processes she lays out in *Le Chantier littéraire*. The reintegration and resurrection of Osiris's fragmented body, of *tu*, requires much work to search for and find all the body parts that are lying around in the mud. Once found, more work is required to put them together again, with *j/e* pouring her own body and soul into *tu*. And after the work of re-memberment and reassembly, Isis, *j/e,* brings Osiris back to life through her language: "j/e décrète que comme par le passé tu vis Osiris" [*I* decree that you live as in the past Osiris]. When we read *tu* as being language itself, as a body that's no less real or alive for being textual, the process of dismember-

---

67. Radicalesbians, *The Woman-Identified Woman*.
68. As Marie-Hélène (now Sam) Bourcier, the translator into French of *The Straight Mind*, puts it, "Wittig is the only one to not prescribe identification to woman only, to leave the door open to bearded lesbians." "Wittig la politique," in *La Pensée straight*, 33.

ment and resurrection reads very much like the process of writing described in *Le Chantier littéraire*.

Wittig conceives of writing as requiring violence against language to strip it down to its raw, originary state, if these words are to be able to be brought back as a real body alive with potential:

> [...] l'ensemble des mots, le vocabulaire, est pris dans la glu du sens, des sens conventionnels (de ce que Barthes a appelé 'la cuisine du sens'), ils arrivent chargés et sont tout sauf 'bruts'. [...] Il faut faire sur le langage une opération de réduction qui le ramène 'au degré zéro,' qui le dépouille de son sens conventionnel afin de le transformer en un matériau neutre, brut. [...] Cette opération n'est pas une opération mineure et à vrai dire je ne sais pas qu'on ait déjà parlé de ce sujet de façon systématique. Tout écrivain doit prendre les mots et les mettre à nu.
>
> Il faut obtenir un mot brut tel qu'un diamant avant d'être taillé, un mot dans sa gangue, gros de possibilités. Et au départ ils sont tels quels (tels qu'on les connaît à la fois dans la langue et le langage littéraire), aussi éloignés de l'état brut que des images de messieurs et dames attifés et encore corsetés le sont du corps nu. (96–97)

> [The totality of words, vocabulary, is stuck in the glue of meaning, of conventional meanings (of what Barthes called 'the kitchen of meaning'), words arrive weighed down and anything but 'raw.' [...] It's necessary to perform an operation of reduction on language that takes it back 'to degree zero,' that strips it of its conventional meaning in order to transform it into a neutral, raw material. [...] This operation isn't a minor one and to be honest, I don't know that anyone has already spoken of this subject in a systematic way. Every writer must take words and strip them down.
>
> It's necessary to obtain a raw word like a diamond before it's been cut, a word in its gangue, fat with possibility. And at first, they (the way we know them both in speech and in literary language), are as removed from this raw state as images of decked out and corseted gentlemen and ladies are from the naked body.]

Wittig insists on the primary work of the literary worksite as being that of turning ordinary language, which comes to the writer already used by others in speech and in other texts, and thus already coated in meaning and steeped in ideology (discourse, in other words), into *le langage brut*—language that can be worked with as a raw material. Wittig uses anthropomorphic vocabulary to speak of this process and language's embodiment: the writer must strip words of their meaning, strip them naked, remove the corsets and vestments with which these words have been covered, dressed up, and ultimately, constrained. (For Wittig, as for Sarraute, words are best experienced in the nude.)

This stripping is a major process, as seen in *Le Corps lesbien*'s anatomical text, which Wittig glosses in *Le Chantier littéraire*, explaining that this anatomical text is used to get language back to its brute state:

> D'où l'apparition systématique, manifeste du corps de mots décrivant le corps humain dans ses termes cliniques et médicaux, choisis comme appartenant à un vocabulaire technique et scientifique et à cause de cela moins totalement investi par l'idéologie [. . .]. Il m'a semblé que les mots réduits à leur plus simple forme, pourraient ainsi, gisant comme corps de texte parallèle au texte qui s'écrit, quand employés dans ce corps de texte, partir à neuf comme si de rien jamais n'avait été, dans la jubilation de leurs lettres et de leurs formes, appelés là uniquement pour le plaisir. C'était aussi leur donner carte blanche et leur donner toute l'impulsion rêvée (qu'ils soient entiers, qu'ils bouleversent tout) afin qu'ils accomplissent si faire se peut une transformation de la réalité sociale. Une bande de chevaux de Troie, désarmés, offrande à une déesse. (109)

> [Hence the systematic appearance, manifested in the body of words describing the human body in clinical and medical terms, chosen as belonging to a technical, scientific vocabulary less totally vested with ideology [. . .]. It seemed to me that words reduced to their simplest form, motionless like the body of text parallel to the written text, could thus, when employed in the body of that text, start over as if nothing had ever happened, in the jubilation of their letters and their forms, summoned there solely for pleasure. This also entailed giving them carte blanche and whatever impulse they dreamt of (that they be whole, that they turn everything upside down) so that they might accomplish, if possible, a transformation of social reality. A band of Trojan horses, disarmed, an offering to a goddess.]

Each word in its brute state is a Trojan horse, but in this case they are disarmed, not yet used, not yet sent out into the city of the reader's mind—they are in a state of potential. This language is one of possibility, a possibility founded in jubilation and pleasure, a desirable and desiring language, a language conceived of as immanently political and universal.

The most beautiful and striking sentence in this passage is the last one, where Wittig refers to language, liberated from ideology, meaning, and convention, as an *offrande à une déesse* [offering to a goddess]. Which goddess is Wittig referring to when *Le Corps lesbien* is replete with goddesses, from

Ishtar and Isis to Aphrodite and Artemis? Wittig answers the question when she writes, "Tes dents l'une après l'autre j/e les arrache [. . .] j/e les regarde briller, elles sont prises avec leurs racines, à laquelle en faire offrande sinon à Sappho la très lointaine" (143) [*I wrench out your teeth one by one* [. . .] *I see them gleaming, they are removed with their roots, to whom should I offer them if not to Sappho the most distant*] (127). The offering is to be made to the poet Sappho, who, while not part of the usual pantheon, is elevated to such status by Wittig, who invokes her far more often than she invokes any deity. Sappho occupies a privileged position in Wittig's imaginary as a writer of lesbian texts. Her accession to divinity comes from her power to use language. Wittig's deity, instead of a Christian God who is the Word made Flesh, is a woman of flesh who makes words. The offering *j/e* makes to Sappho of extracted teeth is a bodily analogue for the band of Trojan horses described in *Le Chantier littéraire*. Each tooth, with its exposed roots, is a tooth that cannot be used in its toothy capacities to bite, chew, and produce speech. These teeth that Wittig would offer up are effectively disarmed and unable to be deployed, like the Trojan horses she offers. They lie still, like the anatomical words that punctuate the novel. Wittig, as the authorial *j/e*, gives these teeth, this brute language, to Sappho, who represents literary creation and the jubilant and pleasurable space of a culture and language outside the straight mind. She offers up her body and the body of her beloved *tu*, language, in service to this liberated and liberatory writing.[69] Although it means having to perform a violence akin to that of pulling out teeth by their roots or of having her entrails ripped out like Prometheus, Wittig is willing to do so because this passion is passion in all sense of the term—suffering, as well as intense physical and emotional love.

As with Sarraute, writing, which requires the entire mind and body, isn't an easy task for Wittig. The stakes are high, unto death, but this death results in life as a writer, and the life of language through the text. Wittig doesn't try to break language just to do violence to a language that has been used to do violence to her, a linguistic tit for tat, but rather, to recuperate language for a new kind of literature, which can be shared. This literature, animated by a passionate relationship with language, results in a reciprocal unbecoming: the reader and writer unbecoming subjects, freed into subjectivity, and language's constraints unbecoming, disintegrating, its body's freedom restored.

---

69. Here, *tu*'s double meaning as not only the second-person pronoun but also the past participle of *taire* [to silence], emerges. The teeth, these brute parts of language, in their potential, are silent—they do not speak yet: they are offered up to a goddess who will use them to speak—an integration into yet another subjectivity, another life.

As the principal dynamic between language and human, this reciprocity enables Wittig, in addition to entering language and taking its body apart and putting it back together as a lesbian body, to be herself entered by language and acted upon. She is torn apart, no longer the unitary body stable in its deadening individual identity, but something closer to a universe without contours. Just as language can be reappropriated from masculinity through a pronoun, a small target that results in repercussions for all of language, language, when it enters Wittig, can affect her in her body's totality:

> [Les mots] caressent l'œil mais ils ne s'en tiennent pas là, le corps est gagné comme dans l'amour, un geste de caresse commence à un endroit précis et de là le corps est touché dans son ensemble. Et comme dans ces caresses carnales qui parfois sont plaisantes simplement mais peuvent aller jusqu'au dérangement, ainsi font les caresses des mots.
>
> [[Words] caress the eye but they don't stop there, the body is won over as in love; a caressing gesture begins in a specific location and from there the entire body is affected. And as with these carnal caresses, which are sometimes simply pleasant but can also disturb, so too with the caresses of words.][70]

Wittig's language is clear here. The writer's role has been reversed, and, instead of being the one to touch and manipulate words, down to their viscera, she is touched and manipulated—in a state of *dérangement,* overcome by language. In her possession of and by language, her caresses of and by language, she is never language's proprietor or master. The moment we open the pages of *Le Corps lesbien* and enter the text, regardless of what sex we are, we're given access to the band of Trojan horses, to the uprooted teeth, and we're asked, through the syntactical ordering and assemblage of our reading, to arm and assemble them. We are invited to become *j/e,* to unbecome and be broken. Through our intervention, that raw language—those words lying still in the writer's quarry, those dismembered parts of a body—becomes a lesbian text, a lesbian body, language's living body.

GARRÉTA: "TO THE LOST ONE"

Dérangement is an apt characterization of Garréta's reaction to language. Her experience of language, as it is represented in her work, is profoundly disturbing, both for the reader, as seen in her hostile and queer use of pro-

---

70. Wittig, *Le Chantier littéraire,* 122.

nouns in *Sphinx* and *La Décomposition*, and for the writer, as we will see in the *dérangement* that pervades *Ciels liquides* (1990) and *Pas un jour* (2002). Unlike Sarraute and Wittig, who both write of a present passionate encounter with language, Garréta's passion, as is appropriate for someone who identifies with a melancholic postmodernity where true collectivity is impossible, is relegated to an irretrievable past. Garréta's writing expresses a passion for language that's always already passed into memory. Her passion is marked as much by language's absence as by its presence. This tension between presence and absence is a fault line through which desire for language emerges as the core of Garréta's work. In *La Décomposition*, for instance, we see the narrator's pursuit of aesthetic perfection entail the maiming of both human bodies and of the body of Proust's magnum opus. In a darker echo of Wittig, this aesthetic fulfillment is unable to be realized save through violence of an absolute, fatal nature, which doesn't result in resurrection. In *Ciels liquides* and *Pas un jour*, Garréta is *à la recherche de la langue perdue* [in search of lost language], and those two novels are filled with both thematic and textual violence—her response to a desire that's both unrealizable and irremovable. While Wittig's violence toward language summons and resurrects a language that's alive and present, in Garréta's writing, this gesture comes too late—it's an attempt to bring back a language that has slipped away or is yet to come. In what follows, I examine first *Pas un jour* and then *Ciels liquides*, going in reverse chronological order, to show the trajectory from desiring a language that's slipped away to desiring a language that is yet to come. By going backward, Garréta's desire for language becomes more apparent.

Pas un jour, for which Garréta won the Prix Médicis, is a novel ostensibly produced under an Oulipian constraint: write from memory, for five hours a day, about a woman the author has desired or been desired by, faithfully transcribing what memory dictates. Though published as a novel, the coincidence of Garréta the biographical subject with the narrator, compounded by the photograph of Garréta herself peering out from the Livre de Poche edition, makes it difficult not to read this as an autobiographical work.[71] On a structural level, Garréta, in keeping with the etymology of *dérangement* as a disordering, flouts the order that is supposed to govern *Pas un jour*: in the last section of the novel, entitled "Post Scriptum," Garréta confesses to not only breaching the autobiographical pact but her contract with her self-imposed constraint by having inserted a completely fictional section. She provokes us

---

71. See Killeen, "Esquives, pièges et désaveux" for a reading of *Pas un jour* as an autofictional text that tries to operate in an anti-confessional mode in an attempt to open up new possibilities for a self-writing that can bypass confession.

by commanding us to "Cherchez la fiction" [Look for the fiction].[72] Garréta's structural bad faith is a form of textual violence that casts uncertainty onto the whole text as we become *dérangées* as readers, unable to find the fiction, either giving up the task, or taking the novel in its entirety to be fiction, which may be Garréta's point all along, one of her aims in the novel being to wean readers off any facile adherence to the concepts of identity and subjecthood that validate the idea of the autobiographical author. The *dérangement* does not stop at the structure, however, and I want to turn away from this structural disordering to look instead at what sort of *dérangement* language produces in the writer and the desire that it reveals, provokes, and sustains.[73]

Pas un jour has contradictory aims: on the one hand, to narrate desire by recollecting the women the narrator has desired and been desired by—"l'alphabet bégayant du désir" (11) [the stammering alphabet of desire] (4)—and on the other, to evacuate desire from the narrative and channel the constraint as a way of separating memory from a direct and free contact with desire—"Le récit ne sera que cela, le dévidage de la mémoire dans le cadre strict d'un moment determiné" (12) [That will be the narrative: the unwinding of memory in the strict framework of a given moment] (5). In other words, the point is not to relive those past desires. The writing is not to stir up feeling, the past is not to contaminate the present in an unfettered way: "Froideur du récit, consonante à la froideur du désir" (90) [A cold narration, consistent with the coldness of desire] (53). This desire will be handled and contained, with a fixed beginning and end, and none of the urgency and heat we normally associate with it. At the same time as she points to the force of the desire that inhabits her memories through the imposition of a constraint to keep them in check, the narrator also undercuts this desire by insisting that her subjectivity, as attached to a notion of the self, is nowhere to be found

---

72. Garréta, *Pas un jour*, 144; Garréta, *Not One Day*, 87. All subsequent references will be made in-text, and the translation will be occasionally modified.

73. After having just articulated Garréta's will to disarticulate the biographical, flesh-and-blood author from the narrator, I want to recognize that I perform a slippage between them, a slippage I perform with Sarraute and Wittig, as well, when I attribute desire or intentionality to them as opposed to their narrators. I think this is justified: when I speak of the writer, I'm speaking of her as a person in relationship with language. Through their narrators, who may or may not correspond to the biographical and social data that is collated to the social entities that these writers also are, writers create fictional persons, who, for being fictional, are not any less real. I believe that narrators are transposed onto the writers who give them shape, form, and substance, and that a narrator's relation to language reflects the writer's own relation, as the writer is the animating force for the narrator's language, a force that cannot but leave traces. Given that I am seeing a certain relationship to language that is present in all their works—a consistency across their corpus even as the narrators change—I think it's fair to point to the writer behind the narrators.

in the novel. Desire—"le passe-partout de la subjectivité" (10) [the one key to unlock the secret of our subjectivity] (3)—opens a door onto nothing. Or does it? This key, which she implies is false, has a real function. If the self and attendant subjectivity of an (auto)biographical Garréta whose life experiences can be mapped onto the episodes do not exist, if there is no transparent and one-to-one connection between the self who writes and the self who lives, if Garréta, the person endowed with a passport and civil status who writes, isn't the person whose desires are being recounted, there is still a subjectivity that's evinced—the desire for language that is unwound throughout the text along with memory. This desire and subjectivity—how can one have desire without subjectivity?—do not originate from without the text, but from within it.

Garréta's desire for language, unlike the desire for and of women that constitutes *Pas un jour*'s narrative thread, cannot be unwound and recounted in the strict frame of a given moment: unlike these memories, this desire isn't something that belongs to the past, existing solely through recollection. Instead of being re-counted, it is still being counted, and is behind the recounting of these other desires. It passes through these episodes of a past and passed desire and makes itself known, in the writing of these encounters with women, as a very present desire. Over the course of the twelve sections that correspond to eleven episodes of desire with eleven women—one of the sections, entitled "I," is not devoted to a specific woman but to the American landscape as experienced on the road, and reads as an ode to the Interstate—Garréta paints portraits of very different women, from a high school crush to the stepdaughter of a writer, to an older colleague at a university. But they all have in common the way women stand in for language as surrogates: Garréta doesn't avoid describing sexual encounters in physical terms, and the book is filled with women's bodies, but the language she uses to describe their seduction (of and by her) and their coupling is as textual as it is sexual. She relates to and treats these women's bodies as if they were texts: what she pursues in pursuing them is an experience of their bodies as language. Garréta's writing doesn't suggest that language's corporeality is the same as human corporeality. Instead, in the wake of a language that seems inaccessible and absent, the human body stands in as an inadequate substitute for language's body.

In the closing line of the Ante Scriptum that introduces the novel, Garréta writes, "Car la vie est trop courte pour se résigner à lire des livres mal écrits et coucher avec des femmes qu'on n'aime pas" (16) [For life is too short to resign ourselves to reading poorly written books and sleeping with women we don't love] (8). In juxtaposing badly written books with unloved women, Garréta sets up a parallel between reading and sex, where an encounter with a textual body can be considered in the same light as a sexual encounter with a physical body—an erotic current subtends both. In the very next sentence that follows, which opens the section on the woman known as B*, Garréta continues this elision, writing: "Mémoire du corps: son inscription dans un espace, son ancrage dans une lumière" (17) [Memory of a body: inscribed in a given space, anchored in light] (9). Garréta chooses language that casts the human body in linguistic, textual terms, as something inscribed, and *ancrage* [anchoring] evokes its homophone *encrage* [inking], which evokes writing. Instead of choosing *souvenir* to refer to the memory of B*'s body, Garréta opts for the ambiguous *mémoire*, which, without an article to indicate its gender, could signify both *memory* (*une mémoire*) and *essay* (*un mémoire*). "Mémoire du corps" could mean both the body that is represented—remembered—and the body that represents.

The section continues with the narrator's analysis of her seduction by B* at a villa for academics where both are in residence. The narrator is attracted to B* and desires her body because it is the vessel for her language—it's B*'s language, her voice and the things she says with it, that are compelling:

> Tu y revenais, tu l'esquissais, cette nuit virtuelle avec B*, et il te semblait que tu aurais à son corps le même délice qu'à sa parole, qu'elle aurait au jeu de l'amour la même souplesse et fermeté qu'au jeu du langage et de la pensée, que le corps à corps aurait même vigueur sensuelle, même inventive vitalité. (22)

> [You kept coming back to it, sketching out this virtual night with B*, and it seemed to you that her body would offer the same delight as her words, that the lovemaking would have the same sensual vigor, the same inventive vitality.] (12)

The narrator desires B* insofar as her body is a figuration of her language, of the way B* speaks and writes and thinks. She imagines getting to the human body as a way of getting to language. The body is the promise of a language made tangible, translated into flesh—the same vitality that animates B*'s language is bound to be found in her body, even if it is not language's body itself.

This same will to access language through a woman's body, to treat human flesh as a window onto language that can be seen through, opened up, and entered into, continues throughout the novel. For example, with C*, the narrator identifies the source of desire as C*'s language: "Dans les phrases, dans le souffle qui porte les phrases, dans la voix qui profère les mots qu'avait-elle glissé, quel charme . . ." (29) [In the sentences, in the breath that carries the phrases, in the voice that pronounces the words, what had she slipped, what charm . . .] (17). The women that populate *Pas un jour* are idealized *récit-femmes*, women-narratives, the fusion of human corporeality and language, and they are appealing for that reason: the narrator gets to desire both the human and linguistic objects of her desire simultaneously. Even when Garréta writes an episode where the narrator desires and is desired by a woman whose language seems to lack the charm and virtuosity of B* and C*'s language, she is still able to anchor desire in language by turning the woman's body itself into language, as is the case with Z*, whom she bites hard enough to leave a mark:

> [Z*] la sent comme une brûlure sourde dans son dos, ou encore un trou dans sa peau, n'ouvrant sur rien, sans fond ni bord. Quand tu y songes, elle ressemble sans doute à toutes les empreintes que laissent des dents sur la chair vivante. [. . .] Tandis que vous cheminez, tu la presses soudain d'imaginer que ton avion s'écrase: la trace dont elle souhaite la disparition, de peur qu'elle la trahisse, et toi avec elle, cette trace, combien elle lui deviendrait chère quand aurait disparu celle qui l'imprima sur sa peau. [. . .] Tu lui dis encore de s'imaginer jour après jour la sachant s'évanouir, nuit après nuit plus pâle dans le miroir voilé d'un deuil tenu secret, la mémoire de toi s'effaçant enfin de son corps et ce signe palimpseste des sens qu'elle seule—qui ne le voit pas—, et toi seule—qui ne serais plus—auraient su déchiffrer, devenir lettre morte. (136–38)

> [[Z*] feels it like a dull burning in her back, or else a hole in her skin, opening onto nothing, with neither bottom nor edge. [. . .] While you stroll together, you suddenly urge her to imagine your plane crashing: the trace that she wants to disappear, out of fear that it betray her, and you also, that scar, how it will become dear to her when the one who imprinted it on her skin will have died. [. . .] You tell her again to imagine, day after day knowing it will vanish, night after night more pale in the mirror veiled by a mourning kept secret, the memory of you fading at last from her body and this palimpsest sign that she alone—who cannot see it—and you alone—who will no longer be—would have known how to decipher, will become a dead letter.] (83)

Though Z* is not endowed with a seductive, charming language, the narrator supplies her with that language through her body. Z* is transformed into a text: her body is treated as paper and the narrator's mouth as printer. Even while the mark is fresh, Garréta already pushes this scene of writing into the past, turning the still fresh *lettre* into a *lettre morte*, a letter cut off from its destination, which goes unheeded, unremarked—out of reach. Garréta builds her representation of Z*'s body as text, as a site of signification, on the condition that the narrator, in the authorial position, be dead, unable to enjoy it, unable to assume the position of reader vis-à-vis her creation.

The desire for language is articulated most clearly in section "D*," which treats most directly the activities of reading and writing. With D*, "une femme hétero" (42) [a straight woman] (24), the narrator doesn't desire her, but she allows herself to be desired by D*, giving in to D*'s demands for clandestine sex. In this episode, where their encounter is marked not by passion but by fatalistic submission, a retrospective sense of disgust, and the desire to forget that this ever happened, her desire is still present. This time, it's framed completely outside the human body. As an alternative to D*'s desire for the narrator's body and the botched story it results in, the narrator articulates instead her desire for texts:

> Tu achètes—car tu ne saurais résister au désir d'un volume qui te promet des transports de pensée ou d'imagination—des livres que tu ne te résous jamais à abandonner derrière toi (pourquoi te faut-il garder la trace de tes transports? pour les pouvoir réitérer?), tu te lestes de leur poids, et le désir du transport s'achève en malédiction de la possession et de l'accumulation des signes, des objets. Tu as fait franchir l'Atlantique dans les deux sens à des milliers de volumes; tu t'y es **courbatu les reins, rompu les bras**. Tu dissémines le fric que tu oublies de dépenser sur de multiples comptes, car tu n'as de désirs que pour des livres [. . .]. (37, my emphasis)

> [You buy—for you wouldn't be able to resist the desire of a volume that promises flights of fancy or thought—books you can never resolve to leave behind (why must you keep traces of your transports? To be able to reiterate them?), they weigh you down, and the desire to be transported ends in the accursed possession and accumulation of signs, objects. You have carried thousands of volumes both ways across the Atlantic; **you have the backaches and sore arms to prove it**. You scatter money that you forget to spend in multiple accounts, for you have desire only for books [. . .].] (21)

The parallels between the desire for books and the narrator's encounter with D* are striking. With D*, the narrator gives in to D*'s desire despite her better judgment, and this ambivalence is reflected in Garréta's writing about the narrator's giving in to her desire for books, something that results in *malédiction* and physical pain. Garréta's description of the narrator's body post-book mirrors her description of her body post-D*: "A l'issue de ces trois jours, des crampes irrémissibles dans le poignet, les doigts raides à ne plus pouvoir tenir un stylo, les reins courbatus, les bras, les épaules, la nuque douloureux, le dos lacéré" (46) [At the end of these three days, shattered, your wrist inexorably cramped, fingers stiff and unable to hold a pen any longer, loins sore, arm, shoulders, neck aching, back lacerated] (27). The repetition of sore arms and back links, once again, the act of reading, or taking in language, with the act of taking in a body. This link is reinforced by the notion of "accursed possession and accumulation of signs," which connects to Garréta's description of D*'s body as the site for the possession and accumulation of signs, part of a signifying economy.

The narrator chalks up her attraction to D* as having stemmed from the interplay of signs and semiotic possibility that D* had signified:

> A y resonger, une part cruciale de ton attraction pour D* a tenu à cela: la secrète captation des signes qui, au milieu d'une société aveugle et sourcilleuse tout ensemble, permettaient la reconnaissance initiatique du désir. [...] Tu ajouteras ici deux choses. Que D* n'a pas été la seule femme à t'offrir le vertige de cette communication ésotérique du désir. Et que, dans ce que la langue commune s'acharne à désigner sous le nom d'homosexualité, la part qui a eu toujours sur ton imagination l'emprise la plus forte n'est autre que la sémiotique et l'herméneutique si singulières qui découlent des situations de secret qu'elle peut impliquer. Enfin, c'est ce plaisir des signes, de leur labyrinthe où cacher et capter ce qui ne se peut dire, car hors la loi des codes, des langages institués et publics [...]. (42)

> [On second thought, a crucial part of your attraction for D* was tied to precisely that: the secret grasping of signs which, in the middle of a society both blind and supercilious, permitted the initiatory recognition of desire. [...] You will add two things here. That D* was not the only woman to offer you the vertigo of this esoteric communication of desire. And that, in what the common language persists in designating by the name of homosexuality, the part that always had the strongest pull over your imagination is none other than the semiotics and hermeneutics, so singular, that stem from situations of secrecy that homosexuality may involve. Finally, it's this pleasure of signs that you hold dear above all else, their labyrinth where one hides and captures that which cannot be said (for it is outside the law of normative codes and public languages) [...].] (24–25)

It isn't so much D*'s body in and of itself that is attractive, but the way her body acts as a signifier—something to be decoded and intercepted. The sexual act and its attendant pleasures are simply the physical manifestation of "ce plaisir des signes" [this pleasure of signs], of coming into close contact with a woman's body that is semiotic in its constitution. Without the body's semiotic potential, there is no spark of attraction, no impelling need to possess, no overwhelming desire.

Garréta takes seriously the model of textual erotics and erotic textuality that Roland Barthes, an intellectual influence,[74] puts forth in *Fragments d'un discours amoureux* [*A Lover's Discourse*] (1977) and *Le Plaisir du texte* [*The Pleasure of the Text*] (1973). *Pas un jour* combines *Le Plaisir*'s positing of the text as having corporeality, as being "an anagram of the body," its contours delineating "a body of bliss consisting solely of erotic relations,"[75] with the sort of semiotic sleuthing Barthes undertakes in *Fragments*, where he decodes the various signs that are housed in and produced by the object of his desire and recounts how this amorous discourse seduces him.

Time and time again throughout *Pas un jour*, Garréta sets up women as texts to be decoded, read, understood. Saussure puts forth the notion of the sign as made up of the *signifié* [signified] and the *signifiant* [signifier], and Wittig refers to the latter as the *charpente acoustique* [acoustic structure/skeleton].[76] For Garréta, each woman operates as a collection of signs, and her body is the signifier to the signified it contains—it is a *charpente charnelle* [fleshy structure]. Even in the episodes that don't recount a specifically sexual desire, the body still operates as the fleshy framework for a text. For example, section "L*" recounts an encounter with a ten- or eleven-year-old girl, the stepdaughter of a writer attending the same academic conference as the narrator. The girl has a crush on the narrator. While there's no real sexual tension or dynamic in play, the narrator describes herself, the object of desire, as having been textualized in the process of being desired: she's assumed the role of Prince Charming, a figure in a book come alive for the little girl (100–101; 60).

Even in section "I," which is about the American road and not about any human body, Garréta treats this geographic body in the same way, as a text to be read. The section features the narrator with her Rand McNally, mapping out the American landscape with proper names. She names the roads she takes (*I-95, New Jersey Turnpike, US-33* (75–76)), the cars she drives (*Pontiac Grand Am, Buick Regal, Chevrolet Lumina, Toyota Solara* (74)), the places she passes through (*la côte Est* [the East Coast], *les Appalaches* [the Appalachians], *New York, New Haven, Houseatonic* [sic], *Newark, Philadelphie, Virginie de l'Ouest* [West Virginia], *Marmet, Charleston, Ripley, Ohio, Pomeroy, Michigan, Illinois, Géorgie, Caroline, Chesapeake Bay, Tappan Zee Bridge* (75–77)). Gar-

---

74. Garréta, in conversation with me, recounted having attended the last season of his seminar at the Collège de France (December 1979–February 1980), before he died after being struck by a laundry truck.

75. Barthes, *The Pleasure of the Text*, 17.

76. Wittig, *Le Chantier littéraire*, 106.

réta traces the contours of this American body through the names of the roads the narrator has driven on, the cities that act as points of articulation for these roads. The narrator possesses and experiences America through the names she conjures up to capture it, these instances of language a way to touch the country and attach it to her memory, but also to recreate its body.

Garréta conceives of this section as an allegory, a sublime figure of desire: "Aurais-tu pu concerter plus belle allégorie, figure plus sublime du désir?" (83) [Could you have devised a more beautiful allegory, a more sublime figure of desire?] (49). The desire in question is for "la Grand Am de Pontiac, cette grand-dame ou âme américaine que tu ne cesses de désirer, objet de tes désirs les plus constants" (82) [the Pontiac Grand Am, that *grande dame* or *âme*, American soul that you never stop desiring, object of your most constant desires] (49). The narrator needs to name the American landscape, this allegorical figure of her desire, and she traces its topography—contact with the road an automotive analogue for making love to a woman's body—through descriptions of the places, which act as an overlay to this inventory of their names and the contours they sketch out.[77] It is as if these names have a talismanic power, and the narrator takes evident pleasure in invoking them, sounding out the un-French *charpente acoustique* of these words in her French mouth. As with the other, humanly embodied objects and subjects of desire in the novel, Garréta's America is an assemblage of names, a text to be read, and in that sense is as much woman as the other initials who stand in for the flesh-and-blood women of the other episodes.

Pas un jour exemplifies Derrida's oft-quoted dictum that *Il n'y a pas de hors-texte*, that there is nothing outside of text,[78] which certainly proves to be true for desire in the novel. Here, desire is inseparable from language, from textuality. As much as desire acts on the senses and the body, it does so with signification at stake: corporeality is tied to signification, desire to reading and writing. In *Pas un jour*, the body only matters insofar as it can read and be read, signify and be interpreted. But the passionate encounters with these women-texts are all accessed retrospectively, and Garréta seeks to contain

---

77. One could criticize Garréta here and see an uncomfortably close parallel between this charting out of the American body and the ways place-names bear the traces of a both imperialist and patriarchal conquering of "virgin territory." The white conquerors and explorers come in, raping native women and giving the geographical features of the conquered country sexualized names, such as the Grand Teton mountain in Wyoming, which means literally "Big Breast." The ex-French colonies and French territories are especially rich in this regard: e.g., Les Mamelles [Breasts], in the Seychelles, Trou de Madame Coco [Madame Coco's Hole] in Guadeloupe. For more on the erotics of place names, see Kristin Graves, "Mapping *La Belle Créole*" (PhD diss., Yale University, 2014).

78. Derrida, *De la grammatologie*, 227.

them temporally in another moment, another carefully delineated frame. She casts the narrator as a solitary figure who stays up at night, revisiting these past desires and textual-sexual moments in those quiet hours when no one else is awake. Garréta writes this solitude explicitly into the text as she has the narrator describe herself as wearing headphones in the middle of the night, planted in front of her computer, the machine into which she writes all these desires: a portrait of the modern writer (73–75; 43–44). Her desire for the pleasure of signs is a solitary one, channeled through the absence that these women, these instances of signs and language have left behind. The Garrétian writer has only the traces of language to remember.

The desire she has for a language lost, a desire for something absent, becomes clearer when *Ciels liquides,* Garréta's second novel, is taken into consideration: elegiac in tone, it directly evokes the loss of language. As we move now toward *Ciels liquides,* what I want to take away from this examination of *Pas un jour* is the intensity of this desire for language, rendered equivalent to erotic desire, and the melancholic frame within which this desire circulates. Looking at *Ciels liquides* will take this desire for language outside the human realm, and place the desire that emerges in Garréta's writing alongside Sarraute and Wittig's in conceiving of the body of language as being something other than human.

Ciels liquides, like *Sphinx,* is narrated by a young student, but here the anonymous narrator studies political science instead of theology, and we know the student is male. The novel is divided into two narratives: the frame narrative, in italic type, places the narrator at his family's country home, inside its cellar, with limited food and supplies, waiting out some sort of nuclear apocalypse that has left him the sole survivor. This frame narrative begins the novel and is set in the present. The framed narrative, in regular type, recounts the narrator's life before the cataclysmic event. It recounts how this member of France's elite, slated to become part of the next generation of leaders, loses his language when he's stricken by aphasia. He first suffers gaps in his vocabulary, no longer able to name the things he used to be able to, then becomes incapable of reading or writing, and finally entirely loses his capacity to speak and to understand what others say to him. *Ciels liquides* is a tale of language lost, of language found, and of what other things are lost along the way.

Garréta pays close attention to the physical body in its language-less state, and, throughout the novel, she continually associates the corporeal with the linguistic and conceives of the narrator's desire for language as a bodily one. What distinguishes the staging of language vis-à-vis the human body in this novel versus that of *Pas un jour* is the way the drama of the relationship between human and language, between language and corporeality as it is commonly understood, plays out primarily within the narrator's body in *Ciels liquides*. The narrator's body is considered the source and originary site of language, and language is concentrated within that particular body in a way that departs from the proliferation of corporeal sites of language we find in *Pas un jour*. *Ciels liquides* can be read as a laborious progression from a somewhat instrumentalizing view of language where a human engages in a deeply corporeal, physical relationship with language (but takes language as an object and something that can be incorporated or assimilated into the human body), to a view of language that treats it as autonomous, other, non-human, although close to the human.

At the beginning of the novel, before the narrator's fall from linguistic grace, he gorges himself on language and his desire to learn language is akin to a physical hunger: "Je passai des mois entiers à me gaver de nourritures et d'idiomes exotiques" [I spent entire months stuffing myself with exotic food and languages].[79] Language is described as something that can be taken in and absorbed by the body. Garréta continues this association between language and body, or more accurately, between language and a certain bodily assimilation of it, by describing the earliest stage of the narrator's aphasia as one where his mind is likened to a page and his thoughts to ink:

> Je parvins à cacher quelque temps cette infirmité récurrente dont j'éprouvais plus de honte que de peur. C'était un soudain trou d'ombre, une tache d'encre que je sentais poindre et s'étendre puis se résorber avant qu'une vague de nuit ne vienne recouvrir les vocables et ne me contraigne d'interrompre la conversation engagée, la phrase commencée.
>
> Je rusais un temps: prévenant la lame obscure, je renvoyais à mon interlocuteur sa parole, répétant très vite ses derniers mots avant qu'ils ne fussent eux aussi engloutis, ou bien encore laissais choir sur la page trois gouttes de cette encre soudain inondant mon crâne. (27)
>
> [For some time, I managed to hide this recurring infirmity about which I felt more shame than fear. It was a sudden pocket of shadow, an ink stain that I felt arrive and expand and then diminish before a wave of light came

---

79. Garréta, *Ciels liquides*, 15. All subsequent references will be made in-text. Some might object to my translating *idiome* as language, but I agree with Derrida, who writes regarding this distinction: "I do not know where we can find *internal* and *structural* features in order to distinguish rigorously between a language, a dialect, and an idiom." Derrida, *Monolingualism of the Other*, 8.

to cover the root words and force me to interrupt the conversation entered into, the sentence begun.

I tried to trick people for a time: anticipating the dark blade, I returned to my interlocutor their speech, repeating their last words very quickly before they too were swallowed up, or else let fall on the page three drops of that sudden ink inundating my skull.]

Already, here, Garréta moves away from the idea of language as part of the human or as able to become part of the human body, and emphasizes language's alterity: with ink on a page, one can maintain a distinction between the paper and the ink that is indelibly on the paper, whereas food, once it is broken down by the digestive system and absorbed into the blood stream, can no longer be recognized as food as such, but has effectively become part of the body. Language and human are figured as different from each other, and as the novel progresses, this difference becomes more pronounced, and the two are granted, respectively, more autonomy from each other. Even just a few pages later, for example, Garréta describes the narrator's inability to produce words (the next step in his aphasia, after first being unable to understand them), in quite Sarrautian terms: "En marchant, je toussai par deux fois, tâchant de racler au fond de ma gorge des lambeaux de langue" (30) [While walking, I coughed twice, trying to scrape away shreds of language from the depths of my throat]. Language isn't simply something the body produces through the use of one's vocal cords and mouth, but it has a physical, material presence and exists within the body as a foreign body, like one of Sarraute's earlier figurations of language's autonomy.

When the narrator's aphasia completely sets in, his parents hospitalize him. The medical team, in attempting to diagnose him, treats the narrator's language-less, mute body as a text to be analyzed: they put electrodes on his skull and attach them to a machine that reads and records the signals his brain sends out; they treat his skull as a sheet of paper onto which they inscribe circles and arrows in red pencil—a medical code only they are able to read. The narrator rebelliously rubs off these inscriptions and resists being treated as if he were language. While hospitalized, the narrator has no freedom, as he is confined to a bed where he is constantly surveilled. But even as he loses the capacity to move freely, he gains a new sort of freedom: he's no longer subject to the social and academic responsibilities he shouldered when he was a promising young student. This liberation from parental ambitions is concretized when a mysterious artist named Céleste comes to visit him at the hospital and kidnaps him—we aren't given any sense of her motivation or rationale or of how she knows about him. Céleste undoes the restraints that had been put on the narrator to prevent him from erasing the marks the doctors made on him, dresses him, and takes him to her artist's loft where she feeds him, sleeps with him, and works on a sculpture of an angel.

The nameless narrator is thus the mute witness to Céleste's representation of a celestial creature whose purpose is to be a messenger—to carry a text, in other words—as the angel has been figured and understood in Christian theology.[80] In her studio, she has a body without language and a body that stands in for language. Céleste takes the angel, made of wood and cloth, and has the narrator accompany her to the Seine where she proceeds to try to hang the angel from a bridge—it's unclear what sort of statement this is meant to convey to the Parisians and tourists who would see it—but she falls to her death when a gust of wind sweeps the angel, and her along with it, into the river's waters.

Céleste's death is a turning point in the novel: the narrator is completely alone in the world, cut off from society by his inability to speak and be spoken to, identity-less and without any material resources. This first moment of complete alienation and solitude anticipates the post-nuclear holocaust world with which the novel begins, and reverses it: the novel begins with the narrator who has language but no world to live in; this turning point places the narrator in the world but with no language with which to navigate it. In the second part of this framed narrative, the narrator follows the city workers who fish the angel out of the river and take it to a cemetery. He discovers an empty vault in the cemetery, which he makes his home—a foreshadowing of his post-apocalyptic existence in a lifeless world. He then learns to provide for himself, in a way. He collects flowers from graves, sells them to passersby, and exchanges what coins he receives for bread, depending on other people to count out the proper amount of money for him. He stumbles across some paper and proceeds to begin making rubbings of the tombstones that surround him, able to procure and possess language in that way, and to "write" by reproducing text. Even if he cannot understand what he is copying, he understands that it is language. After he starts collecting these instances of mortuary language, regaining language in an impoverished way, he crosses paths with a man whom he recognizes as his doppelganger. He follows this other man who has his body and face but, unlike him, is endowed with language. He tails him from his workplace, the morgue, to a brothel, and then witnesses his double's decapitation. The narrator takes advantage of his double's death to take the dead man's clothes and wallet and the identity that the papers inside the wallet promise him. Armed with the congruence of his own features, he starts working at the morgue, cleaning and cataloguing bodies and assisting

---

80. *Angel* derives from the Greek *angelos* via the Latin *angelus*, both meaning "messenger."

in autopsies, but possesses this other identity as incompletely as he possesses the language of his rubbings.

The narrator at this point, with his rubbings and job, discovers desire, in the form of a sunbather whose gender Garréta doesn't reveal. The sunbather chooses to frequent the cemetery to sunbathe and the narrator falls in love with the beauty of this body, eventually working up the courage to approach them. He gives the beloved body a rubbing as a way of making contact and communicates through gestures, sounds, and laughter. Emboldened by the regularity of the interactions that follow, the narrator decides to declare his passion, but, on the chosen day, the sunbather does not show up as is their habit. Crushed by his love object's absence, the narrator goes to work only to discover the sunbather's body in the morgue on the coroner's table.

This discovery is a world-shattering one for the narrator. Confronted with the sunbather's lifeless body, the narrator recognizes the body that Céleste's angel was modeled after: "Sur le billard d'acier froid, dans la lumière étale, gisait l'ange, son cadavre de chair, son modèle, sa statue" (143) [On the cold steel operating table, in the still light, lay the angel, its fleshly cadaver, its model, its statue]. Céleste's angel, as a sculpture, had led the narrator to his cemetery home, and as a living body, had visited the narrator in it. The narrator witnesses the angel's autopsy in a state "sans vie ni voix" (144) [of lifelessness, voicelessness], and identifies deeply with the dead body, feeling every cut made into the cadaver in his own body:

> Je sens à mesure de la dissection de l'ange tous mes viscères, veines et artères ligaturées, ligaments sectionnés, un à un déroulés, décollés, séparés, extraits de leurs gangues membraneuses, pesés, leurs replis fouillés par le couteau, s'en aller de moi. (145)

> [With the dissection of the angel, I feel leaving me all my viscera, ligated veins and arteries, cut ligaments, one by one uncoiled, detached, separated, extracted from their membranous envelopes, weighed, their folds excavated by the knife.]

It's as if the angel's body were his own, and this empathic projection of his senses onto the angel's now insensate body can be seen as a visceral manifestation of the narrator's desire for language—the angel exists to be a message—and this desire for language is for an embodied language, as seen in the narrator's falling in love with the angel's body. In this scene, which is a sort of reciprocal vivisection, Garréta's relationship to the angel parallels Wittig's *j/e*'s passionate relationship to *tu* in *Le Corps lesbien*. But Garréta's version sees no resurrection. This mutual dismemberment, rather than leading to life, leads to as absolute a separation as possible from the angel—this language-body—and the narrator is deprived of the reintegration that Wittig narrates.

The angel's death is a devastating one and when the narrator returns to his cemetery home, he discovers that his vault has been razed. The framed narrative in regular type comes to an end with the narrator wandering around homeless, bereft of language, identity, and love—things we take to be foundational to being human. He comes across a train station, and, while looking at the signs that indicate the trains' destinations, all his language suddenly comes back to him when he's able to recognize the name of the town he used to go to every summer, where his family has a country home. This is the seam that connects the two narratives, and in making the leap from this retrospective narrative to the present, post-apocalyptic one, Garréta suggests that the narrator took that train to his family's country home only to have the whole world go up in nuclear flames.

The frame narrative, which punctuates the framed one at irregular intervals, is a much simpler one in terms of plot: nothing happens—it's the narrator's monologue to himself in a grimmer version of Noah's Ark where he waits out disaster, but, unlike Noah, has no company save himself. The narrator tries to pass the time by debating with himself whether it's safe to venture outside the cellar. In his deliberation, he becomes convinced of someone else's presence, some malicious entity who's watching him, waiting for and wanting his death:

> *Il y a là dans ma nuit auprès de moi un autre qui, malgré la nuit, me voit et se joue de moi. [. . .] Il veille quand je dors et me souffle mes rêves. Dans la nuit je suis en son pouvoir. Autour de ma tête il resserre un étau. Il veut s'en emparer. Son souffle est sur moi. Il m'étouffe. Je me débats.* (163)

> [There, next to me, in the night, is another who, despite the darkness, sees me and dupes me. [. . .] He watches when I sleep and blows my dreams to me. In the night I am in his power. He tightens a vice around my head. He wants to seize it. His breath is on me. He suffocates me. I struggle.]

This other presence is a breath that blows out the narrator's precious matches, his only light source after the last light bulb goes out—a breath that wants to remove the narrator's breath and keep him in darkness (165).

It's unclear who this maleficent other is. Rather than try to identify this other as a specific, singular other, I think it would be more productive to take this other as protean, able to assume multiple forms. The language of tightening a vice around the narrator's head and taking possession of it suggests that this other is none other than his doppelganger, here to get his head back as revenge for the narrator's appropriation of his identity. Or, perhaps, it is the angel, turned malevolent. In the narrator's past life, before his language was restored, the angel was a desirable figure, and a benevolent one. In this apocalyptic time and space, this other presence reads like that of an angel of death who has come to take the narrator's life, who desires his body (and particularly the head, where the processes of speaking, reading, and interpreting take place) in a fatal inversion of the narrator's desire for the other angel's body.

In this terrible world with language but no one with whom to share it, the narrator resigns himself to his imminent death after leaving the cellar and discovering that the outside world holds no life or possibility of it. What follows, in the final pages of the novel, is the narrator's inventory of all the objects that inhabit the cellar with him, which will be the objects of his last will and testament, the legacy he leaves behind. The novel ends mid-sentence, with the narrator's breath suddenly cut off, when the other presence, this angel of death, takes over: "*Il y a l'ovale émaillé d'un ci   *" (180) [*There is the oval adorned with a ci   *].[81] The book ends in the middle of a word. The abruptness with which the text ends is disturbing: we witness the text's cutting off as the narrator witnessed his double's decapitation. Garréta seems to be suggesting that the reader is the narrator's double, inhabiting his *je*, his *I*, the way the narrator inhabited his double's identity. And just as he witnessed his double's death, the reader is also present at his demise, which can be read as a metaphor for the text's termination.[82] Rather than allow the reader to have a quiescent end to the novel and to our reading experience, Garréta cuts language off violently and suddenly, the way Céleste and her angel fall, and the artist and her creation are removed from the narrator as Garréta and *Ciels liquides* are removed from us.

Ciels liquides features an extraordinarily complex plot that operates through the dynamic of doubling: the narrator and his double, the angel and its double, the narrator and the angel, the rubbing that is a double for the tombstone off which it is taken, the double narrative structure, and the reader as a double for the narrator. In the midst of all this doubling, the angel emerges as a crucial figure and is an allegory for the embodiment of language. The angel's appearance introduces the narrator to desire, a desire for language as much as for the sunbathing body—it's only after "speaking" to the angel that the narrator feels compelled to confess his passion. It's through an

---

81. Spaces were inserted to retain the visual impact of this ending. This sentence has no period.

82. Perhaps the maleficent other is none other than the reader.

approximation of language that inchoate desire is given a concrete form. The angel as a site of language is more desirable than the angel as body alone. The narrator, in desiring contact with the angel before he knows it is the angel, desires a body that provides him with the first instance of conversation in the novel in his aphasic state: "La conversation était engagée; il n'était que de la soutenir" (132) [The conversation had been started; it was only a question now of sustaining it]. The cruel irony of Garréta's novel is that this conversation, with and in language, is unsustainable. What the narrator experiences as a moment of real engagement and intimate communication—"le ton devint très vite plus intime" (132) [the tone very quickly became more intimate]— gives way to the angel's death, which then gives way to the restoration of the narrator's language.

It's essential that the narrator's interlocutor is the angel because the angel, as a messenger, is an entity whose sole function is to carry language. Even though the sunbather may not seem to be the angel insofar as the angel was a sculpture, the sunbather is the angel's cadaver and its origin, its beginning and end. The narrator treats the sunbather as the angel, and so I do as well. The sequence of the angel's death and the narrator's subsequent restoration to language points to a zero-sum economy of language and desire that Garréta sets up: you can either have your angel (the body of language, the incarnated message-text) or your language (the ability to use language, to speak, read, and write). The narrator's re-entry into language—the narrator's becoming a writer—is thus built upon his mourning the loss of the angel. For him as for Garréta, to write is to always write after a passionate encounter—with the angel, in *Ciels liquides,* with the women-narratives, in *Pas un jour.* Garréta, unlike Sarraute and Wittig, never gets to have her language and eat it too.

At this juncture, I'd like to turn to an essay Garréta wrote on the invisibility of French lesbian writing entitled "In Light of Invisibility," which is instructive on two counts: first, it indicates how we might be able to read *Ciels liquides* and *Pas un jour* together, as coherent and interconnected parts of her corpus, despite how different each novel is in tone, construction, and plot. And second, it ends with a surprising and unanticipated invocation of the angel, which, when read as a gloss of *Ciels liquides,* serves to bring us back to language as an autonomous, corporeal entity, whose autonomy and corporeality are at the heart of a poetics of unbecoming that spans the twentieth century into the twenty-first through Sarraute, Wittig, and Garréta's respective *corps-à-corps* with language.

This essay was published in 1996, six years after *Ciels liquides,* as part of the published proceedings of a conference that had taken place at the Yale French Department the previous year, *Same Sex/Different Text?: Gay and Les-*

bian Writing in French. This issue of *Yale French Studies* takes up the question of whether homosexual writing exists, and if so, what constitutes it.[83] Garréta thwarts the question and writes against the idea of a homosexual essence or gay subjectivity in literature, arguing that "the empirical self and the writing (or reading) self are not identical; fiction is the realm where identities, far from being reinforced, may be displaced."[84] As we saw in Chapter 3, Garréta is averse to the idea of the self as the site of subjecthood and identity. We can thus treat the distinction she makes here between the empirical self and the writing (or reading) self as follows: the empirical self corresponds to a subject endowed with an identity, whereas the writing/reading self denotes subjectivity as the site of experience but not identity—subjectivity without subjecthood. The displacement that she sees fiction as capable of effecting, to anti-identitarian effect, is enacted exemplarily in the splitting and doubling we find in *Ciels liquides*. The essay thus brings together both *Ciels liquides* and *Pas un jour*, speaking to the continuous, consistent rejection of the subject and of identity evident in Garréta's work. Present in an early work like *Ciels liquides* are the seeds for what would become a very explicit critique of subjecthood and identity in *Pas un jour*.

The essay elucidates what I've outlined in this chapter as Garréta's version of the passionate relationship with a living and embodied language through a rather surprising turn toward the angelic as it comes to a close:

> The contemporary passion for unmooring all our categories from their metaphysical foundations seems to have given rise to a desperate and equally violent attempt at consolidating self-identifications: the text should resemble its author; readers should be able to recognize themselves in the text. Such mirrorings are fantasmatically invested with the power to anchor and insure self-identical subjects. [. . .]
>
> I have often wondered at the insistent recurrence of a figure in queer fictions, from Proust to Genet to Marie-Claire Blais's *L'ange de la solitude*, the figure of the angel. It is said that Sodom and Gomorrah were destroyed because their inhabitants did not recognize the angels, mistaking them for mere bodies. Bearers of light and disincarnate, luminous, and intangible, angels displace the body/light equation that commands visibility. The annunciation of the Word they perform precedes its incarnation. They are there to show that there is more to vision than not being blind and that the

---

83. Mahuzier et al., "Editors' Preface."
84. Garréta, "In Light of Invisibility," 212–13.

passage from the transcendent realm of the word to the immanent realm of bodies requires more than a mirror.[85]

This passage provides a gloss for Garréta's own *Ciels liquides* and its angel(s). She takes the biblical tale of Sodom and Gomorrah as a cautionary tale, a warning about the dangers of misrecognition, of not seeing the Word contained in the angelic body, but also of another type of misrecognition, that of seeing self where it isn't. The angel works to disrupt our usual sense of optics and identification. The angelic body, figured here, is light, whereas the human body isn't light but merely reflects it. The reflected light enables us to see and apprehend the human body, to believe in its incarnation and identify it. The angelic body, on the other hand, is not apprehended through vision or reflection, but through annunciation—a linguistic act. (Hence the narrator's inability to ever establish physical contact with the angel's body, save in death, when this body is no longer language's, but simply a human body.) And in language, we cannot see ourselves—"the passage from the transcendent realm of the word to the immanent realm of bodies requires more than a mirror." What we should see instead is language, and, I would add, the bodies of a transcendent language.

It makes sense that Garréta invokes the untouchable, intangible angel to speak of language, where Wittig invokes the touchable, tangible goddess. The angel is that which even in its presence is always absent or removed because of its provenance from the spiritual realm. The angel never stays for longer than it takes to speak its message—it embodies "le dévidage de la mémoire dans le cadre strict d'un moment déterminé" of *Pas un jour*. And it does not desire, it is only desired. The Wittigian goddess, on the other hand, is not constrained to a determined moment and desires the human in the space of a passionate present.

Garréta's writing, which bears witness to her deep desire for language, reveals a language that can be found in (but not of) human bodies, as in *Pas un jour*, where human bodies are desirable in their capacity to give the writer an experience (however partial or limited) of language. By invoking the angel, Garréta posits language as autonomous and other, unable to be conflated with the human or taken as an extension of the human (the women-texts in *Pas un jour* aren't to be taken for language's real bodies). Her desire for language is a desire deflected—mediated through human corporeality and time—and it is particularly keen because it mourns the loss of a language that is cut off as soon as it's experienced. Garréta punishes her narrator for mistaking the angel

---

85. Garréta, 213.

as a body by cutting him off from the angel. She does not seem to be able to indulge the desire for language the way Sarraute and Wittig do.

Sarraute follows and patiently waits for language, accepting it in its intermittence and capriciousness, and experiences what we might call a plenitude of subjectivity in those moments that language appears for her in its living- and embodied-ness. Wittig wrestles with language, embraces it and tears it apart and receives its caresses, experiencing in her contact with language what she calls *dérangement*. But Garréta appears to cut her own desire off short, in what seems to be an attempt to prevent it from having to enter into a present that will inevitably be lost, irretrievably turning into the past. The immanence of human bodies, time, and subjectivity cannot withstand the transcendent, angelic body of language, which *is*, which doesn't reflect. The human always falls short of language. If Wittig presents a theology of the present with her exuberant goddesses and offers herself to a goddess, Garréta presents a theology of anticipation and of mourning, of after. As with the women-texts of *Pas un jour*, the angel-body-text of *Ciels liquides* is experienced in its absence or loss, which can be read into *Ciels liquides*'s dedication, "To the Lost One."

Garréta addresses a language that is lost because it was desired and experienced, and could not be held on to. This sense of loss and the destructive nature of desire goes all the way back to *Sphinx*, where one of the first bodies Garréta ever wrote into being—that of the dancer A***—is also taken away from the narrator once they've had the opportunity to realize their desire and the narrator has had the chance to experience A***'s body. It's hardly a coincidence that A*** is rendered a vessel for language, in this case, African American language. In Garréta's writing, one can never seem to hold on to what one desires, be it a human body, or language itself. The two are never far apart, caught up as they are in the same circuit of desire. And therein lies the conundrum: as a writer, she desires language, to touch it and work with it in the *chantier littéraire* in order to produce a text, but to do so is to lose it. Garréta's writing, then, is always in memoriam. But because language is absent for Garréta, it becomes present for us, and there is no reason that readers need to adhere to her melancholic, privative, ascetic theology. Indeed, as seen in Chapter 3, through the very act of reading her texts, we unbecome because we are encountering the body of the language Garréta uses in all its materiality and vitality.[86] The text's existence makes it possible for us to experience language for ourselves, with as many types of relationship to language possible as there are subjectivities, each one a sign that we are alive with language.

---

86. While my discussion of *Pas un jour* has concentrated on mining the content to elucidate Garréta's view of language, the novel, like *Sphinx* and *La Décomposition*, operates on a formal, material level through her use of the pronoun *tu* to make subjecthood uninhabitable. See my "Autofiction Infiltrated."

From Sarraute, where language is our guide, to Wittig, where language is the *amante* whom we are to love with a deadly, vital passion, to Garréta, where language is an angel who might take our breath away, each of these writers presents language as something vital with which we can be in a dizzying, *dérangeant* relationship, even if, in the case of Garréta, that relationship is always filtered through loss. But, as Alfred Tennyson famously wrote, "'Tis better to have loved and lost than never to have loved at all."[87] It is better to have been consumed and transformed by love, opened by and to the other, than to remain imperviously, implacably oneself, a self contained and made by identity. It is better to unbecome someone than to become something. Our unbecoming as humans depends on the body of language: we have access to unbecoming language only insofar as we have access to it as a body, which, in its non-humanness, is able to make us become more than the fragmented categories of humanity that we have been told make up who we are. Perhaps we can see Sarraute, Wittig, and Garréta's works as a call to love and be loved by language: they all invite us to lose ourselves in a passionate *corps-à-corps* with language and unbecome, at least for a while.

---

87. Alfred Tennyson, "In Memoriam A. H. H. OBIIT MDCCCXXXIII: 27."

CONCLUSION

Unbecoming Language

I'VE BROUGHT TOGETHER the works of Sarraute, Wittig, and Garréta as a collective corpus of writing against difference, against identity, and of writing for language, for an experience of language that enables us to unbecome. To use Sarrautian vocabulary, each of these writers works to strip language of the socially determined and deterministic meaning it is clothed in. They denude language, enabling readers to have a fresh experience of a living, vibrant language not already domesticated by the dictates of the social order. In the nudist colony of their literary production, Sarraute, Wittig, and Garréta's writing invites us to also strip ourselves bare of our identity clothes.

Sarraute does this through exploiting rapidly shifting pronouns and situating the action of her narrative inside the psyche, where she can bypass the identification and the interpellation of subjectivity as a subject—the corralling of persons into identity categories—that is an inevitable consequence of living and participating in our current regime of sociality, or life as we know it.

Wittig takes on a less interiorized perspective than Sarraute and views her texts as Trojan horses, literary weapons to be deployed against the difference at the heart of forms of oppression like sexism and racism. Like Sarraute, Wittig exploits pronouns to forcibly unseat the masculine subject from its position of presumed universality and replace it with the feminine or neutral as a corrective to a false universalism.

Garréta pushes her readers to remove their identity clothes by writing texts that cut off the usual processes of readerly identification with characters—narrating and narrated subjects—and turn against readers. Her texts make it impossible to slip inside as unobtrusive readers. In them, it's uncomfortable to hold on to the idea of the reader as a subject endowed with identity: she imputes to the reader's identity repugnant views or makes the reader the object of a hostile narrator's abuse, for instance. She drives us to let go of our identity if we do not want to be interpellated in an alienating way by her narratives.

Examining Sarraute, Wittig, and Garréta individually, there are many possibilities for what their legacies might be, what innovations and contributions they are or will be remembered for. We could point to Sarraute's modernist experiments in redefining what constitutes a novel by eliminating clearly delineated characters and plots, which have characterized and continue to characterize the form, and by pursuing a realism that bears little resemblance to the realist novels that came before. We could take her tropisms as a way of exploring hidden recesses of human psychology and previously unexplored realms of human relationality. We could admire Wittig's feminist resolve to create a lesbian corpus that created a new language to wrest universality away from the masculine and destroy gender with the very language that creates it. We could marvel at her writing's intertextuality and her uncanny ability to cannibalize the canon. We could laud the elaborate construction of Garréta's works and the deployment of constraints that garnered her a place in the Oulipo. We could point to her ability to write with classical language about modern and contemporary things. We could see her as a bold voice in an otherwise rather shallow field of queer French literature.

Sarraute, Wittig, and Garréta are extraordinary writers in their own right. But in *Unbecoming Language,* the point has been to take them together. This is not to devalue their individual corpora or say that they cannot stand, or stand less firmly, on their own. Rather, it's to show how, when their works are read together as a collective corpus of writing, an original poetics of unbecoming emerges that would otherwise remain submerged: Sarraute's language makes Wittig's possible, and Wittig's language in turn opens up anti-identitarian possibilities for Garréta.

The foundation for this unbecoming poetics is the affective and corporeal relationship they have with language, itself an embodied and vital entity. Their embodied, sensuous encounter with language's body forces a confrontation with the deadened and mortified language of a social and political order that has used language to build structures of inequality through the construction of identity categories. In their writing, language is not merely embodied, it is unbecoming—it drives what I see as the political process of shedding the categories and the identities that we've been coerced into becoming.

I want to reprise Chapter 4 to insist on Sarraute, Wittig, and Garréta's affirmation of the non-humanness of language's corporeality. Sarraute, Wittig, and Garréta do not equate language with the human, and despite what might seem like anthropomorphizing representations of language, its corporeality is always rendered other, imbued with a non-human dimension. In Sarraute, that non-human takes the form of the animal, vegetal, and microbial. In Wittig, the non-human takes the form of a *tu* that, even as it is human, is more than that—goddess, animal, spore. As with Sarraute, the human is an unstable metaphor and it cannot be an exclusive point of reference. And in Garréta, the angel displaces language from being considered in human terms, and the human cannot adequately account for or stand in for language.

By maintaining the non-human corporeality of language, Sarraute, Wittig, and Garréta create and hold open the space of difference between language and the human. Their treatment of language as both corporeal and non-human challenges us to rethink both our relationship to language (to stop reifying and instrumentalizing it and make room for an affective and sensate relationship to and with it) and our conception of the human body. Unlike *écriture féminine*, where the (feminine) body is what is written, turned into language through the workings of the libido, with desire operating at an unconscious level, in this unbecoming poetics, desire is consciously directed toward an embodied language that responds to and receives that desire. Writing emerges as the product of that encounter. Each of these poetics preserves a form of difference, or has difference as a motor. In *écriture féminine*, the operative difference is that of sexual difference—it's the feminine libido that is capable of transforming human corporeality into language. In the poetics of unbecoming, sexual difference—and any kind of intrahuman difference, as a difference created discursively by humans and reinforced socially—is rejected, and the difference that is foregrounded is instead the difference between human and language.

By shifting difference from the difference between various categories of humanity to this human-language difference, which is grounded in an experience of language as a living body, Sarraute, Wittig, and Garréta's writing takes pressure off the human body as a site of differentiation between humans by treating the human body as a body made truly universal in its relationship with and to language. Language does not distinguish between the categories of human as humans do. The human body, in its contact with language's body, is stripped of the layers of identity clothes it wears. To be with language as Sarraute, Wittig, and Garréta are with language in their writing, is to unbecome.

It's difficult to process the idea of language having a body because of how easily we produce language—we open up our mouths, and there it is. We command our fingers to type or to grip a pen and move it around on paper, and there language is. Sarraute's laborious approach to the tropism rightly signals the intense effort it takes to become conscious of language as an autonomous body, and to relate to it as such. Within the formalized context of literature, we pay increased attention to language, but even that is insufficient and we must assume a Sarrautian level of meticulous regard. The Russian formalists paid attention to language in order to render it strange as poetic language, but that attention to the materiality of language resulted not in a sense of language as embodied and living, but rather, as a vehicle for meaning.

Meticulous regard is not enough to reveal language's living body. That body cannot be found in the greetings we exchange, the grocery lists we jot down hurriedly, those manifold and seemingly omnipresent instances of language that only reinforce categories and identity and (intrahuman) difference. I would argue that just as biological life-forms have specific habitats—e.g., some fish can live in fresh water, and others only in salt water—language does as well. Language is able to be alive and embodied in a particular kind of habitat, the literary one created and preserved by Sarraute, Wittig, and Garréta, which we might describe as a habitat of innovation. They are all innovative writers writing against convention. It's in that writing against the literary flow, that push to do something new with language, that language becomes accessible as something autonomous and alive. The poetics of unbecoming, the becoming body of language that makes the human unbecome, occurs within a literary space of experimentation and innovation. But just because this space is rarefied—the conventional is conventional insofar as it dominates—doesn't mean its ramifications for how we might rethink human embodiment are any less important.

Desiring and having a passionate encounter with a body that isn't human opens up the radical possibility of not having embodiment, desire, and relation determined by a difference that leads immediately to hierarchy. In the difference between human and language, what kind of hierarchy could one establish? Hierarchies are only able to operate insofar as the two terms being compared are taken to have something in common, to share some common quality. Hierarchies of race and sex only hold insofar as the different races and sexes are recognized as human, despite the dehumanizing treatment those deemed inferior are subjected to. The poetics of unbecoming insists on a difference that cannot be recuperated for hierarchy, on subjectivity that relinquishes the subjecthood that falls into hierarchical modes of being.

With Sarraute, her quest to find the tropism sets up language as an antisocial body that draws the human subject out of its sharply delineated contours of self that sociality requires, and brings it into a living reality that is limitless, turning the subject into a universe without contours. For her, finding and coming into contact with this living language is an expansive, universal experience that breaks open the self and the world to introduce an infinite universe in their stead. Wittig takes this living language and sets it up as one half of a pair of *amantes* where the human-*amante* breaks open the language-*amante* and vice versa so that the two can come together and be reintegrated as bodies liberated from the oppression of phallocentric culture and influence. The transformation that results from this new and regenerative way of experiencing language necessarily entails a new way of experiencing the body. For Wittig, making love to and with language, with a violence that enacts the death of old language, brings both human and language into a new life and reality. This dynamism embodies the utopian spirit that animates her literary works and is a product of her participation in the revolutionary movements of May '68 and the MLF. Garréta's experience of language lacks the exuberant togetherness and community that Wittig's utopian writing expresses, and the violence that permeates her writing does not lead to a blissful afterlife for language. Instead, Garréta's writing shows two possibilities for language: either a language to be desired that remains intact in the potential of unrealized desire, or a language that's been desired and encountered, made love to, known, and as a result, lost. But reading texts even as melancholic as Garréta's still enables the reader to enter into the *chantier littéraire* and into a relationship with the language to be found therein.

These three writers present three different visions of language as a living, embodied entity: Sarraute's language is alive, but vulnerable and constantly endangered—its life could be snuffed out at any moment—while Wittig and Garréta offer opposing versions of language's afterlife. Wittig's language is triumphantly resurrected, its body impervious to violence and dismemberment; Garréta's language has died, or, in its absence, might as well be dead, and there is no sense of an ineluctable return. But their corpora all reflect the rich anti-identitarian possibility of a literature that results from an encounter and a relationship with language's body—in its fragility, immortality, or absence—and the possibility for readers to encounter that body as well. They are different modalities and temporalities of a poetics of unbecoming.

From Sarraute's antisocial experience of language's body to Wittig's exuberant erotic textuality, to Garréta's more pessimistic textual erotics, these writers give us entry into a language that is not just acted upon and manipulated, but that acts upon the human, that guides, that moves unto death, unto life, that leaves its imprint on human bodies. As readers, we are not voyeurs observing their relationships with language from a distance, obtaining gratification through the indirectness of our involvement. Instead, we are interpellated, hailed as being already caught up in the very same language that caught them up. Their *corps-à-corps* encounters with language could be called instead a *corps-à-corps-à-corps,* where they seize us and place us also in front of that vast panorama of language, which, like Garréta's angel, can cut off our breath and make itself known, leaving its trace on our bodies with its own, erasing the marks that the social and political order has made on us. This cutting off of the breath is not a fatal one—the human does not die in the encounter with language, but unbecomes. Language, as a body, is unbecoming, and it is ours.

BIBLIOGRAPHY

"À quoi servez-vous?" *La Nouvelle critique,* no. 120 (November 1960): 85–88.

Abecassis, Jack I. "Montaigne in Brooklyn: Paul Auster's Body Writing." *MLN* 129, no. 4 (2014): 1035–59.

Althusser, Louis. "Ideology and Ideological State Apparatus (Notes Toward an Investigation)." In *Lenin and Philosophy, and Other Essays,* translated by Ben Brewster, 85–126. New York: Monthly Review Press, 2001.

Andrews, Chris. "Intertextuality and Murder: Anne F. Garréta's *La Décomposition* and *À la recherche du temps perdu.*" *Australian Journal of French Studies* 54, no. 1 (April 1, 2017): 71–83.

Apter, Emily, Ed Atkins, Armen Avanessian, Bill Brown, Giuliana Bruno, Julia Bryan-Wilson, D. Graham Burnett, et al. "A Questionnaire on Materialisms." *October* (January 1, 2016): 3–110.

Armstrong, Nancy. *How Novels Think: The Limits of British Individualism from 1719–1900.* New York: Columbia University Press, 2005.

Asso, Françoise. *Nathalie Sarraute: Une écriture de l'effraction.* Paris: Presses universitaires de France, 1995.

Auclerc, Benoît. "Le tropisme ou comment ne pas y croire dur comme fer." *Fabula-LhT,* February 1, 2012. http://www.fabula.org/lht/9/auclerc.html.

———. "Wittig et Sarraute." In *Le Chantier littéraire,* by Monique Wittig, 201–205. Lyon: Presses universitaires de Lyon; iXe, 2010.

Badiou, Alain. *The Adventure of French Philosophy.* Translated by Bruno Bosteels. London: Verso, 2012.

Balibar, Étienne. "Is There a 'Neo-Racism'?" In *Race, Nation, Class: Ambiguous Identities,* by Étienne Balibar and Immanuel Wallerstein, 17–28. New York: Verso, 1991.

Balén, Julia. "The Straight Mind at Work at the Heart of Queer Theory: Excavating Wittig's Radical Lesbian Materialism from Misappropriation." *Trivia: Voices of Feminism*, no. 16 (Spring 2014). http://www.triviavoices.com/the-straight-mind-at-work-at-the-heart-of-queer-theory.html.

Barad, Karen. *Meeting the Universe Halfway: Quantum Physics and the Entanglement of Matter and Meaning.* Durham, NC: Duke University Press, 2007.

Barthes, Roland. *The Neutral: Lecture Course at the College de France (1977–1978).* Translated by Rosalind Krauss and Denis Hollier. New York: Columbia University Press, 2005.

———. *The Pleasure of the Text.* Translated by Richard Howard. New York: Hill and Wang, 1975.

———. *The Rustle of Language.* Translated by Richard Howard. New York: Farrar, Straus, and Giroux, 1986.

Benmussa, Simone, and Nathalie Sarraute. *Entretiens avec Nathalie Sarraute.* Tournai: La Renaissance du livre, 1999.

Benveniste, Émile. *Problèmes de linguistique générale.* Vol. 1. 2 vols. Paris: Gallimard, 1966.

———. *Problèmes de linguistique générale.* Vol. 2. 2 vols. Paris: Gallimard, 1974.

———. *Problems in General Linguistics.* Translated by Mary Elizabeth Meek. Coral Gables, FL: University of Miami Press, 1971.

Berger, Anne-Emmanuelle. *Le Grand théâtre du genre: identités, sexualités et féminise en "Amérique."* Paris: Belin, 2013.

Bersani, Leo. *Homos.* Reprint ed. Cambridge, MA: Harvard University Press, 1996.

———. "Is the Rectum a Grave?" *October* 43 (December 1, 1987): 197–222.

Bewes, Timothy. "Reading with the Grain: A New World in Literary Criticism." *Differences* 21, no. 3 (2010): 1–33.

Blanchot, Maurice. *The Infinite Conversation.* Minneapolis: University of Minnesota Press, 1993.

Bordo, Susan. *Unbearable Weight: Feminism, Western Culture, and the Body.* Berkeley: University of California Press, 1993.

Bouchardeau, Huguette. *Nathalie Sarraute.* Paris: Flammarion, 2003.

Bourque, Dominique. *Ecrire l'inter-dit: La subversion formelle dans l'œuvre de Monique Wittig.* Paris: Editions L'Harmattan, 2006.

———. "On dirait une révolution: L'originalité formelle de l'œuvre de Monique Wittig." *Tessera* 30 (June 1, 2001): 92–98.

———. "Shattering the Gender Walls: Monique Wittig's Contribution to Literature." In *Literature and the Development of Feminist Theory,* edited by Robin Truth Goodman, 114–27. Cambridge: Cambridge University Press, 2015.

Braidotti, Rosi. "Thinking with an Accent: Françoise Collin, Les Cahiers Du Grif, and French Feminism." *Signs: Journal of Women in Culture and Society* 39, no. 3 (March 1, 2014): 597–626.

Brooks, Carellin. "The Body in the Text: All-Seeing 'I's." In *Every Inch a Woman: Phallic Possession, Femininity, and the Text,* 61–88. Vancouver: UBC Press, 2006.

Butler, Judith. "Critically Queer." *GLQ: A Journal of Lesbian and Gay Studies* 1, no. 1 (November 1, 1993): 17–32.

———. *Gender Trouble.* New York: Routledge, 1990.

———. "Wittig's Material Practice: Universalizing a Minority Point of View." *GLQ: A Journal of Lesbian and Gay Studies* 13, no. 4 (2007): 519–33.

Canning, Kathleen. *Gender History in Practice: Historical Perspectives on Bodies, Class, and Citizenship*. Ithaca: Cornell University Press, 2006.

Cairns, Lucille. "Queer Paradox/Paradoxical Queer." *Journal of Lesbian Studies* 11, no. 1–2 (August 1, 2007): 70–87.

Caserio, Robert L., Lee Edelman, Judith Halberstam, José Esteban Muñoz, and Tim Dean. "The Antisocial Thesis in Queer Theory." *PMLA* 121, no. 3 (2006): 819–28.

Chambers, Samuel Allen. "The Politics of Literarity." *Theory & Event* 8, no. 3 (October 4, 2005).

Chen, Mel. *Animacies: Biopolitics, Racial Mattering, and Queer Affect*. Durham, NC: Duke University Press, 2012.

Cixous, Hélène, Keith Cohen, and Paula Cohen. "The Laugh of the Medusa." *Signs* 1, no. 4 (July 1, 1976): 875–93.

Collectif, ed. "MLF: Le mythe des origines." *Prochoix*, no. 46 (Winter 2008).

Coole, Diana, and Samantha Frost. *New Materialisms: Ontology, Agency, and Politics*. Durham, NC: Duke University Press, 2010.

Cope, Karin. "Plastic Actions: Linguistic Strategies and Le Corps Lesbien." *Hypatia* 6, no. 3 (1991): 74–96.

Costello, Katherine. "Inventing 'French Feminism:' A Critical History." PhD diss., Duke University, 2016.

Cott, Nancy F. *Root of Bitterness; Documents of the Social History of American Women*. New York: Dutton, 1972.

Courson, Nathalie de. *Nathalie Sarraute: La peau de maman*. Paris: L'Harmattan, 2010.

Crowder, Diane. "Bio." http://www.moniquewittig.com/bio/bio.html.

———. "From the Straight Mind to Queer Theory: Implications for Political Movement." *GLQ: A Journal of Lesbian and Gay Studies* 13, no. 4 (2007): 489–99.

Cusset, Francois. *French Theory. Foucault, Derrida, Deleuze & Cie et les mutations de la vie intellectuelle aux Etats-Unis*. Paris: La Découverte, 2003.

Daroczi, Sandra. "Monique Wittig." Accessed May 11, 2018. https://modernlanguages.sas.ac.uk/research-centres/centre-study-contemporary-womens-writing/languages/french/monique-wittig.

Davis, James D. *Beautiful War: Uncommon Violence, Praxis, and Aesthetics in the Novels of Monique Wittig*. New York: Peter Lang, 2010.

Delphy, Christine. *Classer, dominer: Qui sont les autres?* Paris: La Fabrique, 2008.

———. "The Invention of French Feminism: An Essential Move." *Yale French Studies*, no. 97 (2000): 166–97.

Derrida, Jacques. *De la grammatologie*. Paris: Éditions de Minuit, 1967.

———. *Monolingualism of the Other, or, The Prosthesis of Origin*. Stanford: Stanford University Press, 1998.

———. *Of Grammatology*. Baltimore, MD: Johns Hopkins University Press, 2016.

———. *Of Spirit: Heidegger and the Question*. Chicago: University of Chicago Press, 1991.

Descarries, Francine. "Language Is Not Neutral: The Construction of Knowledge in the Social Sciences and Humanities." *Signs: Journal of Women in Culture and Society* 39, no. 3 (March 1, 2014): 564–69.

Devarrieux, Claire. "'J'ai connu la guillotine.'" *Libération*, June 17, 1999. http://www.liberation.fr/livres/1999/06/17/j-ai-connu-la-guillotine_276051.

Disch, Lisa. "Christine Delphy's Constructivist Materialism: An Overlooked 'French Feminism.'" *South Atlantic Quarterly* 114, no. 4 (October 1, 2015): 827–49.

Duchen, Claire. *Feminism in France: From May '68 to Mitterand*. London; New York: Routledge, 2013.

Duffy, Jean. "Rereading "L'Opoponax" by Monique Wittig." *Revue critique de fixxion française contemporaine*, no. 8 (May 24, 2014): 156–73.

Duggan, Lisa. "Queer Complacency without Empire." *Bully Bloggers* (blog), September 22, 2015. https://bullybloggers.wordpress.com/2015/09/22/queer-complacency-without-empire/.

Durand, Alain-Philippe. *Un monde techno: nouveaux espaces électroniques dans le roman français des années 1980–1990*. Berlin: Weidler, 2004.

Duras, Marguerite. "Une œuvre éclatante." In *L'Opoponax*, 283–87. Paris: Minuit, 1983.

Écarnot, Catherine. *L'Écriture de Monique Wittig: À la couleur de Sappho*. Paris: L'Harmattan, 2002.

Edelman, Lee. *No Future: Queer Theory and the Death Drive*. Durham, NC: Duke University Press, 2004.

Epps, Bradley S., and Jonathan Katz, eds. "Monique Wittig at the Crossroads of Criticism." *GLQ: A Journal of Lesbian and Gay Studies* 13, no. 4 (2007): v-454.

Eribon, Didier. *Théories de la littérature: Systèmes du genre et verdicts sexuels*. Paris: Presses universitaires de France, 2015.

Fausto-Sterling, Anne. *Sexing the Body: Gender Politics and the Construction of Sexuality*. New York: Basic Books, 2000.

Feole, Eva. "Le déchaînement littéraire: 'Sphinx' d'Anne Garréta et 'Le corps lesbien' de Monique Wittig." *Revue critique de fixxion française contemporaine*, no. 12 (April 27, 2016): 110–19.

Finas, Lucette. "Nathalie Sarraute: Mon théâtre continue mes romans." *La Quinzaine Littéraire*, no. 232 (December 1978): 4–5.

Foucault, Michel. *The Archaeology of Knowledge*. New York: Pantheon Books, 1972.

———. *The History of Sexuality: An Introduction*. Translated by Robert Hurley. New York: Vintage Books, 1990.

———. *The Order of Things: An Archaeology of the Human Sciences*. London: Routledge, 2002.

Fouque, Antoinette. "Femmes en mouvements: hier, aujourd'hui, demain." *Le Débat*, no. 59 (January 1, 2011): 122–37.

Fouque, Antoinette, and Mouvement de libération des femmes. *Génération MLF, 1968–2008*. Paris: Des femmes, 2008.

Fourest, Caroline. "Le féminisme pour les nuls." *Le Monde*, October 9, 2008, sec. Idées. http://www.lemonde.fr/idees/article/2008/10/09/le-feminisme-pour-les-nuls-par-caroline-fourest_1105039_3232.html.

Freed-Thall, Hannah. *Spoiled Distinctions: Aesthetics and the Ordinary in French Modernism*. New York: Oxford University Press, 2015.

Garréta, Anne. *Ciels liquides*. Paris: Grasset, 1990.

———. "Fins de romans, XVII(e)–XVIII(e) siècles: Stylistique, rhétorique, poétique d'un lieu textuel." PhD diss., New York University, 1988.

———. "In Light of Invisibility." *Yale French Studies*, no. 90 (1996): 205–13.

———. *La Décomposition*. Paris: Grasset, 1999.

———. *Not One Day*. Translated by Emma Ramadan. Dallas, TX: Deep Vellum Publishing, 2017.

———. *Pas un jour*. Paris: Grasset, 2002.

———. *Sphinx*. Paris: Librairie générale française, 1986.

———. *Sphinx*. Translated by Emma Ramadan. Dallas, TX: Deep Vellum Publishing, 2015.

———. "Wittig, la langue-le-politique." In *Lire Monique Wittig aujourd'hui,* edited by Benoît Auclerc and Yannick Chevalier. Lyon: Presses universitaires de Lyon, 2012.

Gazier, Michèle. "Nathalie Sarraute: Une aventurière intérieure." *Télérama*, February 26, 2002. http://remue.net/spip.php?article186.

Gerard, Sarah. "States of Desire: An Interview with Anne Garréta." *The Paris Review* (blog), December 11, 2017. https://www.theparisreview.org/blog/2017/12/11/states-of-desire-an-interview-with-anne-garreta/.

Graves, Kristin. "Mapping *La Belle créole*." PhD diss., Yale University, 2014.

Grosz, Elizabeth. *Becoming Undone: Darwinian Reflections on Life, Politics, and Art.* Durham, NC: Duke University Press, 2011.

Günther, Renate. "Le Chantier Littéraire (Review)." *French Studies: A Quarterly Review* 66, no. 2 (2012): 274–75.

Haget, Henri. "On se tutoie? Faut voir . . ." *L'Express*, September 13, 2001. http://www.lexpress.fr/actualite/societe/on-se-tutoie-faut-voir_491511.html.

Halberstam, Jack. "Straight Eye For the Queer Theorist—A Review of 'Queer Theory Without Antinormativity.'" *Bully Bloggers* (blog), September 12, 2015. https://bullybloggers.wordpress.com/2015/09/12/straight-eye-for-the-queer-theorist-a-review-of-queer-theory-without-antinormativity-by-jack-halberstam/.

———. *The Queer Art of Failure*. Durham, NC: Duke University Press, 2011.

Halberstam, Judith. "Unbecoming: Queer Negativity/Radical Passivity." In *Sex, Gender and Time in Fiction and Culture,* edited by Ben Davies and Jana Funke, 173–94. New York: Palgrave Macmillan, 2011.

Halicks, Ruth Ann. "Interview with Nathalie Sarraute." *Artful Dodge*, 1980. http://artfuldodge.sites.wooster.edu/content/conversation-nathalie-sarraute.

Hemmings, Clare. *Why Stories Matter: The Political Grammar of Feminist Theory.* Durham, NC: Duke University Press, 2011.

Hermann, Claudine. "L'Écriture a-t-elle un sexe? Questions à des écrivains." *La Quinzaine Littéraire*, no. 192 (August 1974): 27–30.

Hewitt, Leah Dianne. *Autobiographical Tightropes: Simone de Beauvoir, Nathalie Sarraute, Marguerite Duras, Monique Wittig, and Maryse Condé.* Lincoln: University of Nebraska Press, 1990.

Higgins, Lynn. "Nouvelle Nouvelle Autobiographie: Monique Wittig's 'Le Corps Lesbien.'" *SubStance* 5, no. 14 (1976): 160–66.

hooks, bell. *Feminist Theory: From Margin to Center.* 3rd ed. New York: Routledge, 2014.

Huffer, Lynne. *Are the Lips a Grave?: A Queer Feminist on the Ethics of Sex.* New York: Columbia University Press, 2013.

———. "Foucault's Fossils: Life Itself and the Return to Nature in Feminist Philosophy." In *Anthropocene Feminism,* edited by Richard Grusin, 65–88. Minneapolis: University of Minnesota Press, 2017.

———. *Mad for Foucault: Rethinking the Foundations of Queer Theory.* New York: Columbia University Press, 2009.

Huppert, Isabelle. "Nathalie Sarraute." *Cahiers du cinéma*, no. 477 (March 1994): 8–14.

Irigaray, Luce. *An Ethics of Sexual Difference.* Ithaca, NY: Cornell University Press, 1993.

———. *This Sex Which Is Not One.* Translated by Catherine Porter and Carolyn Burke. Ithaca, NY: Cornell University Press, 1985.

Jagose, Annamarie. "Feminism's Queer Theory." *Feminism & Psychology* 19, no. 2 (May 1, 2009): 157–74.

———. "The Trouble with Antinormativity." *Differences* 26, no. 1 (2015): 26–47.

Jameson, Fredric. *Postmodernism, or, The Cultural Logic of Late Capitalism.* Durham, NC: Duke University Press, 1992.

Jardine, Alice, and Anne M. Menke, eds. *Shifting Scenes: Interviews on Women, Writing, and Politics in Post-68 France.* New York: Columbia University Press, 1991.

Jefferson, Ann. *Nathalie Sarraute, Fiction and Theory: Questions of Difference.* Cambridge: Cambridge University Press, 2000.

Kaplan, Alice. "On Language Memoir." In *Displacements: Cultural Identities in Question*, edited by Angelika Bammer, 59–70. Bloomington: Indiana University Press, 1994.

Kelly, Joan. *Women, History & Theory: The Essays of Joan Kelly.* Women in Culture and Society. Chicago: University of Chicago Press, 1984.

Khatibi, Abdelkebir. *Maghreb pluriel.* Paris: Denoël, 1983.

Killeen, Marie-Chantal. "Esquives, pièges et désaveux: Les 'Anti-confessions' de Nelly Arcan et d'Anne Garréta." *Études françaises* 53, no. 2 (2017): 171–87.

Kim, Annabel. "Autofiction Infiltrated: Anne Garréta's *Pas un jour.*" *PMLA* 133, no. 3 (2018): 559–74.

Klapisch-Zuber, Christiane. *Culture et pouvoir des femmes: essai d'historiographie.* Paris: A. Colin, 1986.

Kornbluh, Anna. "We Have Never Been Critical: Toward the Novel as Critique." *Novel* 50, no. 3 (2017): 397–408.

Kosnick, Kristina. "Reading Contemporary Narratives as Revolutionaries: Radical Texuality and Queer Subjectivity in the Works of Monique Wittig, Anne F. Garréta, and Nina Bouraoui." In *Sexuality, Eroticism, and Gender in French and Francophone Literature*, edited by Melanie Hackney and Aaron Emmitte, 1–16. Newcastle upon Tyne: Cambridge Scholars Publishing, 2011.

Kristeva, Julia. *Desire in Language: A Semiotic Approach to Literature and Art.* Edited by Leon Roudiez. Translated by Thomas Gora and Alice Jardine. Revised ed. New York: Columbia University Press, 1980.

———. *Revolution in Poetic Language.* Translated by Margaret Waller. New York: Columbia University Press, 1984.

Lacan, Jacques. *The Four Fundamental Concepts of Psycho-Analysis.* Translated by Alan Sheridan. New York: Norton, 1977.

Lauretis, Teresa de. "Queer Theory: Lesbian and Gay Sexualities. An Introduction." *Differences* 6, no. 2–3 (1991): iii–xviii.

"Le corps lesbien." Les Éditions de Minuit. Accessed September 30, 2016. http://www.leseditionsdeminuit.fr/livre-Le_Corps_lesbien-1895-1-1-0-1.html.

Lebovici, Élisabeth. "La bonne, la brute et la truande." *Romanic Review* 107, no. 1–4 (January 2016): 173–91.

Leduc, Violette. *La folie en tête.* Paris: Gallimard, 1970.

Lerner, Gerda. *The Woman in American History.* Specialized Studies in American History Series. Menlo Park, CA: Addison-Wesley Publishing Company, 1971.

Lindon, Mathieu. "L'assassin théoricien." *Libération,* September 23, 1999. http://next.liberation.fr/livres/1999/09/23/a-quoi-ca-sert-parmi-les-divers-usages-de-la-litterature-anne-f-garreta-et-alain-fleischer-en-propos_284965.

Livia, Anna. *Pronoun Envy: Literary Uses of Linguistic Gender.* New York: Oxford University Press, 2001.

Lotringer, Sylvère, and Sande Cohen, eds. *French Theory in America.* New York: Routledge, 2001.

Love, Heather. *Feeling Backward: Loss and the Politics of Queer History.* Cambridge, MA; London: Harvard University Press, 2009.

Mahuzier, Brigitte, Karen McPherson, Charles A. Porter, and Ralph Sarkonak. "Editors' Preface." *Yale French Studies,* no. 90 (1996): 1–4.

Marlatt, Daphne. "Musings with Mothertongue." *Tessera* 1 (January 1, 1984): 53–56.

Mathieu, Marie-Ève. "Des corps textuels." *Postures* 1 (1997): 113–18.

Mauriac, Claude. *L'Allitérature.* Paris: Albin Michel, 1958.

McCarthy, Mary. "Everybody's Childhood." *New Statesman,* July 15, 1966.

Minogue, Valerie. *Nathalie Sarraute and the War of the Words.* Edinburgh: Edinburgh University Press, 1984.

Moi, Toril. *Sexual/Textual Politics: Feminist Literary Theory.* 2nd ed. London; New York: Routledge, 2002.

Moses, Claire Goldberg. "Made in America: 'French Feminism' in Academia." *Feminist Studies* 24, no. 2 (1998): 241–74.

O'Meara, Lucy. "Georges Perec and Anne Garréta: Oulipo, Constraint and Crime Fiction." *Nottingham French Studies* 53, no. 1 (March 1, 2014): 35–48.

Perreau, Bruno. *Queer Theory: The French Response.* Palo Alto, CA: Stanford University Press, 2016.

Perrot, Michelle. "MLF: 'Antoinette Fouque a un petit côté sectaire.'" *Le Figaro,* October 9, 2008, sec. Société.

———. *Une histoire des femmes est-elle possible?* Paris: Rivages, 1984.

Picq, Françoise. *Libération des femmes: Les années-mouvement.* Paris: Seuil, 1993.

———. "MLF: 1970, Année Zéro." *Libération,* October 7, 2008. http://www.liberation.fr/societe/2008/10/07/mlf-1970-annee-zero_112802.

Pivot, Bernard. "Pendant la campagne électorale lisez des romans." *Apostrophes,* March 7, 1986. http://www.ina.fr/video/CPB86005337.

Poel, Ieme Van Der, Sophie Bertho, and Ton Hoenselaars, eds. *Traveling Theory: France and the United States.* Madison, NJ; London: Fairleigh Dickinson University Press, 2000.

Puar, Jasbir. *Terrorist Assemblages: Homonationalism in Queer Times.* Durham, NC: Duke University Press, 2007.

Rabaté, Dominique. *Poétiques de la voix.* Paris: José Corti, 1999.

Rabaudy, Martine de. "Nathalie Sarraute: L'exploratrice des mots." *L'Express,* May 21, 1998.

Radicalesbians. *The Woman-Identified Woman.* Pittsburgh, PA: Know, Inc., 1970.

Rambures, Jean-Louis de. *Comment travaillent les écrivains.* Paris: Flammarion, 1978.

Rancière, Jacques. *The Flesh of Words: The Politics of Writing.* Palo Alto, CA: Stanford University Press, 2004.

Rawson, C. J. "Cannibalism and Fiction: Part II: Love and Eating in Fielding, Mailer, Genet and Wittig." *Genre* 11 (1978): 227–313.

Reber, Dierdra. *Coming to Our Senses: Affect and an Order of Things for Global Culture.* New York: Columbia University Press, 2016.

Ross, Kristin. *May '68 and Its Afterlives.* Chicago: University of Chicago Press, 2008.

Ruti, Mari. *The Ethics of Opting Out: Queer Theory's Defiant Subjects.* New York: Columbia University Press, 2017.

Rye, Gill. "Uncertain Readings and Meaningful Dialogues: Language and Sexual Identity in Anne Garréta's 'Sphinx' and Tahar Ben Jelloun's 'L'Enfant de Sable' and 'La Nuit Sacrée.'" *Neophilologus* 84, no. 4 (October 2000): 531–40.

Rykiel, Sonia. "Quand j'écris, je ne suis ni homme, ni femme, ni chien." *Les Nouvelles,* no. 2917 (February 9, 1984): 39–41.

Rykner, Arnaud. *Nathalie Sarraute.* Paris: Seuil, 1991.

Salles, Alain. "Grasset retrouve son rang dans les prix littéraires." *Le Monde,* November 8, 2002. http://www.lemonde.fr/archives/article/2002/11/08/grasset-retrouve-son-rang-dans-les-prix-litteraires_297362_1819218.html?xtmc=anne_garreta_pas_un_jour&xtcr=12.

Sarraute, Nathalie. *Between Life and Death.* Translated by Maria Jolas. London: Calder, 1970.

———. *Childhood.* Chicago: University of Chicago Press, 2013.

———. *"disent les imbéciles."* Paris: Gallimard, 1978.

———. *Lecture.* Audio CD. Gallimard, 1998.

———. *Œuvres complètes.* Paris: Gallimard, 1996; 2011.

———. *The Age of Suspicion.* Translated by Maria Jolas. New York: George Braziller, 1963.

———. *The Golden Fruits.* Translated by Maria Jolas. New York: George Braziller, 1964.

———. *Tropisms.* Translated by Maria Jolas. New York: G. Braziller, 1963.

———. *You Don't Love Yourself.* Translated by Barbara Wright. New York: George Braziller, 1990.

Sartre, Jean-Paul. *Being and Nothingness.* Translated by Hazel E. Barnes. Reprint ed. New York: Washington Square Press, 1993.

Savigneau, Josyane. "Un genre énigmatique." *Le Monde.fr,* April 4, 1986. http://www.lemonde.fr/archives/article/1986/04/04/un-genre-enigmatique_2917458_1819218.html.

Shaktini, Namascar. "Displacing the Phallic Subject: Wittig's Lesbian Writing." *Signs* 8, no. 1 (1982): 29–44.

———. "Monique Wittig's New Language." *Pacific Coast Philology* 24, no. 1/2 (1989): 83–93.

———, ed. *On Monique Wittig: Theoretical, Political, and Literary Essays.* Urbana: University of Illinois Press, 2005.

Smith, Barbara, ed. "Combahee River Collective Statement." In *Home Girls: A Black Feminist Anthology.* New Brunswick, NJ: Rutgers University Press, 1983.

Sonnenfeld, Albert. Review of *Review of The Opoponax,* by Monique Wittig and Helen Weaver. *NOVEL: A Forum on Fiction* 2, no. 2 (1969): 185–86.

Spivak, Gayatri Chakravorty, and Donna Landry. *The Spivak Reader: Selected Works of Gayatri Chakravorty Spivak.* New York; London: Routledge, 1996.

Stryker, Susan. "My Words to Victor Frankenstein above the Village of Chamounix: Performing Transgender Rage." *GLQ: A Journal of Lesbian and Gay Studies* 1, no. 3 (1994): 237–54.

Suleiman, Susan, ed. *The Female Body in Western Culture*. Cambridge: Harvard University Press, 1986.

Surkis, Judith. *Sexing the Citizen: Morality and Masculinity in France, 1870–1920*. Ithaca, NY: Cornell University Press, 2006.

Weil, Kari. "French Feminism's *Écriture Féminine*." In *The Cambridge Companion to Feminist Literary Theory*, edited by Ellen Rooney, 153–71. Cambridge: Cambridge University Press, 2006.

Weiss, Shusha, and Jason Guppy. "Nathalie Sarraute, The Art of Fiction No. 115." *Paris Review*, no. 114 (Spring 1990). http://www.theparisreview.org/interviews/2341/the-art-of-fiction-no-115-nathalie-sarraute.

Wiegman, Robyn. *Object Lessons*. Durham, NC: Duke University Press, 2012.

———. "Sex and Negativity; or, What Queer Theory Has for You." *Cultural Critique* 95, no. 1 (July 6, 2017): 219–43.

Wiegman, Robyn, and Elizabeth Wilson. "Introduction: Antinormativity's Queer Conventions." *Differences* 26, no. 1 (2015): 1–25.

Wilder, Gary. *Freedom Time: Negritude, Decolonization, and the Future of the World*. Durham, NC: Duke University Press, 2014.

Willging, Jennifer. *Telling Anxiety: Anxious Narration in the Work of Marguerite Duras, Annie Ernaux, Nathalie Sarraute, and Anne Hébert*. Toronto: University of Toronto Press, 2007.

Williams, Caroline. *Contemporary French Philosophy: Modernity and the Persistence of the Subject*. London: The Athlone Press, 2001.

Winter, Bronwyn. "(Mis)Representations: What French Feminism Isn't." *Women's Studies International Forum* 20, no. 2 (March 1, 1997): 211–24.

Wittig, Monique. "Author's Note." In *The Lesbian Body*, translated by David Le Vay, 9–11. New York: William Morrow, 1975.

———. *Brouillon pour un dictionnaire des amantes*. 2nd ed. Paris: Grasset, 2011.

———. *La Pensée straight*. Paris: Éditions Amsterdam, 2013.

———. *Le Chantier littéraire*. Lyon: Presses universitaires de Lyon; iXe, 2010.

———. *Le Corps lesbien*. Paris: Minuit, 1973.

———. "Le Déambulatoire. Entretien Avec Nathalie Sarraute." *L'Esprit Créateur* 36, no. 2 (1996): 3–8.

———. *Les Guérillères*. New York: Viking Press, 1971.

———. *L'Opoponax*. Paris: Editions de Minuit, 1983.

———. "One Is Not Born a Woman." *Feminist Issues* 1, no. 2 (Winter 1981): 47–54.

———. "Some Remarks on The Lesbian Body." In *On Monique Wittig: Theoretical, Political, and Literary Essays*, edited by Namascar Shaktini. Urbana: University of Illinois Press, 2005.

———. *The Lesbian Body*. Translated by David Le Vay. New York: William Morrow, 1975.

———. "The Literary Workshop: An Excerpt." *GLQ: A Journal of Lesbian and Gay Studies* 13, no. 4 (October 1, 2007): 543–51.

———. *The Opoponax*. Translated by Helen Weaver. London: Peter Owen, 1966.

———. *The Straight Mind*. Boston: Beacon Press, 1992.

INDEX

A***, in Garréta's *Sphinx*, 129, 134–37, 142, 146, 232
aesthetics, 128, 213; in Garréta's works, 16, 143–44, 150–52, 213; of literature, 18, 101, 114, 117, 128, 143, 151, 192; politics and, 18, 41, 74–75, 101, 114, 144; Sarraute and, 40, 49n27, 66; Wittig's, 18, 85, 103, 125
agency, 18, 26, 45, 128, 192n43, 194; of language, 172, 179, 182, 185, 188, 189
affect, affects, 4, 72, 169, 172
African Americans, in Garréta's *Sphinx*, 129, 135–42, 232. *See also* blackness, blacks
alienation, 61, 180, 205; in Garréta's writings, 22, 159, 225, 235
allegory, 49, 86, 141–42, 221, 228
alterity, 136, 137, 141, 165, 184, 187, 192, 224
Althusser, Louis, 25
Amazons, 195
anatomical text, in Wittig's *Le Corps lesbien*, 195–99, 197 fig. 2, 203, 203n60, 207, 210, 211
angel, angels, 225, 230; in Garréta's *Ciels liquides*, 226–27, 228–29, 231–32, 233, 236, 239
antecedents, in Garréta's *La Décomposition*, 148, 157

anthropocentrism, 102, 170, 171, 192, 192n44, 193n45
anti-difference French feminism, 2, 3, 3n5, 32, 33, 34, 165; Wittig and, 13, 45, 130n10
anti-identitarianism, 31, 32, 150, 230; in Garréta's *La Décomposition*, 150–51, 153–55; queer theory and, 22, 77, 127n6, 163; of Sarraute, 31, 41, 44–45, 64, 70, 77; of Sarraute, Wittig, and Garréta, 8, 28, 29, 37–38, 165. *See also* identity, identities
aphasia, in Garréta's *Ciels liquides*, 222–24, 229
Apostrophes (television program), Garréta on, 14–15
Armstrong, Nancy, 2, 131n11
ars poetica, 180; Wittig's *Le Chantier littéraire* as, 12, 45, 83
art for art's sake (Gautier), New Novel writers and, 9–10, 20
Asso, Françoise, 54n33, 58
Auclerc, Benoît, 44n15, 60–61n42
Auster, Paul, 171
autobiography and autofiction, 104n22, 151–52, 152n40, 213, 214
avant-garde, 36, 40, 104. *See also* New Novel [*Nouveau Roman*] movement

251

Badiou, Alain, 27
Baker, Josephine, 134
Balibar, Étienne, 140
Balzac, Honoré de, 8, 24, 37n2; novels of, 49, 104, 105, 131n11
Barnes, Djuna, 91
Barthes, Roland, 3n5, 26, 42n12, 49, 85, 209; *Fragments d'un discours amoureux*, 87, 220; influences Garréta, 16, 220, 220n74; *Le Plaisir du texte*, 168n10, 220
Baudelaire, Charles, 111
Beauvoir, Simone de, 39, 42, 80, 165, 165n1; *Le Deuxième sexe*, 24, 80
Beckett, Samuel, 36; as New Novelist, 10, 37 fig. 1
being, Being, 41, 72, 76, 202
Benmussa, Simone, 69–70n53
Benveniste, Émile, 26, 70, 110–11, 111n31, 147–48, 184n37
Bersani, Leo, 5n8, 30n66
Bibliothèque nationale de France, 126; Sarraute's papers at, 11, 14n32, 59n39
bildungsroman, 104n22, 109; Wittig's *L'Opoponax* as, 20, 86n11, 104, 109–10, 133
biopower, 43–44, 44n14
blackness, blacks, 62, 138n22, 146; fetishization of, 138–39, 140–41; in Garréta's *Sphinx*, 129, 135–38, 140–42; language of, 137, 140, 141, 142. *See also* African Americans
Blais, Marie-Claire, 230
body, bodies, 134, 142, 169, 170–78, 194, 206, 220, 224, 231; of America, 221, 221n77; explanation of, 169–70, 169n11; in Garréta's novels, 135, 213, 223, 225; language and, 175, 215–17, 222–23, 236; metaphor and, 169–70, 194n47; race and, 135–36; in Wittig's *Le Corps lesbien*, 193–94, 199–200, 201–2, 204. *See also* body of language; corporeality; *corps-à-corps*; female body
body of language, 168, 170, 175, 179–80, 192, 193, 231–33, 238, 239; as non-human, 222, 236; Sarraute, Wittig, and Garréta's encounters with, 173, 235–36; violation of, 188–89, 206; in Wittig's *Le Corps Lesbien*, 194–95, 203–8

Brecht, Bertolt, 116
Brée, Germaine, 80
Brouillon pour un dictionnaire des amantes [*Lesbian Peoples: Material for a Dictionary*] (Wittig and Zeig, 1976), 76, 81n3, 86n11, 114, 133; lesbianism of, 12, 19
Butler, Judith, 80, 84, 134, 134n19; *Gender Trouble*, 13n30, 80–81, 82n6, 163
Butor, Michel, 8, 10, 10n16

categorization, categories, 16n40 73, 119, 150; Garréta's works and, 16, 125–28; identity and, 32, 65, 165; queer theory destabilizes, 22, 163; Sarraute and, 1, 10, 37, 38–41, 44, 46, 61n42, 64, 75, 76; undoing of, 131, 236; Wittig and, 92, 119. *See also* difference; identity, identities
Catherine Legrand, in Wittig's *L'Opoponax*, 104, 104n23, 110n29, 112, 113, 115
Céleste, in Garréta's *Ciels liquides*, 224–26
chambre noire [darkroom], in Garréta's *La Décomposition*, 154–55
Chantier littéraire, Le [*Literary Worksite, The*] (Wittig, 2010), 81n3, 84, 103, 110–15, 117, 161, 191; corporeality in, 178–79; as doctoral thesis, 83, 86–87; footnotes in, 87–88; foundation and structure of, 92, 93; importance of, 82, 83, 103; language in, 153, 187–88, 193; on literature and subjectivity, 27, 45, 157; materialism in, 82n6, 101–3, 193; publication of, 81, 83, 84–85; quotations from, 88–89, 93, 94–95, 96, 97, 98, 99–100, 132–33, 178–79, 197–98, 207, 209, 210, 211; Sarraute and, 12, 45, 83; translation of, 81n4, 84–85; Trojan horse and, 85–90, 123, 210
charpente acoustique [acoustic structure/skeleton], in Garréta's *Pas un jour*, 220, 221
Chatounowski, Pauline (Sarraute's mother), 8, 176
Chen, Mel, 6n11, 171–72
childhood, children, 105, 114, 176; narratives of, 104, 104n22, 109, 115; in Wittig's *L'Opoponax*, 105–6, 108
Ciels liquides [*Liquid Skies*] (Garréta, 1990), 15, 21, 22, 127, angel in, 225, 226–27, 228–29, 233; Céleste in, 224–26; *dérangement* in, 213; desire and passion in, 226, 228, 229; Garréta's *Pas un jour* and, 229–32; language in, 222–31; narrator in, 222–25,

226, 227, 228, 229, 231–32; plot of, 224–28; post-apocalyptic France in, 224–26, 227; quotations from, 223–24, 226, 227, 228, 229, 232; reader and, 228; violence and death in, 213, 225, 226, 227, 228, 229

Cixous, Hélène, 3, 3n4, 3n5, 25, 130n10, 165, 166; écriture féminine and, 2, 168

class, classism, 1, 2, 24, 32, 59, 78n65, 136, 137, 138n22, 141; bourgeoisie, 52, 59, 60n39, 78n65, 117–18; women as, 13, 62

clichés, 51, 52, 55, 58–59, 59n38

Colette, *Claudine à l'école,* 104n22

Condé, Maryse, 39

conformism, 60n39, 61, 61n42, 63

consciousness, 7, 36, 71, 156–57, 168n10, 181; feminist raising of, 2, 19; identities and, 72–73; Wittig on, 178, 179

Constant Journey, The [*Voyage sans fin, Le*] (play; Wittig, 1984), 12

constraint, constraints, 18, 126, 148n37, 213; Garréta and, 125, 128, 128n7, 214, 235; on language, 210, 211; Oulipo and, 15, 15n36, 134, 151; on women, 23, 121

content of language, 94, 96, 98, 100–101, 108

corporeality, 171, 193; human, 201, 221, 231; in Garréta's *Pas un jour,* 215–16, 217; of language, 172–73, 177–78, 194, 194n47, 220, 223, 229, 236; in Wittig's works, 178–79, 194–95

corps-à-corps, 172n19, 239; relationship to language as, 172–73, 229, 233; Wittig and, 191, 205, 207; Wittig's *Le Corps lesbien* and, 193, 205

Corps lesbien, Le [*Lesbian Body, The*] (Wittig, 1973), 76–77, 81n3, 86n11, 103, 114, 115, 208; anatomical text interruptions in, 196–98, 196n53, 197 fig. 2, 203, 203n60, 207, 210, 211; body in, 193–94, 199–200, 201–2; corporeality of language in, 194–95; description of, 193–94, 195; goddesses in, 194n46, 206, 210–11; lesbian politics of, 12, 19, 193, 195; pronouns in, 133, 195–96, 200, 201, 202–3, 203–4, 204n62, 205, 211n69, 212; quotations from, 195, 197 fig. 2, 199–200, 202–3, 203n60, 204, 211; translation of, 195–96n51, 196n53; Trojan horses in, 212; violence in, 196, 199–200, 202, 203, 226–27; Wittig on, 195

corpus, Sarraute, Wittig, and Garréta's works as collective, 235

Cott, Nancy, 19

Dans l'béton [*In Concrete*] (Garréta, 2017), 15, 15n37

Dante, *Divine Comedy,* 86n11, 133, 191

death: in Garréta's *Ciels liquides,* 225, 226, 227, 229; in Garréta's *Sphinx,* 142, 143; in Wittig's *Le Corps lesbien,* 200, 201, 202–3. *See also* murder

Décomposition, La [*Decomposition*] (Garréta, 1999), 15, 21, 127, 129, 147; anti-identitarianism in, 150–51, 153; murder in, 22, 148–49, 149n38, 150, 151, 152, 153, 158, 159; narrator in, 148–49, 152–57, 159, 160, 160n47, 161, 162; plot of, 148–49; pronouns in, 147, 148, 150, 155, 156–63, 212–13; queerness of, 163–64; Proust and, 139n24, 148n37, 148–49, 152–54, 158, 213; quotations from, 149, 150–51, 152–53, 155, 156–57, 158–59, 160n47

deconstruction, deconstructionism, 3n5, 22, 80, 77, 139, 180

De Gaulle, Charles, 12, 116

de Lauretis, Teresa, 29

Deleuze, Gilles, 3n5, 25, 25n56, 26, 27, 28

Delphy, Christine, 3, 3n5, 34, 80n2, 165

Denoël, publishes Sarraute's *Tropismes,* 9, 9n15, 46n23

dérangement, 212, 213–14, 232, 233

Derrida, Jacques, 3n5, 22n50, 26–28, 85, 221; deconstruction and, 25, 25n56; language and, 170, 223n79

Descartes, René, 25

desire, 168, 205, 214, 215, 220; écriture féminine and, 168, 236; in Garréta's *Ciels liquides,* 226, 229; in Garréta's *Pas un jour,* 214–16, 218, 221, 226, 231; Garréta's works, 232; language and, 193, 213, 222, 226, 229, 231–32; of reader, 135, 135n21. *See also* passion

destruction, 21n49, 201; in Garréta's writings, 21, 22–23; in Sarraute's writings, 57, 73

Dickens, Charles, *Dombey and Son,* 131n11

difference, 18, 20, 25, 25n56, 29, 32, 33, 41, 45, 74, 141, 142, 143, 168, 173; categorization and, 1, 10, 65; as constructed, 13, 142; cultural, 136, 137; fetishized, 129–30; in French feminism, 2–3, 24, 165, 166; Garréta and, 127, 136–46; hollowing out, 34,

35, 46, 111, 140, 145; language and, 31, 130, 132, 137, 142, 145; racial, 129, 130, 135–36, 139, 140, 147, 234; rejection of, 42–43, 146; social order and, 5, 32, 33; Sarraute, Wittig, and Garréta against, 1–2, 21, 23, 77. *See also* categorization, categories; sexual difference

differences (journal), 29, 163

differentialist French feminism, 2–3, 19–20

discourse, 102, 103, 110, 120, 121, 121n46, 167, 170, 209; Foucault on, 101, 130; language and, 130–31, 131n13, 145, 157, 165

doubling, doubleness, 131; in Garréta's *Ciels liquides*, 228–29, 230; of language, 93, 100

Duras, Marguerite, 38n4, 39, 82, 104, 114n36

écriture féminine, 3n4, 74, 78, 130n10, 166–68, 194, 236; defined, 2, 166; poetics of, 3, 45

Edelman, Lee, 5n8, 30n66

Éditions de Minuit, 10, 10n16, 10n17; republishes Sarraute's *Tropismes*, 9, 46n23

Éditions iXe, publishes Wittig's *Le Chantier littéraire*, 84

EHESS (École de Hautes Études en Sciences Sociales), Wittig's doctoral work at, 83

Enfance [*Childhood*] (Sarraute, 1983), 29n65, 46n21, 58n36, 75n60, 175, 191; quotation from, 176–77

English language, 140–41; gender in, 129n9, 134

Enlightenment, 15, 16n40, 29

Entre la vie et la mort [*Between Life and Death*] (Sarraute, 1968), 179–92, 204; quotations from, 180, 182–83, 184–85, 186–87, 188, 189, 190–91; reader and, 192

epic, 133

epistemology, epistemes, 7, 90, 171

Ère du soupçon, L' [*Age of Suspicion, The*] (Sarraute, 1956), 9, 36n1, 180

Ernaux, Annie, 39

Eros mélancolique (Garréta and Roubaud, 2009), 15

erotic, erotics, 221n77; textual, 220, 238

essentialism: biological, 136; strategic, 23n51, 34, 136

experience, 4, 17, 88, 164; language and, 18, 31, 40, 45, 55, 57, 65, 75, 206–7, 215; of selves as subjectivities without subjecthood, 5, 7, 60, 71

experimentation with language, 4, 5, 237; Garréta's, 133, 157. *See also* innovation, literary

female body, 2, 168, 194, 195, 220; in Garréta's *Pas un jour*, 215, 216–17, 221; in Wittig's *Le Corps lesbien*, 199–200

feminine, femininity, 70, 166, 234; degendering, 113, 113n34; rejection of, 165, 208

feminism, feminist theory, 2, 7, 13n30, 42, 77, 85, 102, 130, 165; anti-, 20n47; feminist movement and, 19–20, 21, 23, 23n51, 80; feminist studies and, 82, 84; Garréta and, 15, 15n38, 24, 138; queer theory and, 81, 130; wave model of, 23, 23n51, 138, 138n22; white, 138, 139; Wittig and, 4, 12–19, 79–80, 165. *See also* anti-difference French feminism; French Feminism

fiction, 5, 6, 16, 35, 165n1, 214n73, 230; auto-, 151–52, 213n71; Garréta and, 139–40, 149–50, 151–53, 157, 161, 162–63, 213–14, 230; as possibility, 75, 230; pure, 152, 152n40; reality vs., 153, 155, 161–62; Sarraute and, 27, 49, 118, 123; as theory, 27, 28; Wittig and, 64, 86, 102, 118, 123, 193, 208. *See also* genre, genres; literature; novel, novels

Flaubert, Gustave, 111; *Madame Bovary*, 143

footnotes, in Wittig's *Le Chantier littéraire*, 87–88

form of language, 90, 96, 97, 119; content and, 94, 98, 100–101, 108; new, 101, 103, 111, 118, 174; in Wittig's *L'Opoponax*, 105–6, 114, 126

Foucault, Michel, 14n30, 16, 16n40, 22n50, 27, 28, 44n14, 81, 85, 130, 142; *assujettissement*, *assujetties*, 5, 6; on discourse, 101, 130; *Histoire de la sexualité*, 130, 146

Fouque, Antoinette, 19–20, 20n47, 80n2

France, 23, 36, 79, 104; culture in, 136–37; Paris, 8–9, 12, 129–30, 144, 225; politics in, 21–22, 126n2; race in, 24n53, 136, 138n23; in World War II, 9, 10n17, 44, 75n60, 79

French Feminism, 2–3, 3n4, 25–26, 130n10, 166. *See also* anti-difference French feminism

French language, 16, 75, 158, 221n77; gender in, 54n32, 69, 131n13, 134, 141; in Sarraute's *Enfance*, 175–77; translations from, 81n4, 84–85, 91, 106n25, 125n1, 188n39, 195–96n51, 223n79

French literature, 2, 82, 104n22, 111; Garréta and, 4, 127, 235; queer in, 127, 235. *See also* literature

Fruits d'or, Les [*The Golden Fruits*] (Sarraute, 1963), 46, 75, 180, 181; ellipses in, 66, 67; gender in, 65–69; pronouns in, 66–67, 68, 69, 70; quotations from, 67–68

Gallimard, 10n17; Pléiade collection of, 8, 11, 11n23, 37n1; Sarraute and, 9, 10, 24, 180

Garréta, Anne, 1, 4n6, 20, 22, 23, 29n65, 123–24, 127–28n7; anti-difference poetics of, 3, 77; author and, 129–30, 135n21; Barthes and, 16, 220, 220n74; difference denounced by, 129–30, 130n10, 138, 144; experimental literature of, 5–6; influences on, 16, 22; language and, 7n13, 212–13, 231; literary sketch of, 14–17; as *normalienne*, 14, 129; Oulipo and, 2, 4, 15, 125n1, 125–26, 133, 148n37, 213, 235; queerness of, 28, 127, 163–64; Sarraute, Wittig, and, 85–86, 128; as scholar, 14–15, 26; Wittig influences, 2, 15n37, 16, 17, 18, 20–21, 126, 128, 130, 132

Garréta, Anne, on: angels, 230–31; Butler, 13–14n30; *La Décomposition*, 161; early modern literature, 16; Lacan 154, 154n42; novels, 149–50; reading, 4; self, 230; *Sphinx*, 132, 135; Wittig's influence, 132; Wittig's *Le Chantier littéraire* and, 83–84; Wittig's universal, 16–17n43

Garréta, Anne, works of, 128n7, 139, 164, 232, 234–39; anti-identitarian core of, 127, 139, 143; *Ciels liquides* (1990), 15, 21, 22, 127, 213, 222, 223–32; constraint in, 125, 126, 128n7; *Dans l'béton* (2017), 15, 15n37, *La Décomposition* (1999), 15, 21, 22, 127, 129, 147, 148–63, 164, 213, 232n86; against difference, 127, 130; "In Light of Invisibility" (1996), 229–31; politics of, 126, 127, 127–28n7, 128; queerness and, 22, 127, 127–28n7, 163; *Eros mélancolique* (2009; with Roubaud), 15; *Pas un jour* (2001), 15, 21, 127, 127n5, 128, 157n44, 213–23, 229–32; *Sphinx* (1986), 14, 15n37, 18–22, 29, 125n1, 127–29, 130–48, 150, 163, 213, 222–32, 232n86

Gautier, Théophile, 9–10

gender, 2, 33n69, 42, 70, 92, 99; erased from Garréta's *Sphinx*, 129, 134, 147, 149n38, 150; in Garréta's *La Décomposition*, 148–49, 149n38; genre and, 20, 133; as identity category, 34, 40, 73; language and, 76, 98–100, 119, 129n9, 132, 147, 235; pronouns and, 107–8, 109–10, 112–13, 147; in Sarraute's *Les Fruits d'or*, 65–69; studies of, 21, 21n50, 134; writing and, 37, 42

Genet, Jean, 230

Genette, Gérard, as Wittig's thesis advisor, 83

genre, literary, 86, 104, 151, 180; gender and, 20, 133

Germany, German language, 9, 41, 44, 75n60, 79

GLQ, Wittig issue (2007), 14, 84–85

goddess, goddesses, 194n46, 206, 210–11, 211n69, 231, 232

Grosz, Elizabeth, 6n11; *Becoming Undone*, 6–7

Guérillères, Les [*Guérillères, The*] (Wittig, 1969), 70, 75n61, 76, 81n3, 86n11, 103, 114, 115, 194n46; lesbianism of, 12, 19, 80; pronouns in, 69, 70, 133; Wittig and, 99

Guillaumin, Colette, 3, 165

Günther, Renate, 84

Halberstam, Jack, 29n64, 30n66, 30–31

heterosexuality, 31, 111, 134, 135; normativization of, 22, 127; regime of, 80, 201, 207

hierarchy, 167n8; as conceptual foundation for oppression, 2; difference and, 237; division and, 16; identity categories and, 1; pronouns and, 158

history, historicity, 9, 17, 17n43, 18–24, 29, 124, 144–45, 195; language and, 76, 90, 131

homosexuality, homosexuals, 2, 22, 105, 130, 195, 207, 219, 230; Proust and, 144, 145; sexual encounters of, 134, 135; in Wittig's *L'Opoponax*, 104, 104n23

human, humans, 5, 102, 168, 170, 183, 227; humanity and, 1, 70, 80, 102, 133, 184, 233; language and, 102–3, 128, 168, 170, 171, 184, 184n37, 212, 224, 236; neutral-

ity of, 41–42, 76; non-, 22, 33, 47, 102, 169, 170, 172, 184n37, 223, 233, 236; post-, 77, 102–3; subjectivity of, 25n54, 75, 76, 102–3, 120, 147–48, 157. *See also* anthropocentrism; body, bodies
Huppert, Isabelle, 77–78

identity, identities, 2, 5–7, 22, 25n56, 28n61, 32, 34, 41, 60, 73, 75–78, 114, 130, 142–43, 154, 163, 230; blurring of, 53–54; categorization of, 33, 43; clothes of, 73, 78, 234, 235, 236; consciousness and, 72–73; destabilization and decomposition of, 70, 150, 157, 163; difference and, 1, 25n56; in Garréta's *La Décomposition*, 153–57; Garréta suspends and rejects, 15n37, 230; identitarianism and, 28n61, 61n42, 135; language and, 31, 165, 236; performative, 134, 163; politics of, 28n61, 127–28, 154; pronouns and, 69, 161–63; queer, 25, 127n6, 127n6; self-, 6, 28, 162–63, 230; Sarraute sheds, 24, 46, 234; unfixing of, 50, 55; writing against, 21, 44–45
ideology, 17, 25, 90, 199, 209; language and, 131, 198, 210
immanence, 5, 232; body and, 169, 231
indeterminacy, indeterminism, 29, 32, 49, 66; Garréta and, 16, 133, 135, 143, 145, 147, 160–61; in Sarraute and Wittig's fiction, 82, 112; in Sarraute and, 36–78; sexual, 129, 129n9
innovation, literary, 101, 104–5; Garréta and, 126, 213n71, 213–14; Sarraute and, 8, 38n3, 40, 116–17; of Sarraute, Wittig, and Garréta, 235, 237; Wittig and, 20, 85, 96, 103, 105; in Wittig's *Le Corps lesbien*, 194, 196–97; in Wittig's *L'Opoponax*, 107–8, 114, 114n36
interiority, 66, 73, 74, 118, 120, 122; *je* and, 108, 110, 110n29, 112; Sarraute and, 65, 73, 234
intimacy, 104n23, 159; language and, 121, 164, 171, 189, 191, 229; of Wittig's *Le Chantier littéraire*, 86, 87, 92; of Wittig's footnotes, 87–88
Irigaray, Luce, 3n4, 3n5, 81, 165–66, 167n5, 168, 174n24; as differentialist French feminist, 3, 25, 130n10
irony, 150, 153, 207
Isis, 202, 203, 208, 211

Jardine, Alice, 39–40, 84
Jefferson, Ann, 44n15, 191
Jesus Christ, 170, 203
Jews: Sarraute as, 8, 10, 11, 31, 44–45, 74, 75n60, 79; in World War II, 44–45, 75n60, 79, 105
jouissance, 5, 5n8, 164, 167n5, 168n10

Kaplan, Alice, 175, 179
Kelly, Joan, 19
Khatibi, Abdelkebir, 171
Klapisch-Zuber, Christiane, 19
knowledge production, 1, 7, 44n14, 86, 143
Kristeva, Julia, 3n4, 3n5, 81, 165, 166, 167n5, 168n9; as differentialist French feminist, 3, 25, 130n10

Labé, Louise, 111
Lacan, Jacques, 3n5, 25, 25n56, 26, 27, 168n10; Garréta on, 154; Wittig on, 154n42
langage brut, le, Wittig on, 209–10, 212
language, 15, 25n56, 90, 112 126, 128, 134, 147–48, 170, 194n46; agency of, 179, 185, 194; autonomy of, 173, 199, 205, 224, 229; of blacks and African American, 137, 140–42, 232; corporeality and, 171–72, 177–78, 193–94, 194n47, 215–16, 223, 229, 236; dead, 182, 184, 187, 189, 192; difference and, 32–33, 130, 132, 142, 145; discourse and, 130–31, 131n13, 145, 157, 165; double nature of, 93, 100, 107–8, 115; embodiment and, 173, 178, 193–94, 209, 226, 228, 230, 232, 236–38; experience and, 18, 40, 43, 45, 55, 57; fiction and, 5–6, 7, 25, 105; Garréta and, 213, 222–31, 223n79; gender and, 70, 75n61, 98–100, 119, 132, 147, 199, 235; grammar and, 104, 106, 204; human and, 33, 102, 123, 179, 184, 184n37, 212, 236; intermediate space of, 47, 50, 59, 60, 78; linguistic turn and, 6, 25, 25n54, 85, 170n13; loss of, 213, 231–32; love and desire and, 215, 221, 222, 231–33; materiality of, 7, 7n13, 92–93, 97–98, 101–3, 115, 120–23, 131, 143n28, 150, 169, 171–72, 179, 182–83, 193, 197–98, 205, 232, 237; mobility of, 181–82, 189; neutrality and, 43, 199; normative, 57–58; phallocentric, 70, 167; physicality of, 90, 92, 179; pornographic, 195, 198; potential of, 84, 131, 157, 174; powers of,

10, 50, 53, 55, 102; raw, 97, 101, 120, 131, 198, 209, 212; reality and, 77, 92n16, 93, 100, 105, 115; Sarraute and, 180–93, 204, 224; sensation and, 47, 51, 64–65, 71, 178; social contract and, 94–95, 110; subjectivity and subjectivation and, 30–31, 43, 110–11; tongue and, 176–77; tropismic, 50, 60, 173–74, 189n40, 192; unbecoming, 32, 34–35, 41, 233, 234, 239; of universalism, 16–17; violence and, 201, 203–5; vitality of, 92, 95, 102, 120, 172–73, 183, 187–88, 193, 205, 233; Wittig and, 14, 76, 92, 132, 195, 204–5, 212. See also body of language; French language; literature; living language; pronouns; punctuation; relationship to language; tropisms

Leonardo Da Vinci, Vitruvian Man, 194

Leopardi, Giacomo, 111

Lerner, Gilda, 19

lesbianism, lesbians, 22, 105, 127, 133, 207; body of, 208, 212; feminists as, 20, 80; language and, 194n46, 205; literature of, 195, 235; as provisory concept, 114, 114n37; Wittig and, 4, 12, 13, 14, 19, 21, 21n49, 77, 81, 145, 193

Le Tellier, Hervé, 126n2

Lévi-Strauss, Claude, 26

libido, feminine, 166, 168, 236

Lindon, Jérôme, 37 fig. 1, 10n16

literary criticism, 9, 88, 89, 101, 166

literary worksite [le chantier littéraire], 81n4, 89, 173, 232; innovation in, 64, 96, 114; inside view of, 87–88; le langage brut in, 109–10; readers in, 193, 238; Sarraute's, 99; Trojan horses and, 94, 123, 164; Wittig's, 64, 82, 90–94, 96, 103, 114, 115, 120. See also Chantier littéraire, Le

literature, 2, 24, 35, 122, 143, 150, 152, 166, 181, 230; absence of territory in, 16, 27; aesthetics of, 18, 143; committed [littérature engagée], 9, 20; early modern, 15–16, 16n40, 27, 142; experimental, 5–6, 125, 126; French, 2, 4, 10, 15, 18, 104, 111, 127, 151, 235; gender in, 131, 131n11; identity and; innovation in, 8, 40, 85, 96, 116–17, 237; language and, 90, 100–101, 237; philosophy and, 99, 149–50; politics and, 2, 18, 22, 40–41, 40n9, 84, 90–91, 100, 101, 127–28; potential and possibilities of, 2, 16, 22, 35, 74, 117, 118, 125, 143n28, 210, 238; queer and lesbian, 127, 195; revolution and, 116–17; subject and subjectivity in, 4, 128; theory and, 27–28, 85; as Trojan horse, 94–101; universality of, 16–17, 92; Wittig and, 115–16, 120. See also fiction; genre, literary; innovation, literary; novel, novels

living language, 45, 51, 58–60, 62, 78, 120, 164, 172, 193, 230, 236; eludes mastery, 182; encounter with, 238; metaphors for, 183; in Sarraute's Entre la vie et la mort, 180, 181, 184, 187–88, 192, 193, 232; Sarraute, Wittig, and Garréta's visions of, 238–39; Wittig and, 143n28

love story, Garréta's Sphinx as, 14, 15n37, 22, 129, 133

Malherbe, François de, 111

Mallarmé, Stéphane, 167n5, 171

Manifeste des 121, Le, 79, 116

Marin, Robert, 9

Marlatt, Daphne, 170

Martereau (Sarraute, 1953), 9, 65

Marx, Karl, 26

Marxists, 12, 90, 124; journals of, 13, 116–17; Wittig as, 79–80

masculinity, 113n34, 195, 199, 205, 212; default universalization of, 147, 235

materiality, materialism, 7n13, 90, 101–3, 169n12, 171–72; of anti-difference French Feminism, 3, 3n5, 13, 165; of language, 7, 89, 92–93, 97–98, 120–21, 123, 131, 143n28, 150, 182–83, 193, 197–98, 205, 232, 237; new, 6n11, 6–7, 25n54, 85, 121n46, 192n44; of Wittig, 82n6, 101–3

Mathieu, Marie-Ève, 171

Mathieu, Nicole-Claude, 165

matriarchy, 21n49, 167

Mauriac, Claude, 37 fig. 1, 37n2

May 1968 student uprisings, 21, 116, 123; Wittig and, 12, 79–80, 238

McCarthy, Mary, 114, 114n36

meaning, 6, 91, 98, 111, 209–10

medium, language as, 97, 100–101, 121, 150, 171, 182, 187

Menke, Anne, 39–40

Mensonge, Le (Sarraute, 1966), 180

metaphors, 178, 179, 192, 194n47, 199, 208

Minogue, Valerie, 38n3, 45n18, 73n59

Mitterand, François, 21
MLA (Modern Languages Association), Wittig and, 13
MLF (Mouvement de Libération des Femmes [Women's Liberation Movement]), 13, 13n27, 19, 21–22, 116, 124; Psychépo and, 19–20, 20n47; Wittig and, 2, 12–13, 13n27, 19, 20, 80, 80n2, 238
modernism, 10, 124, 235; avant-garde and, 36, 40, 80, 104
Mouvement de Libération des Femmes [Women's Liberation Movement]. *See* MLF
multilingualism, in Sarraute's *Enfance*, 175–76, 177
murder, 143; in Garréta's *La Décomposition*, 22, 148–49, 149n38, 150–53, 158–59

narrative, 27, 49, 50, 66, 115, 156, 217; frames of, 222, 225, 227; Garréta's, 215, 235
narrator, 214n73; in Garréta's *Ciels liquides*, 222–32; in Garréta's, *La Décomposition*, 148–49, 152–60, 160n47, 161–62; in Garréta's *Pas un jour*, 213–21; in Garréta's *Sphinx*, 134–43, 147, 222
nationality, nationalism, 1, 43, 28n61, 136; biopower of nation state and, 43–44, 44n14
negativity: in Garréta's novels, 125, 162; queer, 5n8, 27–28, 30, 30n66
neutrality, 42n12; Sarraute's, 41–43, 45, 75–77, 95; Wittig's, 195, 234
New Novel [*Nouveau Roman*] movement, 10n16, 37 fig. 1, 38n4, 114; gender and, 38–39; Sarraute and, 2, 8–11, 36–40, 37 fig. 1, 38n3, 46, 81, 124–25, 180; Wittig and, 12, 20, 80, 204–5
normativity, 22, 28n61, 29, 57, 59; Garréta and, 22–23; Sarraute and, 31, 46n21
novel, novels, 1–2, 26n59, 76, 131, 150, 180; conventions of, 65, 104, 235; Garréta on, 149–50; realist, 4, 8, 20, 104, 231; reality and, 118–19, 152; within novels, 65, 65n49

Oedipal complex, 25n56, 153
OEuvres complètes (Sarraute, 1996), as Pléiade edition, 11, 11n23
Ollier, Claude, 10, 10n16, 37 fig. 1
ontology, 7, 102, 132, 171

Opoponax, L' (Wittig, 1964), 15n37, 81n3, 86n11, 99, 127, 194n46; as lesbian bildungsroman, 20, 86n11, 104, 115; pronouns in, 69, 107–10, 110n29, 111–14, 132; reviews of, 114, 114n36; Sarraute and, 17, 104; subversive intertextuality of, 105–6, 111–12; Trojan horses in, 107–8, 110, 113–15; wins Prix Médicis, 80, 104; as Wittig's debut novel, 12, 80, 103
Osiris, 202, 203, 208
Oulipo (Ouvroir de Littérature Potentielle [Workroom of Potential Literature]), 15, 15n35, 15n36, 126, 126n2; Garréta and, 2, 4, 15, 125n1, 125–26, 133, 148n37, 213, 235
Ouvrez (Sarraute, 1997), 45n18; as Sarraute's last publication, 11, 37n1, 178n28
Oxford University, Sarraute at, 9

paradise, 123, 191
paragraphs, missing from Wittig's *L'Opoponax*, 105
Paris-la-politique (Wittig, 1999), 12, 19
Pascal, Blaise, 205
passion, 221, 231, 237; deadly, 203, 233; in Garréta's *Ciels liquides*, 226, 228, 229; for language, 92, 101, 172, 184, 185, 193, 207, 213, 221, 229, 230–31, 233; between Sarraute and Wittig, 17, 82; in Wittig's *Le Corps lesbien*, 193, 195–96, 203, 211, 226. *See also* desire
Pas un jour [*Not One Day*] (Garréta, 2001), 21, 127n5, 157n44, 232, 232n86; body and language in, 214–22, 229, 231; description of, 213–14; desire in, 214–16, 218, 221, 230; Garréta's *Ciels liquides* and, 229–32; narrator in, 128, 213, 214, 216–21; as Prix Médicis winner, 15, 213; quotations from, 128, 214, 215, 216–17, 218–19; violence in, 213, 214
patriarchy, 19, 21n49, 40, 85, 110n29, 208, 221n77; violence of, 167, 201, 203; Wittig resists, 44, 85
Pensée Straight, La (Wittig, 2001), 113n34, 205–6, 207. *See also Straight Mind, The*
Perec, Georges, 15n36, 104, 104n22, 104–5, 105n24
Perrot, Michelle, 19
phallocentrism, 130n10, 194, 195, 200, 238; language of, 205, 208; non-, 194n46, 198

Pinget, Robert, 10, 37 fig. 1
Pivot, Bernard, 15–16
Planétarium, Le [*Planetarium, The*] (Sarraute, 1959), 9, 10, 24, 65, 66, 78, 180
Plato, 26, 40n9
plot: absent in Sarraute's fiction, 65–66, 75, 235; in Garréta's fiction, 149, 227, 228, 229; as novelistic convention, 8, 9, 16, 20, 39, 104; in Wittig's fiction, 103, 194
poetics, 128, 168; of anti-difference, 3, 165–66, 168; feminist, 2, 45, 165; of unbecoming, 8, 18, 31, 32, 45, 166–73, 229, 235–37
politics, 34, 79, 126n2; identity, 28n61, 127–28, 154; literature and, 2, 18, 22, 40n9, 40–41, 43–46, 74, 90–91, 99–101, 114–16, 127–28; in Wittig's works, 12, 19, 80, 116, 123, 129, 193–95, 206–7
pornography, 195, 198; violence and, 196, 199
Portrait d'un inconnu [*Portrait of a Man Unknown*] (Sarraute, 1948), 65; Sartre and, 9, 38, 58–59, 59n38
posthumanism, 77, 102, 103, 171
postmodernism, 16, 16n42, 123, 213
poststructuralism, 22, 101, 102; French, 3n5, 21–22n50, 25, 25n54, 29, 165
power, 90; bio-, 43–44, 44n14; of language, 10, 50, 53, 55, 102
Prix Médicis: Garréta receives, 4, 12, 15; Wittig's *L'Opoponax* receives, 80, 104
Prometheus, 211
pronoun, pronouns, 33, 33n70, 69, 70, 74, 76, 107, 120–21, 264; in Garréta's *La Décomposition*, 148, 150, 155–63; in Garréta's *Sphinx*, 134, 146–47; Garréta's use of, 128, 161, 212–13, 232n86; in Sarraute's *Les Fruits d'or*, 66–68; in Sarraute's *Tu ne t'aimes pas*, 71n55; tropisms and, 48–52, 52n31, 53–57; in Wittig's *Le Corps lesbien*, 133, 195–96, 200–204, 204n62, 205, 211n69, 212; in Wittig's *Les Guérillères*, 69, 70, 133; in Wittig's *L'Opoponax*, 107–10, 110n29, 112–13, 132
proper names, in Garréta's *La Décomposition*, 148
Proust, Marcel, 16, 91, 144, 145, 230; *À la recherche du temps perdu*, 144, 148–49; in Garréta's *La Décomposition*, 139n24, 148n37, 148–49, 152–54, 158, 213
psyche, 52, 181, 234

Psychépo (Psych et Po; Psychanalyse et Politique), 19–20, 20n47
psychoanalysis and psychology, 26, 29, 147, 167, 168, 177n27, 235; Wittig on, 181n34, 154, 154n42
punctuation, 104; ellipses in Sarraute's *Les Fruits d'or*, 66, 67; slashes in Wittig's *Le Corps lesbien*, 195–96n51, 204, 204n62, 205

queer, queerness, 14n30, 15n38, 23, 29n65, 31, 127; Garréta and, 1, 13–16, 28, 31, 82, 126–28, 163, 212–13; literature and, 22, 230; negativity and, 28, 30, 30n66; studies of, 13, 21, 21n50, 82, 84, 134
queer theory, 5n8, 22, 23, 29n64, 29–31, 81, 85, 163, 163n50; Garréta and, 16, 24, 124; identity in, 25, 28, 28n61, 77, 130, 134
Queneau, Raymond, 15n36, 104n22, 104–5, 105n24

Rabaté, Dominique, 47, 60
Rabaudy, Martine de, 192
race, racism, 1, 2, 77, 95, 133, 138n22, 234; in Garréta's *Sphinx*, 129, 136–42, 146
Rancière, Jacques, 16, 40n9, 143, 143n28
Rawson, C. J., 196
reading, reader, 43n13, 49, 142, 161, 191; Garréta's fiction and, 4, 103, 143, 158–60, 228; *dérangement* and, 212, 214; desire and, 135, 135n21, 221; labor and, 139–40, 141; sex and, 215–16; of Wittig's *L'Opoponax*, 113, 115; writer and, 100, 115, 120, 123, 192n43
real, reality, 7, 49, 58, 85, 102, 103, 131, 167; fiction and, 152, 152n40, 153, 161–63; language and, 77, 92n16, 93, 100–101, 105, 115–16; new, 101, 108, 111, 115, 119, 120; Sarraute on, 118–19, 118n43; tropism and, 46–47, 60, 173–75
récit d'enfance [narrative of childhood], 104n23, 105n24; Wittig's *L'Opoponax* as, 104, 114
relationship to language, 5, 116, 121, 123, 168n10, 174, 183, 192, 230, 232, 238; changing, 33–34; Garréta and, 214n73, 222–23; in Sarraute's *Entre la vie et la mort*, 180–89; Wittig on, 96, 98–99, 102–3; in Wittig's *Le Corps lesbien*, 206–7,

211–12; of writers, 180–81; in writings of Sarraute, Wittig, and Garréta, 172, 173, 235–36, 238–39

resurrection, 208, 213, 227; in Wittig's *Le Corps lesbien*, 202, 203

Robbe-Grillet, Alain, 8, 9, 10, 37 fig. 1, 46, 46n21, 104

Rothenburg, Marcia, 13

Roubaud, Jacques, 15, 126n2

Rousseau, Jean-Jacques, 16, 104n22, 142n27

Russia, Russians, 237; language of, 41, 175–77; Sarraute and, 8, 10, 11, 24, 31, 41, 74, 176

Salles, Alain, 4n6

Sappho, 211

Sarraute, Nathalie, 1, 26, 29n65, 31, 43, 74, 79; biographical sketch of, 8–11; as canonical French writer, 4, 8, 11; categorization of, 10, 37, 38–41; childhood of, 176–77; collected papers of, 11, 14n32, 59n39; connections between Wittig, Garréta, and, 85–86, 129; country house of, 17, 79; daughters of, 45, 45n17; death of, 83; difference rejected by, 3, 42–43; experimental literature of, 5–6; historicity of writings of, 23–24; interviews of, 69–70n53, 77–78; identity rejected by, 10–11, 45; indeterminacy and, 36–78; influences Wittig, 2, 17–18, 20, 44n15, 82, 120, 123; language and, 7n13, 17, 185, 224, 232, 233; as lecturer, 10; long career of, 36, 37n1; neutrality and, 41–43, 45, 77; New Novel and, 2, 8, 10, 11, 36–40, 37 fig. 1, 38n3, 81, 124, 125, 180; physical appearance of, 36, 37 fig. 1; politics and, 43–46, 44n15, 116, 126; scholars of, 11n23, 38n3, 40, 44, 44n15; singularity of, 37n2, 38; Wittig and, 12, 14n32, 17, 71–72, 77, 91; Wittig's *Le Chantier littéraire* and, 12, 17, 27, 45–46, 82–84, 88, 99–100; in World War II, 44–45, 75n60, 79; writing and, 17, 46

Sarraute, Nathalie, on: Barthes, 26; form and content, 98; gender in writing, 39; her singularity, 10; her work, 182n35; infinite selves, 7–8; innovation, 116–17; listening, 178; *Le Planétarium*, 78; psychoanalysis, 26; real, 118–19, 118n43; on sexual difference, 41–42; *sous-conversation*, 36, 174; subjectivity, 6; tropisms, 36, 43n13, 174, 235; on Wittig's *L'Opoponax*, 104; on words, 51

Sarraute, Nathalie, works of, 199, 234–38: *Enfance*, 29n65, 46n21, 58n36, 75n60, 175–77, 191; *Entre la vie et la mort*, 179–92, 204; *L'Ère du soupçon*, 9, 36n1, 180; *Les Fruits d'or*, 46, 65–70, 75, 180–81; "Le Langage dans l'art du roman" ["Language in the Art of the Novel"], 51; *Martereau*, 9, 59, 65; *Le Mensonge*, 180; *OEuvres complètes*, 11, 11n23; *Ouvrez*, 11, 37n1, 45n18, 178n28; politics of, 43–46, 60–61n42, 118, 125; *Le Planétarium*, 9, 10, 24, 59, 65, 66, 78, 180; *Portrait d'un inconnu*, 9, 38, 58–59, 59n38, 65; pronouns in, 66–68, 71n55, 163, 234; "Roman et réalité" ["The Novel and Reality"], 118–19, 174; *Le Silence*, 180; *Tropismes*, 9, 9n15, 24, 46–65, 46n23; *Tu ne t'aimes pas*, 46, 70–76, 120; *L'Usage de la parole*, 58n36; *Vous les entendez?*, 59

Sarraute, Raymond, 9, 24, 44–45

Sartre, Jean-Paul, 9, 79n1, 116; Sarraute's *Portrait d'un inconnu* and, 9, 38, 58–59, 59n38

Saussure, Ferdinand de, 26, 27, 168, 220

Scève, Maurice, 111, 113

Sciences Po (Institut d'études politiques de Paris), Queer Week, 127, 127n4

Sedgwick, Eve Kosofsky, 16, 163

self, 66, 98, 147; decomposure of, 28, 30; Garréta and, 149, 230; rejection of, 11, 162; Sarraute and, 71–72; shattering of, 5, 5n8, 30, 30n66

sensation: language and, 47, 178; tropism and, 50, 51, 53, 64–65, 71, 175

sex, sexuality, 22, 31, 41, 133, 195, 199; as category of oppression, 1, 2; in Garréta's fiction, 134, 146, 215–19, 221; reading and, 215–16; sexism and, 12, 234. See also sexual difference

sexual difference, 2, 20n47, 39, 41, 25n56, 42n12, 69, 75–78, 95, 111–12, 166–67, 234, 236; in Garréta and, 129–30, 130n10, 134, 139, 141–44

Shaktini, Namascar, 13, 194n46

signification, 131, 168, 168n10, 194, 221; body as site for, 170, 218

signified, 169, 220; Wittig on, 93–94, 96

signifier, signifiers, 25n56, 97, 220; body as, 169, 194n46, 219; Wittig on, 93–94, 96, 220

Silence, Le (radio play; Sarraute, 1964), 180

Simon, Claude: New Novel and, 8, 10, 37 fig. 1, 112; Wittig and, 82, 104, 112–13

social contract, 98, 123, 207; language and, 94–95, 110; Wittig on, 94–95, 121

social order, 1, 60, 69, 73, 75, 154, 239; categorization and difference in, 5, 32–33, 146, 234; language and, 78, 235–36; society and, 42, 43n13, 59, 105, 106, 146, 165; writers and, 180, 190

Sodom and Gomorrah, 230, 231

Sonnenfield, Albert, 114n36

Sorbonne, 9, 12

sous-conversation [sub-conversation], 36, 47, 174

Sphinx (Garréta, 1986), 29, 127, 146, 232; A*** in, 129, 134–37, 142, 146, 232; characters in, 129, 129n9, 134; English translation of, 125n1, 127, 129, 134; Garréta on, 132, 135; as Garréta first novel, 129, 132, 139; gender erased from, 14, 15n37, 22, 129, 129n9, 134, 150; irony in, 140, 142; laborious reading of, 139–40, 141; marketing of, 125n1, 127; narrator in, 134, 136–43, 147, 222; pronouns in, 134, 146–47, 163, 212–13; quotations from, 135, 136–37, 140, 141, 146; race and racial difference in, 135–41; racial clichés and stereotypes in, 137–40, 142; sexual encounters in, 134–35, 146; Trojan horses in, 138–39, 142–45, 163; Wittig and, 18, 21, 129, 163

Spivak, Gayatri, 34

straight mind, 114; Wittig and, 1, 114n37, 119, 144

Straight Mind, The (Wittig, 1992), 13, 21n49, 81, 81n3, 82, 84, 91, 99, 114n37; on literature and subjectivity, 27, 90–91; politics and political theory of, 80, 83, 85, 90–91; quotations from, 131–32, 145; Sarraute in, 17–18. See also *Pensée straight, La*

structuralism, 25, 101

subject, 7, 25, 77, 121, 147–48, 206; Garréta rejects, 128, 148, 149, 230; minority, 205–6

subjecthood, 42n12, 59, 73, 168n10, 230; dissolving of, 28, 128; in Garréta's fiction, 127, 156–57, 161n49, 161–62, 232n86; subjectivities without, 5, 7, 17, 26–27, 31–32, 41, 74, 86, 128, 168, 230, 237; as unbecoming, 6, 17, 30

subjectivity, subjectivities, 5n8, 20, 25, 34, 42n12, 68n51, 69–73, 77, 108, 121, 147–48, 215, 232; contourless, 59, 60, 162, 175; difference and, 25–26, 74, 142; in Garréta's fiction, 148, 214; human, 1, 25n54, 75–76, 102–3, 120; language and, 110–11; lesbian, 21, 21n49, 111, 205; masculine, 69, 74; pronouns and, 69, 114, 161; splitting of, 109, 110; without subjecthood, 5–7, 17, 26–27, 31–32, 41, 74, 86, 128, 168, 230, 237; unbecoming, 7, 17, 30, 74, 122, 128, 168, 168–69n10, 211; Wittig and, 14, 108–10, 114; of writer, 186–87, 191

substance vivante [living substance] of tropism, 173–74, 185, 190; living language and, 181–82

suffrage, women's, 23, 24, 24n53

Symbolists, 171

syntax, in Wittig's *Le Corps lesbien*, 198–99, 204

Tcherniak, Ilya, 8, 176

text, texts, 90, 126, 221, 238; Barthes on, 26, 168n10, 220; bodies into, 166, 224; lesbian, 203, 205, 211, 225; reader and, 103, 155–56, 171; violence against, 149, 213, 214; women's bodies as, 215, 217–18, 231, 232; in Wittig's *Le Corps lesbien*, 194–97, 201; writers and, 89, 155–56, 171

Their Majesty the I, in Garréta's *La Décomposition,* 156–57

theory, 44n15: French, 3n5, 21–22n50, 25n54, 25–28, 166; literature and, 27–28, 85

Trojan horses, 85–86, 94, 117, 122, 164, 193, 234; in Garréta's *Sphinx*, 138–39, 142, 143–44, 145; literature as, 94–101; Wittig and, 96, 131–32, 144n29, 144–45; in Wittig's *Le Chantier littéraire*, 85–90, 94–101, 123–24, 179, 210–12; in Wittig's *L'Opoponax*, 103–4, 107, 110, 113–15

Tropismes (Sarraute; 1939, 1957), 46–65, 59, 60, 67; quotations from, 47, 48, 49, 52, 53, 55–56, 57; writing and publication of, 9, 9n15, 24, 46, 46n23, 64

tropisms, 41, 46–47, 70, 74, 76, 120, 180–81, 190; language and, 59n38, 181, 189n40,

192, 193; runaway, 61–64; Sarraute and, 36–37, 43n13, 46–60, 82, 119, 174–75, 181n34, 235, 237–38; *substance vivante* of, 173–74, 181, 185, 190; after *Tropismes*, 64–75; sensation and, 50, 51, 71

Tu ne t'aimes pas (Sarraute, 1989), 70, 71, 75, 120; extracts from, 72, 73; as late-career work, 46, 76

typography, in Wittig's *Le Corps lesbien*, 196–97, 197 fig. 2, 199

unbecoming, 26, 28, 30, 32, 34, 35, 43, 86, 128, 168–69n10, 233; Halberstam on, 30–31, 30n66; language of, 34–35, 41, 234, 239; as state of radical neutrality, 7, 17; as subjectivities without subjecthood, 6–7, 17, 30, 74, 122; Sarraute, Wittig, and Garréta's connected writing of, 17–18, 168, 237; in Wittig's *Le Corps lesbien*, 211, 212. See also poetics: of unbecoming

uncertainty, 48, 49, 51; in Sarraute's writing, 54–55

United States, 21n50, 166, 171, 208; landscape of, 215, 220–21, 221n72; Wittig in, 12, 13, 15, 81

universal, universalization, 1, 115, 17n43; of masculinity, 147, 234, 235; Wittig and, 144–45, 198, 205, 234; in Wittig's *L'Opoponax*, 112–13, 115, 133

universalism, universality, 16–17, 29, 92, 114, 120; false, 29n65, 109, 234; Garréta and, 17n43, 29n65; lesbian writing and, 105, 114–15, 235; of literary worksite, 95–96

universe without contours, 41–43, 75, 78, 92, 238

Usage de la parole, L' (Sarraute), 58n36

utopianism: in Garréta's works, 21–22, 42n12; in Wittig's works, 19, 193, 196, 238

vagina, vaginas, in Wittig's *Le Corps lesbien*, 198, 199, 200

Valerie Borge, in Wittig's *L'Opoponax*, 104n23, 113

violence, 91, 238; against language, 201, 203–5, 213; in Garréta's novels, 161, 213, 228; in Wittig's *Le Corps lesbien*, 196, 199–203, 206, 211. See also murder

Virgil, 107, 111, 191

Virgile, non [*Across the Acheron*] (Wittig, 1985), 12, 19, 81n3, 86n11, 103, 133

voice, voices: disembodied, 66, 74, 75, 201, 216

Warner, Michael, 163
Wiegman, Robyn, 28, 29, 29n64, 73, 84
Wilson, Elizabeth, 29, 29n64
Wittig, Gille, 11n24, 13
Wittig, Monique, 1, 3n4, 4, 20–21, 27, 60–61n42, 81, 82, 82n5, 85–86, 143n28, 191; as activist, 14, 20, 79–80, 116, 238; as anti-difference writer, 3, 3n5, 130n10, 165; arrest of, 13, 80; Benveniste and, 147–48; biographical sketch of, 11–14, 19; death of, 13, 14, 83; experimental literature of, 5–6; false universalism and, 29n65, 147; feminism and, 23, 82; Garréta and, 2, 15n37, 16–18, 21, 126, 129; language and, 7n13, 107, 119, 130–31, 143n28, 212, 232–33; lesbianism and, 12, 19, 21, 21n49, 28; as political writer, 44, 81–86, 126, 129; psychoanalysis and, 154, 154n42, 181n34; Sarraute and, 2, 14n32, 17–18, 20, 44n15, 71–72, 74, 76, 77, 82, 83, 120, 123; Trojan horse and, 139, 144n29, 144–45, 234

Wittig, Monique, on: *corps-à-corps*, 207; *Le Corps lesbien*, 207, 210; difference, 167; gender, 70; lesbians, 13, 19, 21, 21n49; literary criticism, 89; metaphors, 178, 179; psychoanalysis, 154n42; relationship to language, 96, 98–99, 102–3; Sarraute's language, 45, 60, 121; signified and signifier, 93–94, 96, 220; social contract, 94–95, 121; Trojan horse, 96, 131–32, 144–45; universality, 144–45; writing and language, 89, 122, 204, 209

Wittig, Monique, works of, 18, 20, 82n5, 125, 234–38; *Brouillon pour un dictionnaire des amantes*, 12, 19, 76, 81n3, 86n11, 114, 133; *Le Chantier littéraire*, 12, 27, 45, 81, 81n4, 82–103, 110–17, 131, 153, 157, 161, 178–79, 191, 193, 197–98, 207–10; "Combat pour la libération des femmes," 13; *The Constant Journey*, 12; *Le Corps lesbien*, 12, 19, 76–77, 81n3, 86n11, 114–15, 133, 193–212, 226–27; *Les Guérillères*, 12, 19, 69, 70, 75n61, 76, 80, 81n3, 86n11, 99, 114–15, 133; innovation in, 20, 85, 86, 96, 101; "The Mark of Gender," 70,

98, 99, 113n34; *L'Opoponax*, 12, 15n37, 17, 20, 69, 70, 81n3, 82, 86, 99, 103–16, 127, 132; *Paris-la-politique*, 12, 19; *La Pensée straight*, 13, 113n34, 205–7; "Some Remarks on The Lesbian Body," 207; *The Straight Mind*, 13, 17–18, 21n49, 27, 80–85, 81n3, 90–91, 99, 145; tonal shift in, 19–20, 77, 115; utopia in, 82, 127; violence in, 213, 238; *Virgile, non*, 12, 19, 81n3, 86n11, 133

woman, women 13, 19, 29, 39, 133, 207–8; Garréta and, 160n47, 214–19, 222, 229; Sarraute as, 10, 11; suffrage and equality for, 23–24, 24n53, 201, 203; as texts, 220–21, 231–32; as writers, 37–40

Woolf, Virginia, 4

World War II, 9n15, 10n17; Sarraute during, 9, 44–45, 75n60

Wright, Barbara, 105

writer, writers, 28, 120 145, 161, 190–91, 212, 214n73, 222, 232; *dérangement* of, 212–14; innovation by, 96, 116–17; language and, 92, 172, 207; obligations of, 118, 184–85; in Sarraute's *Entre la vie et la mort*, 180, 184, 186–87, 190–91; Wittig's instructions to, 97–98

writing, 44, 50, 204, 221, 229, 230, 231; gendered, 37, 38; language and, 187–88; non-gendered, 39, 42; in Sarraute's *Entre la vie et la mort*, 180, 181; Wittig on, 89, 204, 209

Yale University, 229–30

Yourcenar, Marguerite, 39

Zeig, Sande, 12, 13, 76

Zola, Émile, 150

www.ingramcontent.com/pod-product-compliance
Lightning Source LLC
Chambersburg PA
CBHW030132240426
43672CB00005B/110